ALSO BY JAMES S. GORDON

*Comprehensive Cancer Care: Integrating Alternative, Complementary,
and Conventional Therapies* (with Sharon Curtin)

*Manifesto for a New Medicine: Your Guide to Healing Partnerships
and the Wise Use of Alternative Therapies*

The Golden Guru: The Strange Journey of Bhagwan Shree Rajneesh

The Healing Partnership (with Raymond Rosenthal, MD, MPH)

New Directions in Medicine (with Raymond Rosenthal, MD, MPH)

EDITED BOOKS

Mind, Body and Health: Toward an Integral Medicine
(edited with Dennis Jaffe, PhD, and David Bresler, PhD)

Health for the Whole Person: The Complete Guide to Holistic Medicine
(edited with Arthur Hastings, PhD, and James Fadiman, PhD)

Reaching Troubled Youth: Runaway Centers and Community Mental Health
(edited with Margaret Beyer, PhD)

FOR YOUNG ADULTS

Stress Management (vol. in *The Encyclopedia of Medicine* (ed. Solomon Snyder, MD, DSc)

Holistic Medicine (vol. in *The Encyclopedia of Medicine* (ed. Dale Garell, MD)

MONOGRAPHS

Final Report of the White House Commission on Complementary and Alternative Medicine Policy
(with the other commissioners)

"Caring for Youth: Essays on Alternative Services"

Special Study on Alternative Services
(vol. 2, *Report to the President's Commission on Mental Health*)

unstuck

YOUR GUIDE TO
THE SEVEN-STAGE JOURNEY
OUT OF DEPRESSION

James S. Gordon, MD

THE PENGUIN PRESS
NEW YORK
2008

THE PENGUIN PRESS
Published by the Penguin Group
Penguin Group (USA) Inc., 375 Hudson Street, New York, New York 10014, U.S.A.   •
Penguin Group (Canada), 90 Eglinton Avenue East, Suite 700, Toronto, Ontario,
Canada M4P 2Y3 (a division of Pearson Penguin Canada Inc.)   •   Penguin Books Ltd,
80 Strand, London WC2R 0RL, England   •   Penguin Ireland, 25 St. Stephen's Green, Dublin 2,
Ireland (a division of Penguin Books Ltd)   •   Penguin Books Australia Ltd,
250 Camberwell Road, Camberwell, Victoria 3124, Australia (a division of Pearson Australia Group
Pty Ltd)   •   Penguin Books India Pvt Ltd, 11 Community Centre, Panchsheel Park, New Delhi –
110 017, India   •   Penguin Group (NZ), 67 Apollo Drive, Rosedale,
North Shore 0632, New Zealand (a division of Pearson New Zealand Ltd)   •
Penguin Books (South Africa) (Pty) Ltd, 24 Sturdee Avenue, Rosebank,
Johannesburg 2196, South Africa

Penguin Books Ltd, Registered Offices: 80 Strand, London WC2R 0RL, England

First published in 2008 by The Penguin Press,
a member of Penguin Group (USA) Inc.

Excerpts from *Tao Te Ching* by Lao Tzu, a New English Version with foreword and notes by Stephen
Mitchell. Translation copyright © 1988 by Stephen Mitchell. Reprinted by permission of HarperCollins
Publishers.

Publisher's Note

Neither the publisher nor the author is engaged in rendering professional advice or services to the
individual reader. The ideas, procedures, and suggestions contained in this book are not intended as a
substitute for consulting with your physician. All matters regarding your health require medical supervision. Neither the author nor the publisher shall be liable or responsible for any loss or damage alleg-
edly arising from any information or suggestion in this book.

Names and descriptive details have been changed to protect the identities of the individuals involved.

LIBRARY OF CONGRESS CATALOGING IN PUBLICATION DATA

Gordon, James S. (James Samuel)
Unstuck : your guide to the seven-stage journey out of depression / James S. Gordon.
p.   cm.
Includes bibliographical references and index.
978-1-59420-166-0
1. Depression, Mental—Popular works. 2. Depression, Mental—Alternative treatment.
I. Title.
RC537.G663   2008
616.85'27—dc22   2008001598

Printed in the United States of America
5   7   9   10   8   6

DESIGNED BY STEPHANIE HUNTWORK

ILLUSTRATIONS BY MEIGHAN CAVANAUGH

For Gabriel Gordon-Berardi and Jamie Lord

CONTENTS

>>>>> Depression is not a disease, the end point of a pathological process. It is a sign that our lives are out of balance, that we're stuck. It's a wake-up call and the start of a journey that can help us become whole and happy, a journey that can change and transform our lives.

This book is the story of that journey and a detailed map of its challenges and rewards. I'll be your guide. I'll show those of you who've been suffering with "clinical depression" how to move, step by step, through and beyond its dense darkness. And I'll walk with all of you who are simply unhappy, anxious, or confused, and help you to discover ways to help and heal yourself.

This journey, which is as old as recorded history, has seven stages. In *Unstuck,* I'll give you the tools and the compass you need to successfully navigate each one of them. And I'll share with you the stories of people— the ordinary, and yet remarkable, men, women, and children—who've taken this journey with me. Like them, you too can move through and beyond depression and distress, learn from and be healed by your experience, and find fulfillment, even delight.

I've been preparing to write this book for more than forty years, since

I myself had an experience of clinical depression that lasted many months.

One late-winter morning in 1965 in New York, six months into a pathology research fellowship, between my second and third years at Harvard Medical School, I awoke in a sweat. The sheets were twisted around my body, and I was clutching the blankets to my chin. My mouth was dry, and my head ached. My chest hurt when I breathed, as if a hand had pushed my sternum up against my spine. I felt feverish, but didn't seem to have an infection. I didn't know if I could heave my body out of bed, but I knew I didn't want to.

Several weeks before, my girlfriend and I had broken up. Now the irritable unhappiness of our last months together, the loss of our love, seemed to be breaking open in my body, weighing me down. The doubts and frustrations of my first years in medical school—of long days in dry lectures and tedious labs—rushed back. My mind was filled with anxious, accusatory questions. What had I done wrong? Why hadn't I been able to love better? How could I ever find fulfillment in medicine? What was the matter with me?

I told myself to get over it. I was young, privileged, healthy. Perhaps my girlfriend and I would get back together. In any case, there would certainly be other women I could love, wouldn't there? I knew I should be able to sort out my confusion and pain about medical school, to embrace my upcoming years of work with patients, and find a way to become the kind of doctor I wanted to be. I said these things to myself, but none of them seemed to make any difference. I felt worthless and hopeless, ashamed of my weakness, horribly lonely, without strength or will or direction. It felt like the end.

It was actually the beginning.

In the months that followed, I was wrapped up in and constrained by the damp heaviness of my depression. It looked to my frantic parents and bewildered friends as if my easy, confident, forward progress had come to a crushing halt. It felt that way too. I resigned my fellowship, left New York, moved back to Cambridge, Massachusetts, and began to see a psychiatrist. Before, I'd always been sociable, often laughing. Now I spent many of my days alone, crying for lost opportunities, relentlessly examining and judging my faults, missing my girlfriend. I plodded slowly, head often down, through Cambridge's lovely spring and summer. And yet I felt something new, something very necessary and overdue, was growing in me.

When I returned to medical school a half year later, I was still unsettled in many ways, but I felt different, more solid, as if my center of gravity had begun to drop from my head to my heart. My own suffering, and the early days of my own journey of self-discovery, had opened me to people who were dealing with situations far worse than mine. On the Beth Israel Hospital surgical ward, I sat with ancient Jewish men and women, some of them Holocaust survivors, as they moaned through late-night pain and early-morning loneliness. On my medical rotation, I held a giant, bewildered black man who, believing he had to "fly or die," was trying to pry open the windows at Boston City Hospital. While sitting with and caring for these people, and many others, and sometimes helping them find strengths they'd forgotten they had, I began to discover my own strength and purpose and meaning.

In the fifteen years afterward, as a student at Harvard, a psychiatry resident at the Albert Einstein College of Medicine, and a researcher and clinician at the National Institute of Mental Health (NIMH), I continued to be impressed by the strength and resiliency, as well as the vulnerability, of troubled and suffering people. I respected the people I was helping as full partners in our therapeutic work, and I began to think of them as fellow travelers on a healing journey. I developed programs that actively engaged deeply depressed and psychotic adults and adolescents in their own care and, later, a national program for runaway and homeless youth.

During those years and since then, I've worked closely with and learned deeply from some of the great physicians and researchers of our time. I've also studied with remarkable traditional healers from India, Tibet, Africa, China, and the Americas, exploring ways of understanding and treating depression that have been used successfully by cultures around the world for thousands of years. With the help and guidance of these men and women, I developed and refined the comprehensive, practical, individualized, non-drug approach to depression that I'll teach you in this book.

This "*Unstuck* approach" will equip you with the perspectives and attitudes and the mental, emotional, and physical techniques you need to sustain yourself as you make the journey through and beyond depression. It includes:

>> Simple, effective meditations that can enhance the biology of your brain and body, and make it far easier for you to deal with and transform the beliefs and fears that have inhibited and overwhelmed you.

>> Clinically tested experiments with words, images, drawings, movement, yoga, and dance that can help you mobilize your intuition—and your body—to move surely and often swiftly through each of depression's seven stages.

>> Detailed, practical plans for using food and supplements, and the ancient, powerful methods of Chinese medicine to balance your physical and mental functioning.

>> Ways to make the world's spiritual wisdom and spiritual practices a sustaining part of your healing journey.

>> Strategies for tailoring all of these approaches and techniques to your unique, individual situation, to *your* life.

In the years since I left NIMH, I've used this model in my own private practice, with many hundreds of depressed people of every age, class, and race. The results, as you'll see, have been deeply satisfying for my patients and for me, and often quite miraculous. Since 1991, as the founder and director of The Center for Mind-Body Medicine (CMBM), I've brought the approaches and techniques I describe in *Unstuck* to tens of thousands of troubled and stressed-out people around the world. Together with my CMBM colleagues, I've created groundbreaking programs for health professionals and medical students who are hoping to live lives of greater professional fulfillment and personal satisfaction. We've helped people with cancer and other chronic illnesses, as well as those who are anxious and depressed, to feel far healthier, vastly more optimistic and energetic, far more in control of their lives. And we've made it possible for many thousands of people who've been depressed and traumatized by war and disaster, in Kosovo, Israel, and Gaza, and in post-9/11 New York City and post-Katrina New Orleans, to find new hope as well as emotional healing.

Now, for the first time, I'm offering this program, this *Unstuck* approach, to you, in a form you can use on your own at home. This *Unstuck* program is not a substitute for consultation with a physician or sessions with a skilled psychotherapist. It *is* a powerful, user-friendly way for you to help and heal yourself, as well as a practical plan for enhancing your experience with the professionals with whom you work.

As you read *Unstuck*, I'll be by your side, explaining and guiding you through every stage of your healing journey, leading you in exercises and experiments that you can use to explore and resolve the difficulties that trouble you. At the end of each chapter, I'll give you simple, practical Prescriptions for Self-Care, methods you can use every day to transform yourself mentally, physically, and spiritually; methods that will help you lift the weight of depression and soar beyond it.

This book will challenge the prevailing "medical model" of depression and the widespread, even epidemic, use of chemical antidepressants. This narrow model of diagnosis and treatment insists that those who feel helpless and hopeless, unhappy and uncertain, have a disease, like insulin-dependent diabetes, that requires a pharmacologic treatment. I'll offer you evidence that strongly suggests that this model is poorly justified, largely inappropriate, limited and limiting, and, often enough, dangerous to your physical, emotional, and spiritual health. The antidepressants that it dictates should be used seldom, as a last resort—and generally briefly—not as a form of primary care.

What I'm sharing with you here is a newer, more hopeful and far more comprehensive and effective model for healing depression—both the clinical depression that is diagnosed in sixteen to eighteen million Americans each year and the chronic, low-grade dissatisfaction, unhappiness, and anxiety that affect so many more of us. It's a model you can start to use right now, one that will meet your unique individual needs and give you positive results that you can begin to experience immediately.

This *Unstuck* approach marries modern science with the perennial wisdom of the world's great psychological and spiritual traditions. It makes use of the remarkable capacity each of us has to recover—physically, emotionally, and spiritually—from the hurts and trauma we have experienced, to transform our fears into teachers, and to restore and renew our brain, body, mind, and spirit.

The path is realistic, hopeful, well traveled. The people I've worked with have learned to reduce their stress and improve their moods. They've changed their attitudes, their biology, their relationships, and their lives in profound, and sometimes immeasurably enriching, ways. In the midst of loneliness, confusion, and despair, they've found meaning, purpose, and peace, as well as love and delight. They feel better—not only better than before they became depressed, but often better, more fulfilled, than they ever have. And so can you.

unstuck

Is There Some Other Way?

>>>>> If you asked to see me as a doctor, to become my patient, I'd talk to you on the phone first. I'd want you to know something about who I am, what we'd do together and how we'd do it. I'd want to make sure, too, that there was a good fit between what you're looking for and what I have to offer—before you ever came to my office or paid me a fee. And most of all, I'd want you to start to feel that your time of helplessness and hopelessness was over; and that I could help you to move, step by step, out of depression.

This introductory chapter is the written equivalent of that phone conversation. It's longer and more detailed, because I want to be sure I give you as complete a picture as possible of how I'll work with you, and because I want to respond to as many of your questions as I can.

In this chapter, I'll explain why I understand depression to be the beginning of an unfolding process of self-awareness, not the grim end of a disease process; how depression's signs and symptoms can be used as opportunities rather than viewed as catastrophes; and why I believe that "clinically depressed," and ordinarily unhappy and confused people, can achieve greater understanding, wholeness, and fulfillment.

I'll outline the seven stages of this journey through and beyond depression—stages that I've adapted from mythologist Joseph Campbell's groundbreaking studies of the world's mythic heroes and heroines. These are stages that my patients and I have moved through and that I'll describe in detail in the next seven chapters of *Unstuck*.

In this introduction, I'll give you a bird's-eye view of the approaches and techniques that you'll be learning throughout *Unstuck*—mind-body approaches such as meditation and guided imagery; yoga and other forms of physical exercise; food, supplements, and herbs; self-expression through words, drawings, and movement; acupuncture and spiritual practice. I'll explain how you'll be able to use them to decrease your levels of stress, lift your mood, and strengthen and enliven your body, mind, and spirit.

I'll also give you some perspective on the current disease theory of depression and tell you about the clinical experience and the scientific evidence that lead me to see antidepressant drugs as a last resort rather than a first choice. And I'll show you how you can enhance your biological and psychological functioning far better, and with far greater satisfaction, with the approaches and techniques that I'll be offering to you in *Unstuck*—without the negative consequences, the uncomfortable and sometimes disabling side effects that drugs bring.

If we were talking on the phone, I might suggest that you call a patient of mine to find out what it's like to work with me. Here, right at the beginning of this book, I'll introduce you to one of them, Theresa, and let you see what our first session is like. Later, in *Unstuck,* farther down the road of both of your journeys, you'll meet her again.

As you read about my work with Theresa, you'll begin to see how you too will make creative, practical, mood-transforming use of the comprehensive approach I present. I believe you'll also feel the earned optimism and the heartfelt hope that I bring to you as we begin this journey together.

THERESA

"This is Theresa," she says when I pick up the phone. Her voice is sweet and a bit rough, like unfiltered honey. She's speaking slowly, stressing each syllable. "I think I'm depressed?" It sounds as if she's asking a question. "My therapist and my internist both say I should be on Prozac. Is there some other way?"

I had first seen Theresa four years before this phone call. She was a lawyer in her midthirties working for women's and children's rights who had come to me with headaches, back pain, and high blood pressure. She had wanted help with the stress of living far from her southern home, at urban high speed, among people who seemed even colder than the climate. She came for acupuncture, manipulation for her back, and advice about her diet. She wanted me to teach her meditation so she could "be more mellow," without relying on after-work glasses of wine.

I saw Theresa weekly for a month, and every two or three weeks for a few months more, and taught her what she wanted to know. Theresa and I talked about her dissatisfaction and stress. When Theresa was a child, black in a not-yet desegregated South, her mother believed that perfection of her daughter's manners and scholarship would protect her and propel her toward success. Now Theresa demanded perfection of herself. She spoke far more about her real or imagined shortcomings as a lover and a lawyer than she did about her good friends or the very good work she did with battered women, dealing with their emotional hurt as well as sorting through their legal options.

After a half dozen sessions, Theresa's headaches and back symptoms subsided, her blood pressure descended, and her anxiety ebbed. Still, I felt a sadness in her, and a sense that life would never measure up to her generous hopes for it. Listening to her now, I remember that this kind, competent, lovely woman—her face as sweet as her voice—worked too hard to take care of everyone who asked for her help, and lavished far too much love on troubled and troubling boyfriends.

In the office the next morning, Theresa gestures toward her body, once svelte, now going scrawny, "I've lost weight, and I don't sleep more than four or five hours a night." She hesitates as if each sentence were a stone she has to lift from her mouth. "I wake up in the morning, and I feel terrible."

At work Theresa is alternately listless and agitated. She puts off making necessary phone calls and finds herself staring out the window or pacing the halls or jiggling her foot at her desk. Tasks that were once routine are now ordeals. She leaves late, guilty about what she hasn't done and anxious that she will have to make up for it the next day. Theresa used to go dancing with friends. Now she tells them she is tired. At home, she watches TV and eats frozen dinners. Sometimes she measures her wine in bottles, not glasses. For the last month, she's felt increasingly hopeless.

When I ask, "What happened a month ago?" she says it was time to end another relationship. It hit Theresa then, perhaps for the first time, that she was almost forty, and didn't have a man who loved her, or a child.

And there is more. A thousand miles away, her mother's arthritis has slowed her to irritated immobility, and her father's sight and vigor are fading. Theresa feels she should be with them, but doesn't want to, and feels guilty about that. "I'm still carrying my whole organization on my back—you know," she says ruefully, "women's rights for everybody except this woman."

I pay attention to how Theresa tells me her story, the way the sentences sink at the end, as well as the pain of what she says. I take note of the "signs," the outward manifestations of the way she feels, as well as the "symptoms," the inner feelings and experiences about which she reports.

These are the signs: Theresa's clothes hang on her. She moves as if she has a fever or is old and afraid her bones might break. Her face, once animated, is almost frozen. She speaks slowly, as if each sentence, each thought shared, was an effort. The symptoms: She tells me that she eats and sleeps little, moves her bowels only twice a week, that her energy is low, and she has trouble concentrating. Along with weight, she's lost the sense of pleasure in her life and interest in what once absorbed her. She feels guilty about her work and her parents. Everything she's done to help others seems unimportant; everything she hasn't done—the men she hasn't married, the babies she hasn't had—haunts her. She can notice, but not feel, her friends' affection, and happiness seems like a distant dream. She feels worthless.

THE DISORDER OF OUR TIME

To qualify for the diagnosis of major depressive disorder, you need five of the nine signs and symptoms that are listed in the *Diagnostic and Statistical*

Manual of the American Psychiatric Association (the DSM-IV) and summarized in the box below. Theresa has eight of the nine, and they have been going on, as is required by the diagnosis, for more than two weeks. Since depressed, discouraged feelings have been around her, shadowing her life like dark, low-hanging clouds, for more than two years, Theresa could also be diagnosed as suffering from the chronic unhappiness of a dysthymic disorder—*thymos* is the Greek word for "courage," and *dysthymia* has come to mean "disordered and depressed mood."

CRITERIA FOR MAJOR DEPRESSIVE DISORDER

>> Depressed mood most of the day, nearly every day, as indicated by either subjective report (e.g., feels sad or empty) or observation made by others (e.g., appears tearful).

>> Markedly diminished interest or pleasure in all or almost all activities most of the day, nearly every day.

>> Significant weight loss when not dieting, or weight gain, or decrease or increase in appetite nearly every day.

>> Insomnia or hypersomnia nearly every day.

>> Psychomotor agitation or retardation nearly every day.

>> Fatigue or loss of energy nearly every day.

>> Feelings of worthlessness or excessive or inappropriate guilt (which may be delusional) nearly every day.

>> Diminished ability to think or concentrate, or indecisiveness, nearly every day.

>> Recurrent thoughts of death (not just fear of dying), recurrent suicidal ideation without a specific plan, or a suicide attempt or a specific plan for committing suicide.

Depression is the defining disorder of our time. Heart disease and cancer will kill more Americans, but depression has become the most disabling of nonfatal conditions in the United States and around the world.

Some thirteen to fourteen million Americans will suffer from a several-week or months-long "major depressive disorder" this year. Another three million have a dysthymic disorder. This means that in any given year, almost one-tenth of our adult population will have a diagnosable, "clinical" depression. One widely cited study estimated that one in five Americans will have an episode of either major depression or dysthymia during their lifetime and another predicted, even more ominously, that one-fifth to one-fourth of *all* U.S. adolescents will experience an episode of major depression by the time they are twenty.

Countless others of us will suffer from what has been labeled a "minor depressive disorder" (two of the nine symptoms listed) or feel "blue" or have physical symptoms (pain, fatigue, confusion, and/or sleeplessness) that are regarded as manifestations of an unhappiness that doesn't, or hasn't yet, reached the threshold for clinical diagnosis.

The losses in productivity of Americans diagnosed with clinical depression alone will likely cost more than *$50 billion* this coming year, a figure that is probably dwarfed by the losses caused by workers whose unhappiness stunts their creativity and blunts their drive. Depression—and chronic stress and unhappiness that may never be diagnosed—may predispose those of us who suffer from it to a host of other chronic and even potentially fatal problems, including chronic pain, heart disease, alcoholism, diabetes, and suicide.

The statistics globally are comparable. According to the World Health Organization, depression is the leading cause of nonfatal disability on our planet, accounting for 12 percent of total productive years lost. And the numbers are going up: From 1990 to 2000, worldwide disability from depression increased by approximately 20 percent.

FROM DISTRESS TO DISORDER AND DISEASE

From earliest times, it was understood that a combination of forces produced what we call depression. Some of these were regarded as "constitutional," that is, present at birth: Two thousand five hundred years ago, the father of our Western medicine, Hippocrates, thought that a child in

whom "black bile" predominated was by definition a melancholic or—
as we would now say—dysthymic type. The Greeks understood as well
that environmental factors—food, climate, emotional shock, and, especially, loss of a loved one—could deepen the experience of depression
or even provoke it in anyone, including people with more "sanguine"
or optimistic constitutions. Some people might be more vulnerable
to depression, but any or all of us could, under particularly stressful situations, experience it.

Early descriptions of depression by Hippocrates and the Greek
physicians who followed him are completely recognizable. In them,
melancholia—depression—is characterized by feelings of deep sadness,
hopelessness, and worthlessness, as well as weight loss, irritability, withdrawal, and suicidal despair. In these descriptions, depression is also
closely linked with fear. Fear is said to produce or contribute to depression, and those who are depressed are likely to be fearful, even of highly
unlikely future misfortune—"groundless despondency," it's called.

For most of the last two thousand years, from the AD second-century
Greek physician Galen to the nineteenth-century Frenchman Philippe
Pinel and the German Richard von Krafft-Ebbing, it was understood that
there was a continuum of depressive symptoms. People who became
depressed "without cause," and whose symptoms lasted for long periods
of time, were of far more concern and were most likely to be labeled as
melancholic. Those who became depressed with cause, after a loss or misfortune, were generally regarded as suffering from ordinary, nonpatho-
logical grief or unhappiness.

The great psychiatrists of the late nineteenth and early twentieth
centuries focused much of their attention on the reasons for, as well as
descriptions of, depression. Roughly speaking, they were divided into two
camps. Emil Kraepelin and his followers believed that depression would
prove to be a manifestation of pathological, and perhaps hereditary, physical lesions in the brain. By contrast, Sigmund Freud and his students
looked for the origins of adult depression in early life experience, particularly absence or loss of love in early childhood.

When I began my psychiatric residency in 1968, these two perspectives were still contending for theoretical supremacy. Meanwhile, most clinicians were relying on a rough-and-ready division of depression into "reactive" and "endogenous" types. Reactive depressions were those that were clearly attributed to recent events in a person's life: for example, loss of a loved one or job. Though the episodes might be terribly painful, they tended to be limited in duration and were regarded as amenable to psychotherapy, the "talking cure." Endogenous depressions were, by contrast, like Hippocrates's melancholia, "without cause." They were more severe, lasted far longer, and were often distinguished by ominous physical signs such as immobility and a profound loss of appetite, and/or by delusions and hallucinations. People with endogenous depression were regarded as good candidates for medication—antidepressants as well as antipsychotic drugs—and sometimes electroshock therapy.

The distinction between reactive and endogenous depression was soon called into question by clinical experience and studies that revealed precipitating causes—often loss of a loved one, a job, etc.—in most people diagnosed with endogenous depression. With the publication by the American Psychiatric Association of the third edition of the *Diagnostic and Statistical Manual* (DSM-III) in 1980, the distinctions between reactive and endogenous depression largely disappeared, even as the territory covered by the term *depression* expanded exponentially.

The diagnosis of depression was now based not on causes or the context (loss of a relationship or job) in which depression took place, but *only* on the DSM symptoms. This made it easier to agree on who had the appropriate symptoms, but it was no longer clear what these clusters of symptoms actually meant—anyone whose ordinary unhappiness lasted longer than two weeks might be grouped, with no evidence or studies to justify it, in the same category of clinical depression as those suffering from crippling, despairing, bed-bound immobility.

Some important studies were beginning to show that simple psychotherapeutic interventions—eight or ten sessions of cognitive behavioral therapy (CBT), which helped depressed people create a more positive and optimistic attitude and way of thinking, and interpersonal therapy

(IPT), which looked at malfunctioning relationships—worked as well, or better than, drugs for most depressed people. Still, public attention and public and private funding were flowing toward drug research and prescribing.

By the time the DSM-IV (in which the criteria for depression are almost identical with those of the DSM III) appeared in 1994, pharmaceutical companies, ever alert to a rapidly enlarging customer base, had begun massive marketing campaigns for drugs they called antidepressants. Soon enough, the concept of depression as a drug-treatable disease was certified by managed-care plans and other insurers.

Eager to save money, these businesses provided economic incentives for primary care physicians to prescribe, in brief visits, drugs for depressed people, while cutting benefits for psychotherapy. More recently, government approval of "direct-to-consumer" advertising—those glossy magazine photos and gauzy TV clips of brows unfurrowed and smiles brightened by drugs—sealed the pharmacological and managed care deal.

Currently, our society and its physicians, including those who, like me, are specialists in psychiatry, routinely treat as a disease any condition that could conceivably be gathered under the ever-enlarging diagnostic tent of depression.

Depression is often compared, in both professional and popular literature, to insulin-dependent diabetes, a condition with predictable pathological findings, a strong genetic foundation, clear biochemical errors, and an obvious pharmaceutical answer. Shots of insulin are necessary to maintain adequate sugar metabolism in the diabetic, whose pancreas cannot manufacture it. So, the analogy goes, depressed people, whose brains cannot produce the appropriate chemicals for normal emotional functioning—neurotransmitters such as serotonin and norepinephrine—require antidepressant medications.

These drugs, of which the selective serotonin reuptake inhibitors (SSRIs) such as Prozac, are now by far the most widely used, are regarded as the treatment of choice for virtually everyone who is depressed. In 2005,

U.S. physicians wrote some 189 million prescriptions for antidepressants for people diagnosed with depression and also—as the definition of disease expanded still further—for a vast array of others who seemed inhibited, shy, anxious, in pain, unhappy, or just plain out of sorts. This year patients, insurance companies, the federal government, and its taxpayers—that is, all of us—will pay about $12 billion for these drugs.

At present, those who do not view their depression as a disease in need of pharmacological treatment are routinely regarded by psychiatrists, other physicians, and public health officials as poorly informed, "resistant," or self-destructive. And physicians who are reluctant to prescribe antidepressants may be accused of malpractice or worse. Ten years ago, one of the most powerful health administrators in America, Alan Leshner, PhD, then director of the National Institute on Drug Abuse, was quoted in the *New Yorker* as saying, "My belief is that today, in 1998, you should be *put in jail* [emphasis is mine] if you refuse to prescribe SSRIs for depression."

DEPRESSION IS NOT A DISEASE

In fact, there is no good evidence that depression—whether major depressive disorder or dysthymia—is a disease in the way that insulin-dependent diabetes is. There are no consistent pathological postmortem findings in the brains of those who are depressed. The genetic association, though present, is hardly overwhelming, and the studies that describe it are significantly more problematic than most accounts indicate. Meanwhile, a fifty-year research effort has turned up no consistent biochemical abnormalities in the brains, spinal fluid, or blood of depressed people.

Though some studies do show an association between low levels of serotonin and depression, there is still no proof that most people with low levels of serotonin or other neurotransmitters—or their chemical breakdown products—are depressed, nor have most depressed people been demonstrated to have low levels. Nor is it clear whether any such altered level of neurotransmitters might be the cause, or the consequence, of depression, or what relationship it might actually have to depression. Indeed, recent research strongly suggests that stress and the action of stress hormones are more likely causes of depression and of observed changes in neurotransmitter levels. In any case, no tests are used in clinical practice to pinpoint either those who do have lower levels of neurotransmitters or which substance might be lower or, indeed, who might best respond to which antidepressant.

There is, moreover, surprisingly little evidence that the antidepressant drugs that are all but universally prescribed are more effective than a variety of other approaches, which I'll discuss later. In fact, when you look at the studies closely, it seems that antidepressants may be only marginally more effective than the placebos, the sugar pills, to which they are compared in most scientific studies.

On the other hand, there is an increasing body of information on the uncomfortable, destructive, and potentially disabling side effects of taking—and even ceasing to take—these medications. There is data emerging, too, on the very real suicide risks of the supposedly safer, newer antidepressants, the SSRIs. Finally, even when antidepressant pills do provide depressed people with relief—quieting their anxiety or making them less preoccupied with their unhappiness—many report that their range of feelings is seriously "limited" or that they feel "numb."

The story of how interesting but limited observations, wishful thinking, and genuine concern have been compounded—under the enormous pressure exerted by the hugely profitable pharmaceutical and managed care industries—to expand the domain of clinical depression and to justify and ceaselessly promote pharmacologic treatment of depression is well told in books that I list in the bibliography. In the following section, I'll share with you evidence that leads me to conclude that antidepressant drugs are a flawed last resort, to be used only when all other, less side-effect-burdened approaches—the ones I'll teach you in *Unstuck*—have proved inadequate, or in certain emergencies and special cases that I'll discuss later.

The Logic and Limitations of Antidepressant Drugs

What follows is a critical overview of what we do know—and what you may well want to know—about the disease theory of depression and its treatment, and of the promise and the very real limitations and dangers of antidepressant drugs. This is important information for you to consider in deciding whether to take, or continue taking, antidepressant drugs. In the notes at the end of *Unstuck,* you'll find the many scientific references upon which I base my judgment, references you can read and share with your physician or psychiatrist, or any therapist you may be seeing.

As you will see, I am quite critical of the use of antidepressants and also of the evidence upon which their prescription is based. Still, even if you're thoroughly convinced by what I say, if you are presently using them, *you should not just stop taking antidepressants.* Because the drug withdrawal symptoms are potentially dangerous as well as unpleasant, you should go off them slowly, under medical supervision. You should also, ideally, use some of the techniques I recommend later in *Unstuck* to mitigate the emotional and physical pain that often accompanies withdrawal.

I am not saying that you should *never* take antidepressants. So far as I'm concerned, they should be used *rarely,* and generally for brief periods, in occasional life-threatening emergencies or when all other less potentially harmful approaches have been tried for a reasonable period and found wanting.

Finally, though, if you *are* taking antidepressants, you can certainly continue taking them while you also take the healing journey that I describe in *Unstuck.* A number of people I've worked with have done so until they were ready to stop taking them.

GENES AND MOOD

The standard textbooks of psychiatry point out that genetically identical twins who have been separated at birth—a time-honored way of focusing on heredity and factoring out environmental influence—have a significantly greater "concordance" for (or likelihood of experiencing) depression than do genetically different fraternal twins who have been similarly separated: approximately 30 to 35 percent versus 2 to 5 percent. There is, many scientists conclude, a real genetic contribution to depression, a characteristic it has in common with other diseases.

I agree with the data but, along with other critics, disagree with the certainty of the conclusions.

I, along with many other psychiatrists, see the genetic contribution as more like a predisposition. It make sense that some of us will be more shy and fearful, more likely to be vulnerable to loss, or more easily traumatized than will others, just as some of us will likely be more angry, impulsive, outgoing, intelligent, athletic, musical, or artistic. These qualities do not constitute disease. And our predisposition to them is only our constitutional beginning. Our subsequent development—including our relationships with parents and other key people and the environments we live in—will largely determine how, how often, and how prominently these tendencies, these predispositions, manifest.

In fact, a recent, landmark study—on variations in the 5HTT gene, which controls serotonin activity and is widely assumed to be linked to depression—bears out the complexity of the relationship among genes, the environment, and depression. Those with two variants of the gene were indeed more vulnerable to depression than those with a third variant but *only after they had experienced high numbers of stressful events* (particularly financial setback). There was, however, no evidence of a direct effect of variations of the gene on the overall incidence of depression.

Our genetic makeup may contribute to our vulnerability to depression, but the influence is likely to be far more modest than is generally believed. Even more important, genetic predispositions that may be modifiable with prescription drugs may well be more effectively altered without them—by social changes, such as improving the quality and security of employment, and by adopting the approach and using the techniques taught in *Unstuck*.

EARLY SORROW, LATER DEPRESSION AND BRAIN CHANGE

There is an important and growing literature on the effect of early life experience, particularly profound psychological trauma, on the brains and later development of both animal and human infants. One of the most striking findings is the loss of cells in the hippocampus. Later in life, these children appear to be more vulnerable to depression, a finding that confirms decades of theory and observations (which I'll discuss in chapter two) that early loss and depression predispose us to depression later in life.

It appears, too, that episodes of depression in adult life are also accompanied by changes in brain functioning: Positron emission tomography (PET) scans and magnetic resonance imagery (MRI) have revealed changes in glucose metabolism (glucose is our primary brain food) and blood flow in some areas of the cerebral cortex, and the limbic, or emotional, areas of the brain, during episodes of depression. Interestingly, similar changes can be provoked in nondepressed people when they read stories that recall episodes of sadness.

Autopsies of a small group of chronically depressed people have revealed decreases in hippocampal volume and in numbers of glial (or supportive) brain cells in the frontal cortex. This association between brain changes and depression does seem to be real, but it doesn't mean that depression is a disease, and it certainly doesn't mean that drugs are its logical treatment.

One of the most striking and frequently cited studies by proponents of the disease theory is by Grazyna Rajkowska and her colleagues. It showed changes in the glial cells in the brains of twelve people, seven of whom had committed suicide. All these people, it turned out, had been treated for long periods, sometimes with antipsychotic drugs as well as antidepressants. It is impossible therefore to know if their depression was the cause or consequence of brain damage, or indeed whether the brain damage may have been caused by long-term drug use. Moreover, it is impossible to know what general conclusions about the vast majority of depressed people can be drawn from this small study of long-term, heavily drugged, tragically depressed individuals.

Finally, it's crucially important to understand that changes in brain function and structure that may result from depression may also be able to be reversed. In recent years, scientists have discovered that even our adult brains have a very significant capacity for regeneration and growth—for *neuroplasticity*—and that this process can be stimulated by a number of the simple, nondrug approaches that you'll be learning in *Unstuck*. Psychotherapy, for example, has been noted to change brain function in ways that are associated with improved mood. Exercise (at least in animals) has been demonstrated to stimulate new brain cell growth in the hippocampus. And meditation not only can change brain function—decreasing activity in centers associated with unhappiness and increasing it in others that are crucial to love, compassion, and happiness—but can also alter the anatomical structure of our brains: One recent, remarkable study shows significant thickening of the cerebral cortex in regular meditators.

DRUGS FOR DEPRESSION?

The history of drug therapy for depression is fascinating, revealing, and disturbing. During the early 1950s, physicians noted that Iproniazid, a medication that was being used to treat tuberculosis, significantly elevated the mood of some patients. Iproniazid, a monoamine oxidase inhibitor (MAOI), stopped the breakdown of neurotransmitters (including serotonin, dopamine, and norepinephrine) by the enzyme monoamine oxidase (MAO), thereby prolonging and enhancing their effect on the brain cells with which they were communicating. This led to the development of a class of antidepressants, the MAOIs, that are still prescribed, particularly for some severely depressed people and those with so-called atypical depression. These drugs did appear to elevate mood, but they had significant side effects, including dangerous, high blood pressure–producing interactions with foods that contain tyramine (a monoamine compound derived from the amino acid tyrosine), such as aged cheese, chocolate, processed meat, and alcoholic beverages.

Observations on MAOIs paved the way for the development of the "biogenic amine hypothesis," a theory that depression is caused by abnormally low levels of neurotransmitters (such as dopamine, norepinephrine, and serotonin) that contain a molecular group called an amine, in which nitrogen is bonded to three other atoms.

In 1957, imipramine (its trade name is Tofranil) was discovered. It appeared to increase the amounts of the amines serotonin, norepinephrine, and dopamine at the junction between nerve cells in the brain, presumably by blocking their reuptake and inactivation. Imipramine has a three-ringed chemical structure and it, and its successors (amitriptyline, trade name Elavil, is the best known), were therefore called tricyclic antidepressants. The effect of these drugs on depression was widely studied and documented. Though there were significant side effects, including potentially life-threatening irregular heartbeat, urinary retention, and a horribly uncomfortable dry mouth, and though the tricyclics could be used, in overdoses, to commit suicide, these compounds were regarded for thirty years as the treatment of choice for depression.

Meanwhile, research on the biogenic amine hypothesis proceeded. Scientists who pursued this line of inquiry found less than normal amounts of the chemical breakdown products, the metabolites, of neurotransmitters, in the blood, urine, spinal fluid, and brains (at autopsy) of some, but only a minority, of depressed people. They observed, as well, that some depressed people who had once been treated with antidepressants and were no longer depressed became depressed again if tryptophan, which is a precursor, or building block, of serotonin, was eliminated from their diets. These findings meshed with observations that MAOIs and tricyclics, which raised neurotransmitter levels, also seemed to improve mood.

In the 1970s, SSRIs (selective serotonin reuptake inhibitors) were developed. These compounds—fluoxetine (Prozac) was not the first, but quickly became the best known and most widely used (with annual U.S. sales reaching $3 billion by 2000)—made more serotonin available for intercellular transmission by blocking its reuptake by the nerve cells that produced it. The SSRIs were believed to be—and were aggressively marketed as—more effective and, because more selective (working only on one amine, serotonin), less burdened with side effects and suicidal risks than the tricyclics.

This line of thinking made a certain amount of sense, but this promise has not been fulfilled. There is no evidence that SSRIs, or drugs like venlafaxine hydrochloride (Effexor) that affect the reuptake of norepinephrine, as well as serotonin (the SNRIs), are any more effective than the tricyclics.

It also seems, as the science develops, that drug effects on neurotransmitters are actually of secondary importance. It has long been observed that antidepressant drugs quickly increase brain neurotransmitter levels, but take several weeks to produce a decrease in depressive symptoms. It now seems far more likely that the greater effect of the drugs is exerted on other aspects of brain physiology and anatomy, including most particularly their ability to inhibit the destructive effects of stress hormones, and to promote cellular growth in the hippocampus and in areas of the cerebral cortex that are connected to the regulation of stress. This suggests that approaches that work *directly on stress* which may also affect cortical functioning and stimulate the growth and development of cells in the hippocampus, *and* are free of negative side effects—the approaches I describe in this book—may well be a far better, as well as far healthier option than drugs.

SSRI Side Effects

Though SSRIs do selectively affect serotonin (and not dopamine or norepinephrine) metabolism, the consequences are anything but selective. Because serotonin is so widely distributed in the body (its largest site of manufacture, for example, is in the gastrointestinal tract, not the brain), so, too, are the side effects. Studies have shown that one half of those taking Prozac have gastrointestinal problems; one fifth experience head-aches from the drug; 15 percent find themselves increasingly nervous and agitated (this effect was noted in some of the earliest studies of the drug); large numbers have significant, unwanted weight gain; and a very sig-nificant percentage (60 percent of those who were asked about it in one major study, 70 percent in another) experience various kinds of sexual dysfunction. In fact, almost 40 percent of all depressed patients in the brief (four to eight weeks) SSRI research studies that were done for drug approval dropped out, even before the studies were concluded.

Long-term use of the SSRIs is revealing even more alarming side effects. One well-documented study of people taking SSRIs shows dete-rioration of brain function in the frontal lobe of the cerebral cortex. Research has also shown that over time SSRIs increase one vital neuro-transmitter, serotonin, at the expense of depleting another, dopamine. This decidedly "unselective" effect may well account for the reports of people on SSRIs who have developed disorders of movement that resem-ble the crippling, dopamine-depleted neurological condition Parkinson's disease.

It's also entirely possible that the long-term—even lifetime—use of SSRIs, which has become increasingly common, will produce even more alarming, unpredictable, and as yet undetected problems. It took twenty years for the medical community to realize that fenfluramine (of the widely and carelessly prescribed fen-phen diet pill combination), which is, like the SSRIs, a serotonin-enhancing drug, can cause *potentially life-threatening damage* to heart valves.

Stopping SSRIs is also unpleasant and can be dangerous. The SSRIs are, contrary to pharmaceutical manufacturers' denials and euphemisms— *discontinuation syndrome* is the term they most often use—psychologically habituating and physically addictive. This is obvious to both physicians and their patients. People on SSRIs often must take ever larger doses to maintain the same effect (habituation) or require frequent additions to, and changes of, medication. When they stop taking the drugs— paroxetine (Paxil) is the most dramatic and dangerous example because it leaves the body quickly—they often experience severe withdrawal symptoms. These include agitation, irritability, diarrhea, fainting, sweats, headaches, a panoply of physical and emotional distress, and heightened feelings of depression and desperation that bear a painful resemblance to what we see in the withdrawal profiles of heroin and cocaine addicts.

Finally, the SSRIs may actually have as much suicidal potential as the tricyclics. Though SSRI overdoses are less likely to be lethal than those with tricyclics, they are not uncommon. Approximately one hundred Americans are reported to die each year from serotonin syndrome, a high-fever-inducing brain intoxication for which SSRIs are often wholly, or partly, responsible.

Even more disturbing, SSRIs may actually precipitate suicidal thoughts, feelings, and acts. For more than fifteen years, highly skilled psychopharmacologists have observed the self-destructive, and destructive, tendencies of some people on SSRIs. This effect is most apparent in the first days or weeks of use—and may include a profound and desperate agitation and, with it, suicidal and sometimes homicidal feelings and actions in people who had never before felt or acted this way. In fact, some epidemiological data from Great Britain show markedly increased rates of suicide in people on SSRIs, as well as an increase in suicidal feelings in healthy volunteers who were given the SSRI sertraline (Zoloft).

In recent years, reevaluation of drug company data and additional studies in Britain and the United States have shown an *increase* in suicidal thoughts, feelings, and behaviors among children, adolescents, and, most recently, young adults who are taking SSRIs. This data has been convincing enough for the U.S. Food and Drug Administration (FDA) to compel pharmaceutical companies to relabel the drugs, with a strong "black box" warning about their potential hazards for those under twenty-five. Thus, SSRIs may be less likely to be a means for suicide than the tricyclics, but they may well be more likely to set the stage for, or indeed, precipitate it.

Given the nature and extent of the side effects of antidepressants, the oft-noted tendency—sometimes referred to as Prozac poop out—for them to stop providing relief over time, and the unknown hazards of their long-term use, it is vitally important to examine how effective they actually are.

DO DRUGS WORK?

When I first began, about a dozen years ago, to carefully examine the evidence for the efficacy of antidepressants, I was far more troubled than I expected to be; in fact, I was shocked. I certainly didn't begin as a pro-drug partisan. Though I had met a number of people who felt their mood was improved and their anxiety decreased, I had also seen many who found antidepressants ineffective. I'd also observed that the drugs often seemed to blunt emotions and to push people toward passivity, to block the understanding that profound change and growth were necessary. Still, I expected the studies that justified their use to be convincing, to show that they regularly and reliably relieved symptoms of depression. This turned out not to be the case.

To begin with, the studies originally done to demonstrate that antidepressants should be allowed to be marketed were much less impressive than we physicians and the public were led to believe. The total numbers of people who were studied prior to drug approval by the FDA were small. In the years since drug approval, tens of millions of people have taken Prozac, but only seventeen hundred were involved in placebo-controlled trials *prior* to approval, and the final decision to approve the drug was, according to one critic of the process (who used the Freedom of Information Act to obtain the data), based on results with "fewer than 300."

The period of study (four to six, or sometimes eight, weeks) bore little relationship to the time for which drugs would usually be prescribed—months, years, a lifetime. On top of that, large numbers of studies that showed poor results were never published (the so-called file-drawer effect), presumably because the drug companies that sponsored them wanted to present only the best face of their highly profitable products.

As I talked with thoughtful colleagues and reviewed the studies myself, I discovered that many studies that were done—*before and after* FDA approval—were flawed for other reasons: They eliminated, at the beginning, people who were likely to get well even without the drug (the so-called placebo responders); ignored the importance of the often substantial personal contact that accompanied the dispensing of drugs in studies; and put too much weight on studies that relied on reports of "observers" who might for a variety of reasons (including the sums paid them as drug company consultants) tend to see more positive changes with the drugs than on how the patients themselves felt.

The "Best" Studies Are Not So Good Either

There was one further and important problem that called into question the results even of positive drug studies. It appeared that few of those that were initially done to obtain FDA approval or, later, to document the effects of approved drugs, used "active" placebos, substances that caused side effects that resembled those of the antidepressants. This is crucial because both the patients taking the antidepressants and the professionals evaluating their effects were able, in the overwhelming majority of these cases of "inert placebos," to identify whether or not the patients were taking the drug being tested, thereby "unblinding" the experiment.

This probably led those who experienced side effects to feel confident that they were getting the drug and therefore probably enhanced its effect. Conversely, those who knew they were not getting the drug most likely had their confidence undermined, therefore diminishing the placebo effect. Finally, since those who were recording the effectiveness of the drugs—many of whom were being paid by the companies that manufactured the drugs they were testing—knew who was, or was not, receiving them, their judgment may also have been affected. A recent study by the highly regarded Cochrane Collaboration concludes that where active placebos were used, the differences in symptom relief between drug and placebo, *however evaluated,* were "small."

The studies that have been done in the years since drug approval and the meta-analyses (reviews of multiple studies) by groups other than Cochrane have been contradictory. Though antidepressants appear to be more effective than inert placebos in relieving symptoms, there is significant disagreement about even the size of this effect. One "systematic review," published in 2000 in the prestigious *Annals of Internal Medicine,* showed that antidepressants were, on average, 50 to 60 percent more effective than placebo. Though most of the placebos used were inert, thereby calling the results into question, this percentage (which has been replicated in some subsequent studies) is generally accepted and cited by physicians who prescribe antidepressants.

On the other hand, another review, published in the equally prestigious *Archives of General Psychiatry* the year after, painted a far less favorable picture. This article, which reviewed clinical trials, unpublished as well as published, done between 1987 and 1997, revealed that in the longer term trials, which were more likely to reflect actual patterns of clinical use, tricyclics were only 12 percent more effective than (the usually inert) placebo *and SSRIs were even less effective, only 8 percent greater than placebo.* Another review article published the following year showed that in 69 percent of the placebo-controlled studies there was *no difference* between tricyclics and placebo.

And, most recently, in 2008, a "Special Article" that appeared in the *New England Journal of Medicine* definitively confirmed the existence of bias in published studies on antidepressants. Reviewing seventy-four FDA-registered studies, the authors found that positive findings were almost inevitably published, while two-thirds of the negative results never appeared in scientific journals. Aggregating the data from all these studies, they concluded that the *actual benefits of antidepressant drugs are significantly less than is generally believed, and, indeed, only slightly greater than placebo.*

Finally, it's important to understand that in many studies the improvement that was noted was only *partial*—according to the widely used Hamilton Depression Rating scale (HAM-D), a "reduction" in symptoms of 50 percent rather than a "remission" of most or all symptoms.

Antidepressants or Short-Term Psychotherapy

Antidepressants thus appear to be only slightly more effective at symptom relief than inert placebos, though with a host of side effects and potential risks that placebos, of course, do not have. It does not appear that they are more effective than brief (ten- to twelve-week) trials of either cognitive or interpersonal psychotherapy (the former focuses on self-defeating ways of thinking, the latter on resolving interpersonal issues related to depression).

Perhaps the best known of the comparative studies is the National Institute of Mental Health Collaborative depression study. This multi-year, multicenter effort concluded that there was *no difference* in overall effects between imipramine and brief trials of both cognitive therapy and interpersonal therapy. The drugs were rated as slightly superior for severely depressed patients by the observing clinicians, but, and I think more important, not by the patients themselves.

In an eighteen-month follow-up, both psychotherapies produced better (though not statistically significant) outcomes than the drug. In addition, patients who received imipramine were, presumably because of increased distress, more likely to have symptoms of depression and more likely to seek out treatment during this follow-up time.

More recent research has generally shown equivalent results for drugs and psychotherapy, and somewhat better outcomes for a combination of drugs and therapy. These studies, however, don't usually compare—as they should, if we are going to rely on the results—psychotherapy with drugs to psychotherapy with an *active* placebo. And one well-done, and widely cited study noted a subgroup of people—those with chronic depression and a history of childhood trauma—for whom the combination was "only marginally superior to psychotherapy alone."

Interestingly, several studies done in recent years have shown that both antidepressant drugs and psychotherapy (interpersonal therapy as well as cognitive behavioral therapy) produce significant changes in brain functioning, along with symptomatic improvement, but that the changes produced are different from one another.

.   .   .

All this doesn't mean that antidepressants can't be helpful to some people. They can. But these studies and my forty years of clinical experience do lead me to conclude, as I've said earlier, that these drugs should be a rarely used last resort: "First do no harm," Hippocrates long ago admonished his students. They are not, as they are almost universally presumed to be, the treatment of choice for most people who are depressed. And they are most emphatically not an intelligent or effective response to the vast array of problems—including low self-esteem, anxiety, shyness, adjustment to college, menopause, or ordinary unhappiness—for which they are promiscuously prescribed.

ANOTHER WAY

The treatment that does make the most sense, for ordinary unhappiness as well as significant clinical depression, combines a variety of kinds of psychological guidance and instruction with a number of other approaches including:

>> Exercise
>> Meditation
>> Guided imagery
>> Self-expression through words, drawings, and movement
>> Yoga
>> Nutrition and supplements
>> Acupuncture and herbal therapies
>> A variety of spiritual practices

Each of these techniques has been *demonstrated* to improve mood in significant numbers of people and to bring about physiological and, in some instances, anatomical brain change, without blunting the emotions or producing noxious and debilitating side effects. *Each by itself* may yield results that are better than placebo, and may very well be as good as, or better than, antidepressants. Common sense urges us to consider that an approach that combines and carefully individualizes these techniques to each of our needs—an integrative approach—is likely to produce better results for most people than chemical antidepressants, at far less physical and emotional cost.

This approach—the *Unstuck* approach—which I describe in this book, has many other advantages. It addresses causes—the underlying physical, emotional, mental, and spiritual blocks and imbalances that produce stress and depression and inhibit our normal functioning and blight our relationships—rather than symptoms. Drugs may produce passivity and dependency. The integrative approach I'm describing mobilizes us and enhances our capacity to help ourselves. It brings hope and life-affirming connection to others. And every one of us, regardless of education, economic status, age, degree of depression, or other therapeutic activities, can use it.

THERESA TALKS OF HER PAIN

Theresa, who had seen some friends unchanged and others numbed and agitated by antidepressants, really doesn't want to take Prozac. But she feels helpless and hopeless, ashamed of past bad choices and current "weakness." She is desperate for relief.

Her present pain has revived—as it so often does in those of us who are depressed—long-buried images of hurt and loss. Her boyfriend's dissatisfaction and criticism are churning up frightening memories of her mother's censure and punishment. His departure evokes the terrible pain of early emotional abandonment. Images and feelings flood her: an arm raised to threaten, her mother's back turning, loneliness.

Theresa closes her eyes for a few moments, breathes deeply and slowly. Her shoulders and chest shake, and tears overwhelm her words.

There is every reason, it seems to me, for Theresa to be depressed. The life she's been living, however admirable, is no longer serving her. In some ways, it hasn't served her for many years. The loss of her lover and, she now fears, of her hope to have a family, echoes and deepens earlier losses. These losses undermine the structure of cheerfulness and caretaking, of skillful action and achievement that she erected as a child to ensure that those she loved were approving, satisfied, and loyal and that the larger hostile world was kept at bay. Theresa is kind, caring, and competent, but she has for years been ruled by others' expectations and her own harsh self-judgment, unable to appreciate her virtues or savor her own strength.

Theresa is depressed and even somewhat disabled. She does not, however, have a disease that requires drugs. Though now stuck, she is also at a turning point. The signs and symptoms of depression, as well as her losses and her understanding of them, can be a wake-up call to change, a new beginning.

It seems so peculiar and shortsighted, as well as disrespectful, to look at Theresa's symptoms in isolation from the broader tapestry of her life, to prescribe drugs for them, to attempt—in a particularly unappetizing and widely used psychiatric phrase—"to restore her premorbid personality." Taking pills may indeed numb her to her pain, but perhaps this is pain she needs in order to feel. Drugs may shore up walls—defenses against living more fully, and more for herself—that need to come down. Though they may provide short-term relief, they may also obscure the message that depression is bringing her, and discourage her from making changes that can transform her life.

"Depression is an impasse to be navigated, an imbalance to be corrected," I tell her. "It isn't like a virus or bacterium," a hostile pathogenic invader to be repelled, or a genetic error to be reversed. Depression can certainly be a crisis, but as the Chinese written characters for "crisis" reveal, it offers opportunity as well as danger. And depression, for Theresa, or any of us, is not simply the end point of a pathological process. It can be a call to psychological and biological transformation, a catalyst to deeper self-knowledge and to a richer experience of who we are, the beginning of a journey toward healing and wholeness.

IS DEPRESSION BIOLOGICAL?

None of this means that depression is not biological. We live in a body, and all our experience is, among other things, biological. If you call me an unpleasant name, it may hurt my feelings and make me angry, and it will also likely alter my biology. My heart rate and my blood pressure will probably go up, my breathing will get shorter and faster, my muscles may tense as if in preparation for fighting or fleeing from you. Some neurotransmitter levels may go up, others down. If I depend on you and you're also abandoning me, my fight-or-flight response may soon be compounded by other biological changes.

Fight or flight—with its shallow breathing, tensed large muscles, high heart rate and blood pressure, hypervigilance, dilated pupils, and decreased intestinal activity—is governed by the sympathetic nervous system, one-half of the body's autonomic (or automatic) nervous system, and mediated by the epinephrine, the adrenaline, it secretes. It is the natural response of all vertebrates to potential threats. Think of television images of the gazelle on Africa's Serengeti Plain sighting the lion and turning to flee.

Animals do, and our human ancestors generally did, move rapidly through the fight-or-flight response. They escaped, or fought and won, or were caught and killed by predators. The biological changes of fight or flight quickly vanished. Five minutes after escaping the lion, the gazelle is happily grazing.

When large-brained, "civilized" humans are stressed, we often carry the lion, our "threat," with us, remembering him long after we have escaped. He is there every time we experience the loss that has made us desperate, or condemn ourselves for what we have or haven't done, or think about a day in our conflict-filled office, or contemplate making a change that seems impossible.

When our fight or flight persists, the stress response becomes operative. Our thoughts and feelings and memories, and the images that give them form, continue to stimulate the hypothalamus, one of the brain's central switching stations. The hypothalamus secretes corticotropin-releasing hormone (CRH). CRH stimulates the nearby pituitary, or "master," gland. The pituitary in turn secretes adrenocorticotropin hormone (ACTH), which flows through the bloodstream to the adrenal gland, where it causes the release of cortisol and the other stress hormones. Now our hypothalamic-pituitary-adrenal axis (HPA) is in overdrive.

If the stress is chronic, our adrenaline and, with it, our blood pressure and heart rate stay high, as do our levels of cortisol; our muscles remain tense and our gut is in turmoil. The cortisol keeps our blood sugar elevated, and our immune system weakens. Every organ and every cell become more vulnerable, including those in the emotional centers of our brain.

Prolongation of the fight-or-flight response—chronic stress—may negatively affect our immune response and predispose us to infections, arthritis, and heart disease, as well as persistent anxiety and depression. The more distressing the events and our experience of them are, the longer they persist, and the earlier in life they occur, the more likely they are to cause long-term biological changes. And those who do experience painful or stressful early-life losses of love seem to be more vulnerable to the same kind of stress and trauma later in life, and to depression.

Some people who are depressed or "stressed out" may have ongoing dysfunctions in the circuit that connects the brain, the hypothalamus, the pituitary gland, and the adrenal gland. Overactivity of this HPA axis may produce the increased levels of cortisol that can be seen in depression. Prolonged overactivity may also eventually lead to adrenal exhaustion, and with it very low levels of circulating cortisol, more fatigue, and a depression that may be even deeper.

Depressed people may also have decreased metabolism in various parts of the frontal lobe of the cerebral cortex. Continuing high levels of stress hormones may destroy cells in the hippocampus, an area of the brain intimately connected with memory and emotion. And there may be abnormalities in the levels of the various neurotransmitters.

These beautifully intricate and individually variable but still imperfectly understood biological responses to stress and loss do not, however, constitute a disease. Nor do they exist in isolation. They are intimately connected to and can be *profoundly influenced by:* the way we think and feel; how we act and express ourselves; what we eat and whether or not we meditate or exercise; how we relate to others, and how close we are to them; what work we do and where we do it; as well as our income and our gender. Low-income and unemployed people and those with fewer close connections to others, for example, are far more likely to be depressed, and women are diagnosed with depression almost twice as often as men.

USING THE *UNSTUCK* APPROACH TO AFFECT YOUR BIOLOGY

All these aspects of our lives—biology, attitude, activity, relationships, vocation, social status, gender, and income—are interpreted and experienced in ways that are shaped by our belief in, and our commitment to, our ability to help ourselves. If we feel helpless about our situation and hopeless to change it, we will likely remain depressed. If we mobilize our hope, understand that it is reasonable and entirely justified, and then act on it, our mood will likely improve. As we express our feelings, make a commitment to helping ourselves, act on our own behalf, and reach out to others, we are already on our way to reversing the biological markers of chronic stress and depressed mood, to moving through and beyond depression.

Simply by thinking about the world differently (for example, realizing, as cognitive behavioral therapy teaches us, that the glass can be half full rather than half empty), we lower the levels of our stress hormones. We can lower stress hormones by writing in a journal about what we're feeling. Just by talking with another human being, a Guide who is trained to listen empathetically—a psychotherapist, a physician, perhaps even a friend—we may begin to straighten out our disordered brain functioning.

The easily learned mind-body approaches, such as meditation, guided imagery, and biofeedback, that are central to the *Unstuck* approach all quiet the fight-or-flight response. And all have a direct effect on our levels of anxiety and stress. Each can recalibrate our malfunctioning HPA axis; help shift brain functioning from areas of the cortex associated with distress to those that mediate happiness and compassion; regulate the level of our stress hormones and neurotransmitters; perhaps even replace dead or damaged hippocampal cells with healthy new ones; and improve our mood. As I noted before, a recent study shows significant thickening in the cerebral cortex of the brains of regular meditators. All these mind-body approaches, as you'll see, also offer us a more relaxed, less fearful, and less depressing perspective on the mental and emotional issues that disturb and deplete us.

Physical exercise has similar direct effects on the biology and psychology of depression. Exercise increases levels of neurotransmitters that may sometimes be depleted and releases relaxing and pleasure-inducing endorphins. Exercise has been demonstrated in animals to increase the numbers of new, healthy neurons in the hippocampus. Exercise also helps us feel better about our bodies, which, when we're depressed, often seem alien and burdensome. Exercising, we discover that feelings of helplessness and hopelessness begin to fade. Several impressive scientific studies have shown that exercise may *by itself* be as effective as antidepressants or psychotherapy in reducing the symptoms of depression.

Nutrition can make a difference as well. For a number of people, eliminating or cutting down significantly on certain foods (sugar and caffeine, for example) may enhance mood, decrease anxiety, and increase energy. Some depressed people seem to have a sensitivity to certain foods—among them, wheat, milk, and soy—that may contribute to their altered mood. Inadequate levels of some nutrients—including B vitamins, selenium, chromium, and magnesium—can cause clinical depression and anxiety. Supplementation can bring relief.

There are other approaches, too, from many of the world's great healing traditions, that mobilize our capacity for self-healing and help lift us out of depression. Acupuncture can improve mood, decrease levels of anxiety and agitation, enhance sleep, and raise levels of the very neurotransmitters toward which antidepressant drugs are directed, with none of the negative side effects, along with a number of additional physical and emotional benefits. Herbal therapies can also be powerful: A simple herb, Saint-John's-wort, has demonstrated significant effectiveness in relieving mild and moderate depression; individualized combinations of herbs that address each person's specific emotional and physical imbalance may hold out even more hope.

And then there are all the other aspects of our lives that can offer us emotional and physical healing—our relationships with others and with the social and natural world that surrounds us.

When we neglect the nourishing roots of family and friends, jobs, neighborhoods, nature, and culture, our lives begin to dry up. When we're able to appreciate close family and friends, or to be enthusiastic about and committed to our work, we are less likely to become depressed. If, once depressed, we can spend time in nature or reach out to others or engage ourselves in work that feels useful and productive, we're likely to move through the experience with greater ease.

Depression also signals a spiritual crisis. When we are depressed, our lives seem purposeless, empty of meaning. All the world's religions and all the great spiritual traditions recognize this depleted, despairing state. And all offer deep truths and powerful experiences that can open us up to a sustaining connection with some "thing," or some "one," larger than ourselves—a "higher power," God, nature, the Tao—and, yes, lift our spirits and our mood. The wisdom of these traditions and the hope and healing they bring are available to all of us.

When I work with depression, I know that sooner or later I will address each of these dimensions—attitudinal, physical, mental, emotional, familial, social, vocational, ecological, economic, and spiritual. Each is part of who we are. All are interconnected and have a profound effect on one another.

In the chapters that follow I'll show you how to make use of all of these aspects of your existence intelligently, creatively, joyously, and in ways tailored to your unique need for healing. I'll help each of you to mobilize your capacity for hope, action, and passion to relieve the symptoms of your depression, *and* to transform your life.

OUR WORK BEGINS

This work of healing is grounded in hope, connection, and a more meditative approach to our lives. It starts with knowing that you can make a difference in how you feel, in how you live your life. In this next section,

I'll talk a little about the hope and connection that make this approach possible and support it, and teach you a simple meditative technique that will ease all the steps of your journey, and give you the confidence that you can successfully complete it.

I want you to feel that depression is an imbalance and a challenge, not a disease and misfortune; I want to help you recognize that as you begin this journey with me, you are opening the door to change and healing. You are no longer thinking of yourself as a victim of a disease process that's out of your control. You're becoming an active participant in a process of learning and growth, change and healing.

The practical and self-validating approaches and techniques that I'll teach you will likely help you to feel somewhat better very soon. If you learn them well and use them faithfully, you'll probably feel *much* better.

Instead of relying on a belief in an unproven theory, or a pill and the pharmacologic lift it may give you, you'll be making real, manageable changes; experiencing the physical, emotional, and spiritual well-being that you yourself have created, the natural healing that is available to everyone. You will feel better and you will *know* that you are helping and healing *yourself.*

Hope and Connection

It is likely that hope led you to this book, just as it brought Theresa to see me. In fact, hope is the necessary medium of this work. It is a clear antidote to depression, and is itself a force for healing and restoring wholeness. People who are hopeful generally feel better than those who are not, regardless of their biological status or physical disability. Hope for the power of a pill together with faith in the one who prescribes it are what make a sugary placebo almost as powerful—in a number of studies, *as* powerful—as a chemical antidepressant. The demonstrable effect of meditating or exercising or changing your diet, of deep breathing or using your imagination, will increase your hope exponentially. As you read about the rapidly accumulating scientific evidence for the effectiveness of these techniques, your hope will be reinforced. Hope supports the powerful changes you make as you use these techniques. The results you experience from them will, in turn, justify and sustain still greater hope.

Connection—imaginative, physical, emotional—is critical for almost all of us. It means reaching out, sometimes even when we, like Theresa, feel most like retreating. Reading this book, you are connecting with me and with the people whose stories I'm telling—with what I've learned on my own journey and from my patients and friends, with the ways I've helped others, with the optimism my clinical experience inspires in me, and with the guidance I'm offering.

Meditation

Because meditation is fundamental to our work together, I want to begin teaching it to you right here at the beginning of our journey. Meditation is not difficult or esoteric. You don't have to go to some faraway mountain retreat or strange place or put on different clothes to do it. And you certainly don't have to pay a fee or join a group or renounce your religion. Meditation is practical and easy to learn. It decreases the stress that keeps you confined in depression and produces the relaxed, moment-to-moment awareness that allows change to happen. Meditation quiets your body and allows you to observe more calmly the mind-generated terrors that may alternately agitate and immobilize you. And meditation nourishes the courage and persistence you will need as you make the journey through and beyond anxiety, despondency, and fear.

The word *meditation* comes from *medi,* the same Sanskrit and Greek root that is the origin of our word *medicine. Medi* means "to take the measure of" and "to care for."

There are three basic types of meditation. In concentrative meditation, we focus on a sound (like the Sanskrit *Om*), an image (the sight of ocean waves lapping the shore), or words (a repeated prayer like the Lord's Prayer). Concentrative meditations are part of virtually all the world's spiritual traditions and religions. We'll do one, together with Theresa, very soon.

The second type of meditation, awareness or mindfulness meditation, appears to have originated with Buddhism in South Asia, where it is called *vipassana*. It encourages moment-to-moment awareness of thoughts, feelings, and sensations as they arise. We'll discuss its importance and its use in detail in chapter four.

Both concentrative and awareness meditation have been studied extensively, and their positive effects on mood and anxiety have been widely documented in the scientific literature.

The third kind of meditation, expressive meditation, is the oldest one on the planet and is still central to the practice of many aboriginal and tribal people. It includes fast, deep breathing; shaking, dancing, and whirling; and spontaneous emotional expression. Though it has not yet been studied by scientists, it's enormously useful, particularly when you're anxious, depressed, or angry. In chapter three, I'll teach you several forms and show you how they can be powerful tools for energizing your body, relaxing your mind, and healing your depression.

THERESA BEGINS WITH SOFT BELLY

The technique I most often use myself, the one I'll teach Theresa in this our first session, is called Soft Belly. Soft Belly is a biologically powerful concentrative meditation and is grounded in slow, deep breathing.

I teach it at the very beginning of our journey because I hope Soft Belly will be your constant companion, quieting, steadying, and reassuring you at every stage of your journey. When you do Soft Belly, you simply allow your belly to rise with the in breath and fall with the out breath, while you focus on the image of a soft, relaxed belly.

When your belly is soft, your lungs, together with the muscular, dome-shaped diaphragm that separates the chest from the abdomen, expand more and the volume of air you inhale increases. The exchange of oxygen in the lower part of your lungs, where the blood flow is greater, improves. When your belly is soft, all the other muscles in your body begin to relax as well. Soft Belly can help quiet the mental and physical agitation, the persistent fight-or-flight response, and the chronic stress that are almost always present—along with exhaustion, hopelessness, and self-condemnation—when we are depressed.

Slow, deep, relaxed breathing mobilizes the parasympathetic nervous system, the half of the autonomic nervous system that balances the fight-or-flight response of the sympathetic nervous system. It creates what Harvard cardiologist Herbert Benson, who did some of the early research on this phenomenon, called "the relaxation response." Conscious use of deep breathing overrides the pattern of fast shallow breathing that leads to, and results from, anxiety, and offers us more of the oxygen that is necessary for efficient and relaxed mental functioning. It stimulates the vagus (from the Latin for "wandering") nerve, which balances the functioning of a number of our most important internal organs.

Slow, deep breathing also decreases our blood pressure and our heart rate, smoothes out our intestinal functioning, and lowers our levels of the stress hormone cortisol, our blood sugar, and, in some studies, our cholesterol as well. When we meditate regularly, using techniques similar to Soft Belly, the portions of our brain associated with fear and anxiety, and with unpleasant thoughts, quiet down. PET scans and MRIs show us that slow, deep meditative breathing lights up the parts of our brain that are intimately connected with happy thoughts and good feelings.

I first learned Soft Belly thirty years ago in a workshop on death, dying, and loss, given by Stephen Levine, an experienced and wise traveler on the journey out of depression and despair. I've used it almost every day since. I like it because it's graphic and concrete. It uses words and a physical image to enhance and deepen the experience of breathing, to gently focus our ever-wandering minds. I like it, too, because it is utterly nondenominational, and because it so subversively cuts against the grain of our culture's stress-producing position of choice: the tightly pulled-back shoulders and sucked-in gut.

As we focus on the words and image of Soft Belly, we slowly, gently move the thoughts that disturb us toward the periphery of our consciousness. As we relax, we gain perspective on the worrisome way we are accustomed to think. We're able to concentrate better.

Used regularly, slow deep breathing rebalances the hypothalamic-pituitary-adrenal axis. It stills the agitation that makes us despair when we're depressed. It quiets the racing heart of 3:00 a.m. terrors. It helps us gain perspective on the thoughts—and the ways of thinking—that agitate and depress us. It improves our mood. Using Soft Belly, you will likely find, little by little, that you are taking control of your physical and emotional state, making positive, powerful changes in how you feel.

Here's how, toward the end of our first session, I taught Soft Belly to Theresa.

SOFT BELLY BREATHING

Sit quietly in a comfortable chair. It's good to have things around you that make you feel peaceful and comforted: a work of art, a photo of a loved one, some flowers, a religious symbol. It's better if the lights are somewhat dimmed. You can start with five or ten minutes of Soft Belly. Use a kitchen timer to tell you when your session is over.

Sitting quietly, close your eyes. Breathe slowly and deeply, in through your nose and out through your mouth. Allow your belly to be soft as you breathe, expanding on the in breath, relaxing on the out breath.

You might say to yourself as you breathe in, "Soft," and as you breathe out, "Belly." This will focus your mind and remind you that you want your belly to be soft. When thoughts come, let them come, and let them go. Gently bring your mind back to the phrase, "Soft . . . Belly," "Soft . . . Belly."

As you repeat this phrase to yourself, you're giving your mind something to focus on. Sometimes people have the idea that relaxation or meditation has to do with focusing on nothing. Our minds just aren't built that way. We only make ourselves more agitated and, yes, more depressed, if we try to force thoughts away or judge ourselves harshly because they keep returning. Let thoughts come—even judgments about your thoughts and the way you're doing Soft Belly. Let them go. Bring your mind gently back to "Soft . . . Belly."

As you breathe slowly, focusing on "Soft Belly," anxious chatter about past or present failures and imperfections begins, slowly, to grow fainter. The clamor of doubt and worry about what may happen quiets.

When you're ready—or when your timer rings—open your eyes and bring your attention back into the room.

It's nice to have a special place where you do this meditation, one where you can close the door and be by yourself. And it's good to have a regular time, too. It helps connect you to your practice and gives structure to your days.

You can begin doing Soft Belly for five or ten minutes, perhaps twice a day. As time goes on, you may want to do it for longer periods, or more often. You can do it whenever you feel anxious or uncertain, or when your mind gets locked into repetitive thoughts, guilty feelings, or a preoccupation with how bad you've been, or how hopeless your situation is. If you're feeling really depressed or anxious, this could be several times a day or more.

If you feel too agitated when you sit to do Soft Belly, get up and move around. Do some chores, go for a walk. Then try it again, sitting on a bench in a park after you've walked for a while, or in a coffee shop or a library or church or back home. Little by little, you'll feel the relaxation that grows in you.

Sitting this way will not make the thoughts go away—and trying to force them away will only reinforce their importance—but it will give you some peace and quiet amid them, and a distance from them. They will gradually loosen their hold on you. Your mind will clear. It will function better. Your body will relax. You'll realize you can help yourself. Your mood will lift.

Theresa and I sit for eight or ten minutes, breathing together—Soft Belly—relaxing, being together. We open our eyes.

"How are you now?" I ask.

"Better, calmer," she says, "more in my body, in this chair—even a little happier."

What Helps?

Now that Theresa is more relaxed and has seen that she can create this state herself, she's better prepared to take a larger and more active role in helping herself.

"Is there any time of day," I go on, "when you feel better? Anything you do that makes a difference?" I'm looking now for ways that Theresa knows she can help herself, for experiences she can consciously choose to repeat, benefit from, and build on.

Theresa pauses, closes her eyes, and remembers for a moment. "Yoga," she says. "After I do it in the morning, I feel easier and energized, too." Then she adds, "But I don't do it every day, or for long, and when I rush to the office afterward, sometimes I lose its effect."

"Anything else?"

"My friend Barbara," she smiles. "I look forward to her calls and her visits. I can look like hell or repeat myself or say self-pitying things or even stuff that's politically incorrect, and she's there for me. She loves me, and she doesn't take me too seriously. We're friends."

Theresa has told me two things that she already does that she knows are helpful. And we've experienced a third—the slow deep breathing, the Soft Belly—together. At the end of our session I write them out for her on my prescription pad, reminding Theresa of what helps, that she already knows it helps, and that she can do it again.

THERESA'S PRESCRIPTION

1 Do the yoga every day for at least 20 or 30 minutes. Then take some time to sit quietly or read or listen to music before you go to work.

2 Don't wait for Barbara to call. Reach out to her when you need to.

3 Breathe deeply—Soft Belly twice a day for 10 minutes and also when you're agitated.

Just about all of you—no matter how troubled or confused—have these occasions of relief, these "sweet spots": deep breathing, a walk in the park, watching a favorite show on television, eating comfort food, talking to a best friend, thoughts you have, actions you take, people you connect with. If you just take a few moments, you can become aware of them. If you are aware of them, you can, when you need to, consciously choose to use or experience them.

At the end of this chapter I'll share with you the more complete Prescription for Self-Care that I asked Theresa to develop for herself. Following that, there's space for you to write down what *you* already know is helpful, to write your own prescription. At the end of each subsequent chapter I provide another Prescription for Self-Care. These prescriptions will guide you in organizing your personal healing program. They will help you keep track of the changes you're making, the challenges you're meeting, and the benefits you're experiencing.

Every time you do something for yourself—breathe deeply or do yoga or go for a walk or put music on and dance or read a book—you get the specific benefit of that activity (for example, using Soft Belly to reduce stress, quiet the mind, and get a calmer perspective on depression). At the same time, you address and begin to reverse the fundamental problem of depression (and of ordinary unhappiness and stress): your feelings of helplessness and hopelessness, the sense that you're no longer in control of your life, and that your current misery will never lift.

When Theresa calls or visits with Barbara, she's overcoming the isolation that imprisons her in depression. The same is true for you. When you let yourself feel the sadness or rage that gets stuck and buried in depression and you share those feelings, you are no longer *de*pressed—pushed down and flattened out. You are *ex*pressing yourself and connecting with someone else. And when you do this simple thing, or anything else, for yourself, you're no longer stuck, but moving.

I tell Theresa, "If you pay attention—and much of our work is really about paying attention—to what is happening as you sit in the postures of yoga, or breathe slowly and deeply, or when you open the door to Barbara, you'll feel that change and healing are possible, that they are already happening. Change and healing are the essence of all life, moving you deeper into it, moving you forward on your journey."

THE HERO'S HEALING JOURNEY: BECOMING UNSTUCK

Healing depression and overcoming unhappiness mean dealing more effectively with stress; recovering physical and psychological balance; reclaiming the parts of ourselves that we've ignored or suppressed; and appreciating the wholeness that has somehow slipped away from us, or that we have never really known. But this healing is dynamic and expansive as well as integrative, not just a series of tasks, but an adventure.

Depression almost always brings with it—along with the sense of loss and inadequacy, of gloom and uncertainty—a feeling of immobility, of "stuckness." It feels as if we've broken down, alone and lonely, in some dismal, charmless backwater that no one would ever choose to visit. The beginning of the end of depression comes when we recognize this place, and see it not as the end, but as the beginning, a starting point for the journey through and beyond depression, confusion, and despair, toward wholeness, healing, and delight.

This uncertain, challenging journey is, I believe, the life-defining path that leads us to who we really are, who we are meant to be. And it is, in many ways, like the journeys that have defined our culture and the modern ones that impress and inspire us: Moses's painful pilgrimage, Jesus's mission, Muhammad's flight; the trials of confinement and the later-life challenges of contemporary heroes such as Franklin Roosevelt (crippled by polio before he became one of our most effective and compassionate presidents), Elie Wiesel (the Holocaust survivor and Nobel laureate), Mahatma Gandhi, Nelson Mandela, and former prisoner of war John McCain; the hard-won authority of poet Maya Angelou and television teacher Oprah Winfrey; the steadfast marches of the Reverend Dr. Martin Luther King Jr. The ancient Greek poem *The Odyssey,* the model for both our classic novels of self-discovery and our modern adventure and mystery stories, is the tale of a man "full of woe," who finally finds his way home and to wholeness.

As Joseph Campbell and psychiatrist Carl Jung before him point out, these historic and heroic figures are taking "archetypal" journeys, journeys that reflect and embody timeless truths of human psychological transformation, as well as world-changing action. Their stories can encourage us to accept, rather than flee from, the personal challenges that confront us, to relax with rather than tense against our terror. They show us that patience and courage, awareness, creativity, and judicious action can transform suffering. These heroes and their stories are inspirational. They remind us that others have been there before, that we are not alone.

THE SEVEN STAGES OF
THE HEALING JOURNEY

There are seven stages on this journey. They are—in one form or another—as old as recorded history. My discussion of these stages draws on the sequence that Joseph Campbell observed in scriptures and myths and described in *The Hero with a Thousand Faces,* on my own experience as a traveler on this journey, and on my work with thousands of depressed, discouraged, confused, and conflicted people.

1 The Call: the awareness that we are depressed and that some kind of change, a journey, is necessary.

2 Guides on the Journey: meeting and choosing the men and women who can help, and developing our own inner guidance and wisdom.

3 The Surrender to Change: allowing and encouraging ourselves to let go of what constrains and freezes us, and to move into the current of life.

4 Dealing with Demons: meeting the challenges—self-doubt,

loneliness, procrastination, pride, resentment, perfectionism, fear—and finding in them the unique *daimon,* the source of our own meaning, purpose, and direction.

5 The Dark Night of the Soul: allowing and inviting the deepest life-giving freedom to emerge as we move through the despair that may come to any of us.

6 Spirituality: The Blessing: experiencing the unity and peace, the love and generosity, the connection to something or someone greater than ourselves that can transform our lives.

7 The Return: learning to live every day joyously, deeply, consciously, with ourselves and others, in the light of what we have experienced and are always learning.

In the next seven chapters, I'll give practical guidance and specific techniques to use at each stage of the journey. And I'll provide physical, mental, emotional, and spiritual nourishment that can sustain each of you on your path—instruction in meditation and guided imagery that will quiet your anxiety, raise your energy, promote understanding and improve your mood; detailed information about safe, physiologically balancing, mood-lifting supplements and herbs; insights that can change the way you look at your life; stories about ancient heroes—and the ordinary, present-time ones who populate my consulting room—that can move and instruct you, inspire you, and open the door to your own heroic possibilities and to your own healing.

Not all of you will experience all of the stages, or experience them in the order I describe. Some of you may feel despair in the first hours of the Call and others may have moments of great peace while you struggle with your demons. Guides are always appearing. And challenges that are strenuous, difficult, daunting, even overwhelming, can, after some struggle, become richly rewarding.

This book is written for those of you who are, like Theresa, clinically depressed—who can't get out of bed in the morning, eat incessantly or not at all, who *know* that the glass is half empty, who feel that life has failed you and you it, and that it will always be this way.

It's also for, and is about, all of you who may or may not be diagnosed as depressed but who feel stuck or overburdened or unhappy or dissatisfied. And it is for any of you who may wonder "Where am I going? or "Am I ever going to feel better?" or "Why am I here? or What is my purpose?"

Unstuck is meant to be as useful for the ordinarily unhappy and confused as for the obviously depressed. On the journey toward wholeness, all of us must meet similar challenges and proceed with similar care and courage.

If you flee from and suppress the symptoms of depression—with drugs and/or denial—you run the risk of remaining stuck in self-defeating and repetitive patterns, in habits and ideas and ways of relating to others that no longer serve you. If you see and embrace each stage of the journey, each challenge, as your teacher—an opportunity to see what you've been ignoring and need to know—you enter another universe. Now you can recover parts of yourself that have been denied; stretch and grow in ways that further your development as a human being; reach out in ways that offer, and inspire, love. Now powerful change and healing can and will come.

This book is designed to guide you through the stages of your journey and your life, to help you use times of depression, distress, and confusion, however severe or mild, wisely and well. It can help you find new strengths and possibilities in yourself, and more hope and joy than you have ever imagined. In the process, you may become balanced and wise enough so that you will always be . . . unstuck.

YOUR PRESCRIPTION FOR SELF-CARE:
WHAT NEXT?
At the end of my session with Theresa—and at the end of my first meetings with all of my patients—I write out a prescription. It includes a list of supplements and herbs, instructions about changing diet, advice about which meditation or exercise to do. Among my recommendations there are always actions, techniques, approaches, and attitudes that each person has told me—which she *already*

knows—are helpful. These are the ones I'm asking you to record here, at the end of this introduction.

I suggest that you take some time now, before you go on to the next chapter, to write out your own prescription.

First read the instructions and Theresa's example. Next, sit quietly and close your eyes. Breathe deeply and slowly for three to four minutes with your belly soft as Theresa and I did. Then turn to the following page and begin.

Put your name at the top, just as a physician would on a prescription pad. Then begin writing. Short sentences, even phrases, are good. Write down activities you've already been doing that are helpful to you, modifying them to make them fit the needs you now feel. Add any other activities, like Soft Belly, that may have occurred to you as you read this chapter. And, just as on a prescription pad, write down the frequency and duration of the activity that you're proposing. Be realistic, and be a bit bold too.

At the end, sign your prescription.

If you'd like, copy your prescription and put it on your refrigerator or your desk.

Here's the prescription that Theresa and I came up with, listing activities that had helped and likely would continue to help her to help herself.

THERESA'S PRESCRIPTION FOR SELF-CARE:
WHAT ALREADY MAKES ME FEEL HAPPY OR MORE WHOLE

NAME: THERESA

	ACTIVITY	HOW OFTEN?	HOW LONG?	WITH WHOM?
1	Do yoga in the morning	every day	20 to 30 minutes during the week, 60 to 90 minutes on the weekend	by myself
2	Sit quietly after yoga or listen to music before going to work	every day	10 to 20 minutes	by myself
3	Talk on the phone with my best friend Barbara	every day	anywhere from 5 to 30 minutes	Barbara
4	Visit with Barbara in person	at least 1 to 2 times a week	for dinner or a walk	Barbara
5	Go for a walk during the day	whenever I feel trapped or just need to get out of the office	for as long as I feel like	by myself or with coworkers
6	Go to church	Sunday-morning service	2 hours	the whole congregation
7	Do Soft Belly	2 to 3 times a day or whenever I feel anxious	5 to 10 minutes	by myself
8	Cook good food for myself	whenever possible	whatever it takes	by myself or with a friend

SIGNED: THERESA

YOUR FIRST PRESCRIPTION FOR SELF-CARE:
WHAT ALREADY MAKES ME FEEL HAPPY OR MORE WHOLE

NAME: _____ DATE: _____

	ACTIVITY	HOW OFTEN?	HOW LONG?	WITH WHOM?
1				
2				
3				
4				
5				
6				
7				
8				

SIGNED: _____

CHAPTER 1

The Call:
Finding the Right Way

>>>>>> We need to know that we are stuck—depressed, unhappy, troubled—before we can do something about it; we need to acknowledge our pain, so we can hear its Call to change. This is as true for us now, in twenty-first-century America, as it was for the great heroes of our myths and literature. In the first part of this chapter, I'll show you how to listen to this Call, and help you to respond—to take the first practical steps on your healing journey.

Once you know you're depressed, you need to be sure there are no physical reasons for it. In the second part of this chapter, we'll look at the obvious diseases that may cause or contribute to depression. Then we'll go over the subtle biological imbalances that may be missed or dismissed by conventional physicians, but can also cause the symptoms of depression. I'll tell you who to consult to rule out, or diagnose, these conditions, and what you can do to remedy or reverse them.

Finally, as we prepare to move ahead, I'll give you detailed instructions and a simple, practical plan for using food and nutritional supplements to strengthen you physically and emotionally, to make your journey through and beyond depression easier, swifter, more productive, and more life enhancing.

ANCIENT AWAKENINGS AND MODERN WAKE-UPS

We first meet the hero of Homer's three-thousand-year-old epic *The Odyssey* sitting "in his stone seat to seaward—tear on tear / brimming his eyes." Odysseus, that brave, brilliant, richly gifted, and endlessly inventive man, is at a loss. He lives with the eternally young and beautiful goddess Kalypso. He drinks nectar and eats ambrosia by day and makes love to her at night. It looks like a very good deal, indeed, but Odysseus, "with eyes wet / scanning the bare horizon of the sea," is miserable. He knows his destiny is elsewhere, and is immobilized, trapped, it seems forever, on Kalypso's island.

Dante Alighieri, the thirteenth-century poet, tells us, in the first lines of his *Commedia* that he finds himself "in the middle of our life's journey . . . in a dark wood." He has "lost the right way" and feels his "heart pierced with terror."

The eighth-century-BC Greek hymn of Demeter begins with a pastoral scene: The young and beautiful goddess Persephone is wandering away from her companions when, suddenly, the earth opens up. Hades, the chariot-commanding dark lord of the underworld, seizes her. The earth closes over them. The scene changes. Persephone's mother, Demeter, the goddess of all that grows on earth, is blinded by tears.

One man apparently has everything, but is miserable; the other is lost, disoriented, and terrified. The young goddess is helplessly confined in darkness. Her mother is immobilized by loss. All are, though they do not yet know it, about to embark on journeys that will utterly transform their lives.

In our lives such beginnings are usually less clear and dramatic. Still, there are occasions when we realize that our world is tilting at a persistently awkward angle, mornings when we awaken to find ourselves in another country, where the colors have darkened, or are bleeding together.

If this is our first time, it's bound to be a shock. Why, we ask, am I feeling this way? Am I sick? Did somebody put something in my food or drink? What's going on?

The exact experience of depression is as unique as each person, but certain patterns seem to announce its arrival. Sometimes you wake up and you know, with the blinding certitude of the ridiculously obvious, that you're depressed. That's more or less what happened to me that morning in 1965, and to Theresa.

Sometimes the realization comes over time, against the background of a life that had seemed happy and successful. Nothing that is available or offered satisfies. You can't concentrate or finish what you've started. Day by day your step grows heavier, and sleep becomes elusive or addictive. Enthusiasm and joy evaporate. Food and sex slowly lose their appeal. And then, one day, something happens, something that probes an old hurt in a particularly reminiscent way or opens a new one, some event or feeling that brings you a new, darker perspective—and life's weight suddenly feels unbearable.

If these moments are reminders of a dark world we have for a while escaped or ignored, but which has come once again, like Hades, to claim us, we may feel doubly despairing. "Not again," we protest: "I thought I'd left that behind."

These are common responses to experiencing loss, pain, and disappointment. But being unhappy, even "clinically depressed," doesn't mean we are crazy or have a disease. Our fear, confusion, and vulnerability simply mark us as human. These dark times are a part of, not apart from, our lives. They tell us change is necessary.

Dorothy

Dorothy had lived a lie for a long time. Like many other women of her generation, Dorothy had, as a very young woman, married a man considered both "eligible" and "appropriate." He was the son of the local banker, tall and good looking, physically and verbally gifted, the quarterback on the high school football team, class president, and the captain of the debating society. He wore nice clothes and was ambitious enough to know that he wanted a bigger stage than their midsize midwestern city could ever offer.

In fact, Dorothy had, even at a smitten sixteen, wondered if Todd wasn't too much of an actor altogether: He disparaged teammates whom he had moments before embraced, and the smile faded from his face as soon as an adoring coach or teacher left the room. Still, five years later, Dorothy married Todd. It wasn't that there weren't other opportunities: She was very bright and nice, many thought her beautiful, and she had had more suitors than most. But whenever she inclined toward one of them, she felt herself drawn back to Todd.

"I knew there was something wrong with him, some terrible coldness at the center. His kisses seemed so perfunctory. And I never felt comfortable sharing my hopes and feelings with him. But he was handsome and gallant, and he bought me the most lovely presents. He said that we were meant to be together, and that together we could conquer the world. He was the first boy I'd ever slept with, and every girl I knew wanted to be with him. And I was young and conventional and very much attached to my family, and they were so approving, so delighted with Todd, that I married him as much—no, more—to please them as myself.

"I sometimes think I'm smarter than Todd. That may seem immodest. But his intelligence is so limited. He could memorize anything and even analyze a play or a historical or biblical situation brilliantly, but he missed the essence of it, the heart in it."

Dorothy did everything to advance Todd's career as law clerk, lawyer, and politician. When he ran for the Senate, she took a leave from her job as a teacher to manage his campaign. Those long hours together, in the campaign office, at home, crisscrossing the state, planning and strategizing, were the times she felt closest to him. By the time Todd won his upset election, she was almost as well known as he. She had arranged all the parties at the fund-raisers' houses, then stayed late with their wives to help clean up.

Everything looked so promising when they first came to Washington. Todd was the star in his class of newly elected senators. Dorothy started a consulting business for struggling nonprofits. They were a stunning couple, invited to and warmly welcomed at Washington's A-list parties and charity fund-raisers. Still, Dorothy began to feel her world was actually growing smaller. Work had brought her close to Todd, in a way that conversation, sex, and children never had. And now work was taking him away. He had a large and adoring staff and was, as time went on, far less interested in her counsel, in advice that was sometimes mixed with admonition and home truths. While he worked late, she played ball and music with the children. He traveled the world on Senate committee business, and she ferried the youngsters to after-school lessons.

By the time Todd was up for reelection, Dorothy was seeing a psychiatrist. He helped her remember her doubts about Todd. He explored the origins of her dependency feelings in her close—perhaps, he suggested, overly close—relationships with both of her parents, but he also urged her to scale down her expectations. No marriage is perfect, he assured her. The senator doesn't drink to excess, and he doesn't run around with other women, at least not publicly, and he always talks about your partnership. He seems so genial on television, so sensitive to his constituents' needs, so articulate about the country's destiny.

Dorothy was too polite to say so, and too desperate for someone to listen to her, to risk offending the psychiatrist, but she suspected after a year that he was more interested in her husband, the senator, and in the latest insider gossip than in what was going on inside her. She left therapy.

Todd was reelected once, easily, and then again. The children seemed to be doing well, one at a good college, the other just out of law school and engaged. And Dorothy's business was prospering. But the better Dorothy's life looked on the outside, the worse it felt on the inside. "The therapy helped me do what I do," she later told me, "be the perfect Washington wife, and the good mother, and the trustworthy, successful consultant. I was always trying to make things right—for my clients and Todd and the children. But I was losing my vitality, growing old before my time, sleeping poorly, and eating sweets and drinking coffee and Cokes so I could keep on rushing around."

Dorothy consulted another psychiatrist who saw the signs and symptoms of depression and "strongly advised" her to begin taking an antidepressant. Dorothy liked this psychiatrist and took the pills he prescribed for several months, first Paxil and then, when that proved agitating and unhelpful, Zoloft. She felt "unimproved" and stopped. "I'm living an illusion," she thought, "an elegant, appealing, enviable illusion that's sucking the life out of me. How could drugs help?"

And then, a couple of years later, came the morning in the shower when she felt the lump in her breast. She knew it was cancer. She first had surgery, and radiation, and then, because her lymph nodes were involved, chemotherapy. With chemotherapy came nausea and vomiting, hair loss and bone-weary fatigue. Her oncologist saw that she was depressed and attributed it to the diagnosis of cancer, the treatment, and the uncertain prognosis. He, also, recommended antidepressants. Dorothy asked him for "other options," and he suggested that she call me.

THE FIRST NOTE

There are two parts to the Call, two notes. The first note is straightforward, increasingly assertive, and difficult to ignore. It is the announcement—through emotional pain, troubled dark thoughts, and physical signs and symptoms—that we are depressed. Once we've heard it clearly, we can attend to the second note, the one that calls us to change.

Many of us shut our ears to the first note for as long as we can. We deny the feelings of unhappiness, and the gloom that suffuses our perceptions, or deny that the situation that is wearing us down actually exists. We don't want to see how our lives aren't working, to look at our self-defeating ways of thinking and acting, until we absolutely have to.

This is particularly true for those of us who feel trapped in situations we believe we're unable to change or leave. The answer always seems the same: Nothing we've done, or can imagine doing, seems to change things, and the cost of altering the course of our lives seems too high. We can't see how we can leave the marriage or relationship, or make it significantly better, more fulfilling. Our job feels like a prison without parole. We're stuck.

Sometimes we're reasonable and accepting, at other times angry, frantic, despairing. Why isn't it working? Everything looks so right on paper. We may blame ourselves or others, and still hope that somehow things will get better. Each day we feel a little less happy, a little less strong, and a little more discouraged, and still we hold on.

Sometimes it feels as if there's something that is simply "physical"—a disease that's not yet diagnosed, perhaps not even diagnosable. Theresa wondered about this when she consulted her internist. It's crucially important to find out if this is true, because these vague suspicions can be well founded. There are indeed physical—and pharmacological—causes of depression, and you need to make sure that you're not suffering from them. A capable physician can do a complete physical exam, take a history of your illnesses and medications, look at routine laboratory values, and pinpoint or rule out these disorders. I'll talk about this in detail a little later.

There are also other, more subtle physical causes or contributors to depression: biological abnormalities, sensitivities to particular foods, failures to properly assimilate necessary nutrients, or imbalances in our hormones even when the conventional laboratory values are normal. These may need to be explored as well by a physician with a broader, more "integrative" perspective. I'll also discuss these possibilities and this process.

And then there are those of us who continue to insist, even when all obvious and subtle physical causes have been ruled out, that it's still "physical." Physicians describe these people as "somatizers" (from *soma,* the Greek word for "body") because they express their mental and emotional distress in their body. Somatizers are sometimes treated with condescension, as if their symptoms were products of willful denial or were less sophisticated ways of expressing psychological pain. In fact, physical and emotional symptoms can simply be two different aspects of what we call depression.

Traditional systems of healing, such as Chinese medicine and Indian Ayurveda, understand the complete interconnection of mind, body, and spirit. From their perspective, physical symptoms—loss of appetite and impaired digestion, shortness of breath, poor sleep, mysterious pains, weight loss, fever—are best understood as another aspect of a larger picture that may include a depressed mood and an anxious or frustrated mind. I'll discuss and explain in detail these pictures and their connections when we come to chapter four. I'll show you then how Traditional Chinese Medicine, including acupuncture and herbs, can be effectively used to address *both* physical and emotional symptoms. Right now I simply want to suggest that these physical symptoms may themselves be part of the Call, that our body's troubles may in some way be related to the emotional distress, the sense of "stuckness" that defines our depression.

Giving Depression a Number: The CES-D

Objective tests and the numerical scores they produce—the "hard facts"—can sometimes help us to hear the first note of the Call and to realize we're depressed. Their results may be disturbing at first, but they can also be reassuring and comforting, and spur us to action.

Aaron T. Beck, a psychiatrist who was instrumental in creating cognitive behavioral therapy (CBT), has developed a widely and easily used questionnaire, the Beck Depression Inventory (BDI). The BDI explores and quantifies the negative ways of thinking that Beck and his colleagues see as fundamental facts of depression. I've found it reliably clarifies the first note of the Call.

Beck describes, and his test elicits, evidence of "personalization" (all negative experience relates to us), "absolutism" (it will always be this way), and "magnification" (we are, all appearances to the contrary, the *most* worthless, incapable, etc.), ways of thinking and perceiving that are all too familiar when we're depressed. When we're depressed, we overgeneralize and *catastrophize* (what an apt if clumsy word). For Theresa, a single mistake in a complex project obliterated any satisfaction or perception of success and predicted inevitable future failure. She believed she was responsible for all the ills that befell her, and often enough, others as well, and that everyone who observed her probably shared that judgment.

Her glass, when she became depressed, was never half full, always half empty.

The BDI is available only to professionals, so I can't include it in this book. I've instead chosen the widely used Center for Epidemiological Studies scale (CES-D), which was developed at the National Institute of Mental Health. As you answer the questions in the CES-D, you become aware of the way you look at and think about yourself and your life.

If you score in the "depressed range" on the CES-D, you have evidence that there is something measurably troubled in the way you look at and experience the world. Your suffering has a name. If your score is lower, you will likely be relieved. In either case, your answers hold up a mirror to you. They can encourage you to be aware of the depressive distortions in how you're thinking and feeling.

HEARING THE FIRST NOTE: THE CES-D

Here is the CES-D scale. It is an aid to becoming more aware of what you're thinking and feeling. It's a mirror, and it clarifies the first note of the Call.

If you're unsure of an answer, don't linger too long. Just circle what seems most correct and move on. The scoring scale follows the test, but don't look at it until you're finished.

If you score in the range of "clinical concern," pay attention. Even if you don't score in that range, notice your answers. What areas and issues do they suggest that you need to work on? Remember, this is *just* a diagnostic tool. It's for your use. It provides useful hints and a starting place. *It is not an end point.*

CES-Depression Scale

Begin, using the scale below, by circling the number before each statement that best describes how you felt or behaved *during the past week*.

0 = Rarely or none (less than 1 day)

1 = Some or a little (1 to 2 days)

2 = Occasionally or moderate (3 to 4 days)

3 = Most or all of the time (5 to 7 days)

During the past week

1 0 1 2 3 I was bothered by things that usually don't bother me.

2 0 1 2 3 I did not feel like eating; my appetite was poor.

3 0 1 2 3 I felt that I could not shake off the blues even with help from my family/friends.

4 0 1 2 3 I felt that I was just as good as other people.

5 0 1 2 3 I had trouble keeping my mind on what I was doing.

6 0 1 2 3 I felt depressed.

7 0 1 2 3 I felt that everything I did was an effort.

8 0 1 2 3 I felt hopeful about the future.

9 0 1 2 3 I thought my life had been a failure.

10 0 1 2 3 I felt fearful.

11 0 1 2 3 My sleep was restless.

12 0 1 2 3 I was happy.

13 0 1 2 3 I talked less than usual.

14 0 1 2 3 I felt lonely.

15 0 1 2 3 People were unfriendly.

16 0 1 2 3 I enjoyed life.

17 0 1 2 3 I had crying spells.

18 0 1 2 3 I felt sad.

19 0 1 2 3 I felt that people disliked me.

20 0 1 2 3 I could not "get going."

Scoring

Add up all the circled numbers (questions 4, 8, 12, and 16 are reverse scored, meaning that a response of 3 is scored as a 0 and a response of 0 as 3; similarly, a 1 response is scored as a 2 and a 2 response as 1).

The interpretation of your scoring varies depending on your age and culture. In general, however, if your score is between 10 and 15, you may be mildly depressed. A score of 16 to 25 suggests moderate depression, and scores above 25 indicate that, at least right now, you may be significantly depressed. Remember, however, that these questions and scores are simply one way for you to take stock of how you're feeling *right now*. They are not set in concrete, and they definitely don't mean you have a disease.

You may want to use the CES-D every few months to see how your worldview and the way you're feeling changes. Keep the results if you'd like. They can help you see how you've changed and show you some of the challenges you still have to meet.

It's crucial to hear this first "diagnostic" note, but heard by itself, it can be harsh and without resonance. And heard without context and perspective by physicians and mental health professionals who've been relentlessly propagandized by drug companies, it tends to provoke a rapid, reflexive recourse to pharmacological treatment. This was the response of Theresa's psychotherapist and internist, and of Dorothy's psychiatrist and oncologist.

This pharmacological response may be well meaning, but it is often premature as well as shortsighted and potentially harmful. The drugs may sometimes enable us to do more successfully what we've been doing, but what we've been doing and feeling and thinking is what made us depressed in the first place. Too often, the drugs are a Band-Aid, not a cure. Dorothy put it quite well: "I'm living an illusion. . . . How could drugs help?"

There is, however, another way to hear and understand this first note. Your rumination and self-blame, your unhappiness and exhaustion, your weight loss, sleep disturbance, and pain—all these signs and symptoms—are letting you know that your life is out of balance. They are bringing attention to your current condition and your present distress. They do not condemn you to future suffering. Heard this way, the first note—the one that lets you know you're depressed—is not a closing, but an opening note. It's not a death knell. It's a wake-up call.

THE SECOND NOTE

The first note is a statement: "I am depressed." The second note is phrased as a question. It asks, at first softly and tentatively, "Is there something that needs to change?" The second note suggests not an error to be fixed, but deeper lessons to be learned. It's not about "restoring the premorbid personality" or even simply making adjustments in the way we think. The second note calls us to question aspects of our personality, of our ways of looking at ourselves and the world that may themselves be the problem. The second note is deeper, more resonant, and sometimes more challenging than the first. It tells you that you are on the wrong path. Over time, this second note may become more and more insistent. Its overtones may nag at you, jump through the defenses of your despair, chase you when you run. It tells you that it is time to open yourself to the challenges of a journey you do not yet understand—that it is time to change.

You may resist this second note. That's no surprise. The heroes whose stories inspire us also resisted. "I'm not Aeneas. I'm not Paul," Dante protests. I'm no hero, I can't go down there, to the underworld. But life and his destiny were calling him, and they are calling you as well. You can protest all you want, curse your fate, pretend it's not happening, hide in drink or drugs or denial, but you know the time has come to pay attention, *and* to do something.

Dorothy's Dilemma: A Story and a Scheme

Dorothy liked Soft Belly (which I taught her in our first meeting) because it was "eminently practical and utterly portable." She could do it anywhere—at her desk, in a cab, in the ladies' room, even standing in line at the supermarket checkout counter. A calm space grew in her. She felt a softness in her belly, and then in her arms, and legs, and head. Little by little, a small portion of quietness and peace came to her mind. Still, Dorothy didn't know how to respond to the second note of the Call, to the need for change. Couples counseling—often very useful—had proved unhelpful. And she now believed that staying with the senator would only deepen her depression, perhaps—and here she wondered if she was being too dramatic—"kill" her. She was plagued by paralyzing doubts. How would their separation affect Todd's chances for reelection in a conservative, "family-values" state? What would life be like for a single woman closing in on sixty? How would separating from Todd affect her cancer? And, most of all, how could she do this to the children who were fiercely loyal to Todd and protective of him? What would they think and feel and say?

Each day Dorothy felt more anxious, more irritable, more depressed. She breathed softly and deeply, and relaxed, and, for a while, was "better," but the feelings returned. Weeks became months. She understood that she had to leave, but she kept postponing it. Finally, desperate, she asked if there was any way I could help. I told her I had a story and a scheme.

THE STORY >> I began with the story. I had never told it to a patient and wouldn't ordinarily think of repeating it to such a well-mannered, kind, elegant—and decidedly non-Jewish—woman. But it leapt to my mind and out of my mouth.

"There was an old Jewish couple, the Goldsteins," I began, while Dorothy looked at me with an expression of troubled wonder, "who went to see a psychiatrist. He asked them why they were there, and the man began to talk. 'I'm suffering,' he said, 'and I want to get a divorce.'

"'Why?' the psychiatrist asked.

"'This woman you see before you, my wife, is a shrew. She belittles me and disagrees with me: If I say it's a nice day, for her it's terrible. The food she makes is like poison, and the last time we had intercourse I can't even remember.'

"'What about you, ma'am?' the psychiatrist goes on.

"'This pisher,' the woman begins, fairly spitting out the words, 'is the poorest excuse for a husband I've ever seen. My mother warned me against him, and she was right. He's a slob and rude to everyone who comes to the house. He was a terrible businessman, and even worse in bed.'

"The psychiatrist is a bit nonplussed, but he wants to hang in there with them. 'How long,' he asks, 'have you both felt this way?'

"'About fifty years,' they say in unison.

"'Why,' the dumbfounded psychiatrist asks, 'did you wait until now to think about getting a divorce?'

"'We were waiting,' the wife replies, 'for the children to grow up and die.'"

Silence fills the room between Dorothy and me, and for a moment I wonder if my intuition has totally failed me, if I've committed an unforgivable and, to Dorothy, incomprehensible lapse in taste. Then she shakes her head and laughs. "Jim Gordon, you've got me. 'Waiting for the children to grow up and die.' That about says it."

THE SCHEME >> The story got Dorothy's attention, and the punch line stayed with her, as it had with me. But she also needed a plan. The plan had to be grounded in what she was feeling now. It had to answer questions that were foremost in her mind. The plan needed goals toward which she could orient herself, and it required specific, concrete steps that she could begin to take toward those goals.

For years I, like many therapists, had facilitated this process in an unsystematic way: exploring feelings as they arose; examining goals as they came to my patients' minds; and commenting on steps as they were planned or taken. In recent years, it's seemed increasingly important to help my patients become conscious of the whole process, to write down, right at the beginning of the journey, the answers to the questions that will help to guide them on their next steps.

There are three questions I often use, each one of which is designed to produce a list. Here they are:

>> What's going on right now?
>> Where do I want to be headed and what changes are necessary?
>> What are my first steps for getting where I'm going?

These questions can facilitate your awareness. They can set clear directions. And they can help you take the first steps toward your goals. The lists they produce, as I explained to Dorothy, will inevitably grow and change as time goes on.

I advised Dorothy to answer the questions, to make the lists, as fast as she could, and not to worry about full sentences or grammar or spelling. This, I told her, would help her bypass her inclination to procrastinate and to be a perfectionist—tendencies that many of us who are depressed know all too well. Writing without excessive thinking would give her more direct, uncensored access to her intuition and imagination. I explained that she could always change or rewrite her lists later.

RESPONDING TO THE SECOND NOTE OF THE CALL

The three lists that follow will help you respond to the second note of the Call. They're the same ones that Dorothy made. You can use the space provided below or you can make these lists in a journal—an ongoing account of your journey, which I'll discuss below.

Before you make each of these lists, begin by breathing deeply, doing Soft Belly as we did in the introduction—inhaling, exhaling, relaxing your belly, for a few minutes. Soft Belly will quiet your mind's repetitive chatter and make it easier for you to access the practical, personal wisdom that you need.

The CES-D may have helped you identify some of your thoughts and feelings, some of "What's going on right now?" Write these and any other thoughts and feelings that come to you in the first list. Be as specific as you can about all three lists, but don't belabor them. Understand, too, that the lists will inevitably change. The second note calls you to respond according to *today's* knowledge and wisdom.

Here again are the questions, and the lists that Dorothy came up with.

1. What's going on right now?

These are the feelings and thoughts that Dorothy had as she heard the second note of the Call, the one that kept insisting—in spite of her fears and resistance—on change. Writing these down, she became aware of them, and began to acknowledge and respect them. She realized, too, that they were already moving her, actually agitating her, and demanding change.

>> Sense of paralysis, of inability to leave or do anything.
>> Fear that my children will hate me.
>> Fear that other people will think I'm a fool.
>> Fear that friends will drop me.
>> Fear that I'll be horribly lonely.
>> Fear that I won't know who I am.
>> Fear that my cancer will get worse if I leave.
>> Impatience to do something.
>> Hope that my cancer will get better if I leave.
>> Anger at myself for putting up with my marriage for so long.

"Lots of fear," she noted at the bottom of her list, "and anger, too."

2. Where do I want to be headed and what changes are necessary?

This second list consisted of changes Dorothy saw as truly necessary. This list sets goals that draw us toward them, much as setting a course for a boat guides the direction of its progress. When we're feeling most clueless and hopeless, this list reminds us that direction actually does exist.

>> LEAVE TODD [these are Dorothy's capital letters].
>> Stop feeling guilty about the children.
>> Take better care of yourself.
>> Start doing things just for you.

3. What are my first steps for getting where I'm going?

Change is intimidating, more so when we're depressed. Direction attracts us, but our progress toward it needs to be broken down into manageable steps. This third list is concrete and specific. At first it may be short. It will grow as one step leads to another. This third list is often surprising—it was to Dorothy. As you make it, you may see that there *are* ways to begin to do what had seemed impossible. You realize your journey—just like all journeys—really does begin with a single step.

>> Set a date for leaving Todd.
>> Stop eating so many sweets.
>> Look around for my own friends.
>> Check out apartments in the paper.
>> Begin talking to the children about my distress.
>> *Keep listening to the call to change.*

Now, here are the same three questions for *you* to respond to.

1 What's going on right now?

2 Where do I want to be headed? What changes are necessary?

3 What are my first steps for getting where I'm going?

A JOURNAL FOR YOUR JOURNEY

A journal is a useful and reliable companion on your journey. You can use it to record your responses to the questions throughout this book, including the previous ones, and to write down your Prescriptions for Self-Care. Keeping a journal also stimulates awareness and mental clarity; offers you the opportunity for creativity; provides comfort; and promotes emotional healing.

If you need scientific evidence to encourage you, there's plenty. A number of studies by University of Texas psychologist James W. Pennebaker and his colleagues and students have shown decreases in stress and stress hormones, as well as improvements in chronic physical illness, *after only three days* of writing about emotionally charged experiences.

Your journal provides you with an ongoing permanent record of what you're thinking, feeling, and experiencing. It makes it possible for you to see which goals you've met and what you still have to do; how you've changed and progressed.

KEEPING A JOURNAL

The rules of journal writing can be very simple. Here are mine:

1 Buy a journal that suits you—a simple spiral notebook or an elegant leather-bound version, whatever seems right. Put your name on the inside cover, along with your contact information, so if you lose it, someone will likely return it. (You can, of course, use a computer, but a paper journal is more portable and has an identity all its own.) Now you're ready to begin.

2 Note the date of each entry and write down whatever comes to mind—thoughts, feelings, sensations, stories, dreams, memories, opinions—and also whatever has recently happened to you that seems interesting, important, informative, or, for some reason that you don't yet understand, worth putting on the page.

3 Do it every day, even if you write only "I don't have anything to say."

4 Don't censor yourself. Write down whatever comes.

5 If you're feeling awkward, don't worry. Most people do. This is a new activity. Many of us are not used to expressing ourselves, let alone writing what we're feeling and thinking.

6 If you're feeling intimidated, that's not surprising either. Many of us carry images in our minds that inhibit us—our mother coming into our teenage room, opening our drawers, leafing through our diary; a critical teacher red penciling our papers.

7 Notice any fears and images that come up, acknowledge them, write them down, and let them go. This journal is for *you* and only you.

Your journal is the place to record feelings that may have been too painful or too shameful to share with anyone else. It can give form and meaning to your feelings. It allows you to create something out of the void that threatens you when you're most depressed. And it gives you proof that *you can actually do something*. People often begin writing exhausted and desperate and end, ten minutes or a half hour later, energized.

Your journal provides an ongoing account of your experiences, thoughts, and feelings and a place to record the steps you're taking to help yourself—what it felt like to do the exercises and fill Prescriptions for Self-Care. As you get accustomed to keeping a journal, you'll find it focuses your attention, cuts short rumination, produces surprising insights and answers, and tracks your progress. Even when you're most desolate, your journal is a faithful, reliable companion. Its physical presence is comforting, even defining: This is *my* journal, I'm carrying it. I'm the one writing in it. I write, therefore I am.

Healthier Body, Happier Mind

You've already learned about some of the many ways your mind can affect your body, and how psychological stress can predispose you to heart disease, diabetes, and infections, as well as anxiety and depression. It works the other way as well: Your physical functioning affects the way you feel, think, and act, and your attitude toward the world around you.

This section explores the most important ways that physical illness, biological imbalances, nutritional deficiencies, and your unique biochemistry can disturb your physical functioning and trouble your mind. It gives you guidance in discovering whether your mood is being affected by these forces, and tells you who to consult to help you find out if this is so and why. In the pages that follow, I also explain how you can remove—or deal more successfully with—these biological obstacles to your progress, and how you can use food and supplements to sustain you as you go forward on your journey.

I'm sharing this material with you now because you've heard the second note of the Call and are getting ready to make the simple, practical changes that will help you respond to this Call. I want to help you right now—at the beginning of our work together—to do everything you can to make this journey through and beyond depression as easy and productive, as life enhancing, as possible.

Please read the practical information here slowly and thoughtfully, and explore the possibilities, consult the experts, and take the steps that I suggest. Taking these steps may, as you'll see from the examples, relieve you of unnecessary suffering. They will, in any case, help to make every stage of your journey through and beyond depression easier; and help you to transform what might have been a grim ordeal into the hopeful challenge it should be.

CONSULT YOUR DOCTOR

If you're depressed, consult your doctor. This is not because depression is a disease—it isn't. But depression may be caused by or accompany a physical disease. And even when disease is not present, depression may be caused or complicated by a variety of prescription and nonprescription drugs, imbalances in hormones, sensitivities to food, deficiencies in nutrients, and excess of toxic substances, virtually all of which can be discovered and addressed—with significant positive effects on mood.

There are really three parts to this job of diagnosis and treatment. The first depends on a good conventional workup—a careful history, physical examination, and laboratory tests for the most obvious physical causes and contributions to your altered mood. If you have a primary care physician—a family physician, an internist, an ob-gyn, or, for kids, a pediatrician—whom you trust and respect, he or she can do this. The second part requires a fair amount of education on the doctor's part that is not offered in conventional medical training, and a willingness to look beyond the confines of conventional wisdom for more subtle and obscure biological causes. For the third, therapeutic aspect of this work, a physician needs to be familiar with the nonpharmacological, natural, biological approaches that we'll be discussing throughout this book.

Physicians who describe themselves as "holistic" or "integrative" (from, respectively, the Greek and Latin words *holos* and *integer,* or "whole") are generally better equipped to do the second and third parts of the work that's required, to explore and remedy the subtle imbalances, deficiencies, and disruptions that I'll describe in this chapter, as well as the obvious diseases.

Holistic and integrative physicians are conventionally trained as MDs or DOs (osteopathic physicians who have conventional medical training and also manipulate bones and soft tissues as chiropractors do). Naturopathic physicians or chiropractors, who rely primarily on natural, nonpharmacological remedies, can often fill this role. Dietitians and nutritionists may be very helpful in addressing food-related issues and developing programs of supplementation. In the Resources section, I list organizations that can help you to locate all of these practitioners.

The guidelines below are designed to give you basic strategies for discovering the physical causes of and contributors to depression. They will also help you plan a program of nutrition and supplementation that will deal with many of the biological and nutritional imbalances that may predispose you to depression.

LEARNING FROM YOUR OWN HISTORY

Even before medical students make rounds on a hospital ward, we're taught to make a careful and complete list of the medications our patients are taking—prescription drugs and nonprescription or over-the-counter drugs, supplements and herbs—as well as the foods they eat and the recreational substances, legal and illegal, that they use. Any doctor you consult about depression should do this first, and you should tell her everything that you're doing. If you don't trust her enough to tell her, you either need to get over it or to find another physician.

There are many drugs that may contribute to depression. If you're taking one or more, and are sensitive to them, stopping or changing your pattern of usage may take you a long way down the road on your journey toward health and wholeness. The categories of prescription drugs listed in the table on page 69 are among the most common (though by no means the only) ones that may cause or contribute to depression. If you're taking any of them, your physician should carefully evaluate their continued use. You should talk with her about the possibility of lowering the dosage, or finding a substitute for the drug or, at least temporarily, discontinuing it. This needs to be done in a thoughtful and meticulous way, lest you suffer withdrawal or be overwhelmed by the symptoms of the condition for which the drugs were initially prescribed.

PRESCRIPTION DRUGS THAT MAY CAUSE OR CONTRIBUTE TO DEPRESSION

Antianxiety medicines
Antidepressants
Antihistamines (these can, of course, be purchased over the counter in drugstores as well as be prescribed)
Antihypertensives (a variety of drugs that lower blood pressure)
Anti-inflammatory agents (used for an injury, arthritis, etc.)
Antiseizure medicines (used to protect against epilepsy)
Birth control pills
Chemotherapeutic agents (used to treat a variety of cancers)
Corticosteroids (synthetic versions of the adrenal stress hormones used for a wide variety of conditions from arthritis to asthma and eczema)
Sleeping pills of all kinds

I want to call attention to one often-neglected possibility that may be crucially important: Sometimes the very drugs that are prescribed to relieve the symptoms of depression can, in fact, exacerbate these symptoms, producing increased anxiety, agitation, and sleeplessness, and even deepening the feelings of depression. There is a significant body of data that I discussed earlier that suggests that SSRIs, particularly in the early weeks of use, may provoke an agitated, deeper, occasionally suicidal depression. You—and your physicians—need to be aware of this possibility.

Many of the nonprescription substances we take and, in particular, a number of those we take to improve our mood, may also contribute to our depression. It's well known that alcohol and drugs like nicotine, marijuana, amphetamines, and cocaine provide temporary "highs" but— particularly if they are taken in excess or habitually—may make some people more depressed in the long run: It's certainly possible that Theresa's increased alcohol use may have contributed to the depression she was hoping to relieve by drinking. The same may also be true (Dorothy suspected this) of sugar and caffeine, particularly, it seems, when they are used together and excessively.

Several teaspoons of sugar in each of several cups of coffee may contribute to depression; so, too, may the so-called soft drinks like Coke, Pepsi, and Mountain Dew, which are burdened with up to nine teaspoons of sugar—and considerable quantities of caffeine—in each twelve-ounce can. One interesting study showed that a number of depressed people improved significantly when they stopped their habitual use of caffeine and sugar. Incidentally, so-called diet drinks aren't free from these effects: Aspartame (NutraSweet), which is often used in these drinks, has been reported to produce negative effects on the brain and nervous system—including depression—in some people.

Specific medical illnesses are also known to be accompanied by and/or to precipitate depression. Indeed, sometimes an otherwise inexplicable depression may be the first symptom of an undiagnosed, significant physical illness. Hypothyroidism (low or "hypo" levels of thyroid hormone, which regulates the metabolism of all the body's cells), diabetes, the auto-immune disease lupus erythematosus (in which inflammation in blood vessels in the brain may produce depression and other significant emotional problems), and several kinds of cancer are among the most common and best-known physical causes of depression.

This first group in the table below includes these and others, all of which will be familiar to well-trained psychiatrists and primary care physicians. They're the ones that can be detected by a good conventional medical history and complete physical examination, and by the conventional laboratory tests that the history and physical findings suggest.

MEDICAL CONDITIONS THAT MAY GIVE RISE TO, AND/OR BE ACCOMPANIED BY, DEPRESSION

Acquired immune deficiency syndrome (AIDS)
Adrenal gland overactivity, with hypersecretion of stress hormones (Cushing's disease), and underactivity (Addison's disease)
Autoimmune illnesses, including lupus erythematosus and rheumatoid arthritis, where the body's immune cells attack its own tissue in a variety of locations

Cancer, especially cancer of the brain, where pressure on the brain may contribute to the symptoms, and cancer of the pancreas
Cerebrovascular disease, in particular, strokes, or cerebrovascular accidents, where the blood supply to the brain, and therefore its adequate functioning, is compromised
Chronic fatigue immune deficiency syndrome (CFIDS), a multisystem condition, perhaps precipitated by Epstein-Barr or another viral illness, characterized by extreme fatigue and, sometimes, muscle and joint pain, and depression
Chronic pain
Diabetes, a disease in which major problems in sugar metabolism and in circulation are caused by the body's inability to produce, or adequately use, insulin
Heart disease, including heart failure and heart-valve malfunction; these are often accompanied by shortness of breath
Infections, both bacterial and viral, including Lyme disease
Lung disease, particularly chronic obstructive pulmonary disease, which may be present in longtime smokers, coal miners, asbestos workers, etc.
Multiple sclerosis, a disorder with a variety of symptoms, including visual problems and weakness of limbs, produced by inflammation in the "white matter" that surrounds the nerve cells in the brain
Parkinson's disease, a disease characterized by dopamine deficiency in the substantia nigra of the brain, with symptoms including trembling, especially of hands; muscular rigidity; and difficulty moving
Thyroid disease, including both overactivity (*hyper*thyroidism) and underactivity (*hypo*thyroidism)
Trauma to the head
Wilson's disease, an inherited illness in which abnormal copper metabolism may damage the nervous system and liver

There are other, less common conditions that may also precipitate or contribute to depression. They are often ignored or dismissed by conventional medicine, but are, in my experience, occasionally quite significant. In medical school, we're taught that when we hear pounding hooves, we shouldn't think immediately of zebras. This makes sense. The common causes of depression, the horses, are more likely to be producing the pounding. Still, zebras do exist. And, if all else fails, it's worth looking—and listening—for them. Four conditions, four zebras, that can sometimes be heard galloping, are adrenal insufficiency, chronic yeast infections, heavy metal poisoning, and small intestinal bacterial overgrowth (SIBO).

Adrenal Abnormalities

Some depressed people feel a chronic debilitating fatigue and may be vulnerable to repeated viral, bacterial, or fungal infections. I suggest that if you fit this profile, you ask your doctor to test your adrenal function as well as your level of dehydroepiandrosterone, or DHEA. Significantly elevated levels of corticosteroids, the stress hormones, are a sign of chronic stress and are present in some depressed people. Very low levels may be an indication of impending adrenal exhaustion and are also associated with extreme fatigue and depression. Low levels of DHEA, a precursor of both the corticosteroids and the sex hormones, may be another sign that your adrenals need help.

Treatment involves support of adrenal function by a regime of supplementation I'll describe later, the kind of relaxation techniques and exercise I discuss throughout the book, and the use of herbal remedies, including Panax ginseng. If these levels are significantly and stubbornly low, nutritional physicians may also supplement with DHEA and doses of adrenal corticosteroids.

Chronic Yeast Infections

Yeast infections (candidiases) can manifest as red patches on the skin, as inflammations in the mouth or vagina (thrush), and as gastrointestinal disturbances. Yeast infections are more likely to appear after repeated or prolonged treatment with antibiotics (which destroy the bacteria that ordinarily inhabit our bodies as well as pathological invaders); if our immune system is compromised, as in HIV/AIDS or cancer; or if we're long-term users of cortisone or birth control pills.

For half a century, a small group of physicians and nutritionists has claimed that chronic yeast infections may be an important cause of depression. They have hypothesized that when large accumulations of yeast in our gut break down carbohydrates, they produce alcohol and one of its breakdown products, acetaldehyde. These clinicians believe that acetaldehyde (which is implicated in the common hangover) may exert a direct toxic effect on the brain, perhaps by combining with dopamine and other neurotransmitters.

Physicians and nutritionists who treat depressed people who have candidiasis with anti-yeast drugs and yeast-free diets (no fermented foods and foods very low in sugars) have unfortunately not done any systematic research on their regimen. There are, however, many anecdotes of depressed people (among them several people who have told me about their experience) who have followed this prescription and have significantly improved. I suggest that if you're depressed and think you have a yeast infection (oral and vaginal symptoms are easier to detect; finding out if yeast is causing GI upset will likely require a stool sample), you might want to take a look at the *Yeast Control Handbook* (described in the Resources section) and consult a nutritional physician, naturopath, or dietitian for treatment.

Heavy Metal Toxicity

The belief that heavy metals, which tend to concentrate in the nervous system, are a major cause of neurological and psychiatric problems is a subject of maximum controversy. Most physicians disparage the hair analysis that is routinely used to test for heavy metals and deny that heavy metal toxicity—with the exception of some children obviously impaired by the lead they've ingested from house paint or inhaled from automobile pollution, and a few people in hazardous occupations—is a significant factor in health. A much smaller group of nutritional and "environmental" physicians and dentists find widespread evidence of toxicity—from the mercury in dental fillings to the lead, arsenic, and aluminum that are released in industry, and from canning and cooking.

I think that both perspectives have some merit. The hair analyses that are almost always used have been shown to be at best variable, and at worst highly unreliable. And the tendency to place much of the blame for the ever-increasing burden of chronic diseases on heavy metal poisoning is so far unjustified. On the other hand, there are many anecdotes, and some evidence, that do implicate heavy metals in a variety of neurological and emotional conditions, including depression.

I suggest you consider the possibility of heavy metal poisoning if your depression is accompanied by one or more of a variety of other signs and symptoms, including persistent fatigue, confusion, headaches, tremors, numbness, and tingling; if there is evidence of exposure (if you're a dental assistant or have worked in a lab or a factory that uses these metals); and/or if everything else you've done seems like it should be working but isn't.

If you fall into one of these categories, you need to find a physician who has been specially trained to recognize and treat this condition (in the Resources section, I list several of the organizations to which they may belong). Such a physician knows how to test for toxicity (using, in addition to routine blood and hair analyses, "challenges" with oral or intravenous chelating agents that can pull these metals out of our tissue and into the blood and urine where they can be measured); and to treat toxic levels with nutritional therapies and intravenous chelation. This latter is a controversial and potentially hazardous treatment—when heavy metals enter the bloodstream, they can cause acute symptoms of toxicity—and chelation, in particular, requires a physician with significant expertise. However, for those who are accurately diagnosed, expert treatment can sometimes make a very real and dramatic difference in mood, and in other symptoms as well.

Small Intestinal Bacterial Overgrowth (SIBO)

In recent years, nutritional researchers and clinicians have noted a fascinating connection between gastrointestinal symptoms, including most particularly flatulence, diarrhea, and abdominal pain, and depression. In a number of instances, these GI problems seem to be related to excesses of pathological bacteria (SIBO) and deficiencies of the beneficial intestinal bacterial groups *Lactobacillus* and *Bifidobacterium*. These latter—which promote vitamin synthesis, decrease inflammation, and enhance digestion and absorption of nutrients—may be significantly decreased by stress.

Though the science is in its early stages, numbers of people with GI disturbance and depression from various causes seem to benefit from repopulating their guts with supplemental lactobacillus and bifidus: Their GI symptoms decrease, nutritional absorption and energy levels increase, and mood improves.

I feel confident recommending that any of you who are experiencing chronic GI distress (or such systemic problems as chronic fatigue syndrome, fibromyalgia, or Lyme disease) take a supplement of lactobacillus and bifidus. The dose should be approximately two to three billion bacteria per day (usually obtainable in one or two capsules). You should also consult a nutritional physician who can fully explore the causes of your GI problems and work out a more comprehensive approach for you.

Two other points of interest: Omega-3 fatty acids in fish oil, which I'll discuss later, increase these beneficial bacteria, and multivitamin and mineral supplements, like the ones I suggest to you later, work in concert with them.

In addition to these four potential but occasional causes of depression, there are two others that may be far more common and need to be considered.

Seasonal Affective Disorder (SAD)

Seasonal affective disorder (SAD) is the prime example of a condition that was long ignored but has recently been acknowledged by the medical establishment.

Though a depressed winter mood had often been observed in people who live in northern climates, it was only in 1984, when psychiatrist Norman Rosenthal, feeling poorly after he moved from usually sunny South Africa to a gray winter in New York City, described his "winter blues." Rosenthal hypothesized that his depressed mood was caused by diminished exposure to sunlight and treated himself with artificial light. After light treatment, Rosenthal noticed a significant increase in his energy and improvement in his mood. Soon he began to successfully treat others with the same symptoms in a similar way.

If your depressed mood is characterized by early winter onset, with mood lifting significantly with oncoming spring's longer days, let your physician know and look into purchasing a light box, which provides a full spectrum (similar to sunlight) of light that is 10,000 lux strong. A number of studies have shown that exposure to this light source for thirty minutes in the morning can provide significant relief from SAD. Though side effects of light exposure are rare, some people, particularly those who have the tendency to hyperexcitability that characterizes (along with depression) bipolar disorder, can become agitated. In general, however, light treatment works as well as, and often better than, antidepressant drugs, with far fewer side effects. Interestingly, there is also some evidence that full-spectrum light may be helpful for some depressed people who don't have SAD.

Subclinical Hypothyroidism: A Hidden, and Common, Cause of Depression

When symptoms of hypothyroidism, including fatigue and depression, are accompanied by normal levels of thyroid hormone and elevated levels of thyroid stimulating hormone (TSH), the condition is called subclinical hypothyroidism. Unfortunately, many physicians do not make the diagnosis, particularly when TSH levels are only slightly elevated, and treat it inappropriately with antidepressants. I have, however, seen a number of people with subclinical hypothyroidism (and even a few with normal TSH as well as normal thyroid levels) for whom thyroid supplementation produced significant improvement in mood.

What follows is a story that shows how the accurate diagnosis and treatment of subclinical hypothyroidism can make a world of difference.

When Diane came to see me, she had been depressed for "as long as I can remember." She was preoccupied with the hold her childhood still had on her, the difficulties with men that she and a succession of therapists had traced to her tortured relationship with her alcoholic father—"a charming Irish cop who couldn't keep his hands off the bottle, or me"—who was alternately seductive and abusive.

When Diane's father came home from work, he called his young daughter "Daddy's little princess" and sat her on his lap. As the evening wore on and the alcohol worked on him, he was sometimes tearful, then impatient and irritable. When Diane hit puberty, he became increasingly sarcastic and insulting. Diane's skirts were, he kept telling her, too short, her hand gestures "sluttish." Diane's mother, like many spouses of abusers, absented herself. She tended to Diane's younger brother, fussed in the kitchen, and avoided conflict. Diane became fearful and self-conscious, and, as a young woman, exquisitely sensitive to men's reactions to her. With the end of each relationship, she became "a little bit more hopeless."

Diane and her therapists attributed her low-grade depression and her difficulties with, and disappointments in, men to the still-unresolved emotional consequences of a troubled and confusing childhood. But over time, more physical signs and symptoms appeared, including constipation, dry roughened skin, and a sensitivity to cold weather. For a number of years before she came to see me, Diane had felt overcome by exhaustion. She woke up with it each morning and collapsed under its weight each evening. Exercise helped, but no matter how faithfully she worked out—and Diane was loyal to her sessions on the StairMaster and her daily half hour in the weight room—she just couldn't seem to fully wake up. And no matter how much she exercised or how strictly she dieted, Diane put on pounds. As her weight climbed, her mood continued to sink.

Diane was an economist with the World Bank and liked her work. It was exciting, and she felt worthwhile—helping developing countries to create new small businesses. She was precise and detail oriented, and did her job well, and she loved the travel and the people she met. She knew she was unhappy being single. She wanted to settle down with someone who shared her dream of a family, somebody who valued caring for others, and had a religious, or at least a spiritual, outlook on life. She was forty-two and worried, at every break in her busy schedule, that her dream might never come true.

Diane had been in psychotherapy on and off for twenty years, and in Al-Anon, a 12-step group for relatives and friends of alcoholics. She understood the way her family life had established the pattern of her problems, and she found considerable support in Al-Anon, but she didn't seem able to break free of bad relationships or to shake her lethargy. Her depression exhausted her, and her fatigue depressed her.

Diane had been on several courses of antidepressants, two of the tricyclics, and Paxil and Wellbutrin, as well as Prozac. All of them made her feel "a bit strange." None of them relieved her depression. Several made her more tired, one agitated her. Diane had visited her internist, and he had done the kind of conventional medical examination and testing I described earlier. All of her tests and her lab values were, as we doctors say, "within normal limits." There was "nothing," she was told, physically wrong.

When I took Diane's history, I learned that, about ten years before, she'd had a viral illness that just seemed to hang on. It had been diagnosed as infectious mononucleosis—"mono"—but appeared to have cleared up after about two months. Still, from that time on, Diane had been exhausted. Her internist had measured the titer—the level of antibodies—against the Epstein-Barr (EB) virus that causes mono, to see if her depression and exhaustion were manifestations of chronic fatigue immune deficiency syndrome. CFIDS is a rather mysterious condition that sometimes seems to follow mono, and it is often marked by high titers, or levels, of EB virus in the blood, as well as depression and fatigue. Her titers had been low, and he had concluded that she didn't have CFIDS.

He had also thought that Diane might have hypothyroidism. The thyroid regulates the metabolism, the energetic functioning, of all the body's cells. When it is hyper, or overactive, it tends to overheat the body and produce anxiety and sweating, difficulty maintaining body weight, diarrhea, smooth skin, and fine hair. Symptoms of hypothyroidism—of low thyroid functioning—include sensitivity to cold weather, weight gain, constipation, rough skin, and coarse hair, as well as fatigue and depression. Diane had most of the symptoms of hypothyroidism, but her physician had dismissed that possibility when her thyroid function tests came back "within normal limits" and her TSH level was only slightly elevated.

As Diane told me her story, a phrase by John James Audubon, the great naturalist, came to my mind. Audubon said that when there is a disparity between the bird we are seeing in nature and the picture of the bird in his guidebook, we should "believe the bird, not the book." It seemed to me that Diane's physician, though observant and thorough, had believed the tests rather than the patient and her history, and also had not done all the appropriate tests.

There are, in fact, people who have "normal" thyroid function tests—even near normal or normal TSH—but have the symptoms of subclinical hypothyroidism. They just seem to need more thyroid than other people to function normally. Many of these people have all the symptoms of clinical depression as well as the other symptoms of hypothyroidism. When you put them on a dose of thyroid that is *adequate for them,* the symptoms decrease, or even disappear, and they feel much better.

One test for this variant of subclinical hypothyroidism is simple and time honored. I asked Diane to take her temperature first thing every morning for seven consecutive days. She was to shake the thermometer down to 95° and hold it in her armpit, next to her body, for ten minutes, while sitting or lying quietly. Normal body temperature should be between about 97.5° and 98.6°F. Diane's varied from 96.0° to 96.6°F, strongly suggesting subclinical hypothyroidism.

I put her on a small dose of Armour Thyroid, a natural form of thyroid. Few conventional physicians use this form any longer, preferring synthetic thyroid because the dosage can be precisely measured. On the other hand, natural animal thyroid, like Armour, contains not just one, but both of the major thyroid hormones (T3 as well as the T4 that is usually prescribed) that our bodies actually use, as well as other components that may have a therapeutic effect.

Within several weeks, Diane felt more energetic. She took her temperature for another week, and it was higher, but still low, so we raised the dose. After several more weeks, we found a dose that was appropriate for her. Her hands and feet felt warmer, and she was moving her bowels more regularly. The cloud of exhaustion lifted, and with it her depression. She also began to lose weight. She still had difficulty appreciating her own good qualities and finding men who pleased her, but she had far more energy to deal with them and, in fact, far more energy to find sources of pleasure in her life other than work and the quest for the ideal man.

Diane also had the sense, for the first time, that she need not be condemned even to a residual gloominess: If a new approach could help her deal so successfully with her exhaustion, then it seemed to her she might well be able to find a way to deal with the vestiges of self-deprecation and depression.

Diane's hypothyroidism exerted its negative effects on her physical and emotional life, even though her hormone level was within normal limits. Diane simply needed more thyroid than the average person to ensure the proper functioning of the cells in her body. Her medical history suggested that the viral infection ten years before may have affected her thyroid or somehow reset her body's need for thyroid. In any case, her symptoms—the weight gain and constipation, the rough skin and her low body temperature and sensitivity to cold, as well as her depression—pointed to the problem, and supplemental thyroid went a long way toward relieving it.

If you have some or all of the symptoms Diane had, you may want to take your daily temperature for a week as she did. If it is consistently low, it's time to find a nutritional physician to try to help you.

BIOCHEMICAL INDIVIDUALITY

Diane's situation is not uncommon. All normal limits—whether of thyroid or other hormones, or vitamins or minerals or any other nutrients—are simply averages. They do not take account of what the pioneering biochemist Roger Williams described as "biochemical individuality." Williams's laboratory studies at the University of Texas and the thousands of research papers he reviewed show that each of us may differ vastly in our individual "normal limits" and our needs. Even if we are of similar age, gender, ethnicity, and general health status, I may need ten or one hundred times as much of one nutrient as you do, and you may need as much more of another. *We are each biochemically unique.*

These observations have profound consequences for our understanding of human biology and for the treatment of every condition that may trouble us, including depression. Please keep Williams's work and this principle of biochemical individuality in mind as you read the next sections on food and nutrients—and, in fact, as you consider all the various ways of working with and learning from depression. What is best for you may well be different from what is right for someone else with similar symptoms.

LET FOOD BE YOUR MEDICINE

Hippocrates, 2,500 years ago, exhorted his students to "let food be your medicine, and medicine your food." In recent centuries, against any semblance of common sense, the Western medicine that Hippocrates fathered has avoided or minimized his injunction. It was partly, I suspect, because physicians lost the connection to nature that had nourished our understanding of the therapeutic power of food. But other factors also contributed. In particular, improvements in the quantity of food and its availability obscured our appreciation of the importance of the *quality* of different foods and of the ways they might be combined to enhance or impair health. So long as people in industrialized countries ate enough, and had some variety in their diet, modern doctors believed people were safe from the most obvious and dangerous dietary deficiencies, the ones such as scurvy, rickets, and beriberi that affected only severely malnourished and, usually, terribly impoverished people. Physicians weren't aware of and rarely investigated other, more subtle nutritional deficiencies and imbalances.

For much of the twentieth century, nutrition was all but excluded from the medical school curriculum. Patients—except, in recent years, those with heart disease and diabetes—were told to eat pretty much what they wanted. When I was in medical school in the mid-1960s, physicians generally scoffed at the practices of "food faddists" who experimented with diets they believed could cure or prevent a host of diseases. At that time—and for many years thereafter—physicians told their patients that practices such as vegetarianism, fasting, and "elimination" and macrobiotic diets were likely to be harmful, and were certainly not going to do any good. Medical orthodoxy held that virtually everyone in the United States was well enough nourished. Doctors, using drugs and surgery, would take care of the "real" medicine.

Over the last thirty years, there has been a gradual reassessment of the importance of diet and nutrition in the prevention and treatment of a variety of illnesses and conditions. We have begun to bring scientific method to the study of nutritional needs, to question long-held assumptions about the basic soundness of the American diet, and to reassess other cultures' and our ancestors' use of food.

Studies in the late 1970s, sponsored by the U.S. Congress and the Department of Agriculture, made clear that the American diet had deteriorated terribly and was taxing our health. Processed foods, it turned out, contained only a tiny fraction of the nutrients of whole foods. In converting whole wheat into white flour, for example, we lost 70, 80, or even 90 percent of many of the vitamins and minerals that were present in the whole, unrefined grain.

The chemical and hormonal contamination of food, the extent of refinement and processing, the toxic additives and preservatives that increase shelf life and improve appearance, and the reliance on fat and sugar-heavy fast foods combined to create substances that were ever more removed from their natural origins and, we began to discover, ever more inimical to human health. The chemicals and hormones taxed our GI tract and caused our liver detoxification systems to work overtime, while nutrient-poor, refined carbohydrates overstimulated the insulin-producing part of our pancreas. Meanwhile, all these foods combined to put ever more stress on our adrenal glands. This higher level of stress, in turn, made it more difficult for our GI tract to digest and assimilate the nutrients that did remain in the food.

Epidemiologic studies have demonstrated that, over time, this modern, "civilized" diet has made us more and more vulnerable to the chronic illnesses that bedevil our society, including GI disease, allergies, and chronic pain, as well as cancer, heart disease, diabetes, and obesity. And though the evidence is as yet less robust, it seems that food and the way it is processed and prepared may significantly affect our mood. In fact, I am now convinced, by my reading of the scientific literature and my clinical experience, that there are good, evidence-based guidelines for eating in a way that can help to keep our mood stable and our mind and body flexible and efficient.

I'll give you these guidelines very soon, but first I want to create a context, establish a little perspective, and sound a few notes of caution.

Finding the Right Food for You

There is no subject, with the possible exceptions of religion and politics, that provokes as much controversy and evokes as much dogmatism as nutrition. Every year shelves of new books come on the market claiming that the diet they are promoting is *the* one—to help you be fit, lose weight, live longer, cure cancer and heart disease, have better sex, and, yes, feel better emotionally. There are, of course, good and useful ideas and suggestions in many of these books. And some are far more thoughtful than others. There are also, however, several premises and a few attitudes that make me cringe.

First and foremost of these is the conviction that there is one diet for all people. This is a peculiarly rigid assumption. It flies in the face of the biochemical individuality that Roger Williams and his students have so clearly demonstrated. It also violates everything we know about the variety of dietary habits and eating customs around the world. Finally, it offends common sense.

The second thing that troubles me about the diet books, and the mentality they encourage, is their lack of subtlety. It is true that there are some good studies that show that a high intake of sugar and caffeine seems to predispose some people to depression; but there are also numbers of depressed people who swear they get real relief from their cups of coffee. The point is not for me, or any other expert, to tell you that you should or should not have your morning coffee, but for you to take this information and do your own experiment—a couple of weeks without coffee, perhaps; then three weeks with coffee without sugar; two weeks of decaf, etc. Your experience, your knowing, are more important to you than your following somebody else's command.

Third, food is far more than the sum of the nutrients in it. It is, or can be, a great pleasure, and sometimes even greater when we're feeling depressed. Especially then, when you're low, you should eat foods that satisfy you and make you smile, so long as they don't have the kind of serious downside that I'll discuss later on.

During down times, it can be particularly fun and fulfilling to cook for yourself. I know it's very hard to do anything for yourself when you're really depressed (it may feel both overwhelmingly difficult and singularly pointless). Yet many of my patients and students have found that putting out this effort when they're depressed, or just unhappy, or low in energy, or lonely can be engaging and feel life affirming.

The food can be very simple, but selecting and buying it, cutting and cooking it can be absorbing and even healing. In a time of inertia, you're taking action. You're feeling depleted and still you're rediscovering your creativity. You're making something that pleases you and directly counteracting the feelings of joylessness and helplessness that characterize depression. You are literally and metaphorically nourishing yourself.

Whatever and however you decide to eat, and no matter how much good it may do you, don't condemn others for not eating your way. It makes them miserable. And few things, I believe, are less likely to bring real joy to you than the terrible self-righteousness of dietary fanaticism.

So, with these thoughts in mind, here are some brief discussions of food constituents and general guidelines for eating in ways that will help improve your mood.

MAKING SENSE OF THE MACRONUTRIENTS: CARBOHYDRATES, PROTEIN, AND FATS

Carbohydrates

We all need significant amounts of carbohydrates and the simple sugar glucose—the brain's food and source of energy—into which carbohydrates are broken down. But we should choose our brain food intelligently.

Simple sugars, like ordinary table sugar, honey, and the corn syrup that is present in so many processed foods, consist of one or two molecules of glucose. They are quickly absorbed from the GI tract, and tend to cause rapid rises in blood sugar. This gives them what nutritionists call a high glycemic (sugar) index.

These sugars may give us a transient feeling of energy and even elation, but they stress our bodies, making us put out large amounts of insulin and adrenaline to break down and assimilate the carbs. After the initial rush passes, many people feel let down, tired, or even seriously depressed. They tend to crave yet another jolt of sugar. Simple sugars and refined carbohydrates—carbohydrates from which fiber and a variety of nutrients have been removed to make them more attractive or durable or easier to cook with—should be your occasional pleasure, not your regular pattern.

Complex carbohydrates, like whole grains, beans, and green vegetables, consist of three or more sugars joined in a long chain. They are broken down more slowly in our digestive tract. The glucose in them is released gradually into our blood stream, giving our body time to assimilate the sugar without stress. These foods, which release glucose more slowly, are said to have a low glycemic index. Some complex carbohydrates, like green vegetables, beans, lentils, oatmeal, and barley, have a particularly favorable glycemic index. Make them your constant companions.

CHOOSING CARBOHYDRATES

The prescription is very simple: Eat primarily complex carbohydrates, such as grains, green vegetables, soy- and other beans, and fruits with high fiber and a low glycemic index, like oranges, apples, and peaches.

Cut way down on, or eliminate completely, simple sugars, like white and brown sugar, corn syrup, fruit juices, etc. This means reading the labels of processed food, which will sometimes proclaim proudly that they are sugar free, even though they contain fructose or lactose or maltose—all of which are just as much sugar as sugar.

If you do fall off the sugar wagon, don't wallow in self-blame. This is the time to pay attention to what happens. If you feel energized and then depressed and depleted after you've taken a dose of sugar, it likely means that sugar is not good for you. The experience should be an excellent reminder of why you cut down on sugars in the first place.

SUGAR BLUES >> Everyone can benefit from eating more of the complex carbohydrates, but there is a particular group of depressed and unhappy people who seem to be especially vulnerable to sugar. These are the people who have a "sweet tooth." They crave sugar, and perhaps always have, and find themselves devouring half a loaf of bread while waiting for dinner, or polishing off a pint, not a portion, of ice cream. Some of these people have been, or are, exquisitely sensitive to alcohol or have become addicted to it. Most of them find it very hard to stop eating sweets and starches. If you're one of these people, switching from simple to complex carbohydrates, and generally eating more protein and fewer carbohydrates, may really, and very quickly, change your life.

The research literature on the sugar-depression connection is suggestive, but by no means definitive. It does appear that some people who are depressed are more likely to have low blood sugar (hypoglycemia) and that these low levels of blood sugar in turn produce sugar cravings. It is also known that carbohydrates are the engine that drives tryptophan, the precursor of serotonin, into the brain, and that a carbohydrate-induced increase of brain serotonin may be associated with improved mood. Finally, it seems that sugars may also cause a release of beta-endorphins (mood-enhancing opiumlike substances) in our brains.

People who have low blood sugar crave sugar. The problem is that the simple sugars and starches they eat are a short-term remedy but a long-term problem: In addition to stressing the adrenals and provoking high levels of insulin, the jolt of simple sugars may also, in the long run, over-load the brain's serotonin and beta-endorphin receptors and produce an ongoing, and potentially addictive, higher demand for these substances and, perhaps, depression.

If the research, which was presented in book form several years ago by Kathleen DesMaisons, is still only suggestive, clinical experience is far more convincing. Sugar cravers whom I've treated have experienced withdrawal symptoms—fatigue, headaches, irritability, a more depressed mood—as they began to switch from simple to complex carbohydrates and a higher protein diet. This is a sign that they were, at least in some sense, physiologically dependent on these sugars. Even more impressive, and far more important, is that a number of those who kept the complex carbohydrates and protein high and the simple carbs low felt far happier, calmer, and more energetic, often after only a week or two.

I remember twenty-five years ago when a boy named Dominique was living on an inpatient adolescent psychiatric service that I directed. He was a depressed sixteen-year-old who seemed to have a knack for always irritating everyone and getting into trouble: If four kids were talking in class, he was the one suspended; if there was a fight on the street, everyone split and Dominique ran into the arms of the cops. Dominique had been on and off antidepressants (and antipsychotic drugs) for years and had gotten only more anxious and depressed. On the ward, he couldn't sit still for more than a minute, teased the girls and challenged the boys, talked incessantly, jiggled his legs as if he were having a seizure, and told every-one who would listen how he was going to be killed, or kill himself, before he was eighteen.

I noticed that Dominique ate huge quantities of candy and Cokes and, when he could, everyone else's dessert. I suggested to him that since he was already so miserable, he might be interested in trying an experiment: Stop the sweets for ten days and see what happened. For a while he thought I was the crazy one, but eventually, fed up with his own unhap-piness and the abuse from staff and peers that his behavior provoked, he agreed.

After a rough four days, Dominique was a different kid, and the whole ward a happier, more peaceful place. He wasn't interrupting people, shot pool without causing a riot, and was able to sit quietly reading a comic book. He talked about getting a job and going home.

A week later, I came in one morning and Dominique was screaming at a staff member and punching the wall. What happened, I asked. "Hey, Doc," he said, so fast I could barely understand, "the ten days is up. The experiment worked. I got me some Snickers bars to celebrate."

I don't know if Dominique ever tried the experiment again, but at least he knew that there was something he could do to help himself feel better. I've worked with a number of other people with sugar cravings, including many children and teenagers who've been diagnosed with depression and attention deficit hyperactivity disorder (ADHD). A num-ber have done the experiment and taken it to heart. They've made the switch from simple to complex carbohydrates, and to a higher protein diet, with impressive results.

Protein

Protein's stock has fluctuated wildly in the marketplace of nutritional advice. When I was a kid, more than fifty years ago, eating protein, mostly in the form of beef, was an unalloyed good and, for people with little money, a sign of some success as well as a treat. In the last two decades, amid concerns about the fat, hormones, and pollutants in meat, and the dangers of too much protein (excessive protein intake has been implicated in osteoporosis and kidney disease and may, according to some epidemiologic evidence, be associated with cancer), protein's fortunes declined; complex carbohydrates were king. More recently, however, revisionist nutritionists from Robert Atkins to Barry Sears (who created the Zone Diet) have told us that the balance must be redressed, that protein (with the aid of fat) can make it easier for us to lose weight, and help spare us the stress that carbohydrates put on our systems.

In fact, everyone agrees that protein, like carbohydrates and fat, is essential for life. After all, aside from water, protein is the next largest part of our bodies. When protein is digested, it breaks down into the amino acids that are the fundamental constituents of our muscles and ligaments, of the antibodies that protect us against infection, the genes that provide the blueprint for the structure and function of every organ in our bodies, and, of perhaps most immediate importance for those of us who are depressed, the neurotransmitters that allow our brain cells to function and communicate effectively.

Some of these twenty amino acids can be synthesized in our body; others need to come from our food. This latter group, the "essential amino acids," are the ones that we must make sure are included in our diets. Animal protein—in meat, fish, eggs, and milk—is described as a "complete" protein because it contains all the essential amino acids. Vegetarians, it appears, must combine different foods, each of which contains some of the essential amino acids, to obtain complete protein—for example, beans and rice, corn and beans, or soy and oats. It turns out it's not necessary to have both halves of these pairs at the same meal, but it looks as if they should probably be eaten within the same day.

Since protein is so crucial to every aspect of our functioning, the issue is not whether to eat protein, but how much and which kinds. According to archeological findings, our Paleolithic ancestors consumed large amounts of meat, so there is good reason to think that this pattern conforms nicely to our genetic programming. Unfortunately, the meat they ate is for the most part unavailable to us. They hunted and ate wild game, which was very low in saturated fat. The meat in our supermarkets is not only filled with fat, it is, with the exception of some that is raised organically, saturated with the toxic herbicides and pesticides that have been used to produce the animals' feed, and laced with the hormones and antibiotics that produce bigger animals.

In general, you're probably best off if your diet contains about 30 percent protein, and if a significant portion of it comes from vegetable protein and fish, like wild salmon, halibut, and mackerel, and a distinct minority from poultry and lean cuts of meat. If you can afford it, it's certainly better to eat organic meat from animals that have been allowed to graze or roam freely—the free-range chickens that I used to raise when I lived on a farm tasted like an entirely different and distinctly healthier and more energetic species than the rather mushy and bland ones sold in grocery stores.

In addition to its importance as a building block for all our tissue, protein, which takes some time to digest, helps to prolong the process by which carbohydrates are absorbed into the body—and therefore helps insure that insulin will be secreted in a slower, more regular and more physiologically sound fashion.

Finally, because protein is the source of the amino acids that are the basic elements of neurotransmitters, you can use it wisely and combine it properly with carbohydrates to enhance neurotransmitter function. For example, tryptophan, which is a building block or precursor of the neurotransmitter serotonin, is one of the least plentiful of the amino acids. You can, however, maximize your intake of it by eating such tryptophan-rich protein sources as turkey, chicken, and pork (if possible, organic); and you can increase the amount that flows into your brain by making sure you have a complex carbohydrate (like oatmeal or brown rice or broccoli) after you've had your protein. The carbohydrate evokes an insulin response, which in turn encourages the other, more plentiful, amino acids to be incorporated into muscle, leaving tryptophan behind to go to the brain.

Fats

There is a lot of prejudice against fats, some deserved and some as foolish and shortsighted as any prejudice. The basic problem is once again with quality and quantity, not with "fat" itself.

We Americans haven't increased our consumption of dietary fat in the last hundred years, but we have shifted our intake in the direction of refined and adulterated fat. The net result has been to increase the amount of saturated fat—solid, usually animal fat, in which the carbon atoms are saturated with hydrogen atoms. This intake of saturated fat may be associated with a number of chronic illnesses, most particularly cardiovascular disease and some forms of cancer. In any case, this pattern of fat consumption actually decreases the amount of essential fatty acids—linoleic and linolenic acid—we take in. This, in turn, affects the levels and types of the prostaglandins they form. Prostaglandins are substances named for the prostate gland, where they were first discovered, that are crucial—in the right proportions—to the proper functioning of all the organs and cells in our body.

This degeneration of our diet may contribute, in several ways, to some of the symptoms that are characteristic of depression. First, fatty acids, particularly in the form of phosphorus-containing compounds called phospholipids, are vital components of all cell membranes and, most particularly, of brain cells, which have the highest concentration of phospholipids. When these membranes are composed of essential nonsaturated fatty acids, they are flexible and easily permeable to incoming nutrients. When they consist of saturated animal fatty acids and trans-fatty acids (so called because of the alteration in structure brought about by processing, as with margarine, and in deep-frying), the cell membranes become rigid, and the level of functioning declines.

Prostaglandins, and particularly an imbalance between the different kinds of prostaglandins, may also play a role in some peoples' depression. Basically, high levels of the "good" anti-inflammatory prostaglandins PGE1 and PGE3 (promoted by linoleic acid, an omega-6, as well as omega-3 fatty acids) correlate with good mood and enhanced serotonin activity (as well as more effective immunity and diminished tendency to blood clotting), whereas high levels of the "bad" proinflammatory pros-taglandin, PGE2 (derived particularly from beef and other red meat), correlate with depression, irritability, and easy fatigability (and heart dis-ease, decreased immunity, etc.). When our diet is deficient in omega-3 fatty acids, we are more likely to produce the bad prostaglandin and be depressed.

OMEGA-3s >> The omega-3s seem to be especially important. Epidemiological evidence shows a correlation between intake of fish high in omega-3s and decreased incidence of depression. Several clinical stud-ies have been done that demonstrate quite clearly the effectiveness of omega-3s in helping people in whom depression alternates with "manic episodes" of agitation, excitement, and grandiosity—people with bipolar disorder. And there are also an increasing number of studies that point to the usefulness of omega-3s in treating depression.

In addition to suggesting increasing the intake of fish, which is high in omega-3s, I usually recommend a supplemental dosage of about 3,000 milligrams of omega-3s per day, divided in two equal parts. I tell patients to make sure that the oil comes from fish that are certified free of the toxic heavy metals and pollutants that are so widespread, and that may them-selves contribute to depression.

The particular omega-3s that seem most important are DHA (docosahexaenoic acid) and EPA (eicosapentaenoic acid). You can get 3,000 milligrams of omega-3s from a total of six 1,000-milligram capsules of fish oil, each of which contains approximately 180 milligrams of EPA and 120 of DHA together with other omega-3s. Some of the studies on bipolar disorder and depression suggest that a much higher ratio of EPA to DHA may be even more effective. The researchers who conducted these studies developed a product to these specifications, OmegaBrite, which I sometimes suggest. Each capsule contains 350 milligrams of EPA and 50 milligrams of DHA. The producers recommend starting with one capsule three times a day with meals, and increasing the amount over several weeks, if needed, to up to eight capsules a day.

THE TAKE-HOME MESSAGE

If you're depressed—or if your energy is just low—you might want to experiment with significantly decreasing your intake of the saturated fatty acids in red meat and lard, and eliminating altogether the trans fats that may be used in margarine and fast and processed foods. At the same time, you should increase your intake of fish (which is high in omega-3s) and of vegetable oils that are both unsaturated and unprocessed (for example, extra virgin olive oil and other cold-pressed oils). You should also supplement with omega-3 capsules as above.

You may notice a significant difference in mood as a result of this experiment. At worst, you're helping to lay the foundation for long-term good health.

A Few Words on Fiber and Water

Fiber is a vitally important part of our diet and of a dietary approach to depression. Fiber is made from long chains of glucose that are joined together to form pectin or cellulose. Fiber gives structure to plants and protects seeds. There are large quantities of it in whole grains, beans, lentils, and some fruits. Raw food has significantly more fiber than cooked.

There are two kinds of fiber: soluble and insoluble. Both are necessary and both are generally quite deficient in the American diet. Soluble pectin fiber is found in oatmeal and oat bran; nuts, seeds, and beans; and fruit, such as apples, pears, strawberries, and blueberries. It helps to slow sugar absorption from our gut, to promote the growth of beneficial intestinal bacteria, and to soften our stool.

Insoluble cellulose fiber is present in whole grains and bran, as well as in some legumes (lentils and beans) and a number of vegetables, like carrots, cucumbers, and zucchini. Insoluble fiber promotes bowel regularity; removes cholesterol, hormones, and toxins from the gut; and also helps to regulate and slow sugar absorption.

Significant intake of dietary fiber is known to reduce the risk of heart disease, diabetes, and diverticular disease in the large intestine and to promote regular (once or twice daily) bowel movements. The average American's intake is a meager 12 to 15 grams a day (about one-third of an ounce) instead of the more than 100 grams that our ancestors were, and contemporary aboriginal peoples are, accustomed to eating. Not surprisingly, our bowel movements are far smaller and less frequent than those of our aboriginal brothers and sisters.

Knowledge about fiber intake, healthy stool formation, and the diets that promote them is easily available but generally ignored in medical education and practice. Some physicians still believe, and tell their patients, that it's "normal" to have bowel movements three times, two times, or even once a *week*. The experience of humans through much of the history of our species, and of virtually every living human over the age of fifty or sixty, makes it clear that they are wrong. People feel better physically, and often emotionally, when they have a satisfying bowel movement at least once daily.

Though it's generally recognized that constipation is a *symptom* of depression, most mental health professionals don't address their patients' bowel habits. This can be a significant mistake. There is no need to wait for definitive studies that show that constipation *causes* depression. All of us have everything to gain—physically and emotionally—by eating far more fiber and having larger, more frequent bowel movements. We have nothing, except waste matter, to lose.

You can get the fiber you need by making fresh fruits, vegetables, beans, and lentils a significant part of your daily diet, and eating whole grain bread and cereals. I recommend that, in addition, you add four to six tablespoons of unprocessed oat bran to your morning cereal or put it in a fruit and yogurt smoothie. It's bland and a bit gritty, but most people soon get used to the texture. And for most of us, the added dose of fiber is crucial to good bowel health and the mood benefits that come with it.

Water is important to the proper action of fiber and adequate, satisfying, nonstressful bowel movements. The prestigious Institute of Medicine (IOM) Food and Nutrition Board recommends that women consume 91 ounces (a little less than 3 quarts) of water each day from beverages and foods, while men generally need to consume 125 ounces per day. Since 80 percent of our water comes from beverages, this means eight to nine 8-ounce glasses of water for women, and 12 for men. I also recommend two 12-ounce glasses of water first thing in the morning. When you drink the water on an empty stomach, it activates the gastrocolic reflex, which leads to more efficient emptying of the colon.

THE MICRONUTRIENTS

In addition to carbohydrates, proteins, fats, and fiber—the macro-nutrients—there are a number of other substances that can, if present in amounts that are not adequate for our unique, individual biochemical functioning, contribute to our depression. The most prominent among these micronutrients are the B vitamins, including thiamine (B_1), folic acid, pyridoxine (B_6), and B_{12}; vitamin C; magnesium; zinc; selenium; and chromium.

The crucial points to remember are that the B vitamins are vital to the metabolism of all our cells, and in particular, the cells of the nervous system, and that together with vitamin C they help maintain an efficient adrenal response to stress. Magnesium is important in serotonin production; zinc and chromium help to regulate sugar metabolism and therefore nervous system functioning; and the powerful antioxidant selenium may be crucial to nerve cell functioning.

Besides understanding the importance of biochemical individuality, and the role of specific nutrients in preventing depression, we all need to be aware of another crucial fact of our nutrition: The *majority* of us in the United States, and many other so-called developed countries as well, are deficient in one or more of the essential micronutrients, even by the minimal standards of the U.S. Department of Agriculture's recommended dietary allowance (RDA). For example, one study showed that dietary levels of selenium were far below the RDA and that daily supplementation with 100 micrograms of selenium significantly enhanced the mood of normal, generally healthy, volunteers.

Furthermore, when we're deficient in one micronutrient—selenium, zinc, or any vitamin—it makes it difficult for us to make optimal use even of those nutrients that are present in adequate quantities, compromising even more the integrity of our response to stress, the health of our brain, and the quality of our mood. Finally, when we're under stress, as we are when we're depressed, our need for nutrients tends to increase.

When we put these findings together, it becomes clear that the journey we take through and out of depression may be powerfully affected, for good or ill, by the quality and quantity of the nutrients we take into our body and the way we use them.

A Mood-Healthy Supplement Plan

Since testing for levels of nutrients is impractical as well as quite expensive, and since nutrients other than the ones listed above are also needed for optimal functioning, and since there are no significant side effects from taking them, I generally recommend that each of us who is depressed, or stressed, or feeling low in energy, take a high-dose multivitamin and multimineral and a therapeutic amount of essential fatty acids. These are best divided into morning and afternoon doses.

The suggestions for supplementation that I make in the box below are in addition to, and *not substitutes for,* a diet that is healthy for you. These doses can, however, be used by just about anybody who is depressed or stressed. Still, they should be discussed with your physician, particularly if you're on any medication.

Occasionally, B vitamins may be a little irritating to the stomach, in which case a slightly lower dose should be taken. Rarely, they can be too stimulating. In this case, I suggest you either cut the overall dose or begin by taking the second half of the dose at lunch rather than at dinner.

Sometimes doses of vitamin C at the level of 1,000 milligrams—or even 500 milligrams—twice daily can cause GI irritation and diarrhea. If so, cut back to 250 milligrams, morning and evening, and be sure to take it with food.

There's been some recent concern about the toxicity of very high doses of antioxidants, including vitamin A, particularly for smokers, and of vitamin E. The amounts listed in the box below should be quite safe.

I don't routinely recommend supplements with iron, except for patients who are anemic; excess iron can be constipating and may contribute to heart disease.

Start with the lower doses recommended in the box below. You may increase the amount if there are no side effects if you want to see if a somewhat higher dose is more helpful. Positive effects are usually gradual and subtle. If, however, you're significantly depleted, they may be dramatic and swift.

MOOD-HEALTHY DAILY DOSES

Vitamins

Vitamin A (retinol)	5,000 IU
Vitamin A (from beta-carotene)	5,000–10,000 IU
Vitamin D	100–300 IU
Vitamin E (d-alpha tocopherol)	200–400 IU
Vitamin K (phytonadione)	60–90 mg
Vitamin C (ascorbic acid)	500–2,000 mg
Vitamin B_1 (thiamine)	15–50 mg
Vitamin B_2 (riboflavin)	10–50 mg
Niacin	20–60 mg
Niacinamide	10–30 mg
Vitamin B_6 (pyridoxine)	50–100 mg
Biotin	100–300 mcg
Pantothenic acid	200–500 mg
Folic acid	400–1200 mcg
Vitamin B_{12}	1,000 mcg
Choline	150–500 mg
Inositol	150–500 mg

Minerals	
Boron	1–2 mg
Calcium	500–1,500 mg
Chromium	200–400 mcg
Copper	1–3 mg
Iodine	50–150 mcg
Magnesium	250–750 mg
Manganese	5–10 mg
Molybdenum	10–25 mcg
Potassium	200–500 mg
Selenium	100–200 mcg
Zinc	15–30 mg
Omega-3 fatty acids (at least one half as EPA and DHA)	3,000–6,000 mg

Those with symptoms of SIBO should add a supplement that combines acidophilus and bifidus, approximately two to three billion live bacteria per day.

An additional note: If this level of supplementation and the rest of the *Unstuck* approach do not produce significant improvement in your mood, you may want to consult a nutritional physician who can do the extensive testing required to detect specific deficiencies and imbalances.

FOOD SENSITIVITY

Finally, I want to address food sensitivity. This condition is, I believe, far more pervasive and far more often a cause of, or contributor to, depression than we know. It is also one of the most striking, though controversial, examples of our ongoing individual response to diet, and of the link between specific foods and depression.

True food allergy is, by definition, "mediated," or produced by a specific response of a kind of protein, IgE (immune globulin E), to a foreign substance. Food sensitivity is something else again. Some food sensitivity appears to reflect an idiosyncratic reaction to foods like sugar and citrus. Some, according to those who have long studied it, appears to be mediated by other immune globulins, perhaps IgG. This latter kind of sensitivity, they maintain, is usually caused by the passage of large, reaction-stimulating protein molecules out of an intestine that has been made "leaky" by repeated "insults."

Infections and antibiotics and other drugs may be responsible for leaky gut, but there may be dietary causes as well. Modern diets, which often depend on one or two kinds of foods, are rarely in harmony with our species's genetic programming for eating a wide variety of foods. And refined and processed foods, with their toxic additives, are surely a calculated industrial insult to our evolutionary development. Some of us can handle just about anything; the vulnerability of others produces leaky gut and food sensitivity.

As these large, unfamiliar protein molecules pass across the gut and into the bloodstream, they are believed to provoke defensive reactions in nearly every system in the body and to produce a variety of observable, clinical effects, including depression. Though the theory is far from proven, the clinical examples of non-IgE food sensitivity can be quite striking. Here's one of a number from my own practice.

Jenny's Depression Disappears

Six years ago, twelve-year old Jenny's parents brought her to me in desperation. Formerly a bright, conscientious girl, she had in recent months become sullen and short tempered, unable to sleep or study. Now, she was irritated with her family, despondent about her prospects as a student and a teenager, withdrawn from her friends, and despairing about the querulous, unhappy person she'd become.

The well-known psychologist to whom Jenny's parents brought her had noted a severe "adjustment reaction" to the onset of puberty and also diagnosed Jenny as "clinically depressed." Jenny, the psychologist had said, leaving little room for doubt, needed "intensive, twice-weekly psychotherapy for a year or two," which she would provide. The psychologist referred her to a psychiatrist for pharmacological assistance.

The thought of "one to two years" of twice-weekly psychotherapy—talking about mysterious and ominous problems at which the psychologist had hinted, but which neither Jenny nor her parents could identify—seemed overwhelming, as well as prohibitively expensive. Taking the two antidepressants that the psychiatrist soon prescribed (one to improve her mood, the second to counteract the stimulant effects of the first and allow her to sleep) terrified Jenny and her parents. The three of them left the psychiatrist's office in tears.

When I first saw Jenny, her hair was lusterless and her face pinched. There were dark circles under her eyes, and she was carrying more weight than was comfortable for her. She squirmed and ducked her head and sighed and whined when she spoke, as if every communication had to be a complaint.

I took a history of Jenny's depression. The most obvious symptoms—her irritability with her parents, her tearfulness and sadness, her difficulty concentrating, and the distance from her friends—had appeared only in the last three or four months. A few weeks before they began, she'd been hit in the head by a soccer ball. She hadn't lost consciousness, and her doctor said Jenny was "fine," but since then she had had some mild headaches and a persistent pain in her neck.

I went on to Jenny's past history. It turned out that there had been a few "minor" problems during her childhood—frequent colds, difficulty getting to sleep every night, a certain "restlessness," and constipation that had "always" been present.

"Always?" I asked Jenny's mother. She nodded yes.

"From the day she was born?"

"No," her mother said, "when I think about it, it started at eight or nine months"—the age when Jenny stopped breast-feeding and began to drink cow's milk.

I asked about Jenny's diet. She had, her mother said, always been a "picky" eater, and they'd had innumerable talks and even fights about it.

Though they'd come to a truce, and Jenny had agreed to eat some green vegetables and fruit every day, the vast majority of her diet still consisted of dairy products and wheat—yogurt and bread for breakfast, pizza for lunch, ice cream in the afternoon, macaroni and cheese at numerous dinners.

It sounded to me as though Jenny's problems had begun when she was weaned from breast milk. It seemed to me that she, like others I'd treated, was sensitive to the protein in cow's milk. Perhaps her sensitivity wasn't extreme enough to create massive digestive problems, but it may well have had an impact on her colon (the constipation), on her respiratory system (the colds), and her nervous system (her restlessness and sleeplessness).

Apparently Jenny had managed to live in an uneasy equilibrium with her milk sensitivity, eating milk products continually and suffering annoying and somewhat debilitating, but not disabling, symptoms until the last few months. Like many people, she craved what was harmful to her, and then, hurting, wanted more, so she would "feel better." Then something changed: Her sleeplessness, agitation, and compulsiveness increased and her mood plummeted. Perhaps her head injury had somehow destabilized her; perhaps the onset of puberty had contributed.

I told Jenny that there were things I could do to help: manual manipulation of her spine to relieve the torsion and tension caused by the head injury; acupuncture to relax her; some Chinese herbs to improve her digestion and decrease her tension; the basic regimen of supplementation I've just described. I would teach her Soft Belly to help her quiet herself and sleep, and I advised her to exercise more, and more regularly.

But, I went on, there's something else that I'm pretty sure is even more crucial. "Would you be willing to do an experiment with your diet?" I asked.

Jenny recoiled, like a kid in a horror movie holding up a cross to fend off a vampire.

"The milk," I said.

"No, not milk," she cried. "How can I give up milk?"

"How about doing it for three weeks, along with wheat and sugar?"

"That's everything," she groaned.

"And then see what happens and make up your own mind," I continued.

"What about two weeks?" she bargained.

We shook hands on it.

When Jenny came in two weeks later, she was a different girl. She'd lost some of the puffiness in her face and body, the circles around her eyes were less ominous, and she collapsed happily into her chair. Four days after she'd begun to eliminate milk, wheat, and sugar—long before the Chinese herbs arrived or she'd started her supplements—she'd started to regain her capacity to concentrate. A day or so afterward, for the first time since infancy, she'd gone to sleep within thirty minutes of getting into bed. She was now moving her bowels four times—not twice—a week. "I'm not a bit depressed," she said when I asked, and when I wondered aloud if she'd continue on the diet, she nodded her head.

"What about if I cheat?"

"Try it and see," I suggested.

Within two months, Jenny was fine—sleeping well, getting all As and Bs, moving her bowels daily. When, occasionally, she got tense about her grades or an upcoming class presentation, she did the Soft Belly exercise I taught her, and it helped. She found that she could, without problems, eat pretty much everything except milk and large quantities of wheat or sugar. And when she did cheat, as occasionally happened, or when she didn't realize that there was milk in a food, she paid the price—in agitation, mild depression, low energy, and sleeplessness—for a day or so.

The clues to the causes of Jenny's depression and its successful treatment were apparent. I just needed to take a careful history and be willing to look for and give credence to possible causes of depression that are widely ignored. And Jenny, of course, had to be willing to see the sense of what I was saying, to do the experiment, take its lessons to heart, and collaborate with me.

Eliminating What Harms Us

Sometimes we crave foods that we truly need—salt on a hot sweaty day or protein when we're feeling weak. More often, food cravings, like other addictions, point to problems or imbalances rather than offer solutions. These cravings often go back to childhood, to eating foods that are hard for many of us to handle, perhaps because our guts have become leaky, and to diets that depend on too few foods.

If you suspect food sensitivity, I suggest that you work with an integrative or holistic physician, nutritionist, dietitian, or naturopathic physician to explore this possibility. If one isn't available or you can't afford it, or you'd like to do this yourself, it's easy enough to create your own "elimination diet." These diets, which have been used in one form or another for a hundred years, are described in detail in a couple of books I've listed in the Resources section.

What follows is an easy way to assess yourself for food sensitivities and to take steps to deal with them successfully.

CREATING YOUR OWN ELIMINATION DIET

For three weeks, eliminate those foods that are the main part of many modern American diets and that clinicians have found to be the most obvious and consistent causes of food sensitivity: milk, wheat, sugar, corn, soy, and citrus. Eat a diet of whole foods, preferably organic, and preferably without red meat. And drink plenty of spring water.

During the first few days, as you "withdraw" from the food(s) to which you are sensitive, you may feel worse—even more depressed. This is unpleasant, but it may actually be a good sign, a confirmation of a food sensitivity. In a few more days, these symptoms should subside, and you'll likely feel much better.

Keep a diary and each day record the answers to the following questions: How do you feel? What do you crave? What's the relationship between the time you ate, what you ate, and how you feel?

Are you less, or more, depressed on this elimination diet, more energetic or better able to concentrate? What about other symptoms? Does any of this change over time?

Then, after the three weeks, reintroduce the foods that you've eliminated, *one at a time*. See, for example, how you feel after a meal of conventional wheat pasta (with olive oil rather than cheese or butter). What is it like the next day? Is your mood unchanged or worse? Are you more fatigued? Is your digestion affected? You may want to record the answers in your journal.

Then, a week or two later, experiment with another of the eliminated foods, perhaps milk (or cheese) and so on. If you are truly sensitive to a food, eliminating it should, after several weeks, improve your symptoms, and reintroducing it should reproduce some of the original symptoms.

Sometimes the results of reintroducing foods to which you're sensitive are dramatic. Jenny, who felt fine for two weeks, ate a large bowl of pasta with cheese and, the next morning, had a splitting headache and couldn't concentrate. She found out after several more weeks, as many people do, that if she ate some food she craved, like wheat or sugar, occasionally, and in small amounts, she had only minor ill effects. Other foods, like milk or milk products, could reliably stop her bowels, keep her up at night, and bring on the depressed feelings.

This personal investigation into food sensitivity is inexpensive and, if you're motivated enough—if the depression and other symptoms are disturbing enough—well worth the effort you put into it. It may make a significant difference in how you feel. And it's enormously satisfying to find out what's been troubling you *and* be able to do something about it.

SUMMING UP

As you hear and answer the Call, you realize that you are depressed and that change is necessary. This is the beginning of your journey through and beyond depression.

The first lists you make—of what's troubling you now, the directions in which you need to head, and the steps that you need to take to get there—provide a map for you and will reassure you that it is possible to take the journey.

Removing the drugs that may contribute to depression and ruling out or treating the conditions that may cause it help make it possible for you to take the needed steps. Finding and reversing your physical imbalances and giving yourself optimum nutrition can, as you've seen from some of the examples in this chapter, change the nature of your journey altogether.

In any case, the individualized approach to food and eating and the general nutrition and supplementation plan I've shared with you will help you to function optimally and may well make your progress far easier, far faster.

And each time you respond and act—paying attention to issues or pain you have ignored, setting a goal, making a dietary change or sticking to a supplement regimen—you are reversing the feelings of helplessness that have kept you stuck and lifting off the weight of your depression, giving yourself the opportunity to move ahead, with far more hope, on your journey through and beyond depression.

YOUR PRESCRIPTION FOR SELF-CARE:
The Healthier Body, Happier Mind Checklists

These two brief prescriptions are presented as checklists and reminders. You'll want to go through them to ensure that you're adequately prepared and optimally healthy for your journey. The first, The Investigation, summarizes the steps you can take to explore the possible physical causes of depression. The second, Food as Medicine, highlights the sections on mood-healthy eating and supplementation.

The Investigation

1 A complete history and physical exam and routine lab tests (including thyroid function tests) from a primary care physician. Make sure you disclose all prescription drugs and any nonprescription substances you're taking.

2 If nothing significant appears in your conventional workup, and if your energy is really low and/or you often have other physical symptoms (numbness, tingling, headache, swollen feet, GI upset, etc.) that don't register on conventional testing or fall into a clear, conventional medical pattern, then it's time to consider consulting with a holistic or integrative physician, naturopath, nutritionist, chiropractor, etc.

3 If you are depressed and other causes have been ruled out, and particularly if you have other symptoms like frequent colds, GI upset, or low energy, you may want to see if you are sensitive to any foods. Do the elimination diet as I've described it in this chapter.

Food as Medicine

Here is a brief review of the material on using food and supplementation to promote optimal emotional functioning. It will probably help if you read over the sections I'm summarizing. Please follow these recommendations in a way that gives you pleasure as well as satisfaction. Make them your own.

1 Pay attention to my general guidelines for carbohydrates, proteins, fats, fiber, and water.

2 Almost everyone can begin with the supplement regimen that I've offered. Check with your doctor first. If he or she is OK

with it, then proceed. Record the exact amounts of each nutrient you're actually taking. Make sure you take both daily doses.

3 Pay attention to and record your responses to the changes you make. You can do this in your journal, by keeping track of all foods you eat, how much of them you eat, and how you feel—right after eating and throughout the day. A week of record keeping after each major change in diet should give you most of the information you need.

4 Remember, we are all biochemically unique. What works for me, or even most of us, may not be best for you.

5 Cook for yourself and enjoy eating your own food. Do it slowly, meditatively.

CHAPTER 2

Guides on the Journey

Even after you've recognized that you're depressed, and realized you have to change, you may still be uncertain about how to do it. You may write down your emotions and sketch out steps to get where you want to go, but still feel unequal to taking them. Perhaps you're eating healthier foods and adding the appropriate supplements to them, and experiencing positive changes and feeling good about them. But still you want to feel even better, to make sure you're doing everything you can to move ahead.

And, no matter how determined and conscientious you are, there may still be times of doubt when you feel as stuck as ever, when you cry on the shore like Odysseus, wander like Demeter in fruitless search, or tremble like Dante in the dark wood. These are signs that you need to look for and accept help, that you need to find the Guides who can help you get where you want and need to go, the Guides who can support and sustain you on your journey.

In this chapter, I'll help you choose among the many professional Guides—the various therapists who may be available—to find the one who meets your unique needs. I'll show you how to work most effectively, most happily, with this Guide. I'll also help you reach out to others—

family and friends—who can support you throughout your journey. And I'll teach you to recognize some of the false guides, who may promise much but are even more lost than you are.

Finally I'll show you step by step how to use guided imagery to steady your mind and balance your biology, and teach you a time-honored, powerful technique for learning from your own Inner Guide—the intuition, understanding, and wisdom that will grow stronger with every step you take.

MEETING MY GUIDE

About a month after I awoke immobilized and overwhelmed in my New York apartment, at the age of twenty-three, I called Robert Coles, who was then a young psychiatrist at the Harvard University Health Services. I'd visited with him a few weeks before, when I was beginning to wrestle with my depression. The first time I contacted him, I'd hoped that the gravity of meaningful work would pull me across the opening pit of my unhappiness and help me find meaning and purpose in my own life. I had wanted to go with Dr. Coles to New Orleans, where he was helping black kids and their parents integrate the public schools. It turned out that he was back in Cambridge for the foreseeable future, writing. So there was a welcome, good conversation, and even inspiration, but no work.

Now, in the depths of depression, I was calling just about me. I felt downright pathetic next to the courageous kids he was working with, but I was hurting and felt that he could help me, too.

I told him of my desolation over my girlfriend and my anguish about medical school—how I felt misplaced there, and aggravated by it, and sad that it didn't suit me or I it. He sounded both pained and amused. He'd been there. Breakups were excruciating and the first years of medical school had been a struggle for him, too. Like me, he had cut labs to go to the movies.

Dr. Coles laughed at the image of his own sad, bewildered medical school self, wandering New York, hanging out in jazz clubs. In the middle of my considerable emotional and physical pain and self-pity, I felt our kinship and even began to laugh at myself. I sat on my radiator looking out onto a Lower East Side airshaft, holding the phone as if it were a lifeline. We spoke for two hours. A week later I resigned my pathology fellowship, moved into a furnished room in Cambridge, and began my sessions of psychotherapy with Bob Coles.

There is a saying in the East that when the student is ready, the teacher arrives. Actually, it's more of a principle than a saying, an affirmation of a particularly rich and crucial kind of synchronicity—the connection that psychiatrist Carl Jung described between people and events that arises from their intrinsic affinity, a connection that operates outside the laws of cause and effect.

In the years since then, I've observed two elements that must be part of the student's "readiness." First, there has to be a real need for the connection. It may be deeply felt and long yearned for, or barely conscious, but it's got to be there. Second, there has to be a kind of openness, a capacity to recognize and respond to the teacher—the Guide—who presents herself. You're thinking of options and just then a friend calls about a "wonderful therapist." And then, of course, you need to attend to the conversation.

There's a famous and apropos story that is told about faith, but it is also very much about readiness. A man in the midst of a flood is clinging to the top of his floating house. The man prays to God for help. Shortly afterward, a raft appears. The pilot asks the man if he wants to climb aboard. "No," he says, "God will take care of me." The man's home sinks a little more. Then comes a boat, which he also turns away. And finally, just as his house is going under, a helicopter appears. Once again the man refuses the lifesaving ride.

Drowned and in heaven, the man proudly tells God that he faithfully awaited his rescue. God greets him with a thundering rebuke: "Idiot, who do you think sent the raft, the boat, and the helicopter?"

Bob Coles and other teachers, other Guides, have arrived on rafts and boats and planes—and I've usually had the good sense to climb aboard.

Each of these men and women has taught me much I needed to know—about my self-defeating patterns and my troubled relationships, about kindness, and the possible shape of my future life. They widened my limited perspective, opened my heart to others, and helped me celebrate my relationship to the natural and spiritual world. They've cared for, even loved, me as I've struggled to do, see, and feel. They've helped me to discover who I really am.

It is this kind of connection, this kind of guidance, for which all of you should hope and be prepared. If you are, and are willing to search, the Guides you need will appear.

Bob Coles offered an example as well. He was a doctor, a psychiatrist who was passionate about and fulfilled by his work. He was helping to make the world a better place. Though I felt miserable, alienated, and ineffectual, perhaps I could, like him, find meaning in helping others, and in writing about it.

Bob had one more crucial characteristic of the good Guide, one that you should look for, too. My confidence in him was matched by his confidence in me. From that first weepy phone conversation, I had the unshakable sense, without his ever saying it explicitly, that he believed in me, that he knew that somehow I could and would find my way.

HEARING FROM APRIL

When April called ten years ago, her voice was young and thin but determined. She'd just read a book of mine, *Manifesto for a New Medicine,* and an article in *Health* magazine on my work with depressed people. Like the people in the article—a woman who had loaded a gun and prepared for suicide, another who walked zombielike through her days— she'd felt wooden and depressed for years and despaired about the future. She'd been in and out of therapy and on and off antidepressants for a decade.

April had asked her present therapist to get in touch with me—I remembered the message sitting in a pile—and now she was calling. She knew my voice mail announced that I wasn't taking new patients, except "by special arrangement," and she hoped and believed that I would want to make such a special arrangement to see her. She reminded me of myself calling Bob Coles thirty years before.

April wanted to get off the antidepressant drugs and on with her life. "When I read your book," she said, "I knew you were right. We have so much in us to help us heal. We just have to access it. It's much more *appealing*"—she emphasized the irony of this word—"than taking Zoloft." Finding her own strength and truth also seemed wiser and safer.

The Zoloft, which had fewer side effects than the Paxil and Prozac she'd taken in previous years, seemed to keep her from falling into the deepest circles of her depression, but it also paralyzed her emotionally and constrained her mentally. Not that she couldn't think—she was working in a responsible, well-paid job as a statistician for a congressional committee. It was more that she didn't care much what she was thinking about, or even enjoy the intellectual activity. She felt uninteresting, half dead, stuck.

April's therapist had helped her get a handle on how a cold, distant father and a demanding, deprecating mother had contributed to her uncertainty, pessimism, and fear. But after years of therapy, and at age twenty-eight, she still felt "like a kid"—unable to figure out what she wanted to do with her life, dependent on drugs that she hated, condemned to a job that bored her, and a succession of ardent boyfriends who weren't much more stimulating. April told me that the Zoloft reduced her sex drive, "almost to zero." Orgasms were rare and "feeble." The antidepressant also made her palms sweaty, her bowels loose, and kept her yawning and sleepy.

April was anxious, tired, unhappy with herself, and confused by her life. She'd heard the Call and was ready to make a change and, though she wasn't at all sure what it was, she was convinced that I was the one who could help.

FINDING YOUR GOOD GUIDE

There are certain qualities that you should look for in the therapist or pastoral counselor or physician—the professional—whom you regard as your primary Guide. I'm using a capital G to differentiate him or her from all the other physicians, teachers, clerics, friends, and authors who appear along the way, because this Guide, with the capital G, is the experienced and trained person who'll be there for you on a regular, dependable basis, for as long as needed.

Credentials are helpful in determining who's likely to be a good Guide. Having an advanced degree in one of the mental health professions—psychology, psychiatry, social work, pastoral counseling, psychiatric nursing, marriage and family counseling, etc.—guarantees a baseline of professional education, awareness of emotional and mental issues, and extended supervised experience in treating and counseling other human beings. These people may all be called therapists, from the Greek root *therap-,* or "healing." But this baseline is no guarantee of a good fit between the patient or client (as nonmedical therapists call the people they work with) and the therapist.

What follows are some guidelines for finding and choosing the Guide who is appropriate for you—for discriminating between those with whom you can "make do," and those who will be powerfully and enduringly helpful. At the end of this chapter, in the Prescription for Self-Care, there's a detailed plan for determining the characteristics of the Guide for whom you're searching and for making the choice.

Begin at the beginning. What kind of person are you looking for? Sex, age, profession, and professional and personal points of view are places to start. I wanted a psychiatrist when I was in medical school and thinking about my future probably because I was looking for a role model as well as relief. But nonmedical therapists can be equally good Guides. (I'll go over the training and qualifications required for various professions in the Resources section at the end of the book.) In later years, in times of uncertainty, I've happily found a Jungian psychologist, an ob-gyn who taught me hypnosis, a wise old anthropologist, and a variety of spiritual teachers to help guide me. I wasn't thinking about age or sex when I first saw Bob Coles. He was just the right person at the right time.

Theoretical perspectives are important. Are you looking for a psychoanalyst who mines the past for the origins of repressed and suppressed conflict? A cognitive behavioral therapist who will give you exercises to help you reframe and reform your ways of thinking? A body-oriented therapist who will use breathing techniques and touch to help loosen the physical knots that old trauma may have tied? A Jungian who will explore dreams and your connection to larger patterns of spiritual growth? All can be helpful, but the fit must feel right to you. You can combine what you're learning and experiencing in this book with working with a variety of Guides who have different, but potentially compatible, theoretical perspectives.

If you're pretty sure you want a Guide who has experienced and can lead you on the journey I'm describing in this book, then write that down, too. This would be a clinician who appreciates all aspects of life—spiritual as well as mental and social, biological and emotional, the body as well as the mind—a therapist who will help you to understand and help yourself, a clinician whose work is grounded in the moment-to-moment awareness of meditation, someone who questions adjustment and encourages the possibility of your transformation.

This may sound like a tall order, but fortunately there are such people.

LOOKING FOR A GUIDE: FIRST STEPS

You can begin your search by asking a physician, nurse, or clergyperson whom you trust about therapists he knows. Tell him the kind of person you're looking for. When he gives you a name, ask why he thought that person would be good for you.

You can ask your friends who has been helpful to them. They may have a good hunch about whether the fit between you and their therapist will be a good one. Get them to tell you what the therapist is like and, especially, why they think he or she might be helpful to you.

You can also look at the Web site of The Center for Mind-Body Medicine (www.cmbm.org), which I founded in 1991 and still direct. In all, 2,500 clinicians in the United States and abroad have come through the initial phase of our training in mind-body medicine. Twelve hundred (600 in North America) have completed advanced training in using our work, with individuals and groups, and we've certified almost one hundred. We value those we've certified as colleagues and friends, stand behind them, and will put you in touch with them. Though their levels of competence in working with people who are depressed vary considerably, and we cannot vouch for their ability, those who have completed the advanced training will be familiar with, and sometimes deeply experienced in, the kind of approach I'm describing. And even if they're not appropriate as Guides for you, many of these professionals will be able to help you find someone who is.

Finally, there are Web sites in the Resources section that list therapists by profession and philosophical orientation, as well as location. If you use these sites, you may have to work a little harder to find someone whose perspective fits yours, but you'll be able to do it.

Talking to Professional Guides

Find out whatever you can about your potential Guide before you interview him. Many therapists have written about their work or have a Web site where they describe it. Many more are beginning to provide prospective patients and clients with a description of their practice and their philosophy (I think all of us should). The more you know, the more informed a decision you'll be able to make.

If the person you've been referred to sounds good, call or write. Explain your situation, and ask to talk with him on the phone or in person. Understand that this is a perfectly reasonable request and expect, and offer, to pay for the session. The kind of reception you get on the phone or from a letter or e-mail will give you more clues about whom you're deal-ing with and how you'll be received.

There may also be someone who comes to your mind who seems to be exactly whom you're looking for, someone you've read or heard about, a therapist who helped a friend, or somebody whose article or book you've read. Get in touch with him or her and proceed as above. It worked for me and for April, and for many other people who've called me. Don't worry about imposing—it really is the job of those of us in the "helping professions" to talk to people looking for help, and we should all be per-fectly capable of saying, "No, I can't see you," if we can't. And don't be put off just because somebody is well known. If she seems right, call. And even if she can't see you, she may be able to suggest someone else with a similar perspective who lives near you and can.

If you're looking for someone who sees depression—or your other emotional issues—as primarily a school for wisdom and an opportunity for growth, a journey and not a disease, then raise the issue right away. It's vital that you and your therapist have a shared view of your situation. It's incredibly painful and, yes, depressing if you're looking for one thing and she's offering quite another. At the end of this chapter, I'll share with you a Prescription for Self-Care to help you make your choice.

If your potential therapist tells you, as many I've heard about do, that you have to be on drugs in order to work with him, get one or more other opinions. It may be true in his mind, but it's not necessarily true for you.

As you move ahead in this process, always trust and value *your* sense of who's right for you. All the credentials in the world, the fabulous reputa-tion of this or that psychiatrist or psychotherapist, is worth nothing if you feel in your heart and your gut that he or she is not the right person.

You can use the Inner Guide imagery that I'll teach you later in this chapter to ask yourself if the person you're considering is right for you. I know that when you're depressed and desperate for help, it's hard to be discriminating. Still, you need to listen, as best you can, to the voice of your own intuition.

Welcoming, Generous, Courageous

When you talk to a prospective Guide, in person or on the phone, make sure you feel welcomed, accepted, and understood. This kind of generosity of spirit is what drew me to Bob Coles, and it is the most consistent characteristic of all those people who've guided me in my life. The detached, medically minded clinician, or the therapist who obscures his personality with the "blank screen" that some psychoanalysts and other therapists adopt, may be all right for some people. But there's no reason why you have to work with such a person if that doesn't work for you. I don't find that people like this encourage my trust, so I do my best to stay away from them. Incidentally, Freud, the father of modern psychotherapy as well as psychoanalysis, was no blank screen. A number of his patients knew him, often as friends and colleagues, outside of, as well as in, the office.

If a prospective therapist doesn't offer and promote a sense of safety, and doesn't welcome, encourage, or at least accept, emotional connection, then I'd stay clear of her.

If someone seems and feels right, give him a try. Ask to see him regularly: I generally see people once a week in the beginning, occasionally, if they are in crisis, more often. You may or may not make a great deal of headway in solving your problems in the first few sessions, but you should have a sense that you are understood and that you and your Guide are engaged with each other, and with the issues that concern you. You should, most often, look forward to the sessions, to being with your Guide, and to her support and understanding. On the whole, you should feel better after a session, even if you've looked squarely at some of your most unpleasant and shame-producing faults and flaws. If your Guide doesn't meet these criteria, I suggest that you continue your search.

I believe that Guides, regardless of their profession or level of training, should be courageous. You want your Guide to shepherd you calmly and safely through all the stages of your journey—the troubled territory of past hurt and present fears, resentments, and impulses. You want and deserve someone who will help you to relax with the uncertainty of the future. Guides need to know in their bones that it's possible to make the journey and that, with their help, you can, too.

I suggest you ask your prospective Guide about his or her own personal experience, the sources of his knowledge and wisdom. What qualifies him—in addition to professional training and clinical expertise—to understand you and help you to understand and be yourself? The answers are important, and so, too, is the way the answers are offered. Is he defensive or forthcoming? Does he feel genuine, open, and accessible or remote and blanketed in professionalism?

The doctor or therapist who rushes to the prescription pad at the mention of depression, or even despair and suicide, may be acting out of his own fears rather than in your best interest. There is no reason to take unnecessary risks on the journey—and there may be times when emergency measures, including drugs, are necessary—but it's no service to you for your therapist to push you to reject or run from the challenges that are an inevitable part of your healing journey.

Your Guide must respect and welcome all aspects of who you are. One of the sadder moments in my work with Theresa came in her first visit, when she began to tear up and then quickly apologized for "crying in your office." I was sad, not because of her tears, which were a release for her, but because Theresa's experience with doctors had led her to believe that it was inappropriate to cry in their offices. If not in our offices, where? You should feel welcome to say whatever's on your mind, and to express your fears and feelings, even if they seem horribly embarrassing to you.

CHOOSING A GUIDE YOU CAN AFFORD

What do you do, you ask, if you don't have enough money for therapy, or health insurance that covers psychotherapy? What if all that's offered by your health plan or your local hospital is a few minutes of medical assessment and a prescription for drugs—pills to decrease anxiety or prop up mood? Where and how do you find a Guide then?

This is a depressing and infuriating situation that's all too common in America. As far as I'm concerned, all of us should have access, as a matter of right, to health care, including care for our emotional and mental health and well-being.

Still, even while we're working to achieve good health care for all of us, we can find affordable Guides.

Most therapists, and particularly those who are committed to the kind of perspective that I've been describing, see a few patients for significantly reduced fees (at The Center for Mind-Body Medicine, we ask all those we train to do this). They are also likely to know of colleagues who do the same, and of low-cost clinics whose primary commitment is to service rather than profit.

In addition, many hospitals and clinics, as well as graduate schools, have trainees—psychiatric residents; psychology interns; students of social work, nursing, and pastoral counseling—who provide low-cost or free services. They can be found in virtually every city and university town, and often elsewhere as well.

Of course, the trainees have less experience than staff doctors or fully licensed private practitioners. But they are often idealistic and deeply committed to the welfare of the patients and clients who will teach them, as well as be helped by them. They are eager to appreciate and participate in the richness and complexity of a therapeutic partnership. In general they have good, regular supervision by an experienced clinician, to help them understand your situation and to back them up when they may feel uncertain or overwhelmed.

HEALING EARLY LOSS AND PAIN

I put a great deal of emphasis on the Guide and your connection with her because the relationship itself can be profoundly healing, not only of this episode of depression, but of many of the insecurities and misconceptions, the loneliness, hurt, and loss, that may have plagued you throughout your life and contributed to your depression. Let me explain.

One of the abiding truths about depression is that it's very often triggered by loss. The ancient Greeks knew how important loss was. We read it in their epics and hymns—Odysseus, weeping on his rock for home; Demeter devastated by her daughter's absence. Other cultures, from the indigenous ones of Africa and the Americas to the high civilizations of China and India, have also emphasized the connection between loss and depression. Robert Burton in his encyclopedic sixteenth-century treatise *The Anatomy of Melancholy* devotes more than a third of his text to discussion of the depression that may follow the loss of love.

The loss is usually loss of a person—a parent, child, spouse, lover, or close friend. But the loss of the respect of others, or of intimacy with a partner, or of our job or social role or our status can sometimes be as devastating. Monkeys who lose their status in their group develop a syndrome of social withdrawal, decreased activity and food intake, and have higher levels of the stress hormone cortisol and lower levels of serotonin, just like many depressed humans. Psychiatrist Heinz Kohut, who shaped "self psychology," added shading and subtlety to the concept of loss: We become depressed, he suggested, when we lose our sense of self, the sense of ourselves as integrated beings in the world.

In modern times, Freud pointed physicians and psychologists back to the shaping force of early life events, particularly parental loss and neglect, and to the disorders of emotion and thinking they might later produce. In his 1917 "Mourning and Melancholia," Freud suggested that children's early losses—particularly of a parent—would make them more vulnerable to depression as adults.

In the 1930s and 1940s, Rene Spitz, a physician who had been analyzed by Freud, made direct observations on the effects of the physically adequate but emotionally barren care of institutionalized orphans. These children looked and acted depressed. A number of them developed a wasting physical condition that Spitz called "hospitalism." Some died of it.

Observations on monkeys by primatologist Harry Harlow, and on humans by psychiatrist John Bowlby, confirmed the importance of a secure and reliable bond between human—or primate—infants and their mothers, and the later damage, the depression, caused by its absence. Bowlby and his colleague Mary Ainsworth also observed that children who later received the comfort and closeness that was missing in the earlier part of their lives—from caretakers who offered a "safe haven"— could decrease their levels of stress and develop in a healthier, more interactive way.

Erik Erikson, a child psychoanalyst who had been analyzed by Freud's daughter Anna, described the fundamental importance to later development of a "basic trust" that was established in the child by the presence of a reliable and loving mother. D. W. Winnicott, a British pediatrician and psychoanalyst, emphasized the critical importance of what he called the "good enough mother." The good enough mother offered her child a "facilitating and holding environment"; she was at once supportive and respectful of the child's growing independence, sensitive to his unique needs, and reliable. Heinz Kohut described the importance of maternal "mirroring": the mother giving back to the child, through her glance, touch, and words, a fully formed appreciation of his needs, desires, and concerns, his happiness and distress.

Loss and other traumatic early-life events, we now know, may precipitate intense and prolonged stress reactions, including persistent high levels of cortisol, and produce alterations in the structure and the functioning of the child's brain, damaging and destroying nerve cells in the hippocampus, an area of the brain intimately connected with both memory and emotion. It appears that these changes in function and structure can persist, with distressing consequences, making us more vulnerable to depression in adulthood.

Research on depression, attachment, and loss, on painful separation and its physical and emotional consequences, shows us the origins of much depression in early and later loss. It also helps us to understand how the presence and care of others and, most important in this context, of good Guides may help reverse the damage that depression and loss have done, and heal us when we are depressed.

FINDING A SAFE HAVEN

A number of us who become depressed have suffered painful early loss of love or disruption in a relationship with our parents. But even those of us who have experienced adequate mothering often have, in our time of depression, a need and a vulnerability that resembles that of the uncared-for child. The good Guide attends to that vulnerability and meets, at least in a symbolic way, the same kinds of basic needs as a good mother.

The office in which your Guide meets you should feel like a safe and sacred place, a sanctuary where fears can be faced and caring and comfort are available. You may be terrified of losing yet another source of support, and he is reliably present. You're busy toting up your shortcomings and ignoring your good points. He appreciates your virtues and calmly accepts your weaknesses. You're bogged down and deadly serious, and he has perspective on you, perhaps even a bit of gentle humor with you. You're in despair and he still has faith in you.

The good Guide, the good therapist, gives you back, in his word and glance, an image of yourself that is at once softer and more lovable, stronger and more resilient, than you can now imagine. This is Winnicott's holding environment, Kohut's mirroring, Bowlby's safe haven. The good Guide has about him a quality of steadfast reassurance that is similar to the good mother's, a quiet confidence that all will be well, that in some very real sense, no matter how much distress you're now feeling, all *is* well.

The good mother soothes and reassures the anxious child, gives him the sense of calm that physical closeness and love bring, restores to him a sense of the reliability of his baby world, and makes it possible for him to experience Erikson's basic trust. Similarly, the loving attention of the good Guide helps restore to you the sense, when you're most despondent about, or hateful of, yourself, that you are worthwhile and lovable. He provides, by his continued presence, continuity, a lifeline to which you can, in precarious moments, hold fast.

If you have difficulty thinking well of or trusting others, or yourself, the good Guide offers a new, and potentially reparative, experience. Perhaps you have defended yourself against closeness, for fear of being hurt or rejected yet again, or have been fearful of trusting your own feelings and instincts, because you believe you will be condemned for them. Even as you bemoan your inability to trust or be close, the good Guide will give you an experience of trust and closeness and the opportunity to challenge and test it. And, because you are desperate, and desperately vulnerable, because your image of yourself is shattered, you are, perhaps for the first time, also capable of looking into the new mirror she holds up to you, of seeing yourself in the generous way she sees you.

These good, generous Guides are present and active in the journeys of our culture's great heroes. Reading *The Odyssey,* we sense Athena, the goddess of wisdom, everywhere. Sometimes she's out of sight or disguised, but she's always on Odysseus's side; present when he needs her most. Virgil, the Roman poet whose epic inspired Dante's own, is with Dante as he descends into the Inferno, introducing him to those who suffer there, reminding him of history he's forgotten, explaining what he can't understand, never doubting, even when Dante does, that he can make this journey and grow wiser from it. On the tenth day of her journey, Demeter meets Hekate, the torch-bearing goddess of the moon and intuition. It's Hekate who will lead her to the truth of her daughter's disappearance, and it's Hekate's intuition that will help guide Demeter in redeeming her loss.

Fifty years ago, the influential American psychologist Carl Rogers, a contemporary of Erikson's and Winnicott's, summed up the ideal relationship between therapist and client, Guide and traveler, in a phrase that has since resonated with so many clinicians, clients, and patients: "unconditional positive regard." *To regard* means not only "to respect," but also "to look at." The phrase is at once intimate and biological, philosophical and interpersonal.

This unconditional positive regard is what I hope to offer to those who come to see me. It's what I believe every one of you should look for and expect from your Guide. (In the Resources section, I list a couple of good books on psychotherapy and on what you can expect from it.) This kind of connection may repair psychological damage produced by loss and other forms of early and later trauma. It can be central to your emotional well-being. It may well catalyze physical changes, including beneficial changes in brain function.

The research on the positive psychological effects of a variety of kinds of therapy and counseling, including cognitive behavioral therapy, interpersonal psychotherapy, and even counseling by nontherapist physicians, points to a common factor that transcends theoretical and operational differences: the critical role of our relationship with our Guide.

There are also studies that use physiological measures and sophisticated brain scans to show the positive physical and chemical effects of a variety of kinds of therapy: balancing autonomic nervous system functioning and reducing stress, stimulating parts of the brain associated with well-being that have been underactive in depression, and quieting those that have been agitated. Recent research on neuroplasticity also suggests that this kind of guidance may even be able to help repair structural damage to the hippocampus that has been produced by loss and trauma, and stimulate the growth of new cells, new brain tissue.

Our Guide stands in for the parents whose absence or loss or hurtfulness may have made us vulnerable to later depression. In her office or consulting room—in the embrace of her kind, careful attention and sustaining presence—we recover the safe haven from which we feel we've been cast out. In her presence, with her help, we enter a place of mental, emotional, spiritual, and physical healing. I'll speak often about Guides and how they can help as we continue our journey together.

WHEN YOU DOUBT YOUR GUIDE

Work with your Guide can proceed in a nourishing, supportive way throughout your journey as you move through the stages of depression and deal with all their challenges. Still, at a certain point, you and your Guide will both understand that the time of your frequent and regular meetings is coming to an end. This "termination," as it is rather ominously called in psychotherapeutic circles, needn't be abrupt or, indeed, as threatening as it may sound. Ideally, it will feel right and natural to part— perhaps when you've come to the end of your journey through depression and learned the wisdom and skills your Guide has to offer. Nor does your parting have to be final. Many Guides will offer to be available down the road, in case of emergencies or if periodically you "just want to check in."

There may, of course, be times, particularly when things are really difficult, when you feel mistrust of your Guide, or believe he may have overestimated your capacity to deal with stress or distress. Any of us may have occasion to doubt our Guide and may need, as well, to see if he is really there when we need him most. This is a normal, if uncertain and painful, part of the journey, but also one to be learned from.

At a certain point, with some Guides, you may have the persistent feeling that the relationship isn't what you want, or that what you're being offered is inadequate, beside the point, or just not right for you—or that your Guide is as lost as you are. That's when you need to talk honestly about your concerns. If you don't, the relationship will likely deteriorate: You may begin to feel distant from, and mistrustful of, the Guide who once seemed supportive and trustworthy. If you do discuss your concerns, you may be able to come to a better understanding with your Guide and move ahead. Indeed, you may well help him to clarify problems he didn't perceive or couldn't deal with: Guides don't, and can't, see everything, and obstacles overcome together can be great teachers for your Guide as well as yourself, and create an even stronger bond between you.

On occasion there are signs that it may be necessary for you to end your relationship with your Guide: if, after many months of committed exploration, you still feel stuck; or if you're doing your honest best and you keep being told you're "resisting"; or if the answer to all your doubts and concerns is more of the same approach that's no longer working; or if you feel your Guide is unjustly impatient (though sometimes all of us *do* need confrontation or loving toughness) or inattentive or bored.

It's not easy to leave a Guide who believes you should stay, but it may be very important for you. I've seen many people who felt sincerely helped by a therapist (or, for that matter, a spiritual teacher) for a while and then felt stymied, but stayed and stayed, loyal, unchanging, more discouraged, more depressed, with each successive session. They've become as stuck in this relationship and its ideology as they had been in the ideas, concepts, and relationships that may have originally precipitated their depression.

If this point comes, then leaving the person who's been your Guide—even without his blessing—is the next step on your journey. Leaving doesn't invalidate where you've been together, or what you may have learned, or how you've already changed. And you need to remember that there are others, many others, who can be there to serve as Guides on the next leg of your journey.

MEETING FELLOW TRAVELERS

The power of the good professional Guide, the therapist—our versions of Athena, Virgil, and Hekate—and his unconditional positive regard, can be truly awesome and filled with healing. So, too, can the help that others offer us.

I've already outlined some ground rules for choosing professional Guides and assessing the rightness of the fit between ourselves and them, along with some general qualities that I believe are essential to good Guides. By contrast, the teachings and the assistance that others bring us, and the kinds of people they are, vary wildly, and are far harder to predict. I can't tell you who else will be helpful on your journey. I can tell you that they are everywhere. And I can give you some hints about how to recognize and make the best use of them when they appear.

At the beginning of the journey through depression, you are likely to be in a state of heightened questioning, dismay, inhibition, neediness, and disarray. At this time you are, or can be, more open to new kinds of connections—new people—than when your life seemed to run more smoothly. Though you may continue to live in the same geographical place, both you and the world around you seem different: The pieces of your life no longer fit in the same way; even the ones that are apparently constant may look and feel different. The same is true of the people you know and of your feelings for them. You may be drawn to family members whom you haven't noticed for years and find yourself fleeing from others whom you had always assumed were close. Some old friendships may deepen, others may dry up. I suggest you accept, at least for the time being, the incompatibilities and trust the attractions.

Dorothy Remembers Aunt Grace

Though Dorothy was counted a close friend by dozens of thoughtful and even genuinely compassionate people, she didn't talk to them about her depression or her growing realization that she would have to leave the senator. She feared gossip would find its way into the press, and that everyone she knew would think she was crazy to leave such a distinguished and important man, "especially at my age." In the early months of our meetings, she felt unable to talk to Todd and deeply feared her sons' reaction to her concerns.

One afternoon, I said I thought she needed someone, besides me, with whom to share her feelings and struggles, a friend or family member to give her a more objective perspective on her marriage, as well as some support. She looked at me blankly. There was no one. "Sit for a minute," I said. "Close your eyes, do Soft Belly, and see if someone comes to mind."

When Dorothy opened her eyes there were tears in them. Later in the day, she called the old woman who appeared in her mental image. Aunt Grace listened for a few minutes and let out the closest thing to a war whoop Dorothy had ever heard. "Child," Aunt Grace fairly shouted, "that man's been death on you from the beginning."

From that phone call on, Dorothy and Aunt Grace were in constant contact. Though she'd hardly spoken to her for years, Dorothy discovered she trusted this woman as she did no one else in her busy, all-too-public life. Too old to be impressed by anybody and too ornery to be intimidated by conventional wisdom, Grace was remarkably clear-sighted about her niece and, it turned out, very gratified to be useful and close to her.

This kind of symmetry between the one looking for help and the one offering it is a natural wonder that I've often experienced in my own life and observed in others'. Dorothy found it with Grace, and Theresa, you may remember, experienced it with her friend Barbara. It's really a matter of opening yourself up to the possibility, and of not running away when your friend or family member presents herself, in person, or in your mind's eye. Sometimes the person will be there for you always; sometimes, she will disappear from your life, as if she had only reentered it for this singular kind of communion.

Happy, Hopeful Meetings

There are also people who first enter our lives when we're distraught and depressed, lost and seeking. Sometimes they come and go quickly but are strikingly restorative, like the checkout guy in the supermarket, or the waitress who, just when you had given up on the human race, smiled at you. I've had this kind of experience, and so has almost everyone I know.

Often, new people will appear, as if summoned by the changes that are beginning to take place in you. A few months after coming to see me, April found herself drifting away from many of her old friends. Looking around, she discovered women whom she'd never noticed. Before, they would have been utterly unlikely companions—too serious, too old, too unconventional. They now seemed, in their own struggles and search, altogether congenial and deeply reassuring. The men who approached her changed as well. Before, there had been older guys, often elected officials and lobbyists, generally married, waving plane tickets to Paris or Hawaii. Now there were idealistic congressional aides, artists, and writers. None of them was the soul mate she hoped she might someday find, but they called out a different, less fearful and cynical side of her.

As a general rule, I suggest you assume that everyone who appears in your life may have something to offer you, that they are, in fact, your teachers. This perspective, which I feel is valuable under any circumstances, is particularly helpful when you're depressed. Depression can be understood as a devaluation of yourself, of your experience, and of life itself. If you're willing, at least as an experiment, to regard those who appear in your life as potential instructors, you're automatically reinvesting in and valuing other people, and with them, the world. Human beings are no longer simply reminders of your inadequacy or alienation or unhappiness; they are your teachers. Each encounter becomes a lesson. Even at your most gloomy, you're a student. It may seem strange at first, even naive. Still, I think you'll find that if you adopt this point of view, many of these people will provide support and guidance and help you move through your depression.

Beware of False Guides

This isn't to say that there may not be people who may hold you back, drag you down, or otherwise sidetrack you or get in your way. You can learn from your encounters with them as well, but it's good to learn as quickly as possible. Here are a few types to be on the lookout for.

THE ANSWER MEN >> These are people who are sure they know the way, and I mean *really* know the way. They may be old friends or they may have met you only minutes before, but they've got the answers, not only for themselves but for you as well.

They can be very good at sensing your vulnerability and confusion, and at offering to meet your needs for companionship and certainty. But they often profess to far more concern than they could possibly feel, as well as far more conceptual and emotional competence than they're likely to have. Be wary of the easy answers they offer, particularly if you feel them playing on your fears or into your own prejudices.

Sometimes these people emerge on the periphery of your life, perhaps on the street or in a coffee shop. Sometimes they are planted squarely in your path, old friends who want to help, professionals sitting in elegant offices and using the language of this or that psychotherapeutic or medical approach. They often speak with unearned and unexamined authority, and tend to be offended by probing questions or doubt.

It's not that there may not be truth in their words or the teachings from which they quote or the practices they engage in. It's just that they're more preoccupied with confirming their own beliefs and validating their own experience, more interested in finding new recruits than helping you on your way.

THE SOB SISTER OR BALEFUL BROTHER >> These people have an endless capacity for commiseration. When you're lonely and need some-one to talk to, or reassurance that you're not the only one who's ever felt this way, they can be enormously attractive and, for a while, helpful. The barroom buddy whom you've experienced or seen in movies is a good example. One guy is sitting next to another, a couple of shot glasses and beer chasers in front of them. The first guy is complaining about his wife; the other is telling him about all the terrible things *his* wife has done, and how women can't be trusted, etc., etc.

A little of this goes a very long way. If you're paying attention, what you find is that this kind of conversation quickly becomes repetitive and depressing. A relationship that brought comfort soon turns out to be based only on mutually shared misery. If you start to feel better, you may be accused of betraying the agreement to suffer together. The premise is that endless comfort is needed, that unhappiness and victimization are not only a reality, but the only one, that, in fact, nothing will ever change. As soon as you feel this atmosphere closing in, move on.

THE WORRYWART >> There are some people in whom your situation arouses uncontrollable anxiety and provokes anxious meddling. You can recognize them because they're the ones who ask, too many times, and with crippling solicitude, "How *are* you?" even when, perhaps for the first time in weeks, you're feeling better. They're the folks whom Dorothy was fighting to steer clear of. They're the people who keep "wondering" if you don't really "need" to be back in the marriage or job you knew you had to leave; or, alternately, out of the relationship you feel you can improve; or on the drugs or therapeutic regimen you've resisted, or tried and found wanting.

This is the type I hear about all the time—because they raise all the doubts that are already in everyone's mind, and because there are so many of them. It's possible that some, or many, of these people mean well, but their voices are suffused with fear. You need to acknowledge but not obey this fear; it is the enemy of growth and change and of every step on the journey. Thank these folks for sharing—and move on.

Guides in Print

I'm always on the lookout for books that can serve as guides. In the bibliography in the Resources section, I'll give you a number of titles that my patients and I—as well as my colleagues, students, and friends—have found most helpful in amplifying the approach I'm teaching you in *Unstuck*. Here I want to give you just a few hints about finding books that are right for *you*.

First of all, there is no one right book for everyone. We're all different—temperamentally as well as biochemically. Some people prefer books that are practical: detailed descriptions of cognitive behavioral procedures, manuals that diagram yoga postures or acupressure points that relieve stress and improve mood. Others want theory-rich descriptions of depression's possible causes. Some people find support in reading the diaries and memoirs of ordinary people, or literary figures, or famous people who struggled with depression, or in novels describing journeys through depression. Others crave a larger spiritual perspective on the dilemma they're now facing, and find it in religious scriptures or commentaries on them. All can be supportive, reassuring, and helpful, emphasizing in ways that are right for you what I'm teaching in *Unstuck*.

Second, a book that is right at one time may be irrelevant at another. You may want detailed practical instruction for a day or a week or a month, then crave an inspiring story for broader understanding. A book to which you are indifferent at one point may, at another point, some years later, feel utterly compelling. One of my patients told me that as a graduate student he'd read *Memories, Dreams, Reflections,* Carl Jung's account of his own midlife crisis and depression, and thought it only "mildly interesting." Twenty years later, it was a light in the darkness of his own midlife crisis.

Last, sometimes you choose the book and, at least as often, it just appears; it chooses you. Someone you respect may suggest a book. Since you're already reading my book, I feel comfortable doing this in the Resources section. Still, what I suggest—the title and the words I use to describe the book—has to resonate with what you're looking for. Sometimes you'll be attracted by a prominent person's quote on a book's jacket, or even the feel of the book in your hand in the bookstore. I suggest you trust these nudges, read a few pages, and see if it's right for you.

OPENING OUR EYES

A Guide, a therapist, should help us see farther and better than we can unaided. In fact, "What am I not seeing?" is a wonderful question to ask early and often in therapy, of your Guide and of yourself. A skillful Guide, a good therapist, should also cast new light on what you do see, and help you create situations that will enhance and sharpen your vision.

For me, a Guide's humor can be powerfully clarifying and catalyzing. Not long after I began seeing Bob Coles, I told him that my problems were so small compared with those of the children whose pictures Bob had on his desk, the ones who were braving storms of threats to integrate southern schools. My words were accented with the self-loathing and self-pity that then colored my days. "Oh, you have your problems, too," he noted dryly.

These words stay with me forty years later. They summed up my situation and gently, kindly, turned me toward a new perspective on myself. "Stop comparing," Bob was saying. "Accept who you are."

A good Guide should create ways for you to enhance your own ability to know and be yourself. He can use and assign experiences, challenges, exercises that you can do on your own time—in other words, homework. One of the pitfalls of work with a Guide, of any therapy, is that we become dependent on him and it. Real change, real work, we may come to believe, happens only when we're in her presence. The customary, even clichéd, "We'll talk about that next week" encourages dependency. "Why don't you take time this week to look at that?" implies confidence in your ability to do things on your own.

Specific homework assignments give far greater value and therapeutic weight to life outside the four walls of therapy, and they give you concrete ways to help yourself when the therapist, the Guide, is not around. They help you be self-reliant. And, interestingly enough, homework actually enhances your connection to your Guide and his value in your life: As you do your own work, you also feel the presence of the one who's assigned it.

Incidentally, I believe that cognitive behavioral therapy, which has been demonstrated to be so useful in depression, is effective partly because it addresses self-defeating patterns of thinking and perception, partly because of the relationship between the therapist and client, and partly because it is grounded in homework—therapist-assigned exercises of thinking and planning and activity—that the patient or client has to do on his own.

The approach and methods I'm sharing with you in *Unstuck,* which are based on my own work as a therapist and teacher, rely for their effectiveness on your willingness to participate actively, to make an effort on your own behalf. There are indeed some easy miracles—nutrient supplementation for those who are depleted or the removal of foods to which some people are exquisitely sensitive: think of thyroid-deficient Diane, sugar-craving Dominique, and food-sensitive Jenny. Even in cases such as these, however, we have to participate actively, mindfully, and collaboratively in our own healing.

In fact, our ultimate goal as Guides, the aim of all good therapists, and of this book, is to help all of you whom we're treating and teaching to make use on your own of the awareness, the insight, the knowledge, and the strength you're gaining in your work with us. Ultimately, your dependence on your Guide, and on me, will diminish. We'll still be here—available in a crisis or in your memory or on the bookshelf. But more and more, we and what we've taught will be a part of you.

MENTAL IMAGERY: DISCOVERING YOUR OWN INNER GUIDE

Guided imagery is one of the most direct and potent ways to access the inner wisdom that will help us deal with depression's challenges and facilitate the shift from outer to inner guidance. I'm soon going to share with you an imagery exercise that's a powerfully clarifying part of the homework I assign and a significant source of the wisdom and insight you'll use on your journey.

I've been doing this exercise for thirty years, and teaching it for almost as long. It's similar to one that traditional healers—the shamans of Siberia, the curanderos and medicine men of South and North America, and the healers of Africa—have used for millennia. Carl Jung brought the practice into modern psychiatry and psychology. I learned it originally from the late Ruth Carter Stapleton, a Protestant minister who was President Jimmy Carter's sister. It's called Inner Guide imagery.

The Inner Guide imagery is one of the exercises I often assign in the first weeks of my work with the patients I see, one that we use early on in our groups at The Center for Mind-Body Medicine and in our training programs. It's a way of discovering and calling upon our inner wisdom and our intuition—the internal Guide that has often been sleeping, inactive within us.

Before I teach you to consult your Inner Guide—which requires a series of images—I want to say a few words about "mental" or "guided" imagery in general, and give you a couple of other, simpler exercises. They'll help you to develop your capacity for creating and using images to affect and understand your physical and emotional states, and the second of them, the Safe Place image, will, I believe, be of enduring service to you.

The Lemon Imagery: Experiencing the Mind-Body Connection

Imagery is sometimes described as "the language of the unconscious." It includes auditory, kinesthetic (feeling), gustatory (taste), and olfactory (smell) images, as well as visual ones (using visual imagery only is called visualization). When you create mental images, the areas of the brain associated with that sense light up with activity, just as if you were actually seeing, feeling, hearing, tasting, or smelling something in the outside world. Mental images that make use of several senses appear to be more compelling and more effective than those that use just one.

The centers in your brain where you form images are closely connected with the limbic system (which includes the hippocampus), which governs emotions, and the hypothalamus, which, as you may remember, controls the autonomic nervous and endocrine systems (the sources of the fight-or-flight and stress responses) as well as the immune system. This means that your emotions are likely to produce images. It also means that the images you create can easily affect both your emotions and the parts of your nervous system that control your stress response, as well as the functioning of all the glands in your body and your immune system. Practically speaking, your mental images may be able to decrease your level of anxiety, enhance your mood, affect and improve your physical functioning and change the way you experience all the events of your life.

This first experiment with imagery—Imagining a Lemon—is designed to demonstrate how mental images can directly and profoundly affect your autonomic nervous system and through it your physiological functioning. I like to begin with this one because it can give you an immediate felt sense of imagery's power.

IMAGINING A LEMON

If you're going to use imagery most effectively and most creatively, you need to be relaxed.

So sit comfortably, breathing in through the nose and out

through the mouth, allowing your belly to be soft, relaxing into the chair in which you're sitting. Feel yourself connected to the chair. Feel your back against the back of the chair, and your seat on the seat of the chair and your feet on the floor. Let the breathing deepen. Let your belly be soft. Breathe deeply. Let thoughts come and go.

Imagine now that you're in a kitchen. It could be your own kitchen, or someone else's, or one you've just imagined. Look around. What does it look like? What does it feel like to be there?

Now imagine yourself standing in front of a cutting board. On that cutting board is a nice, big, ripe Lemon. Pick up the Lemon. Feel what it feels like, the weight and texture of the skin. Look at it. Perhaps you'll want to rub it on your skin. What does it smell like? Inhale the fragrance.

Put the Lemon back down on the cutting board. Now take a sharp knife and cut the Lemon in half. Let the two halves fall apart. Look at the exposed surfaces. Perhaps there are tiny drops of juice glistening there. Notice the flesh of the Lemon, the white lining of the skin, the pits. Now, take one half of the Lemon and cut it in half. You'll have two wedges now, two quarters of the Lemon half.

Now imagine you're picking up one of those wedges. Again, smell it, feel what it feels like in your hand. Now, slowly bring it to your mouth. Put it in your mouth. Now, bite down on the Lemon, feeling your teeth breaking the flesh of the Lemon, feeling the juice go into your mouth.

Notice now what's happening in your mouth, what's happening to your face. What are you feeling in your body?

Put the Lemon back down. Breathe deeply for a few moments. Open your eyes and, if you'd like, write down your experience in your journal.

What was the smell like, and the color and the texture? How did it feel to hold the Lemon in your hand? Was it smooth or rough?

What was it like to rub it against your skin? And then, when you bit into it, what was that like? Could you taste it? Did you feel your face puckering up? Maybe you were salivating more, maybe even shivering a little. Write down whatever experiences you had.

Salivation and puckering are functions that are mediated by the autonomic nervous system. What you've done with this image is to create a situation in which you had—or may have had—many of the same responses that you would actually have in biting into a Lemon. This experience gives you a hint of the power of imagery to affect your body.

The Lemon image is only one example of the way imagery can affect the autonomic nervous system and your physical functioning. There are many others. The autonomic nervous system affects our level of anxiety and controls heart rate, blood pressure, and the movement of the intestines, as well as salivation. All of these can be affected by imagery. Much research has been done showing the usefulness of imagery in reducing the nausea and vomiting that accompany cancer chemotherapy, in lowering blood pressure and heart rate, in dealing with irritable bowel syndrome and other intestinal problems, as well as in decreasing stress, pain, and anxiety.

Imagery can also affect the immune system: Remember, once again, that the centers for imagery are intimately connected with the hypothalamus, which is the central switching station for the immune system. And, indeed, imagery has been shown to improve immune functioning in people with serious illnesses where the immune functioning may be compromised, like cancer, and also in healthy people.

Creating Your Own Safe Place

Next, we're going to do the Safe Place imagery, which is often the second image I use with people, individually and in groups. It can be particularly important in giving you relief when you're anxious or depressed, or if you're simply living through a stressful time. The Safe Place is also where you'll meet your Inner Guide.

In creating this Safe Place, you draw upon happy memories—or the imagined end of distress—to create a place, and a feeling, of calm and peace. When you create a Safe Place, you're using your imagination to take you far from current unhappiness or danger. The image promotes relaxation and provides a kind of mental and emotional time-out. It also shows you that even in the midst of pain, anxiety, unhappiness, and feelings of helplessness, you have the power to create your own reassurance, pleasure, and security.

Almost everyone I've worked with enjoys and benefits from the Safe Place imagery (kids, incidentally, are often able to use this and other images far more easily than adults). Occasionally, however, some people become anxious as they allow images to form. If this happens to you, just open your eyes. Don't force it. If it happens more than once, you should consult a Guide. You may need help dealing with the memories, thoughts, or feelings that are coming to the surface as you relax. Some people, for whom there really is no safety—for example, those in a violent, abusive intimate relationship or in a war zone—prefer, at least at first, the words *comfortable* or *special* to *safe*. If that's true for you, feel free to use these alternatives.

SAFE PLACE IMAGERY

Read through the following instructions several times, slowly, until you feel you're familiar with the material. If you like, you can use the CD on imagery in my complete program, "The Best of Stress Management" (the Lemon and Inner Guide imageries are there, too), which is listed in the Resources section, to guide you through this experience. Or you can record this exercise yourself, along with the soft music I recommend in the Resources section, or you can choose instrumental music that you like that will encourage the feeling of comfort and of discovery. Speak slowly when you're recording, so that each word has time to evoke images. Pause between sentences or, where appropriate, between phrases, and at commas.

Once you have your CD, or mine, you're ready to begin.

Now, begin breathing more deeply, in through your nose and out through your mouth, letting your belly be soft. Feel yourself connected to the chair on which you're sitting or, if you're lying down (it's fine to do this lying down if you're not too sleepy), to the floor on which you're lying, or the bed. Breathe deeply, relaxing, trusting that your imagination will do the work it needs to do, that it will take you to a place that's safe, that's comfortable for you. Breathe deeply and relax. Feel yourself supported by the chair or the floor on which you're sitting or lying.

Allow the music, and your imagination, to take you to a place that feels comfortable and safe to you. It may be a place in nature, a spot that you particularly love. It may be indoors, in a place that feels just right for you. It may be a place that you know well or one you've never seen before. Allow yourself to go there, to relax into this place.

If you happen to find yourself moving from one place to another, that's fine. Enjoy that as well. After a while, let yourself come to rest in one place.

Look around you. What does it look like? What does it feel and smell like to be there? If there are sounds, what are they? What's around you? What's the landscape like or the scene indoors?

Make yourself very comfortable wherever you are—sitting against a tree, enjoying a favorite chair, a favorite view. Notice what you're wearing on your body, on your feet. Are you by yourself or is someone else there?

If there's anything you would like to take out of this place—an annoying piece of furniture, a part of the landscape that's blocking your preferred view—please do so. Is there anything or anyone else you'd like to bring in? If there is, please do so. This is your place, your special place, your safe and comfortable place. You can make it look and feel just the way you want it to. Breathe deeply, enjoying this place, the feeling of your body relaxing, the comfort and safety it provides. Take some time to enjoy it, several minutes or more, breathing deeply, relaxing. Know that this is a place to which you can return anytime you want, to relax, to be replenished, to be safe.

And now, knowing you can return whenever you like, slowly bring yourself back into the room where you started. Begin by becoming aware of yourself sitting in your chair—or lying down—breathing deeply, connected to this space. Breathe deeply for a few moments more. Slowly open your eyes and come back into the room.

Take a few moments now to write in your journal. Here are some questions to consider: Was there any difficulty getting to your Safe Place? Did you go from one place to another for a bit? Where did you go? What was the safe or comfortable or special place like? What did it look like around you? Were there sounds? How did it feel and smell? Was anyone else there? How were you dressed? Were you sitting or lying down or standing? What did you bring in or take out? What was it like for you to simply be there, relaxing in your own Safe Place?

Remember as you write all this down that you can always return, that this place—or another Safe Place that you may find—is there for you whenever you need it, whenever you want it. And know, too, that even those who have difficulties when they first use this image can usually find a reassuring, calming, Safe Place the second or third time they do it.

The Safe Place image can be relaxing and reassuring when you're anxious and depressed. It helps remind you that peacefulness and control are possible, even in overwhelming situations. I've used it often, with good results, with victims of abuse, refugees, and even with terrified children in the midst of wars, as well as with people who are depressed or unhappy.

Meeting Your Inner Guide

Having had some practice with guided imagery, you're ready to meet your Inner Guide. Your Safe Place, as you'll soon see, is an excellent place for this meeting.

For Jung, the Inner Guide was an aspect of the collective unconscious. Aboriginal healers believe that the Guide's words are a communication from the spirit world. Some people are sure when they meet their Inner Guide that they're contacting a "higher power." So far as I'm concerned, my Inner Guide is a manifestation of my own unconscious wisdom, my intuition.

All these—and many other—beliefs will work perfectly well. All you need to do to contact your Inner Guide is to approach the experience experimentally, with an open mind. Accept whatever communication comes, even if you don't immediately understand it. If nothing in particular comes, accept that, too. It often takes a while for us to get used to, and to trust, this kind of internal communication and guidance.

FINDING YOUR INNER GUIDE

As with the Safe Place image, read through the words below until you feel familiar and comfortable with them, and then record them with the appropriate music. It's best if you record the Safe Place imagery and then continue with the Inner Guide image so you can move easily from one to the other.

Sit in a comfortable, relaxing chair or lie down. Make sure that the light is soft. Close the door so you won't be interrupted. Put a sign up if you need to.

Now, put on your tape or CD.

Begin as you did with the Safe Place image, following the same instructions I gave you in that exercise, exploring and experiencing your Safe Place in the same way you did in the previous image. It may be the same Safe Place or a different one. After you've found and explored, perhaps rearranged, and fully experienced your Safe Place, take some more slow, deep breaths and prepare yourself to meet your Inner Guide.

Here is some additional guidance—some new instructions that you'll want to record:

The Inner Guide who appears in your Safe Place may be a wise old man, woman, or child, someone you know or someone you've read about, or someone who emerges, now, for the first time from your imagination. The Guide may be human—a friend or family member—or a figure from a religious text or a god or goddess. It may be an animal or a spirit or a creature you've never seen before. Whoever or whatever appears, even if he or she or it seems a little strange, is a Guide who can be very useful to you.

Breathe slowly and deeply for a minute or two with your belly soft, and invite your Inner Guide to appear. Accept whoever or whatever comes, even if he or she or it seems surprising or peculiar. This Guide is a part of your inner mind, a representative of that part of your mind that knows what you need to know, that is here to help the part that doesn't yet know. It is here to help that part of you that may be lost or frightened or curious. Let that Guide appear in your imagination. Perhaps it will be a bird flying by, a figure who appears at your side, a voice speaking softly to you.

Introduce yourself to your Inner Guide and ask the Guide to introduce him- or her- or itself to you. Wait for your Inner Guide to communicate in words, gestures, or expressions.

Ask your Inner Guide if you may ask a question. If the answer is yes, then go ahead. You may want to ask a question that has been vexing you for some time—about difficulties on your journey or some painful, depressing feelings or thoughts—or a question that just pops into your mind. Whatever question you ask is fine. This is just the beginning of your relationship with your Inner Guide.

Wait for the answer. It may be clear and powerful. It may be curious, quirky, even, at least for now, incomprehensible. Accept whatever answer comes. This is just the beginning of your communication with that part of yourself that is your inner wisdom, with the inner wisdom that will slowly grow into your surest guide.

If you want clarification, feel free to ask for it. Let the dialogue continue for several minutes.

When you've heard what you need to, or the dialogue seems over, thank your Inner Guide and say good-bye for now. Know that you can return to this place, and that this Inner Guide, or another, is there for you whenever you want, whenever you need help on your journey through and beyond depression. If the experience has been more puzzling than productive, or if you received no answer, know that with guidance, as with so much else, practice will enhance your experience.

Now become aware of yourself, sitting in your chair or lying down, breathing deeply in through your nose and out through your mouth. Keep on breathing, deeply, slowly. Let your belly be soft, breathing. Feel your back against the back of the chair, your seat on the seat of the chair, your feet on the floor, or feel yourself lying down, supported by the floor or your couch or your bed. Breathe deeply with your belly soft. Slowly, as you're ready, allow your eyes to open and find yourself back in the here and now.

Take some time to record your experience with your Inner Guide in your journal. Here are some questions to consider as you write: Did an Inner Guide come? Did you see, hear, or feel your Inner Guide? Who was it? What was your response when you first encountered him or her or it? Was it surprise, gratitude, discomfort, or something else?

The first Inner Guide who emerges from within our unconscious mind is almost always the one most appropriate to this moment. But you may have had trouble fixing on one. That's OK, too. If more than one appeared, which one did you reject, which one did you accept, and why? What's the Inner Guide's name?

Write down the question, or questions, you asked your Inner Guide and the responses you got and how they made you feel. Do it as close to word for word as you can, recording both your questions and comments and your Guide's answers and other responses. Inner Guides are often quite precise in the way they speak (and our unconscious mind seems fond of puns). Responses that are hard to understand may become clear later.

Write down what the discussion with your Inner Guide brought up for you—feelings, thoughts, new ideas, etc. For example, "The wise old woman said I should 'make a change in my job.' At first I thought she meant to change one aspect of what I'm doing in the job, and then it occurred to me that I may need to consider changing from one job to another."

If You Experience Difficulty . . .

Sometimes, in the beginning, no Inner Guide appears; occasionally, he, she, or it walks away. The first experience usually indicates some initial difficulty in working with the exercise—disbelief, discomfort, unfamiliarity, restlessness. Often an Inner Guide will appear the next time you do the exercise. The Inner Guide who remains silent, refuses to answer or walks away is actually responding. His "nonresponse" may mean that you already know the answer or that you need to do some more work on your own before an answer will be given, or that you simply have to sit with your own question for a little longer.

Sometimes we reject the Inner Guide who comes. One of my patients who prided herself on her strength, independence, and nonconformity was shocked, even offended, when a gentle deer appeared to her. "I wanted a lioness or a wise old witch," she complained, "not Bambi!" She pushed Bambi out of her imagery. No one else came. She was "pissed off." I suggested that perhaps Bambi—gentle, loving, vulnerable—was the one she needed to see and hear and learn from. Try trusting your inner wisdom, I advised her; let go of your preconceptions. See what Bambi has to say.

You can do this exercise—combining Safe Place and Inner Guide images—whenever you feel confused or down or stuck. In the beginning it's good to set aside twenty minutes or half an hour. With practice, communication and useful guidance will come more easily—and perhaps faster. You may, after a while, want to do the exercise without the CD. Remember to write down the guidance you get. And notice how, over time, it may change and evolve.

SUMMING UP

The journey through depression, beyond confusion, requires going back and forth between external and internal guidance. In the beginning, and later, too, in times of crisis and confusion, a human Guide, a therapist, or a teacher is invaluable. She holds you in the reliable healing embrace of her compassion, and holds up to you a mirror that helps you to see and understand yourself more fully, more generously. She also offers you ways to deepen your understanding—perspectives, techniques, exercises, experiments—to help you to continue your journey of self-discovery outside the walls of her office, in every step you take. Take the time and use the perspectives and exercises in this chapter and the Prescription for Self-Care that follows to make sure you choose a Guide who is right for you.

Remember, too, before and after you meet this Guide (or these Guides), that you can learn from and accept support from others as well, from professionals and friends and acquaintances, from books—and, yes, movies, music, and art too—that offer practical advice or a larger perspective on your life; clarity and purpose; companionship and inspiration.

Finally, use the Lemon, Safe Place, and Inner Guide imagery to help you develop confidence in your mind's power to explore its inner wisdom as well as control your physical and emotional functioning. As you learn to trust your inner wisdom about what's right for you—your own wise guidance—you'll also be able to measure what you're learning and feeling with your outer Guide and in the rest of your life against the images and answers that arise from within. You'll be able to find answers to problems that had seemed insoluble, ways to lift your mood that you'd forgotten or never before imagined. Little by little, as you keep on using the Inner Guide imagery, this inner knowing, which will become the surest and most enduring of all your Guides, will grow stronger and stronger.

YOUR PRESCRIPTION FOR SELF-CARE:
Finding Your Guide

Here's a way to organize and record your search for a Guide, a therapist, or a counselor who is right for you.

Sometimes a Guide is relatively easy to find. I resisted the Call and, for a while, help, but when I was ready, Bob Coles, whom I'd already met, was there. All I needed to do was realize it and reach out. You, too, may know exactly whom you want to see, or you may be referred to someone who feels just right for you.

Sometimes, however, the process is more complicated. There may be a protracted search for a referral, appointments to be scheduled, interviews with several candidates, judgments and decisions to be made, financial issues to be considered, forms to be filled out. All these may have to be done before you find an appropriate Guide, while you're feeling anxious and unhappy. This prescription is designed to facilitate the process and focus your decision making.

In the left-hand column below (or in your journal), list the *optimal* qualities you're looking for in a Guide. Draw on the ones that I describe in this chapter and on any others that come to you. Then, in the right-hand column, write down the qualities that are *absolutely essential* for you. For example, it might be optimal to have somebody who is expert in the nutritional approaches I described in the previous chapter, but it's essential to have a Guide with whom you feel comfortable. Perhaps it would be ideal to have a female therapist, but a man who "understands and values a woman's perspective" would be OK. And so on.

Finding My Guide

Write down in your journal the characteristics of your ideal Guide—profession, age, gender, philosophy, and methods; how you would like to be treated; etc. Divide these, as in the two columns below, into optimal and essential qualities.

OPTIMAL QUALITIES	ESSENTIAL QUALITIES

After you've interviewed a potential Guide, look at the two columns again and see how he or she measures up to them. Use the space below labeled "Who Is This Guide?" (or create one in your journal) to make a list of the qualities he actually has.

Who Is This Guide? Qualities He or She Actually Has

Where Am I Now?

Look at the three lists. Does your potential Guide have all of the essential qualities you listed? If not, do the qualities he has make up for the ones he may be lacking? Are all of the qualities that you thought were necessary really vital? Is there anything else about your prospective Guide that is particularly appealing, or that turns you off? Write all this down in the space below or in your journal. Take a good look at what you've written.

Now, give yourself time to reflect on the Guide you're considering. Talk with family or friends whose counsel you value. Once a decision comes to you, I suggest you "sleep on it" for at least one night, maybe more. Then look at your lists again. At this time, you'll probably know whether the person you're considering feels right for you.

If you still have significant doubts, set aside some time to sit quietly and do the Inner Guide imagery. When your Inner Guide appears, ask if the therapist or counselor you're considering is the appropriate Guide for you. Ask any other questions that you'd like, as well as raise any doubts you still have about her perspective or method or her personality or the fit between you.

If the answer you get about the Guide is a clear "yes," then proceed to make a contract with her. If "no," you need to keep looking. If "maybe" comes up for you, you may want to talk with the Guide again and then ask your Inner Guide a second time. This is an important decision. Take the time you need.

Surrender to Change

The journey through and beyond depression requires a balance of action and acceptance. Sometimes, the emphasis has to be on action that moves you forward—finding and choosing a physician or Guide, buying and preparing mood-healthy foods, creating lists to help you respond to the Call. Other times, action precedes relaxation and acceptance. You have to set aside the time to meditate or actively create the images that can reduce your stress or guide your choices. Then you need to relax into the experience, to accept the guidance that comes.

In this chapter, we're going to explore "surrender," to see how letting go of control can actually move you ahead on your journey. Surrender isn't the same as submission. Submission means giving up, resigning yourself to the limitations that are holding you back or keeping you down. In surrendering, you're opening yourself up to the current of your life, which is always moving, always changing. And you're inviting and embracing the deep changes that are starting to work inside of you.

Sometimes, for some of you, surrender may happen easily, with little effort. More often, surrender requires exertion. You have to act consciously to free yourself from the places where you're stuck before you can relax into the new freedom you're discovering.

In this chapter, you're going to learn to use movement and action to break up the fixed, stuck patterns of depression; to help you let go of the self-defeating habits that hold you back; to make it possible for you to relax into, accept, and celebrate the changes that will transform your life.

FROM THE SWAMP OF STUCKNESS TO THE RIVER OF CHANGE

Heraclitus, the pre-Socratic Greek philosopher who lived twenty-six hundred years ago, said that we cannot step into the same river twice. The river is always flowing, continually changing. In fact, we cannot step into the same river even once; by the time the second foot falls, we're already entering a different river. This river of continual change is our life.

There are times when all of us resist the pull of the river. Our resistance hardens when we're depressed. Sometimes it feels as if we're neck deep in a swamp. We can see the river, but we can hardly think or eat or breathe, let alone move ourselves into the current.

As the need for change becomes clearer, as we get closer to making the changes that are necessary for us, our resistance sometimes grows stronger.

You may have heard the Call and found a Guide—and even accessed your own inner guidance—and begun to tend to what and how you eat. Still, you cannot move. Perhaps you know you've made a bad bargain— clinging to a partner or lover or career or point of view or attitude that no longer fits (if it ever did) who you really are. You know your defensive- ness or self-pity, your willful blindness or self-justification is diminishing you. You feel it intensely, yet you persist, rationalizing your words, behav- ior and attitudes, and your inertia: "I really am the victim" or "There's nothing more I can do."

"This is the way things have to be," you may tell yourself. Or you plead, "I'm doing the best I can." Pride and stubbornness and, of course, fear, fix you in a circle of pointless argument and hurt. But it's familiar and seems so safe, so justified. Even as the pain of stuckness becomes intolerable, or life begins to pry your fingers loose, you still hang on.

You're afraid that without your familiar mooring you will lose all hope and, perhaps, life itself. You will not let go, will not move into the current of your own life, will not trust that this current will take you where you need to go. And so you continue to live less than fully, in denial of the change that is possible and necessary. And, as time goes on, as you persist in resisting or blocking your own movement, your depression may deepen.

Now you have to summon your courage. The time has come to let go of the ideas and beliefs and behaviors you have been using to protect yourself; to feel what you've been fearing; to surrender in trust to the life that is in and all around you.

MILTON AND LAO-TZU

There are some people who seem to be able to simply let go of fixed patterns and self-defeating attitudes, of defensiveness and self-justification. Even in the midst of depression they can surrender to the river of change. They're models I like to keep in mind, sources of inspiration to me.

Milton was like that. Milton is a meticulous, highly skilled, African American airplane mechanic and former air force sergeant. Milton was forty-five—wiry and muscular, ramrod straight—when he came to see me. For months he'd been feeling alternately enraged and despondent. He was irritated at work and restless when he arrived home. He found himself waking at four a.m. with clenched fists and aching jaws. A neurosurgeon whose plane Milton had long serviced had noticed Milton's growing impatience and obvious unhappiness and suggested he call me.

In my office, Milton's speech was clipped and careful. He said that for two years, since his wife had left him and moved to California with his six-year-old son, he'd been depressed and angry. Even when his jaw wasn't in pain, he woke up tired and irritable. He no longer enjoyed the food he used to relish and had no interest in sex. He dreaded the weekends he once devoted to his son and avoided his own friends. For some months he was able to escape into the challenges of work, but now he regarded them as tedious chores. Recently, he'd begun to be antagonistic toward his boss. And, worst of all, he found himself angry with his son, as if the boy, who dearly loved him, had willed the separation. When he went out to California to visit, he corrected his son's speech ("He sounded like his mother," Milton told me, his voice dripping with hurt and anger), and the way he walked and threw a ball.

Milton recognized that he was feeling sorry for himself, seething at his ex-wife, and that he'd begun to blame the boy he was horribly lonely for. He knew that his short temper and, recently, his shortened phone contacts with his son, were only making things worse. But knowing it didn't help to free him from his anger or his depression. Nor had the Prozac a psychiatrist had prescribed: "I felt numb after a couple of days" he told me, "and even more irritable and agitated, and on top of that I had to take some damn pill."

I listened to Milton for over an hour, watched his hands clench and unclench, felt his fine mind knotting itself ever more tightly, until it seemed it was strangling speech and even feeling.

I asked him if he was willing to breathe deeply with me, to let his belly be soft while we sat with each other. He nodded, and I talked him through Soft Belly.

After ten minutes, his fists began to open and the cords in his forearms and the tight muscles in his belly were growing soft. I asked him to do Soft Belly every time he felt himself grow tense, every time his stomach rebelled against food or anger rose in his throat. He nodded.

"And one more thing," I went on. "Would you read the *Tao Te Ching* by Lao-tzu? He's a Chinese wise man who lived about five hundred years before Christ."

Milton tilted his head and looked at me sideways. I knew he wanted to do whatever might help, but he was obviously unfamiliar with the book or why I might be suggesting it.

"It's about letting go," I said, hoping that this might make sense to him.

I don't know exactly what I thought would happen: I'd never asked a patient to read Lao-tzu before. The idea just came to me. I knew Milton was conscientious, and I thought that between reading the book and doing the breathing, he would feel a little more relaxed, maybe have a bit more perspective on his obsessive concerns. But I never expected to encounter the man who walked into my office a week later.

Milton looked ten years younger. He moved with a little bounce and a glide. He spoke fluently, almost melodically, and he was grinning at me.

"Well," he began, "I went to the bookstore as soon as I left, and got Lao-tzu. I read it cover to cover, and I thought, 'This is hard, all these strange contradictions about "acting without doing" and "staying behind and being ahead" and so on.' And then I read it again, each of those poems, because I knew you were an intelligent man and that there was something you really wanted me to get, although I couldn't exactly say what it was.

"And the next day I had off, so I read the Lao-tzu a third time, slowly. I did the breathing exercises along with each poem, and after a few hours, it was like each poem was going into my body with my breath, working on me like some beautiful smell or great food, and I was feeling those poems, though I still can't say I understood them. And then I went for a long walk—that's the first time I've done that in months."

Sitting in the park, he read the poems again, very slowly, line by line this time. "The words hit home." And here he recited from memory:

If you want to become full,
Let yourself be empty.
If you want to be reborn,
Let yourself die.
If you want to be given everything,
Give everything up.

"'Damn,' I thought, 'that's it.' And then I had the thought that it was like what Jesus says in the Sermon on the Mount about how the lilies of the field don't toil or spin, and their clothing is more beautiful than Solomon in all his glory. So I got my Bible and read that, and then I went back to Lao-tzu.

"And that was Friday and I had the weekend off, so I decided, 'Well it's just one weekend, and my life has been pretty much a mess for two years, and maybe a lot longer than that, so why don't I just give this long weekend to Lao-tzu and, of course, to myself. It's only three days, and, after all, it's my life we're talking about. So I just kept reading Lao-tzu, and after a while, I thought I was getting more of what he meant.

> *The Master sees things as they are,*
> *Without trying to control them.*
> *She lets them go their own way,*
> *And resides at the center of the circle.*

"And I started thinking about how I was trying to control my life, and my ex-wife and my kid, and how I was getting so angry because life wasn't going my way, and every time I tried to make it go my way, or got angry that it wasn't, it just went more the other way. And finally, on Saturday night, sitting in that damn empty apartment of mine, I got so frustrated and upset I started shouting and cursing everybody and everything, and then my face got all tight and I started to cry like I haven't since I don't know when.

"And then, and you've gotta believe this has *never* happened before, I just started to laugh and laugh at what a fool I was. And it went on for hours, because every time I thought I was going to stop, I just remembered how hurtful I sounded when I was talking to my kid and I felt so bad, and I cried again. And then I thought about how angry I was at my wife, and I wondered why I was angry because actually I was well shut of her, and I should be thankful. And then I started to laugh. And finally, I fell asleep, and when I woke, I had tears in my eyes and I started laughing all over again.

"So that was Sunday morning. And I got up and bought three more translations of the Lao-tzu—I read there were almost as many translations of him as the Bible—just to see if somebody else could give me a better slant on some of the poems. And I read them, and compared, and by afternoon, I realized I had more energy than any day in the last two years, and I hadn't cursed my ex out once, and I was really looking forward to talking to my boy that night.

"My ex picked up the phone, and I asked how she was, and she said,

'What you been smokin?' and I laughed and told her I'd just been breathing and walking and reading. And then I talked to my boy, about the same things as usual—his homework and baseball and what's on the TV—but it was different. I was interested, really interested, and he told me so much more, and I didn't get irritated at all, or correct him and make him feel small, and I was grinning like a fool and just about crying at the same time, I was so happy.

"So here I am, doc, and if I ever need you again, I'll surely call, but between you and me and Lao-tzu, I think I'm just about cured."

And, so far as I can tell fifteen years later, he is.

Since then, when I feel at odds with myself, confused, or unhappy, I remember Milton's miracle and often open the *Tao Te Ching* myself. I pick verses at random and, like Milton, breathe and relax with them. Sometimes I imagine Lao-tzu, the smiling "old guy," as his contemporaries twenty-five hundred years ago referred to him, lying back, floating in a patched inner tube on the current of a river, laughing and waving or holding out a hand to me as I struggle. He's a great companion, and guide, and he's been helpful to countless others to whom I've introduced him.

EFFORT BEFORE SURRENDER

Milton surrendered, first to his reading and then, through it, to life itself. Most of us, when we're depressed or despondent, feel too mistrustful, too overcome with inertia and habit and fear, to move so gracefully on Lao-tzu's "easy way." So for us, particularly at the beginning of the journey, more effort is usually necessary. In order to surrender our will, to be empty, to trust in the "pathless path," to "reside in the center of the circle" that Lao-tzu describes, we first need, paradoxically, to exercise our will. Before we can let go into the flow of the river, we must struggle to its bank and dive to its depths. Energy is required, and some discipline and courage are necessary.

And, often enough, we need the support of others so we can move forward to become who we're meant to be.

I find it reassuring that this is also true of the storied heroes whose journeys are inspirations for and archetypes of our own. Repeated urging and reassurance from Guides buck up heroes who are faint of heart. But action is also necessary. To make the break from Kalypso, Odysseus must build his raft and launch it. Dante, terrified of the descent into the Inferno, has to stand on his own feet, overcome his *"viltade,"* his "cowardice," and turn downward behind and alongside Virgil. Demeter must move across the face of the earth, through the pain of losing her daughter; she must extend herself to care for another child, supervise the construction of a temple, and instruct those who have built it before she can experience her own integrity.

We also have to act, to reach out and connect with others, to feel and move our bodies, to engage completely with life before we can surrender to it.

Dorothy Does It

Becoming aware, acting, and reaching out is a sequence that often precedes surrender. Dorothy discovered it was an ongoing process. Within a few months of our first meeting, Dorothy was looking at the world differently. She'd stopped taking the antidepressants not long after our first visit, and she'd begun to let go of the idea that she was somehow sick or deficient. She'd also stopped blaming herself for every difficulty in her marriage. When she dwelled on the impossibility of leaving Todd, she would sometimes catch herself midthought: "I know," she'd say to herself, "I know, I'm 'waiting for the children to grow up and die.'"

Dorothy was more aware of what she was feeling and was reaching out to friends as well as to Aunt Grace. She was keeping a journal, reading and rereading and acting on the lists she had made. She'd begun, tentatively, to talk to the children about her and Todd's difficulties.

I suggested that Dorothy join a mind-body skills group at The Center for Mind-Body Medicine, and she did. These groups of eight or ten, which we've been offering for almost fifteen years, are sometimes composed of people with similar diagnoses, such as cancer or depression. More often, the groups are mixed. Members come with a wide variety of emotional and physical concerns. Their ages range from eighteen to more than eighty, and they're from every imaginable socioeconomic background.

The group offers all of its members tools for awareness, opportunity for action and self-care, an invitation to surrender. It's a safe place where each member can be whoever she is and admit to, accept, and begin to appreciate the ordinary humanity she shares with all of the others. Group support of a variety of kinds has been shown to improve mood as well as prevent depression. Participation in this kind of safe, practical, self-affirming group nourishes, soothes, and often heals us.

CONSIDER JOINING A MIND-BODY SKILLS GROUP

Mind-body skills groups give you an opportunity to learn about yourself and to practice many of the techniques I describe in this book. And they're based on the same meditative and educational approach as *Unstuck*. Members become aware of their own thoughts, feelings, and sensations as they arise, then share with one another what they're observing and experiencing.

At each weekly group, the leader teaches a new way of relaxing or learning about yourself. Over the course of twelve weeks, these lessons include several kinds of meditation, guided imagery (including the Safe Place and Inner Guide images), biofeedback (which promotes relaxation by control of the fight-or-flight stress response), drawings, written exercises, dance, yoga, and, through a genogram, or "family tree," a meditative look at family patterns—those that undermine you and those that can help sustain you.

At the first meeting, each person begins by saying why she is there, and at the beginning of each subsequent group, he or she checks in again. At check-in, each person says how she's been feeling and how she's used the techniques she's learned in previous groups to help herself—or the troubles she's had with them. Each person has a chance to talk. Nobody is allowed to interrupt or analyze anyone else. The whole idea is to become aware of how you're feeling, to gently witness these thoughts and feelings, and to learn to accept rather than judge what you're feeling. And, if you're judging, to notice that as well. Instead of being patients in need of treatment, the people in our groups become students, learning about themselves and discovering the power they have to help themselves.

Twelve hundred professionals have completed our advanced training in leading mind-body skills groups in the United States and around the world. A number of them are leading these groups, often at low cost, in many locations here and abroad. The professionals we've trained have worked with tens of thousands of people with depression and a variety of other conditions, including anxiety, post-traumatic stress disorder (PTSD), and chronic physical illness. Medical school faculty we've trained are also leading these groups—for medical students, residents, and other faculty—in a dozen U.S. medical schools. We and others are beginning to publish research (the papers are mentioned in the Notes section) that demonstrates their effectiveness in improving mood, decreasing stress, increasing energy, improving professional satisfaction (in health care workers), decreasing symptoms of post-traumatic stress, and enhancing hopefulness.

If you'd like to join a mind-body skills group, take a look at The Center for Mind-Body Medicine's Web site at www.cmbm.org for contact information for CMBM-certified group leaders and those who are not certified but have completed our advanced training. I believe these groups—with their combination of practical instruction, meditative awareness, loving acceptance, and personal support—are a wonderful Safe Place to learn to surrender, and can be a very significant part of your healing journey.

For Dorothy, the group—consisting of three others who were in one way or another depressed or stressed out, two with cancer, and three with a variety of other chronic illnesses—was "a godsend." She held back at first, talking about her cancer but not her depression, omitting her last name, and describing her husband but not mentioning that he was a senator. By the third week, she felt enough trust to speak more freely. She was not, she realized, so different from everyone else.

Two of the other group members, it turned out, were in similar binds with their spouses, and almost everyone felt the same fears of change, the same need to keep up appearances, the same terror that unhappiness would never end, or that illness would cripple them and claim them. "I'm beginning to let go of that sense of specialness I've had," Dorothy told me after the fifth meeting, "and of the idea that I need to take care of everyone else. They make fun of me in the group when I try to solve everyone's problems and call me Dr. Dorothy—and, Jim, it feels so good to be just one person with other people."

Support from the group helped Dorothy to stay faithful to her Soft Belly practice. At times of confusion, she anchored her resolve by rereading her lists. She repeatedly asked for counsel from the Inner Guide. She'd set a date for leaving the senator—"right after the next election." Though leaving still terrified her, having a date gave her a feeling of purpose and hope for her future, "for a time of living for myself, not Todd, or the voters."

Dorothy felt better all around, but nine months after I first met her, she was still "bone tired" from the surgery that had removed her breast and the course of chemotherapy that had just ended. And, off and on, she was still terribly discouraged. Sometimes she feared a recurrence of the cancer, or worried that she wouldn't be able to go through with the separation from Todd, or, even more insistently, that she might never recover her energy and her optimism: "I'm not sure if this makes any medical sense," she began, "but I feel like all those years of unsatisfying marriage and all the misspent energy of keeping life with Todd together were gathered into one tight ball in that tumor. And the treatment it's taken to rid me of it has robbed me of everything else, too."

Dorothy was well embarked on her journey, but her continued fatigue and the sense that she was still holding on to the past—or that it was holding on to her—suggested that now was a time for her to do something physically active to raise her energy, to move ahead, and to let go even more.

I asked Dorothy what kind of exercise she was doing, and she looked at me as if I'd committed a terrible social blunder. "Jim Gordon, I'm a tired out, certifiably clinically depressed fifty-eight-year-old woman with cancer who's taking this ghastly chemotherapy. I'm going to have to use all my strength to leave a powerful and determined man to whom I've been married for almost forty years. I can barely drag myself to the office in the morning, and I have to nap at my desk every afternoon. Where do you think I'm going to find the energy for exercise?"

"I think," I told her, "you'll find it as you do the exercise, and that it will come from the reservoir of untapped energy that feeds the powerful, eloquent, and utterly unconvincing protest I just heard." Dorothy shook her head and laughed.

I went on to remind Dorothy that everything we think or feel is recorded in our bodies as well as our minds. Persistent anger, and particularly the grinding suppressed fury of hostility, have been implicated in heart disease and seem to be a factor in chronic pain. Fear, stress, and anxiety lower our immunity and predispose us to infections. Lack of close connections to others makes us more vulnerable to all physical illnesses— and the affectionate support of others helps us to heal when we are ill, and to stay well.

Depression, I reminded her, is a kind of stuckness, in body as well as mind, a fixed pattern of feeling, thinking, and being. Depressed people, as she well knew, feel burdened physically as well as emotionally, palpably constrained by forces that seem beyond them. Disrupting this fixed pattern—in body as well as mind and spirit—helps make change possible. In fact, working with the body is the most powerful, direct, and reliable route to surrender, change, and freedom.

The larger, more hopeful perspective of our talks—my conviction that depression is better viewed as a journey than a disease—redefined Dorothy's dilemma. The relaxation techniques she was learning were altering the physiological patterns of anxiety and tension that contributed to her chronic depression. Making lists of "feelings," "directions," and "steps" provided a framework for and catalyst to change. She was finding reassurance, emotional comfort, and support—from Aunt Grace, her friends, her group, me, and her Inner Guide—where there had been fear, hopelessness, and isolation. Now was the time for her to use her body to help free her in those places where she was still stuck, to enhance and accelerate her healing.

MOVING AND MOVING ON

Significant physical activity is the natural condition of our species. Visit an aboriginal society of hunter-gatherers or a preindustrial agricultural community and you'll see men and women walking, lifting, carrying, chopping, bending, and hoeing. There is continual, occasionally urgent but usually unforced activity for four, six, eight hours a day. It's often communal. And it helps to keep great-grandmothers and great-grandfathers fit into their seventies and eighties.

In the modern world, those of us who don't work on family farms or in construction call this kind of activity exercise. All of us have to find ways to bring this activity, and its benefits for physical health and psychological well-being, into our lives.

Exercise—movement—alters brain chemistry and with it, mood. Thirty to forty minutes of daily exercise—jogging, biking, swimming, lifting weights, using the StairMaster or treadmill, or walking—reliably raises the levels of serotonin and norepinephrine, the two neurotransmitters that most antidepressants aim at increasing, as well as the endorphins, the brain's pain-reducing and pleasure-enhancing amino acid peptides. Exercise likely increases the number and activity of neurons in the hippocampus that are depleted in depression and seem to be so important to emotional well-being. In study after study, exercise (jogging has been most-often studied) decreases people's depression scores, sometimes by as much as 50 percent, a result fully as good as that obtained by psychotherapy or chemical antidepressants. If exercise were a patentable and profitable pill, it would be hailed on the front pages of every American newspaper, and marketed 24/7 on the television networks.

If you join a class, exercise can also offer you an opportunity for emotional support. Many people who initially find classes intimidating (it's amazing how many of us fear that others are not only going to be more fit and capable than we are, but also critical and judgmental of us) come to love them. The class gives substance and structure to days and weeks that may seem empty. It's supportive and fun to have a sympathetic teacher. Our classmates' efforts to help themselves can encourage and inspire our own.

Exercise has two other great and abiding benefits. Even if it is at first difficult or unfamiliar, we almost always feel better about our body afterward, more at home living in it. And, equally significant, if we exercise, we know that the changes we feel are ones we—and not a pill—have created. This sense of being active on our own behalf may, as I've repeatedly said, be the single most direct and powerful antidote to the feelings of hopelessness and helplessness that are hallmarks of depression.

"Still," Dorothy said, "the thought of a StairMaster or treadmill or jogging makes me ill. But walking, not 'long' and certainly not 'brisk,' perhaps I could do that."

WALKING

I'm going to discuss mindful, meditative walking a bit later in chapter four. Here, I just want to give some suggestions for making walking an easier, more pleasurable, and more regular part of your day.

A FEW THOUGHTS ABOUT WALKING

>> Just about anyone over the age of eighteen months who is not confined to bed or wheelchair bound can walk. Obvious, right? But especially when we're depressed, we, like Dorothy, tend to "forget."

>> You can walk where you like: in a park or on the street, around the ball field or in a mall. And pretty much when you want.

>> You might want to begin by walking more slowly than usual, with your knees a little bent and your feet gently landing on the ground as you move. It's easier on your knees, hips and back, and the rest of your body; a little more relaxed and even musical. This is also, interestingly, the way many indigenous peoples walk. Think of Milton after a few days with Lao-tzu.

>> You can walk when you're tired of being indoors or when you've completed a task at work, or on your lunch hour or when your mind is racing. It's change, and this one change can begin to modify and soften the rigid, fixed patterns that characterize depression. Also, this one change will remind you that other changes are possible.

>> You can easily walk at the beginning and end of your workday: on your way to public transportation or after you've parked your car an unaccustomed few blocks from your work.

>> You can walk with other people. This is a nice, low-pressure way of connecting with others—coworkers during the day or family members or friends in the evenings or on weekends.

At first, it was hard for Dorothy to struggle against the inertia that bound her to her chair, the peculiar attraction that life in a nightgown seemed to hold. But once she had overcome the pull backward and bedward, Dorothy began to feel more alert and able. More energy came as she closed the front door behind her. With each satisfying fall of foot on pavement a sense of accomplishment and even, she had to admit, power filled her.

To start out, Dorothy walked for ten or fifteen minutes at odd times during the day and then, as she grew more fond of it, for thirty or forty minutes every morning. She enjoyed the crispness of the air, the shadows the trees cast on her street, the sound of birds, and the children on their way to school.

"You know," Dorothy told me after several months, "it has changed me. My body feels stronger and more energetic, and I have to admit, my mood is better, but I also feel *myself*. Maybe you don't understand this, but I've never ever taken time like this for myself or met a challenge that was just my own. Everything was always for someone else—Todd or the boys or my clients, my friends, my parents. Even shopping for clothes was so I would look nice for someone else. But this walking is just for me, because it makes me feel good."

One afternoon, Dorothy, looking slimmer, less stooped, and altogether brighter, sat down. "Now, Jim Gordon," she began with considerable gravity, "I have something to tell you. I want you just to be quiet and listen, and not say a word or laugh." A deep breath. "I've hired a personal trainer." A long pause while she studied my reaction. "Well, he's this darling young graduate student, and he comes over to the house twice a week and teaches me my own exercise routine, and I have to say I love it. And I also have to tell you how much I love it when Todd comes home and looks at me like I've taken leave of my senses."

RELAXING INTO MOVEMENT

Sometimes I ask my patients and students to do something physical that seems against the grain of their usual way of living. I'm likely to begin by suggesting that the determinedly sedentary person, such as Dorothy, walk. If people are self-conscious about their bodies, I might recommend dancing in front of a mirror. This kind of activity can help you break fixed patterns, give you the opportunity to discover other suppressed sides of yourself, as well as to move into the flow of your life. Often, however, I work within the context of the activity someone is already engaged in, helping her to do it in a more conscious and relaxed, more meditative, way, transforming customary activity into life-changing action.

April was taking yoga lessons when she came to see me. She liked the postures and "the workout" and the increased vitality she felt afterward. But as she talked about it, it became clear that what should have been a delight and a release was becoming, like the rest of her life, a chore and a burden. She "had to" do her yoga just as she "had to" work as a statistician. She spoke of needing to "put in more time at the studio" and to do more "advanced" poses.

I told April she was making me tired. There's evidence that yoga, done in a variety of ways and according to different systems, improves mood and decreases stress. But yoga is about "liberation" as well as mood improvement. Do fewer postures, I suggested to April. Spend more time at home doing them slowly, by yourself. Take all the time you want and need, I suggested; breathe into the stretches, feel them extending, expanding your body. Let your feelings emerge; allow your body to move as it wants.

I explained to April that as far as I knew, yoga postures originally came spontaneously to the ancient sages when they were in states of deep relaxation, of meditation. Now we try to relax by assuming the postures. In fact, she might find—as I had over the years—that if she relaxed, the postures would come spontaneously to her as well.

And, to April's amazement, after a month or two, in the middle of breathing slowly and deeply, as she held a standard posture, such as the cobra or the warrior, her body began to move on its own. Sometimes it felt as if she were melting into the posture, even becoming the animal it represented—feeling the cobra's peculiar power to rise gracefully, swaying. Sometimes as she held a pose, breathing, relaxing, tears of release, of relief from years of physical and mental tension, trickled down her cheeks. Sometimes she found her body moving into postures she had seen only in books, or had never even imagined.

"It's a miracle to me," she said. It was as if Mother Nature were coming to her in the space and time of those yoga postures, filling her from within. For the first time, April felt moved not by others' expectations or her own fear, but by something within herself, "energy"—she couldn't think of a better word—that seemed to renew itself. Little by little, without her forcing or even willing it, she began to understand that the relaxed and relaxing power that she felt in her body might come to animate the rest of her life—loosen the fear that tied her to self-defeating, isolating thoughts and behaviors, and thaw her frozen emotions.

If you're depressed or just tense and anxious, you can do as April did. You can start with some simple postures that you can learn in a beginners' yoga class. What follows are a few you can relax into on your own, even before you take a class.

RELAXING INTO YOGA

Classes led by well-trained teachers are, so far as I'm concerned, by far the best way to learn the asanas—postures or poses—of hatha yoga. They're available almost everywhere in the United States, and in most other countries as well. The Resources section gives you Web sites to help you find one near you.

I strongly suggest—as I did to April—that you practice yoga in a slow, meditative way, relaxing into the postures (the styles that I know well that are most conducive to this are Kripalu and Integral Yoga). If the class feels competitive or pressured in any way—too many new or strenuous postures, taught too fast, or held too long— find another class, another teacher. You don't need more stress or the injuries that come when committed students push too hard. As you slowly become more familiar with particular postures, you'll be able to hold them longer and relax into them.

What follow are descriptions of a few, very simple poses that you can begin with at home. They're designed to open up your chest, to strengthen your lower body, make your spine more flexible, and deepen your breathing as well as reduce your stress, energize you, and help you relax—surrender—into your life.

To begin, you'll need a yoga mat or a carpet that's yielding but not too soft and thick. Also, the numbers of repetitions of each posture, the numbers of breaths you take, are suggestions for beginners. Do what is comfortable for you and increase them as it pleases you.

Child's Pose

I suggest that you begin, and also end, with the child's pose.

Kneel on the ground first, then sit back on your heels and bend your upper body forward. (If your knees are stiff, don't force yourself to go back on your heels.) Stretch your arms out over your head, so they're parallel to each other, your palms flat on the floor, as they are in the accompanying illustration.

Breathe slowly and deeply, feeling the breath move into and through your whole body, and especially into your lower back. Remain this way for 2 or 3 minutes, breathing slowly and deeply, feeling this posture of surrender.

Warrior Pose

You need to stand up for this one.

You begin with your feet parallel and together. Put your right foot forward and the left back so that your feet are now about 3 feet apart. Turn out the toes of your left (back) foot at about a 45-degree angle. Turn your hips so they are facing front. Bend your front knee, and raise your arms over your head, with your palms facing each other. Now bend your front knee slightly more so the majority of your weight is on the front (right) foot. Your right knee should now be directly above your right foot, as in the accompanying illustration. Breathe slowly and deeply, in and out. Breathe like this 10 times.

Breathing slowly, bring your feet back together.

Take a couple of slow, deep breaths. Now step forward with your left foot and bring your right foot back and do the same pose, this time with your left knee bent and your right foot turned out in back. Once again, breathe slowly in and out, 10 times.

Return to standing with your feet together.

This posture strengthens and energizes the lower body, and opens up the upper body.

Cat and Dog

You're on your hands and knees for this one. Breathe slowly in and out, as you prepare for—and do—this posture.

Breathe slowly and deeply in, and arch your back (as in the illustration) like a cat, with your eyes turning toward the ground. On the second out breath, bring your back down so the open part of the curve is facing up and your eyes are forward. This is the dog position. Once again, breathe slowly and deeply, in and out, twice. Repeat this sequence 5 to 10 times.

This posture brings flexibility to the spine and provides a good focus for your active, or agitated, mind.

Downward-Facing Dog

You can enter this posture from the child's pose. First, separate your feet to the width of your hips. Now, turn your toes under so they rest on the ground and your heels are elevated. As you exhale, straighten your legs and simultaneously push up on your palms. Now you should be standing on your feet, with your palms flat on the floor and your rear end in the air, making a triangle shape with your body, as you see in the illustration. Breathe in and out 5 to 10 times, slowly. Bend your knees and come back down into the child pose.

The most strenuous of the postures I'm giving, the downward-facing dog is both energizing and stabilizing.

Chest-Opening Pose

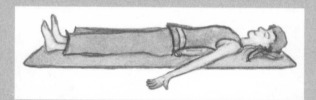

This is a variation on the standard relaxation pose. You'll need to use a blanket folded lengthwise under and along your spine to achieve this position.

Lie on your back, on the blanket, so that the blanket elevates your spine several inches above the floor. Let your head rest on the floor, as in the illustration. Extend your arms to your side with your palms up. Breathe deeply, in through your nose, out through your mouth, with your belly soft. Do this 10 to 20 times.

This pose will help to open up your chest, relax your back muscles, and deepen your breathing. It's another posture of acceptance and surrender.

Lion Pose

Stand up. Your feet should be shoulder-width apart. Bend your knees a little. Extend your arms out in front of you with your palms down and fingers spread apart. There should be tension in your arms, fingers, and hands. Take a deep breath in through your nose and expel it loudly—with a loud lion-like roar—from the back of your throat, through your mouth. Extend your tongue out and down as you roar and look up (see the illustration). You should hear the lion's roar and feel it in the back of your throat. Do this expressive, energizing pose 3 times.

Child's Pose

To conclude the session, assume the child's pose once again, breathing deeply, very slowly—in through your nose, out through your mouth. Breathe like this 10 to 20 times, letting all the muscles of your body relax with each exhalation, letting yourself melt into this posture of surrender.

When you've completed this sequence, which will take about 15 minutes (once you've got it down), give yourself a little time to relax before you move on to your next activity. You can, if you'd like, write down your experience in your journal.

BREAKING PATTERNS, LETTING GO

For Dorothy, simply walking was energizing and liberating, a physical boost and a declaration of independence. For April, yoga was, in addition, a direct opening into a well of suppressed feelings, a profound release, and a vehicle for allowing her to move into, and with, the current of her life.

There are also techniques that traditional healers have used for millennia specifically to raise energy; break up fixed physical, mental, and emotional patterns; and promote surrender. Many of them are, to be sure, strenuous and, at first, a little strange. These are the active, expressive meditations that I mentioned in the first chapter. They're central to my work with depressed, anxious, and traumatized people, and with the chronically ill, as well as with stressed-out and responsibility-burdened health professionals and medical students.

Over the years, I've simplified and shortened the four- and five-stage expressive techniques that I first learned thirty-five years ago from my teacher, Dr. Shyam Singha, an Indian acupuncturist, who learned many of them from his teacher, a wildly controversial Indian guru named Rajneesh. The short forms I've created make them far easier to do and more accessible to more people. I suggest you think of them as I do, as an experiment and an adventure. Do them. See what happens. You might be embarrassed or skeptical in the beginning. That's OK. If you find them helpful, do them often, even daily. At the end of this chapter, I provide specific guidelines to help you use them most effectively and safely.

The simplest one, the one that I often recommend first, is dancing, which has repeatedly been shown to improve mood. I can't even count the number of depressed people, like Theresa, who tell me they love to dance but don't do it anymore. When I suggest dancing, it's not any particular kind of dance. That can be fun, too, but following the steps, whether fox-trot, samba, or electric slide, is very different from simply allowing your body to move into the rhythm, and with the melody, of the music. All you have to do is close the door, find some music that moves you, put it on, and let movement happen.

Shaking and Dancing

The second highly effective technique begins with shaking your body and concludes with dancing. Shaking may require a bit of a leap of faith for you—you may feel that shaking is an undesirable sign of anxiety and fear, or that doing it is silly. It may also seem like too much when you're feeling fatigued, fatalistic, and down. I suggest you put aside your preconceptions. Accept, at least provisionally, that even if it is arduous and/or silly, it may help shake loose some of the chronic tension that restricts and agitates you. If you do, you may well find, as have thousands of people with whom I've done this meditation, that this paired sequence of activities can energize your depressed body, relieve your preoccupied mind, and dissolve your tension. It can also, as you do it regularly, help you feel more at home in your body, and bring you into the moment-to-moment flow of your life.

The technique I use is adapted from Rajneesh's five-stage Kundalini (*kundalini* is a Sanskrit word for the energy that is said to rise up the spine and animate the body) sequence (see the Resources section). It begins with five to ten minutes of shaking followed by five or more minutes of dance.

SHAKING AND DANCING

Create a CD or a playlist. Or, if you'd like, use the CD on breathing and exercise in my Best of Stress Management kit (see the Resources section). You may find that hearing my voice on tape is particularly encouraging.

If you're making your own CD, leave a couple of minutes of silence at the beginning so you can relax into the experience. For shaking, you can use the first segment of the Kundalini CD that's listed in the Resources section. Or you can substitute similar driving, rhythmic music. Begin with 5 or 6 minutes of this. Then, silence for a minute or two. Then add 3 to 5 minutes of music that makes you move.

Sometimes I suggest African songs for this final part—by Youssou N'dour or Oliver N'goma (these and other CDs are listed in the Resources section)—sung in a language you won't understand. The melody will energize, delight, and move you, and help break up repetitive and annoying thoughts. You can also use songs whose words have a particular meaning you may find helpful; for example, if you're frustrated, the Rolling Stones's "You Can't Always Get What You Want." Most of the time, I like to use upbeat, encouraging reggae songs such as Bob Marley's "Three Little Birds" (Everything Goin' Be Alright)" or Jimmy Cliff's "You Can Get It If You Really Want." The most important thing is that the music moves *you*. After a while, or if you're feeling particularly frustrated or stuck, you may want to move for longer periods—10 to 15 minutes each of shaking and dancing.

Begin by planting your feet shoulder-width apart, bending your knees slightly, and relaxing your shoulders. Close your eyes so you're not distracted. Breathe deeply and slowly for a minute or two. "Thank Nature," as Shyam, my teacher, long ago advised me, for this opportunity to move, and move beyond where you're stuck.

As the first rhythmic music goes on, begin to shake your whole body. Shake up from your feet, through your knees, hips, and shoulders, to your chest. Shake to your capacity—vigorously, strongly. Let your shoulders relax and bob up and down with the shaking. Let your head go as you shake. Let your jaws, which carry so much tension, hang open. If sounds come out of your mouth, let them come.

Even if you feel silly or bored or tired, keep going, remembering to shake from the feet on up. Let the shaking take over your whole body. Keep going. If you feel tired or bored, pick up the pace. Keep going. Keep going until the music ends.

Now, stop. Pay attention to your breathing and your physical sensations. Breathe deeply. Relax. Be aware of your body, of your breath.

Now comes the music for moving. Let it move you. Don't follow a particular pattern or dance step. Just let your body move as it will, freely and spontaneously. If you feel awkward or silly, notice that . . . and keep moving. You are alone. No one is watching or judging you.

When the music stops, relax for a few moments, standing, sitting, or lying down.

Write in your journal about the experience.

It's great to do shaking and dancing first thing in the morning, or when your energy is low, or anytime you feel particularly blue or discouraged. It's also a wonderful way, late in the afternoon or early evening, to shake off the burdens of the day. But don't do it just before you sleep; it may be too energizing.

Shaking and dancing can work well anytime you're under stress. My medical students tell me that just before an exam, when they're taut with tension, they sometimes go to the bathroom, lock the stall, and shake for a few minutes. Why? "Better concentration," they say. "Easier exams," "You feel a little lighter," "You don't worry as much," "Better grades."

Dynamic Meditation

I prescribe shaking and dancing often, and always teach it in workshops and training programs. I recommend Dynamic Meditation less often, because it's more strenuous and even stranger. It requires significant physical effort and often brings up quite strong emotions. It is, however, highly energizing and, afterward, relaxing, and it offers a very clear path to surrender. I have done it daily for many months and have prescribed it with great success for men and women whose fixed ideas and remembered pain are constraining their minds, stiffening their bodies, and limiting their lives.

Because these expressive techniques, and particularly Dynamic Meditation, may bring up strong emotions, I suggest you have someone—a Guide, a therapist, a meditation teacher who has experience with these techniques and ease with strong emotions—available to call on and consult.

The original form I learned has five stages. Its instructions and accompanying music are on the Dynamic Meditation CD listed in the Resources section. In chapter five, "The Dark Night of the Soul," I'll tell you why and how I used it with desperate, despairing Madeleine. Here I'm going to describe the less demanding—but still highly effective—two-stage form that I most often recommend.

The fast, deep, energizing breathing is probably unlike any you have done before. If you have significantly high blood pressure, a pacemaker, a history of heart disease, metastatic cancer, or significant shoulder, neck, or head injuries, you shouldn't do this. If you have any questions or doubts about doing this exercise, please consult your physician before you do. Otherwise, you can proceed with the experiment.

DYNAMIC MEDITATION

You'll want to create a CD or playlist for this meditation as you did for the shaking and dancing. Once again, there are two stages separated by a minute or two of relaxation.

The first stage is the Dynamic (or chaotic) breathing, the second, free dance. I like to use the first track of the Dynamic Meditation CD for the fast, deep breathing, but you can use any kind of insistent, rhythmic, repetitive, driving music that will keep on pushing you to breathe faster and deeper. For the second part (the dancing), you can use, as with the shaking and dancing, music that is energizing, inspirational, celebratory for you.

Begin with your feet shoulder-width apart, your knees slightly bent, and, once again, your eyes closed. If you have a problem with balance, however, you'll need to keep your eyes open. Focus on a wall so you won't be unnecessarily distracted.

You're going to breathe in and out *through your nose* as deeply and as fast as you can. This is an energizing, not a relaxing, breath. *Don't breathe through your mouth.* If you do, you may well hyperventilate.

Create loose fists with your hands and bring them close to your chest so they're about 6 to 8 inches apart in front of and to the side of your sternum. In order to deepen and intensify the breathing, raise your elbows and, with them, your shoulders as you breathe in and then bring your elbows forcefully down to your sides as you breathe out. This creates a bellowslike effect that brings more breath deeper, and more forcefully, into your lungs. You'll look a bit like a chicken flapping its wings.

Now breathe as fast and as deeply as you can—in and out through your nose—raising your elbows as you inhale, bringing them down to your sides as you forcibly exhale. Don't worry about keeping a rhythm. Simply breathe as deeply and as fast as you can. If you feel like you're stuck and can't go on . . . keep going. If you have to stop for a moment or two, start up again as soon as you can. If someone were looking at you doing this—and there really shouldn't be any spectators—they might laugh. Don't worry about it. No one's looking. Keep going.

You should be able to do this—even when you begin—for 5 minutes. If that seems like too much, start with 2 or 3 minutes.

In the minute or two of silence following the dynamic breathing, become aware of your ordinary breathing and your body as you stand, relaxed. As you relax, let your thoughts come and go.

When the dance music comes on, let it move your body.

As you feel more comfortable doing this experiment, you can gradually lengthen the time of both the breathing and the dance. You can write down your experience of Dynamic Meditation in your journal.

This technique will probably be even more energizing than the shaking and dancing. Ideally, it should be done early in the day—in fact, early in the morning—and before, *not after,* you eat.

CREATING CHAOS TO BRING ORDER

Over the years, I've learned that the body is the best-equipped vehicle for the ongoing process of surrender. I've described five techniques to promote surrendering in this chapter: simple, straight-ahead physical exercise (walking, jogging, swimming, aerobics); the elegant and subtle postures of yoga, held and entered in a relaxed meditative way; free dance; the somewhat strange but highly effective shaking meditation; and the powerful, demanding Dynamic Meditation. There are many others: The breathing and postures of the Chinese moving meditations, tai chi and qigong, can open our physical and emotional structure just as yoga can; so, too, can whirling, hopping up and down on one foot, or pounding pillows and shouting (which I'll describe and discuss in the next chapter).

All of these techniques put energy into the stuck system that is depression. Through effort, they all help to open us where we've been closed. They give us a taste of a more creative and celebratory way of moving and being, and mobilize our natural healing power. Through effort comes ease; through chaos, order and simplicity; through will, surrender.

There is a significant body of scientific research on the benefits of physical exercise for depressed and anxious people. As I've mentioned before, one form of exercise, jogging, is already proving at least as good as drugs in relieving symptoms of depression. And there are now, as I've said, a number of studies on the effectiveness of yoga and dance in decreasing anxiety and improving mood.

There are, so far, no good studies on the "expressive meditations" such as shaking or Dynamic Meditation, or, indeed, on the psychological transformation that the active meditations can bring. It seems clear, though, that in addition to the increase in neurotransmitters and endorphins, and the feelings of self-efficacy that come from any exercise, something else is very definitely at work. Mind and body are, as I've shown you, interconnected—or better said, everything that happens mentally or emotionally is registered and encoded in the body. These active techniques—fast, deep breathing; shaking and dancing freely; holding a yoga or tai chi pose—raise our energy levels. And that higher amount of energy seems to break up fixed patterns of physical structure, thought, and feeling. It invites other, new movement into both body and mind.

This may sound strange to you, but there is some interesting science that provides a useful perspective on these techniques for mobilizing energy, breaking up fixed physical and emotional patterns, and inviting surrender. Nobel Prize winner Ilya Prigogine's work on "dissipative systems" in chemical reactions is particularly suggestive. At certain "far from equilibrium" points, Prigogine observed, the "perturbation," the disturbance of physical and chemical systems, could bring about a profound and creative change. Out of this chaos, a new, more highly integrated order could emerge. This was a natural process, a result of the unfettered evolution of a system (chemical or physical) and of the free exchange between that system and the world around it.

The analogy seems pretty clear to me. In depression, the natural process of biological and psychological growth and evolution is inhibited. Our muscles are tense and tight, our breathing shallow, our thoughts and feelings limited and constricted. The forms of expressive physical activity I've been describing create the far-from-equilibrium states that disrupt the old habit-hardened physical, mental, and emotional patterns of depression. Chaos arrives, and with it, the possibility of the formation of a new, more open and creative order.

If the science is still in its speculative stage, our collective human experience of these approaches is vast—tens of thousands of years of natural experiments with them, by hundreds of millions of us in cultures around the globe. These are the oldest ways of changing and enlarging consciousness, of helping to free us from our limitations, fears, and self-doubts, from the structures of belief and thought and feeling that limit and cripple us and the societies in which we live.

These were the tools of the shamans of Siberia and of ancient healers and healing traditions around the world. Centuries before Rajneesh rediscovered it, the fast, deep breathing was practiced by the wandering sadhus ("spiritual seekers") of India and the Buddhist monks of Tibet. The shaking has been used in Indonesia; the dancing in Africa, Asia, and the Americas; and whirling by the Sufis of medieval Persia and Turkey. And emotional catharsis is central to the modern expressive forms of Western psychotherapy such as Gestalt and bioenergetics, and their descendants, the various "body-oriented" psychotherapies. "Archaic techniques of ecstasy" is what the great historian of religion Mircea Eliade has called these approaches.

I ask just about everybody I see in my practice to begin with one active expressive technique (walking or dancing or yoga or shaking) along with one quiet meditative technique such as Soft Belly breathing. I suggest you do the same.

As you read on, and perhaps reread these sections, you'll have a better sense of which of these approaches might work best for you. If there is one that speaks clearly to you, you might begin with it; or there may be a technique that seems both odd and appropriate that's a good choice; or even one that seems a bit ridiculous (like shaking) but still nags at your attention. If you'd like, check it out with your Inner Guide. If the answer comes back "yes," then go with it. If you don't get a big yes to any of them, then begin, as Dorothy did, with walking or simply with dancing to fast music. The most important thing is to begin to move your body, to break up the fixed patterns, the inertia that characterizes depression, to move once again into, to surrender to, the flow of your life and of life itself.

GUIDELINES FOR EXPRESSIVE MEDITATION

If you're interested in doing the more vigorous of these experiments—the expressive meditations—on your own, here are ten guidelines to consider as you approach them.

1 You need to begin by raising your energy. The Dynamic breathing—the crazed chicken—is a great way to do it, but so, too, is shaking for ten or fifteen minutes, or doing yoga, or just putting on fast music and dancing. Each of them is a way to break up the fixed patterns in the body and the mental and emotional stuckness that goes with it. Each approach requires energy to initiate, and brings more energy with it. All are doorways to surrender.

2 You need to have the opportunity to let out what's inside, to let the raised energy churn feelings and thoughts, fears and anguish, to the surface, where they can be expressed. This is why dancing follows shaking. You can also increase your energy and release emotions in tandem: For example, you can hold the postures of hatha yoga for several minutes as April did, breathing slowly and deeply, feeling the physical feelings in your body, and then simply allowing—not forcing—your emotions to emerge, like steam rising from the body, as you hold the posture.

3 Understand, too, that even if you have a significant physical disability, you can still move. Patients in hospital beds can wiggle their toes, and open and close their hands and fists slowly, mindfully, as they breathe deeply into their bellies.

4 Do these exercises to the limits of your capacity. Total effort is the most potent prelude to total surrender. *But don't be stupid.* Observe the cautions for Dynamic Meditation. Don't do yoga postures that may aggravate an injury. All these techniques can be useful. Find one that is right—and safe—for you.

5 Whichever technique you choose, do it daily. If it's really hard for you, start with just five or ten minutes, and increase the amount

over time. Twenty minutes a day or more is ideal. It takes some time to warm up and energize our depressed and suppressed self. I suggest you do your practice at the same time each day. This creates anticipation and brings a powerful new rhythm into your life. And do what you've chosen for a period of time. Six weeks of daily practice is good for an initial experiment.

6 Don't do an active expressive practice, such as shaking or Dynamic Meditation or dancing, just before you want to sleep. It really is stimulating. And if you want to do active and quiet practices together, start with the active one and afterward relax into the quiet one.

7 You may well go through some resistance at the beginning (and probably later, too), as well as spells of boredom or rage against the technique and the fool who suggested it, and, perhaps, against all the fools in your life, and even the biggest fool—yourself. That's, as they say, all part of the process. Give yourself a chance to work with the practice, and give the practice a chance to work on you.

8 The expressive techniques are powerful. Before they free us from what constrains us, they may well bring up disturbing, long-buried memories. If you're going to use these techniques, and particularly Dynamic Meditation, I suggest you have available, at least as you start out, someone who understands the power of these approaches and can help you deal with feelings that may come up—a Guide or a teacher. At The Center for Mind-Body Medicine, we've trained many people to be there for you, and there are many others who can help at the meditation centers listed in the Resources section.

9 Give yourself time to relax at the end of your expressive meditation. (This is what I suggested that Theresa do after yoga, on her first visit to me.) This is a time when you feel the effects of what you've done, when your body can experience its freedom, and your mind can enjoy some uncluttered moments. It's wonderful to dance and then do a quiet practice such as a sitting meditation, or to go for a walk, or to just lie down. This stillness after effort is quite

different from the inertia of depression. As Lao-tzu and Milton, the mechanic, might observe, movement has created stillness, and this stillness becomes the source of a new, authentic movement.

10 If your practice seems to be helping you to move into the current of your life, keep on with it. If after a period of time it no longer helps you to feel more energetic, or it stops bringing up thoughts and feelings you need to experience, or it doesn't help you let go of defenses that have constrained you or be a little freer, drop it—and see if there is another that feels right for you now. A Buddhist cautionary tale tells us that we shouldn't carry the boat on our back after we've crossed the river.

SUMMING UP: SOME NOTES ON SURRENDER

>> Surrender can come anytime. Remember Milton.

>> Surrender is completely different from giving up. Surrendering, we move into life's current. Giving up, we slide under it.

>> Surrendering usually requires action. The energy we invest is repaid many times over by the new energy we feel.

>> Exercise is the action the body craves. Many simple forms of exercise will work. Choose one that feels right for you. Consider joining a class.

>> Expressive meditations are ancient and powerful ways to raise our energy level and invite and promote surrender.

>> When we use expressive meditations to put energy into our stuck selves, old patterns begin to break up. This is natural and healthy.

>> With the breakup of old patterns, buried feelings can emerge, new possibilities appear. Often you'll see familiar thoughts and behavior in a different perspective, or as if for the first time. As you go through this process, consult your Guide as you need to.

YOUR PRESCRIPTION FOR SELF-CARE:

Surrender to Change: Recording Your Experience

What follows is a simple protocol for keeping track of what you're doing to open the door to surrender—for recording the active technique you're using and what happens as you do it. Writing down what happens will help you appreciate what you're learning and how you're changing.

I suggest you divide this into four sections.

1 The date and technique you're using and how long you used it for.
2 Why you chose this technique.
3 What happened before, during, and afterward.
4 Any interesting experiences and/or benefits during the rest of the day.

Here's an example:

Pam is a thirty-eight-year-old nurse, neatly, primly dressed, who has been "depressed all my life . . . and sometimes suicidal, too," and on and off antidepressants since adolescence. She loves her husband and his son by a previous marriage. She enjoys being a nurse, but not the mismanagement and time pressure of the clinic in which she's working. She describes herself as "obsessive compulsive" about her work, her demanding mother, and her husband's son, and "colossally guilty" over minor offenses she may have given—to patients and friends, coworkers and her husband. She came to see me for help with migraine headaches as well as depression, and was taking antidepressants when I prescribed shaking and dancing for her.

Here's Pam's record:

1 Day and technique: Oct. 30, 2005; shaking and dancing; 10 minutes each.

2 Why: You suggested I do it, and it's been helping to improve my mood and get rid of my anxiety and migraines. It's also loosened up the tightness in my back and shoulders.

3 What happened today: I felt cranky and down before I started. Resentful toward the doc who runs my clinic. I had a headache. It was like a hangover, but I hadn't drunk anything last night. Then I started shaking. After a few minutes, I felt the tension leaving my body. My head got a little clearer. Then I was enjoying myself, feeling like a kid, remembering, from that swamp of my childhood, some happy times outdoors with my dad. Then I felt strong and started having some sexual feelings—that was nice. For the dancing, I used Carly Simon's "You're So Vain." That was really good. I danced out my anger at my mother and my boss. Afterward, I had a nice long shower and went to work.

4 The day's experience: I saw so clearly the difference between the work I do and the patients, who I love, and the stupidity of the clinic director and the setup there. Every time I looked at my boss, instead of feeling anxious or angry, I started to crack up. He's such a jerk! I realized I have to get out. And yet, even though I know I have to leave, I was still able to relax with all my patients, to really enjoy them. Time seemed to pass so easily. No back or neck pain or headache all day. I'm looking forward to seeing my husband tonight.

You can use this protocol to write in your journal about your own experience with these expressive techniques.

CHAPTER 4

Dealing with Demons

All of us have ways of thinking, feeling, and being that inhibit and constrain us, difficulties we avoid, and addictive, self-defeating habits that fuel our avoidance. Borrowing from Buddhist psychology, I call these patterns "demons." They may contribute in significant ways to our chronic, low-grade dissatisfaction and unhappiness. As you move forward on your journey through depression, demons can rise to confront and challenge you with painful, frightening force.

In this chapter, I'll focus on some of the demons that are most likely to disturb or even disable you, including procrastination, guilt, pride, perfectionism, loneliness, lethargy, and resentment. I'll begin by showing you how April dealt successfully with several demons that had scared and inhibited her since childhood and how she was able to make their daunting power her own and move ahead on her journey more easily and confidently. Afterward, in the heart of this chapter, I offer simple strategies and practical techniques for learning from and dealing with the demons that most trouble each of you, and for making their strength your own. Finally, I conclude with a section on how you can use Traditional Chinese Medicine—acupuncture and herbal therapies—to drain your demons of their power and balance the emotional and physical functions they have disrupted.

DEMON AND DAIMON

The origin of the English word *demon* in the Greek *daimon* gives us the clue we need to understand how to heal ourselves. In ancient Greece it was understood that the daimon was a guide who was both eternal and internal. Plato, in *The Republic,* called the daimon "a divinity" who served each soul; the "guardian" of the soul's life and the "fulfiller" of the choices that soul made when it came into the world. The daimon was also the guiding principle of each individual's life, the source to which you referred in times of trouble and confusion.

The divinity and distinction of the daimon were understood and appreciated well into the nineteenth century. Long before then, however, daimon had generally come to be spelled "demon," and its meaning was all but universally understood in another way. A demon was an evil spirit, manifesting malevolent thoughts and cruel behavior.

The decline and disappearance of the daimon, and its absorption by the demon, represents a turning away from a powerful truth of human life. It's certainly true that some people seem possessed by cruelty—demonic in the modern Judeo-Christian sense of the word. But by focusing only on these terrible exceptions, we have broken contact with the daimon, the sometimes terrifying, but ultimately life-enhancing, life-enriching force that can guide and give meaning and fulfillment to each of us.

Modern biological psychiatry regards the intimidating patterns and terrors of depression not as demons, but as symptoms of a disease. It responds with attempts to mute, deny, and obliterate these symptoms using drugs to take the edge off sufferers' pain, quiet their fears, deny their doubts, and focus them elsewhere. This is understandable but short-sighted and often proves counterproductive, even destructive. Demons denied will keep returning, often with heightened fury. And, by trying to suppress them, we also lose the wisdom they bear.

It is my experience—and one of the fundamental insights of both the modern depth psychology of Freud and Jung and the ancient wisdom of

Buddhism—that the demons that terrify us are those parts of ourselves, of our history, and of life that we have feared, hated, and denied. To heal and become whole, we need to confront, acknowledge, and accept the demons, and to take back the power we have yielded to them. If we are willing to endure the pain of meeting these demons, we will discover the daimons that will show us who we really are, and we will learn how we are meant to live our lives.

Tying Ourselves to the Mast of Mindfulness: A Lesson from *The Odyssey*

We must all find ways to deal with and learn from the demons that will inevitably confront us and to discover our daimons in them. Kirke, the enchantress who becomes one of his Guides, gives Odysseus advice that can benefit us all. Early on the course of his journey toward home, she says to him that he will meet "Seirenes, crying / beauty to bewitch men coasting by. . . . singing [the] mind" of men away, luring them to their death. She tells Odysseus to "plug your oarsmen's ears," but advises him that he may listen, if first his men tie him to the ship's mast.

In gazing on and listening to these beautiful, flattering, seductive, indeed irresistible, demons, Odysseus is opening himself to danger and, most particularly, to the pull of flattery and ease, to promises that will never be fulfilled. At the same time, he is holding fast to his purpose and, quite literally, to the ship that is bringing him to his destiny.

We also have the choice to listen and be steadfast, to act and be aware, and to not react. This is the best posture for confronting, learning from, and taking on the power of all the forces that would constrain, undermine, and depress us. This is the first step in making our demons serve our daimon. The equipment we need, our rope and mast, are the meditation techniques that promote awareness or, as it is sometimes called, mindfulness.

Awareness or mindfulness meditations are the hallmark of the South Asian *vipassana* Buddhist tradition. The practices are also very much a part of Tibetan Buddhism and Japanese Zen and are now used in many

Christian monasteries and nondenominational retreats, workshops, and classes. They are also, with increasing frequency, being combined with a variety of psychotherapeutic approaches to depression, including cognitive behavioral therapy.

I'm going to share with you techniques that you can begin to use immediately. You can learn more about mindfulness and other meditations in classes offered by a variety of traditions (there is some information on them in the Resources section) and from books: My favorites are *The Miracle of Mindfulness* by the Vietnamese Buddhist monk Thich Nhat Hanh and *Zen Mind, Beginner's Mind* by the Japanese Zen teacher Suzuki Roshi.

What follows are two awareness techniques. One is done as a sitting meditation, the other while walking.

AWARENESS MEDITATION

Sitting Meditation

Sit comfortably in a chair. Let your arms rest on the arms of the chair or in your lap. Begin breathing in and out through your nose. You can allow your eyes to close, or keep them slightly open but "soft" and unfocused on a blank wall or out into the middle distance.

Breathe slowly, this time in and out through your nose, noticing the breath as it passes in and out of your nostrils.

Let your attention fall lightly on each thought, feeling, and sensation as it comes, and then on the next. Let them come, let them go. Remember, these are *just* thoughts, feelings, and sensations.

By practicing awareness, you are cultivating, nourishing, and strengthening the observer, or "witness," in yourself, gradually freeing yourself from the hold these thoughts and feelings—most particularly, depressing and obsessive ones—have over you.

Little by little, you'll grow accustomed to the variety of thoughts, feelings, and sensations that arise—to ones that are troubling, puzzling, annoying, and embarrassing, as well as intriguing, satisfying, funny, and uplifting.

You may want to start this practice by doing it for 5 to 10 minutes at a time; twice a day would be good. Gradually extend the periods to 20 to 30 minutes, if you'd like. Use a timer: That way you have one less thing to think about.

I encourage you, as you continue to relax and become aware, to have compassion for the ordinary, confused, conflicted, and peculiar thoughts and feelings that you have. If you talk with others who are doing this practice, you'll find that yours are more or less the same as everyone else's. Relax.

Walking Meditation

Walking meditation is a wonderful complement, or alternative, to sitting. Here is the way I suggest doing it.

Set aside a period of time to walk, perhaps 20 minutes at first. You can bring your timer if it's not too big; otherwise just glance every once in a while at your watch.

Leave all the things that you don't absolutely need—your pocketbook or briefcase or extra clothing—in your home or office. Outside, walk *slowly,* at about a third your normal pace, maintaining silence. (Here keeping your eyes closed is not an option.)

Breathe in and out through your nose. Be aware of the breath as it passes in and out of your nostrils. Continue walking slowly.

Notice everything you see or feel, smell or hear, as well as everything that comes into your mind. As you notice, name the thought, feeling, or sensation to yourself. You may find yourself saying something such as "Breath in right nostril . . . tickle in left eyebrow . . . How long is this going to last? . . . seeing tree bark. . . . feeling roughness under my fingers . . . air around my face . . . Is that woman looking at me? . . . Boy, I'm paranoid . . . Isn't this funny? . . . arms swaying . . . sun over that building . . . How much longer is this going to last?" and so forth.

You may find that walking meditation is a little easier than sitting meditation and more fun, and that you can more easily do it for a longer time.

Walking meditation is not only a wonderful way to develop awareness and to learn to witness your own thoughts, feelings, and sensations, it's also a powerful way to appreciate your surroundings more fully. When I do this exercise with Georgetown University medical students, they're astonished by how much more they see of a campus that they have walked through every day and how much they have previously ignored—"Was that statue there a week ago?" they ask—and by how much more pleasure they now find in this familiar walk.

We can develop mindfulness in any situation, but it's easier in the beginning to set aside a specific time and place to do sitting or walking with awareness. After a while, you'll find yourself mindful in more of the activities of daily life. You'll also be more mindful when the demons, the disturbing thoughts and feelings that so often accompany depression, loom on your horizon or threaten to swallow you up. Then it will be easier to watch your fears and learn from them.

LEARNING FROM THE DEMONS THAT APPEAR

Recognizing and accepting the fear that our demons provoke is a necessary beginning. Everyone, even the greatest heroes among us, has this fear in some measure. In depression it looms far larger. In denying the existence of fear, we are denying a part of ourselves, removing ourselves ever further from a reality we do not want to admit or see. In fighting against fear, we actually perpetuate its power.

The way to free ourselves from the demons we fear is, paradoxically, to get to know them, as Odysseus did: to sit with them, to breathe slowly in and out, to watch them with interest, as they reveal our daimon to us. Then it's possible to take on their strength, to move past them. As we discuss the individual demons that each of us has to face, you'll soon see how this can happen for you.

I was once in a discussion with Ram Dass, the Harvard-trained psychologist and spiritual teacher. Someone asked him about his "neuroses." He said that he still had the same ones that he had had thirty-five years earlier, when after years of psychotherapy and psychoanalysis, he began to meditate. Now, though, they were very different.

Then they were huge, overwhelming, man-eating monsters. Now they were like "shmoos," the harmless, bouncy, bowling-pin-shaped creatures created by *Li'l Abner* cartoonist Al Capp. Instead of fleeing from them when he noticed them, Ram Dass would "invite them," as if they were old friends, "over for tea."

Like Ram Dass, we need to learn that our problems, our demons, can be our friends, our teachers, and our Guides. If we find ourselves being afraid of loneliness, that may be just the time for us to be alone, to sit with our fear of loneliness, to have a discussion with it, to ask why it is arising at this moment. The same is true if we're procrastinating—putting off an important but stressful meeting or decision or task—or feeling fear about an impending loss. The key here is to meet the demon and treat it with the respect you would offer a friend, to move into communication, even communion, with it.

APRIL'S ENCOUNTER

Though mindfulness makes the meeting, the acceptance, and the communion far easier, we often need other approaches to uncover the daimon that our most terrifying personal demons conceal. What follows is a story about how April and I worked together to drain her demons of their power and restore it to her. As you'll see, we used mental imagery to bring her fears of inadequacy, change, uncertainty, and failure into the room with us, to help her relax into a conversation with them. This marked a turning point in her depression and in her life. At the end of this section, I'll give you a technique that you can use, on your own, that will help you to accomplish the same goal.

One evening, almost a year after I began to see her, April, who normally greeted me warmly, stomped into my office.

For the previous two months, she'd been trying to extricate herself from a relationship that was, if not inappropriate, still unsatisfying. She went on for a while about her dependency on Joe and his neediness, but there was no passion in her words. I felt something else was troubling her, scaring her more, and said so.

April first got angry at me for doubting her. Then she smiled. It was true. Neither Joe nor any other guy, for that matter, was really on her mind.

April was hating her secure, status-rich job more and more each day, but she was terrified of thinking about what kind of work she might really want to do. When she allowed herself to consider it, all she could think of was teaching economics in a high school or going back to graduate school in economics, to prepare to be a professor. But, every time a friend offered to help her look at one or the other of these possibilities, she found herself breathing fast and sweating up an anxious storm.

Now, April crossed her arms, slid down in her chair, and proceeded to pout. "I am not," she announced, "talking any more today. I don't feel like it." We sat in silence for a while, she recoiling and seething, and I thinking of appropriate "therapeutic" questions. All of my ideas seemed awkward and irrelevant, so I allowed myself to breathe deeply and relax, and slowly drift into April's world.

"How old are you?" I asked, feeling in that moment that I was speaking not to the thoughtful, lovely young woman in a business suit, but to the angry and disappointed little girl who still lived in her.

"I'm six," she said, looking and sounding very much like it. "And that's all I'm saying."

"What's the matter?"

"I don't know. You don't want to know."

"Could you close your eyes for a minute and look?" I asked, believing that imagery would allow her to gaze in her mind's eye at the demon that was terrifying her.

April closed her eyes. She began to squirm in her seat, breathing fast.

"What do you see?"

"My mother. She's very angry, and disapproving. She's standing over me and she's as big as a house."

April saw herself as a small girl in a yellow rain slicker, frightened, alone, and angry, standing at the front door of her childhood home.

"I hated that coat," she said, her eyes squeezed closed. "And I hated it most of all," she added, "because I wanted another coat so badly."

"What was *that* coat like?' I asked.

Now, she smiled, and her face softened. "It was a purple cloth coat. It was so beautiful and so special."

April had asked for it and her mother had "looked at me like there was something wrong with me. She said it was 'impractical' and 'too expensive' "—April bites off these words—"and that I would have to 'settle' for the same slicker my brother and sister had."

She felt her mother never cared about what she wanted or who she was. All she really wanted, it seemed to April, was to have her daughter obey her and, later, after her father left the marriage, to have April take care of *her*.

April sees herself—the images are flashing behind her closed eyes—as "always frightened." She sees—remembers, really—a little girl waiting for disapproval and disappointment; a teenager stumbling in sports, embarrassed to bring friends home to the bad smell and disorder of her depressed mother's house.

Now April is seeing herself in college, bewildered about choosing a major. On graduation day, there are question marks over her head and in her eyes. How will she ever support herself? She is quiet for a few moments.

"Where are you now?"

"Back with my mother. She's so close and so big. Her voice is so loud. It's like she's scolding and moaning, 'You can't have that coat. Who do you think you are?'"

April starts to cry. They're tight little tears.

"Talk to your mother," I say. "Tell her you want that purple coat, that you love it and will take good care of it."

"She still won't let me have it. She says the yellow slicker is 'good enough' for me." April is really crying.

"Tell her you're grown up now, that you've given her what you could, that now it's time for you to have that purple coat. Say it out loud, please."

And April does, sitting straighter now, speaking softly, through the tears.

"Louder!"

She repeats the words, her voice cracking a little but definitely louder.

"My mother looks so angry. She's angry that I'm talking back to her."

"Speak louder," I urge, speaking pretty loud myself. "Tell her that you're speaking for yourself. Then, when you were six, she could tell you what coat to buy and make you wear it. Now, it's *your* choice, *your* decision."

"It's my choice," says April, her voice deeper, more resonant. "I want"—she's shouting now—"that purple coat!"

April pauses, and shakes her head with disbelief. A smile widens and sweetens her face. "My mother's the same size I am now. And I'm wearing the purple coat and she's wearing the yellow slicker." April is laughing. "And now—this is getting a little ridiculous—she's getting smaller, melting like the wicked witch in *The Wizard of Oz*. I'm certainly not afraid of her, and I don't hate her now."

"How *do* you feel?"

"I feel really pretty in my purple coat, and very pleased with myself."

Mental imagery allowed April to give dramatic form to the demons of fear and shame, unworthiness and helplessness, that had constricted her childhood and still shaped her thoughts and feelings. With guidance and support, April's images transformed. The overwhelming, disapproving mother who had made her feel powerless shrank in size and volume. The fearful, previously silenced, self-protective child spoke up. April began to discover her daimon, the power to define her own life.

This wasn't the end of April's confrontations with her demons or the fulfillment of her alliance with her daimon. It was, however, a powerful-enough glimpse and experience that the course of her life began to shift. Her imagined experience had allowed her to see that she was strong enough to confront what had for so long intimidated her. During this confrontation, April's power grew and that of the demons diminished: Indeed, it looked and felt to her as if she were reclaiming the power she had previously given to them.

April began to make major, real-life changes. Each time she took one step, the next came more easily. April told Joe, without defensiveness or fear, that their romance was over. Next, she used the Inner Guide imagery to ask herself whether she wanted to teach or go back to graduate school in economics. When the answer came back a resounding "Are you kidding?" she was at first dumbfounded, and then delighted. It was no wonder, she realized, that she hadn't been able to make a decision. Neither one was a choice she wanted. Both were yellow slickers. April was relieved for a few days, then panicky.

This is not uncommon. Though demons terrify us, they are familiar and give a certain structure, and clear limitations, to our lives. As we begin to see and relax with them, to find ways to bring their strength into our being, they fade, like April's mother. And, without them, we may feel lost and frightened.

As a child, April had grudgingly allowed her mother to direct her decisions. As she grew older and left home for college, she came to dread both decision making and the anxiety of not knowing what to do. She'd put off many choices and left responsibilities unfulfilled. When she graduated, April became even more anxious. Her depression deepened. She'd internalized her father's worries about her financial survival as well as her mother's dim view of her worthiness and competence. She grabbed the first good-paying job that came along and suffered through its requirements.

Now, April knew she would have to leave the hated job. But she didn't have a clue what she would do, or how she could possibly make a living. How, her anxious mind skittered on, can I keep my apartment? Stay off the street? She had images of herself as homeless and disheveled, a twenty-something bag lady.

I suggested to April that while she prepared for work that really mattered, she could always take a temporary job to make money—for example, be a waitress. April looked at me as if I'd slapped her. She couldn't do that, she said. "I'm a professional person. That's such a cliché, such a—" She didn't really know what.

Was it worse than being utterly miserable, I wondered, feeling like a fraud in her present job, or worrying about being homeless if she left it? Waiting tables was real work. She could probably make a pretty good living at it. It was also a time-out for her, not a career, while she made up her mind about what she really wanted to do. April started laughing, first at my earnest pleading, then at herself.

Just considering being a waitress liberated April from the frustration and distress of trying to choose between unappealing alternatives. She decided to do it because it suited *her* needs right now. Once she'd made the decision, experienced her own autonomy, she could see, for the first time, other possibilities for her future, and other things she might really want to do, right now, just to please herself. She'd been asked to teach a yoga class, and she enjoyed that—it seemed to her "a hell of a lot more relevant and fun" than teaching economics. Maybe she would take a psychology course and a drawing class. She loved to draw and hadn't since she was a kid. And psychology—who knew? She'd certainly spent a lot of her adult life thinking about her own problems.

CREATING YOUR OWN DIALOGUE WITH A DEMON

I guided April in working with images that came spontaneously to her. A few words from me: "How old are you?" "Who else is there?" got her started. And some coaching—"What's happening now?" "Tell her how you feel. . . ." "Louder!"—made it possible for her to explore, experience, and transform her encounter with her demons; to begin to discover her daimon, her own sense of self-worth and purpose. Then she was ready to move ahead with her life, on her journey out of depression.

You can do a similar kind of exploration on your own, using the power of words and images to tap into your unconscious wisdom; to find guidance in moving you ahead on your life's journey. I call the techniques that make this possible a dialogue with a symptom, problem, or issue (SPI). I love this technique—and so do my patients and students, as well as the professionals who come to The Center for Mind-Body Medicine's trainings—and I use it often.

Here's how you do it.

DIALOGUE WITH AN SPI

Think of a symptom, problem, or issue that's troubling you, or one that you'd like to learn more about. It could be the way you're feeling (a sense of hopelessness or fear, loneliness or confusion) or a physical symptom (pain, limitation of motion, an upset stomach), or a problem, such as a craving for food or alcohol or a lack of appetite. Or it could be an issue in your life—difficulty in a relationship, an inability to get started on a project, etc.

It's good to pick an SPI that's front and center for you and to be as specific as possible. The angry April who appeared in my office might have chosen to have her dialogue with "not wanting to talk" or "feeling like a little girl." Dorothy could have picked "breast cancer" or "my fear of leaving Todd." Theresa might have gone with "hopelessness," "fear of not having a family," or, on a bad morning, "my hangover." "Anger at my son" would have been useful for Milton.

Write down a letter to denote the SPI and one that stands for you. For example, one of my patients had a stiff and painful jaw and neck that had resisted his doctors' efforts at diagnosis and treatment. He labeled it "P." His name was David so he was "D."

Once you've identified the SPI and given it an initial, you imagine that this symptom, problem, or issue is sitting across from you in a chair, and that you're about to have a dialogue with it. You close your eyes and take a few deep breaths. When you open your eyes, you let the dialogue unfold and you begin writing.

Usually you'll begin by asking a question. In David's case, D posed the question. Then his pain and stiffness (P) responded. The dialogue goes back and forth as quickly as possible. Here are David's first four entries.

D: What are you doing here?
P: I'm here to remind you.
D: I know, I can't forget you. But of what?
P: Of how stiff you are.

As you go on, the contours of your demon may become clearer, your feelings sharper. David discovered he was filled with suppressed rage.

D: I want the pain to go away.
P: How?
D: Maybe if I open my mouth like this. No, it hurts more.
P: What do you want to say?
D: It's not words. I want to scream! But I'm embarrassed. I don't do screaming.
P: Who doesn't scream?
D: Me. I'm a reasonable man. I'm a businessman, a good citizen, my father's son.
P: Aha! Would you rather be a good citizen with a horrible pain

in the neck, a good boy? Or a guy who screams a little and feels
better?

D: I see what you mean.

P: So go ahead and scream.

Your demon may well help you discover your daimon. In fact,
David's SPI offered a prescription that could help free him from his
anger, dissolve and transform the pain and constriction in his neck,
and put him in touch with the daimon that is his birthright—
self-expression, flexibility, movement, courage, change.

D: I'm screaming at my father now. I hate you!

P: Yes, yes. Keep going.

D: You're so goddamned mean! Why did you try to shut me up? I
was just a kid! Now I'm screaming some more.

P: How does that feel?

D: Better. I can turn my head a little more. And I'm moving my
shoulder now. I'm rotating it back and forth and making
punching motions with my arm. What now?

P: What do you think?

D: Maybe I should do this every day. Maybe I should punch a bag,
too, while I scream.

P: Sounds like an idea.

Trust your intuition and imagination as David did. Let the Zen
motto "First thought, best thought," guide you. Understand that
your symptom, problem, or issue, your demon, may act like a bold,
even sarcastic and confrontational therapist. Don't censor yourself.
Write as fast as you can, and continue for about ten minutes, or
until you come to a natural stopping place.

Time after time, our SPI tells us, as it did David, what we need
to know about why it's there and what function it has in our lives.

Even more important, our SPI also tells us what steps to take to deal with it. In other words, our demon—our large or small SPI—gives us guidance in discovering our daimon.

Many people begin this exercise feeling depleted but find that it gives them energy as well as understanding. It's fast paced and surprising, and often irreverent and funny. And it can be repeated as often as several times a week with the same or different SPI.

If the dialogue with your SPI doesn't feel satisfying, if you don't get the kind of clear guidance that David did, that's OK. Sometimes it takes several dialogues before your inner wisdom helps you find the purpose in the pain, the daimon that your demon has been concealing.

Everyday Demons

When the order of our lives is undermined by sudden loss or illness, undeniable pain, or impending disaster, our demons may become obvious and inescapable: Theresa's self-blame, Milton's resentment, Dorothy's procrastination.

In the fog of the low-level distress in which many of us live, our demons, like April's uncertainties and fears, are harder to discern, easier to rationalize. We may be insecure or envious, indecisive or irritable or lethargic, but who, we ask ourselves, is not? There are good reasons, we tell ourselves—accidents of family or fate—for how we are, for not taking the next steps in our lives. Perhaps there are others who are responsible, circumstances beyond our control.

If we are to free ourselves from these everyday demons, which unconsciously rule and limit our lives and make us anxious and depressed, we first need to acknowledge them. Then, like April or David, we can enter into creative dialogue with them.

If we look clearly at resentment, for example, a demon that is all too easily ignored or rationalized, we can see it for what it is—a suppressed, festering rage—and listen to what it tells us. Knowing and accepting that the anger that fueled his resentment is simply a feeling that comes and goes, Milton began to watch the mask of resentment dissolve, to discover the daimon of compassion.

And so it can go with all the ordinary, disturbing, threatening demons I describe below. Tied to the mast of awareness, you can begin to know and discover them, relax with them, and accept them as part of yourself. Seeing and experiencing their power in ways that I'll describe to you, you can learn the lessons they have to teach. And as you learn that you, like April and David, can take on their power, they loosen their hold on you. Then, awareness, coupled with the simple, effective strategies given in this section, can help you find, behind the demons' masks, the daimon's fair face.

PROCRASTINATION

I'm putting this demon of delay first, for the obvious reason.

If procrastination is holding sway, you're likely to bargain, protest, and plead, "I don't have to do it now, do I?" "Maybe it"—the need to make the call or clean the house or say what we are avoiding—"will go away." As procrastination's influence spreads, every "I have to" bumps into "I can't." Eventually, procrastination may be there in your first morning thoughts, at your desk at work, and on the couch with you in the evening. It can wake you, sweating, at night. Many depressed people describe procrastination as the most disabling and disturbing of their symptoms.

Procrastination may come from fear of being rejected for what you want or need to do or say, or from fear of succeeding or of failing. But understanding procrastination's origins, though helpful, does not dispel the demon. In fact, many people use the need for more understanding as yet another reason for putting off doing or saying what they need to.

It's often useful to begin by asking what you gain and lose from procrastinating, and writing down the answers to these questions in two columns. If you are a procrastinator, you might want to take some time now to make these lists in your journal. Begin by asking yourself what you're putting off now that you need to do. Make two columns as I've done below. Now take a few minutes to do Soft Belly. Then open your eyes and make your lists.

**GAINS AND LOSSES FROM DELAYING OR AVOIDING
WHAT YOU NEED TO DO**

GAINS	LOSSES
1.	1.
2.	2.
3.	3.
4.	4.
5.	5.

The losses column usually turns out to be longer and the cumulative pain caused by procrastination far greater than the results of actions taken. This doesn't solve the problem, but it will help you understand, even when you are in the grip of this demon, that the difficult conversation or project will likely take far less toll on you than weeks of anticipatory worry. You may even remember, as you do this exercise, that you previously discovered that conversations you thought would be so difficult weren't, or that even if they were, you felt better after you had them.

Writing down your losses and gains, you'll likely remember the damage you've done with procrastination in the past. This may increase your pain, but heighten the pressure you feel to move ahead. That may actually be a good thing: Until Dorothy felt utterly miserable and frustrated, she was unwilling to act.

Delaying necessary interpersonal confrontations is a form of procrastination in which almost every depressed person participates. Delay magnifies the original distress manifold. As time passes, and you devote more energy to ignoring or forgetting or rationalizing your avoidance, your anxiety about confrontation is likely to increase, and often, with it, your sense of outrage. You may feel more alienated from the person with whom there's conflict, worse, and, yes, more depressed, about your fearfulness, and angrier at the other person as well as yourself.

If you stay as aware and relaxed as you can, and express your displeasure at someone else's behavior or acknowledge his distress with you, you step beyond the barriers to action you've created, and will likely discover the quiet strength of self-assertion, the daimon concealed by the demon of procrastination. Feeling free of the burden of bad feeling and self-blame that you've been carrying around, expressing yourself, frees you from the current impasse. It also sets an example for your antagonist. Sometimes, he, too, wants to move beyond resentment, fear, and avoidance to a more honest and productive, even a more intimate relationship.

Acting When You Feel Least Able

"That's fine," I hear some of you saying, "if you're just putting off some phone calls or a particular project, or even a difficult confrontation. But what if my whole life is a mess and my procrastination is serious and seriously obsessive?" What if, like Maria, a thirty-year old bookkeeper who's been out of work for months, you produce dozens of iterations of a résumé and still, overwhelmed by anxiety about its adequacy and your prospective employer's response, you can't bring yourself to send it out? Or if, like another patient of mine, Darla, you're accumulating thousands of pages of research—and no finished papers—while your graduate school record gathers incompletes? Or if you find yourself immobilized in the kitchen of your studio apartment, watching your dishes pile up in the sink and spread across the counter, while the trash overflows on the floor?

For those of you who feel utterly disabled by procrastination, active, physical techniques—movement—are often a starting place. They can help pry you loose from where you're stuck. Walking every day, you begin, quite literally, to walk off the anxiety that immobilizes and constrains you. There's a sense of purpose in it, too, one that's antithetical to procrastination. And walking—like running or swimming or yoga or martial arts—acts directly to decrease the physiological and biochemical components of your stress and anxiety, and to elevate your mood. After long, hard months of struggling with the fears that made her procrastination so stubborn—and going on and off antidepressants and stimulants—Maria decided to jog. Her forty minutes a day soon became her "salvation," her prime source of good feeling and hope, the engine that helped her overcome her procrastination.

All the active approaches help you, on a physical level, to overcome your inertia and the sense of victimization that it produces in you. And your body's movement provides the model for movement in your life. Shaking and dancing—Darla ultimately did this—is particularly useful. It breaks up fixed patterns, of which procrastination is very definitely one, and gives you an opportunity to express yourself physically in a new and different way—decreasing anxiety, increasing energy.

For best results, take some time for movement every day, and also every time you feel yourself putting off what you know you need to do. If you keep using these techniques, and repeating them as often as you need to, after some days or weeks, you'll likely feel relaxed and energized enough to take the next step.

At a certain point, we do *have* to act: belly up to the sink to tackle those dishes. There may be trembling at first, maybe even terror, as if an even tighter confinement were imminent. But the rewards of doing what we've put off are palpable, and the feedback immediate. After you finally do act, your breath may come more easily. There may be more space inside your chest, a swing in your arms. Feel free to congratulate yourself, pump your fist, or high-five yourself in the mirror. Later, if you begin to procrastinate again, remember the pleasure of success. It will likely give you energy to do what you're once again resisting.

If you still can't do the task you're putting off, you can, in any case, use your anxiety and your desperation as an engine to propel you forward. Do something else that's also useful or something similar to what you're avoiding. Call a friend who's easy to talk to instead of the boss or lover you're avoiding. If you can't start on the paper that's due, begin with some words in a journal. Darla, who couldn't bring herself to write academic papers that would advance her career, took a summer off from graduate school and enrolled and happily participated in a creative writing class at a community center. After a couple of weeks of jogging, Maria got up the courage to ask a friend for help; together, they finished her résumé and sent it off. Action will melt the inertia that freezes you in procrastination. And action begets more action.

Humor can also be helpful. The punch line of the story I told Dorothy, "We're waiting for the children to grow up and die," is a good example. But so are small comments we can make to ourselves and images we can conjure up. One of my patients who endlessly put off dealing with his employees' poor performance imagined himself on the end of a diving board. He saw himself wobbling ridiculously as he postponed inevitable discussions with them and knew that his scared squirming was far more risky than jumping or even diving into the necessary confrontation.

It's helpful, too, to know that others have similar problems. The knowledge of this company can reduce the self-condemnation that we pile on top of procrastination. And knowing we have very distinguished company may be particularly comforting.

Some years ago, I heard a story about Truman Capote that has helped me deal with my tendency to put off writing papers, reports, letters, and books. I like the story so much because it always seemed to me that writing came easily to Capote, and had from such an early age.

In an interview at the height of his career, he was asked what the most difficult part of his craft was.

"Beginning," he said.

"You mean, Mr. Capote, a new book or story?"

"No," Capote answered. "Beginning every day."

Now, when I feel unable to work on an article or book, I just start by writing anything that comes to mind. Half of it, sometimes all of it, may be completely unusable. But the act of writing, even if the words are self-indulgent, unclear, and ungrammatical, gives me a certain satisfaction. I'm doing what I had feared and avoided. Even ugly or silly words help push open the door so that in time something more satisfying can emerge.

GUILT AND PRIDE

It took me some time to understand that guilt and pride are demons that go hand in hand. They seem an unlikely couple.

Guilt is such a prominent and pervasive part of depression; it looms so large in the thoughts and self-deprecating conversations of depressed people. Pride seems, by contrast, irrelevant or peripheral to the boldface type in which guilt appears in the clinical descriptions and how it manifests in the minds of depressed people. Still, over time I've learned that if I help my patients focus on and accept pride, guilt's controlling force and conviction slowly dissolve.

When you're depressed, you probably have a hard time thinking of yourself as proud. No, you may protest. I'm worthless, useless. I'm not the best or brightest, but the worst, the lowest, the dimmest. I've done and said terrible things, hurt those I love. And besides, all the textbooks, all the doctors, say that we depressed people have poor, or nonexistent, self-esteem.

But, I say, when you're depressed, you often take a certain grim satisfaction—and yes, pride—in your helplessness and hopelessness, in the terrible ways you've behaved and the destructive things you've done. In fact, if you look closely at how you think about yourself, you can see that your guilt and your apparent helplessness may barely conceal feelings of omnipotence. You believe that your every thought and action have been powerful and are powerfully damaging "It was this one act, or these words, that turned her irrevocably against me—ruined our marriage." "That piece of bad judgment doomed my career." "I'm responsible for every ill that has befallen me."

It's usually impossible to argue or charm depressed people out of their guilt. Any attempt at logic or praise or a more balanced point of view may only incite greater conviction and more protests: "You don't really know," the guilty, depressed person says or thinks, "how bad I am, how much harm I've done, and how irrevocable it is."

Though stubborn and firmly protective, guilt's consort, pride, is more accessible. Instead of taking on his guilt directly, I may ask someone to put into words his most terrible thoughts about himself, to make the specific self-accusations: I'll ask him to hear what they sound like, to say them in front of a mirror, or to see what they look like on the pages of a journal.

You can do this yourself. Your accusations may sound and, especially, look a bit extreme, almost as if you are boasting—proud—of the behavior and thoughts that make you feel guilty.

If, after expressing yourself, you're still preoccupied with how bad you really are, you can overcome your embarrassment, summon up your courage, and ask your Guide or a good friend, "Do you think I'm the most loathsome person you know?" Asking the question out loud and hearing the ordinary, commonsense answer that follows may highlight its absurdity and will likely drain your pride—and with it your guilt—of some of its poison.

Regular meditation—the rope tying us to the mast of awareness— will also give you perspective on your pride and on the guilt that goes with it. "Here I am," you may observe, "thinking, declaring once again, that I am the *most worthless*. That I've *always* done the *wrong* thing." As you hear yourself for the tenth or hundredth time, it's enough to make you doubt and wonder, maybe even laugh.

Putting Pride in Perspective

Perspective is crucial to dealing with pride and, indeed, the other demons as well. If you see yourself clearly, you help to dispel the depression-heavy clouds of prideful delusion.

This is, in part, a cognitive approach. But it also requires emotional acceptance and a kind of spiritual exertion. In depression, our pride engorges us with adverbs, such as *most,* and depletes us with adjectives— *selfish, unworthy, miserable.*

If you're willing to see that you've not just been mistaken but also prideful, you may discover that you have been invested in a guilt-laden misery that you've dramatized and inflated. When you alter the way you think—through the questions you ask of a Guide or friend; or rational analysis of your cognitive processes; or concerned coaching, humor, or meditation—you are pruning the branches of your pride. When you acknowledge your investment in your guilt and self-condemnation, you're starving pride's roots.

Seeing and understanding ourselves in the larger context of the familial, social, and natural world are also invaluable for putting our pride in perspective. In our mind-body skills groups we use genograms—four generational pictures of our family tree—to situate ourselves in our families. Drawing and sharing genograms, we may observe multigenerational patterns to which we conform, including depression, and be galvanized to free ourselves from them. We also learn about family strengths—attitudes and actions—that can inspire us and help us move through depression. More generally, we come to recognize both our unique position in the family and our place in it, neither so isolated nor so specially marked for unhappiness.

Taking a walk in the country or in a park in the city can also help put your life and your misery in some perspective. You realize, as you move along, that you are a part of nature. As you observe her forms and rhythms, see how she nourishes and flourishes, and feel the growth and change and life around you, you may well experience a connection that you have lost, and a kinship to something larger than your problems.

Helping Others, Healing Ourselves

Service to others—especially helping people who are more obviously needy and unhappy than we are—helps to undercut pride, assuage guilt, and improve our mood. Caring for a child or a sick friend, you can find meaning and purpose. Volunteering in a homeless shelter, you discover that you're not "the worst off." As you help others, you're also refuting your self-condemning accusations of worthlessness and easing the burden of guilt.

Doing ordinary, concrete tasks for ourselves—washing the dishes, straightening up a desk, buying groceries—can also be helpful for the prideful as well as the procrastinating. It's true that even these actions can sometimes stir up guilt and provoke prideful self-accusation: "How could I have been so stupid, so careless as to let the food rot?" "How could I let my desk disappear under debris?" But the fact of doing these tasks, especially doing them slowly, meditatively, tends to undermine these self-important diatribes, to wear away the abrasiveness of self-condemnation. It's also helpful to allow yourself, for a few moments, to become aware of, imaginatively connected with, all those other humans who are also washing, cleaning, and shopping.

Sometimes when we're depressed, we can even use our concern for others as a weapon against ourselves. One of the subtlest and, in depression, the most frequent forms of pride is the conviction that your suffering, great though it is to you, is actually insignificant compared to that of others, is unworthy of attention, is maybe even illusory. This means you're doubly worthless, first, for wanting sympathy or help, and second, for wanting it for a matter of such small consequence.

Perspective can be very helpful here, too. Your suffering may not be extreme in comparison with that of wartime refugees, or homeless people with AIDS, or abandoned children, but it's real. I've found, time and again, that the simple, graceful acknowledgment of the ordinary reality of our experience and its pain—that we have a right to feel what we're feeling—can be so helpful, so reassuring. Remember Bob Coles reminding me, gently but with humor, that "you have your problems, too."

Sometimes, particularly at first, you will need someone else—a Guide, family member, friend—to hold up to you this mirror of compassion and acceptance. Ultimately, you have to internalize its pride-dissolving, self-affirming message.

Pride's daimon is humility. Humility allows you to navigate safely between the dangers of guilty self-condemnation and those of prideful self-importance and self-absorption. It is the true, ordinary understanding of who you are and what you've done, of the real but not unlimited pain you've caused and may feel—and of your place in a world that is so much larger than you are.

PERFECTIONISM

Perfectionism is a close cousin to pride, a frequent reason for or rationalization of procrastination, and an abiding source of self-torment. If you stake your reputation and, even more intimately, your self-esteem on being perfect, it's hard to act and even harder not to be disappointed, once you do act, with what you've said or done.

The perfectionist brings the geometer's compass, the statistician's computer and standards, to the ever-changing facts of physical appearance and emotional life, and to family, social, and job situations that are, quite literally, beyond our control. And she brings a condemnatory eye to the mistakes she inevitably makes, to her human imperfection.

Perfectionists are likely to feel shame, and to attribute their negative judgments about themselves to others. Often they become more deeply depressed because they believe the loss they have experienced—of a spouse, a job, or a social role—dishonors them and will make others see them as inferior or unacceptable. And these feelings of shame and unworthiness tend to make them avoid others, deepening their isolation and their depression. In fact, this kind of shame is a central element in the paranoia that characterizes some of the most severe depressions.

Perfectionism may or may not mean we are compulsively neat in appearance, handwriting, or speech. But it does bring a defensive quality to the way we deal with the world. We are ever vigilant for flaws in ourselves and others. And so the perfectionist who has been less than perfect suffers.

Perfectionism, I find, almost always puts us a few inevitable feet from depression. I hear it in the sighs of depressed medical students who "have to be at the top of my class"; from women who feel it is their—and often it is *only* their—responsibility to make their relationships work; from women and men who want to be right in every statement, appropriate in each footnote, and masterful in every argument.

If you look closely, you'll see perfectionists populating the pages of the cognitive behavioral therapy texts on depression. The old Groucho Marx joke about not wanting to join any club that would have you as a member is powerfully relevant.

Since pride and perfectionism are intimately related, it's not surprising that perspective is helpful here as well. I find it useful to remind my disheartened and distraught medical students that those who aren't in the top 10 percent of their class also will find fine residency programs and have wonderfully fulfilling medical careers: P=MD (a passing grade means you graduate and become a doctor) is the shorthand that the saner students use.

Perspective is useful, but it goes only so far. We also need to see that perfection is, itself, an illusion. The Zen monks know this. When they create their serene and elegant rock gardens, they deliberately make an asymmetric error. It's a reminder that perfection is always present in nature and cannot be achieved by human activity. Perfection lies in the relaxed, nonjudgmental appreciation of what is—in our lives and in the world, with all the problems and errors that are part of living in this world and being human.

This doesn't mean that we can't or shouldn't work to make improvements in ourselves, or what we do, or the world we live in. But we must change our attitude toward making these improvements and toward the results we strive for and achieve.

The Serenity Prayer that is attributed to theologian Reinhold Niebuhr and used by Alcoholics Anonymous is a good guide here:

> *God, grant me the serenity*
> *To accept the things I cannot change;*
> *The courage to change the things I can;*
> *And the wisdom to know the difference.*

Acceptance is always a necessary step as we meet our demons and discover our daimon. Here, acceptance is both the means for exorcising the demon and the name of the daimon that will appear.

LONELINESS

Loneliness is a terrible demon and sometimes, I think, the most terrifying of them all. It's ever present with some of us. Others discover it, as if it had emerged from a previously unnoticed place inside us, only when we've lost someone who has been central to our lives. In losing that other, we feel, as Theresa did, that we've lost ourselves as well, that we are adrift and isolated. Perhaps we've never before consciously experienced this feeling. Perhaps it reawakens long-buried memories of a lost and lonely childhood.

Some people say they no longer feel physically solid or substantial. After her husband left her for a younger woman, a friend of mine came to think of herself as "transparent." She who had always loved good company and moved with authority through the world refused to answer her phone and became suicidally depressed.

Paralyzed and diminished, we may believe ourselves unworthy of the attentions of those who might care about us. When someone does express concern, we're not sure how to respond, as if this were a skill we'd forgotten. Our attempts to reach out to others may feel forced, and the connections we do make seem painfully awkward and tentative. Efforts that feel like failures may fuel further withdrawal.

In addition to working with a Guide who can provide a reparative experience of support and comfort and a bridge back to the rest of humanity, I recommend three basic strategies for moving out of loneliness: accepting the experience wholly; raising your energy; and, in spite of past difficulties and disappointments, reaching out once again.

Sitting with loneliness is a meditative, mast-bound discipline. Breathing deeply, experiencing loneliness fully, feeling it work painfully on you, change may well happen by itself. Slowly your muscles relax. You may begin to feel, perhaps for the first time in some time, the substance, the reality of yourself, mourning your lost connection, here and now and perhaps long ago as well. Tears may come, and tears, over time, soften the rigidity and self-protectiveness with which you've defended yourself against the pain of abandonment or indifference. Tears can also melt the walls you've erected that keep you from others. I've seen this happen with people such as Theresa, Milton, and Madeleine (whom you'll meet in the next chapter) and hundreds of others whose emotionally impoverished childhoods and later-life losses have led them to feel despairingly lonely and empty.

Pema Chödrön, a Tibetan Buddhist teacher, writes beautifully and simply—and from her own experience—of this process of "being with" loneliness in *When Things Fall Apart* and her other books. When we accept and embrace our loneliness, we feel it more deeply and find comfort as well.

When we write about our loneliness, the words we use, paradoxically, keep us company. As I mentioned before, research by psychologist James Pennebaker and his colleagues has shown that expressing our emotions in writing significantly lowers our stress levels. Expressing your loneliness can also connect you to others, in your life and throughout history, who have also felt this way.

Music works, especially music that echoes, articulates, and amplifies our feelings. The blues and those country songs about lost lovers, as well as symphonies and opera, invite us to feel connected to something beyond us—rhythm, melody, meaning—that reassures, soothes, and inspires.

Many people I've worked with find that movies, often sentimental ones that their critical, perfectionistic mind would reject, can be quite useful in helping them to experience, understand, and move beyond their loneliness. Interestingly, many of these films seem to appear almost automatically and without any conscious effort at odd hours on television or on an airplane screen they happen to be watching.

Films of parents and children who can't connect, because of absence, obstacles, hurt, or misunderstanding, and then find one another were particularly important to one of my patients who was in a nasty custody battle. *I Am Sam,* in which Sean Penn plays a mentally retarded, dedicated, and persistent father struggling against fate and bureaucracy to claim his beloved daughter, held a mirror up to his own powerless longing and deepened his feelings of loss and loneliness; it recalled the childhood hurt and isolation that gave these feelings such extra weight, but also reminded him of what might be possible, the loving intimacy that he treasured.

Inspirational stories about others who've suffered in isolation and learned and changed through adversity also can help. *The Power of One,* a John Boorman movie about a South African boy who stands up and fights for love and equality amid the hatred and division of apartheid has helped several people I know to feel, buried among their own feelings of hurt and powerlessness, the caring and courage that can bring connection.

Physical activity and exercise are also important allies in dealing with loneliness. They undermine the agitation that loneliness brings and clear away some of the rumination that clutters your mind and cuts you off from others. Exercise also replenishes the energy you need to overcome your resistance against reaching out. And sessions of exercise—walking, dancing, yoga—themselves create a connection to your moving, feeling body.

Reaching out to other people is an obvious antidote to loneliness, but it often proves disappointing or feels fruitless. This may be partly because you want it so much and hope for so much from it. The best and easiest strategy that I've found (and now you'll hear echoes of the Guides chapter) is to reach out to those to whom you feel drawn, those whose names or faces or phone numbers arise unbidden in dreams, or through guided imagery, or in the course of happy accidental encounters: Dorothy's Aunt Grace, Theresa's friend Barbara.

Connection is loneliness's daimon. Accept who comes. Enjoy them. Don't burden your meetings, or them, with expectations. Experiencing one connection, you will realize that you know, if you let yourself, that others are possible. Any connection, however improbable or tenuous, can be the bridge to the next.

LETHARGY

Lethargy is the mud in which the wheels of our journey's forward progress are stalled. It's akin to procrastination and often deepens loneliness.

When we are overcome with lethargy, it feels as if we can't possibly do anything. Meaning and purpose have been drained from all the relationships and activities that once held them. It feels as if there's no way to act and there's nothing worth doing. It is these feelings that often mark, sometimes along with paranoia, the deepest depressions, or the darkest times within them.

Lethargy is a particularly disturbing demon because it threatens our place in the social order, as well as our sense of well-being and self-respect. We can, albeit with terrible pain, get along in our loneliness. Perfectionism agitates but doesn't totally disable us. Procrastination leaves us some room for adequate functioning. Lethargy simply sidelines us.

Thomas Moore has written eloquently about lethargy in *Care of the Soul*. He says that its function is precisely this—to force us to stop. He calls these times, following the custom of the Renaissance, Saturnian, after Saturn, the planet traditionally associated with difficulty acting and with inertia. These periods of enforced inaction, when all doors seem closed and all options foreclosed, keep us, Moore suggests, from heading heedlessly in directions that no longer serve us, from the ways of thinking and doing and being that led us to become depressed.

These times, Moore suggests, offer us the opportunity for deep, internal change. Moore uses the adjective *alchemical* for this transformation and refinement and tells us that it *must* take place away and apart, in darkness and dreams, silence and solitude.

Occasionally, lethargy becomes overwhelming and insupportable, a refusal to move or act or even eat that is truly dangerous and must be quickly attended to by family, friends, and physicians. Far more often, the degree of lethargy you experience is mercifully proportionate to your need for it and to your ability to accommodate it. Incapacitating lethargy is, in my experience, relatively rare in women who have to raise and care for children.

Lethargy is most common in older people facing or following retirement; in the well-to-do who can, quite literally, "afford" it; and in people such as Theresa and Dorothy, who are being forced, finally, to admit that their anxious striving in relationships and/or at work is no longer bearing healthy fruit. It's especially common among confused and uncommitted young people who are on the threshold of making major life choices of careers and partners.

Erik Erikson, the psychoanalyst who wrote so eloquently about our entire life cycle, describes this late-adolescent, early-adulthood time of taking off, or withdrawal, as a "moratorium." This time of leaving behind the past, which may often be marked by lethargy, can precede a rebirth; a new direction; indeed, a new life. This modern moratorium has a kinship with the rites of passage of indigenous societies—the ordeals often endured in isolation or darkness that mark transitions, particularly from childhood to adulthood. Both moratoria and rites of passage may be the necessary prelude to discovering one's identity as an adult member of society, as well as a necessary interlude in which that discovery can be made. And the need for these often lethargy-heavy moratoria is not restricted to the young.

Lethargy can last months and be quite debilitating. In other cases, lethargy may hold sway for only one or several hours a day or over weekends. All these times, large and small, may signal a need to take time out to consider our lives—to step off our career path or simply take a few hours off from our job each week; to refrain from committing to a new relationship or from rushing to end an old one.

I've found that if you permit yourself your allotted Saturnian time—the lethargic morning hours that are characteristic of depression, the "unproductive" weekend days, even the weeks when you "just can't get going"—it tends to yield, in its own time, to movement in a new, more authentic, direction. Think of April stalled in her efforts at career change, waiting (a nice pun) on tables. These can be times of simple labor, of reading, thinking, crying, meditating, or just lying about. They're also excellent times for talking with a Guide.

When in the course of a day or at the end of some weeks your energy does begin to rise, you need to nurture and foster it. If yoga stretches are familiar, they're a good place to start. Do them at your own pace. Walking works, too, as it did for Dorothy. So does putting on music and letting your body move to it. After twenty or even ten or five minutes, you'll likely feel a difference.

If, after you've begun to reenter your customary activities or start on a new path, you feel overwhelmed by rumination or returning lethargy, stop for a while and do something else, something easy: Read the paper or have a cup of tea or do both. Don't judge whether or not you "should." And if you're exhausted, take a nap and start up where you left off. Sometimes even five minutes of sleep are restorative.

After you've done something physical (and sometimes instead of it), you can do something practical. Start with something easy, maybe a small part of something you need to do or (as with procrastination) a small task that resembles a larger one that still seems overwhelming: Write a brief letter before working on a long report; straighten a desk before you think of tackling a room or a house; buy a few things in a nearby store before you do a week's worth of shopping.

Being active in small ways lets your mind and body know that movement and change are, even when you consciously doubt it, still possible, that lethargy is a stage, not a permanent state.

Memory is also a powerful aid. Remember change and movement that happened yesterday. There's a possibility that they will come tomorrow, and in the days after that. And be patient through this process. Balance your efforts with an appreciation of your limitations.

Acceptance of the demon lethargy prepares the way for the daimon ease. If you are willing to let lethargy work on you, it can be your friend, helping you to refrain from acting before you are ready, nurturing, like a seed in quiet darkness, your necessary internal change.

RESENTMENT

This demon is hunched and clawed—angry, deformed, and hypervigilant. Think of Shakespeare's Richard III, hunchbacked and ranting, cursing and killing innocents. Resentment isolates us in fear and self-protection and spoils possibilities that might help us revive or thrive.

Anger comes and, like a thunderstorm, goes, perhaps leaving us cleansed. We nurture resentment and fertilize it with justification. Milton's resentment toward his ex curdled his love for his son and made the boy an object of his disdain.

Resentment often owes its origins to spoiled affection. Think again of Milton and his wife; April and her mother; Dorothy and Todd; of yourself when you've felt hurt or rejected or ignored by a parent, spouse, lover, or boss whose favor you vainly craved.

And resentment keeps us bound to whomever or whatever we resent. April's unresolved resentment confined her in fruitless struggle with her mother. Instead of leaving, Dorothy seethed silently at Todd. When you point your finger at someone, your hand assumes the shape of a gun. Then, as the street saying goes, you're pointing one finger at the other person and three back at yourself.

When we're resentful, we're deeply invested in the view that others have, or life itself has, wronged us. We're zealous in marshaling evidence to prove our point. We are, as the biblical verse puts it, keenly aware of the "mote" of offense in our neighbor's eye and blind to—blinded by—"the beam" in our own.

Anticipating offense when none has yet been given, we often produce it. If I act as if you're going to hurt or disrespect me, I become suspicious, defensive, pugnacious, and may indeed produce exactly the kind of response that I fear. Milton—ready to fight with his wife and correct his son—unearthed opposition, defensiveness, and, yes, resentment, in them. And so the cycle continues.

You have to become aware of what you're doing and withdraw your complaints against others—"She did this" or "The system did that"—at least for the moment. Meditation can help this happen. When you move into each moment, you are free. Milton, becoming Lao-tzu's student, suddenly, surprisingly, let go of—perhaps even forgot—what he'd been holding on to. "How're you doing?" he asked his ex cheerfully.

As you become aware of and acknowledge resentment, you can begin to feel its self-protective, perverting effect, the pain its tortured satisfaction causes you, the way it deforms you as well as your perceptions. When you've experienced just how bad it can get, when you're fed up enough, you may choose to stop pointing your finger.

Then you can become aware of, accept, and take responsibility for your own feelings. You no longer have to justify them. There may be anger, but it's clean and clear, directed at a real person for whom you once cared, for whom perhaps you still care. You can draw a picture of it or write it down or pound pillows or shout it out loud. And, like other emotions, it now can pass. You're no longer trapped in the grotesque, hateful mask you've fashioned for yourself, no longer perceive such overwhelming ugliness in the person you resent. Like April's mother, the object of your resentment may melt or shrink, allowing you, no longer threatened or threatening, to experience the daimon of compassion.

EXPRESSING THE ANGER THAT FUELS RESENTMENT—AND OTHER DEMONS

All of Milton's feelings were tied in knots in his muscles' tightness and his mind's preoccupations. He didn't need to express these feelings physically; he was somehow able, under Lao-tzu's tutelage, to let them go. But many of us, especially those of us who are struggling with resentment, can benefit by expressing with our bodies, as well as with words, the anger we have held in.

It may seem strange—even frightening—to physically express all those feelings you've been taught not to feel, and especially the ones of which you're most ashamed. If you were talking to me about them in my office, I might encourage you to express yourself in words, tears, and movement, in screams and pounding on pillows, while you were with me. If you want to do it, if it feels like it might be just right for you, you can also do it at home. Here's how:

LETTING OUT THE ANGER THAT FUELS YOUR DEMON

Set aside some time in a place where you won't be disturbed or disturb others.

Put several pillows (not the ones you sleep on) on the floor. Kneel down in front of them. Take a few deep breaths, relaxing your body. Now raise your arms above your head and begin to pound down on the pillows. (Make sure the pile is thick enough so you don't hurt your hands or arms.) Pound with full force, leaning back and bringing your fists, or your open hands, and your arms down on the pillows.

Perhaps images of those toward whom you feel resentment, or those who have disappointed or abandoned you, will come to your mind. Perhaps as you continue you'll feel the full force of your rage. Pound for 5 minutes or, if you feel like it, for longer—until you can't do it anymore. If loud noises won't provoke your neighbors to outrage, yell and scream out your hurt and pain and anger as you pound. If you can't yell, simply growl and grunt.

After you've stopped—pretty tired and sweaty, maybe a little hoarse by this time—relax, sit quietly, or lie down. Become aware of what's happening now.

Write down in your journal what it was like for you. How did it feel to pound? What thoughts and words and sounds came? Was there someone—or many someones—whose image(s) came to you?

If this feels helpful, you can do it daily for weeks or months, increasing the pounding time if you feel it's needed. The best time to do this is early in the morning so you can get out all the tension, all the anger, all the resentment and hurt before you begin your day.

After the first, or the fifth, session, you may well feel softer, sadder, more vulnerable. You may also be more relaxed, perhaps energized, rather than resentful and angry. You may even find yourself laughing with relief. As you repeat this exercise over and over, you may discover that acknowledging and expressing your hurt and the anger that fuels it is releasing you from resentment. You may also experience compassion and even generosity, the daimons that resentment conceals, that all the demons of depression have obscured.

In the previous section, I've given you guidance in transforming some threatening and representative demons. They're not, of course, the only ones you may confront, nor are the ways outlined the only possible ways to deal with them. I think, though, that you'll be able to adapt the approach and the techniques to any demons that may be particularly troublesome to you. In the final section of this chapter, I want to demonstrate how Traditional Chinese Medicine provides a larger context for understanding all your demons and practical tools for dealing more successfully with them.

Traditional Chinese Medicine: Repairing Damage, Restoring Balance

MAKING THE MIND-BODY CONNECTION

Our demons—the fears and preoccupations that constrain and deform our thoughts and feelings—may seem to us abstract and conceptual. They have, however, an intimate connection with, and a shaping force on, our bodies and the way they function. Conversely, our physical functioning and the physiological and biochemical processes on which it depends, directly affect our emotional and mental life and the demons that trouble it.

This mind-body connection is what gives the long-held anger of hostility the power to raise our levels of the stress hormone cortisol and, with it, our blood sugar and cholesterol; to elevate our blood pressure, close our arteries, clot our blood, and stop our hearts. It's because of this mind-body connection that the longing of loss and loneliness can diminish our immunity, even as it depresses our mood. These connections can, of course, be turned to good therapeutic use as well. They are what make the mind-body techniques we've been using—the various forms of meditation, guided imagery, dance, and yoga and the expression of emotions—so effective in dealing with our demons, in relieving depression and anxiety, and also in treating and preventing chronic illness.

Millennia before the physiological consequences of emotional states were scientifically documented and quantified, the world's systems of traditional medicine understood the central importance of the mind-body connection and developed methods for addressing the complex variety of physical, emotional, mental, social, and spiritual imbalances, and their consequences and interactions. It was understood in Asia, Africa, and the Americas that depression could be caused by any or all of these imbalances and that it could and should be effectively dealt with at all of these levels.

Many of the techniques I've described, including the use of food, breathing, images, movement, and emotional awareness and release— and the meditative perspective that's so crucial to dealing with demons— were, and are, an integral part of these comprehensive systems of healing. So, too, are other techniques—for example, hands-on spiritual healing and massage, and the manipulation of our joints and bones. All can enhance our capacity for self-healing and help restore the psychological, physical, energetic, and spiritual balance that's disturbed in depression.

In this section, I'm going to discuss one such comprehensive approach, Traditional Chinese Medicine (TCM). TCM is an integral part of my work with every depressed person I see, and it is now widely available in the United States and Canada, Europe and South America, as well as in

Asia where it originated. I strongly suggest that you make it part of your own program of care.

TCM understands and treats the connections between mind and body, and among a variety of physical and emotional symptoms, in a way that is very different from, and still largely incomprehensible to, Western scientific medicine. It makes it possible for us to make coherent pictures of the diverse emotional symptoms and patterns—the demons we've been discussing—as well as the fatigue and hopelessness that are depression's hallmarks, and the apparently unrelated physical manifestations that plague depressed and discouraged people. TCM also gives us tools to address and resolve these complex, otherwise mystifying patterns of imbalance, in comprehensive, systematic, and highly beneficial ways.

In the remainder of this chapter, I'm going to focus on how TCM helped my depressed and anxious patient Michael to deal successfully with a variety of physical and emotional symptoms that had long disabled him and frustrated his physicians' and psychotherapists' best efforts to help him. TCM, as you'll see, made it much easier for him to work with and transform his demons and discover his daimon. Afterward, I'll discuss ways you can make TCM—and other traditional forms of medicine—a part of your own healing journey. Finally, I'll help you find skilled practitioners of acupuncture and Chinese herbalism (and other forms of traditional medicine) who can offer this healing opportunity to you.

MICHAEL'S MYSTERIOUS SYMPTOMS

At forty, Michael was tall, boyish, handsome. He also was, if you looked closely, a little paunchy and a bit stooped, as if he were bearing some heavy, awkward burden, or ducking away from a blow. His blond hair fell across his forehead, and he smiled sheepishly as he listed his complaints during our first meeting.

To the world, Michael confided, he seemed a success, at work and at home. He was an advertising copywriter who obviously enjoyed the work and regularly won awards, as well as praise and raises, for his ad campaigns. Away from work, he had a good marriage to a loving and supportive woman, and two bright and happy teenage sons.

Still, underneath his attractive surface, Michael was a bundle of self-doubt, depressive symptoms, irritability, and mixed feelings. He had a variety of inexplicable and unyielding physical symptoms and was often overwhelmingly fearful about what they might mean.

Michael sometimes questioned his abilities at work and, at the same time, wondered if his job provided adequate latitude for the full range of his talents. Though he almost never expressed it, he often found himself annoyed and impatient with coworkers. He loved his wife and loved making love to her, but something about her—he couldn't say exactly what—irritated him as well. And he wondered, in spite of her reassurance, whether he was satisfying her sexually.

Michael had many sources of distress, many demons that constrained and deformed his life. There were the perfectionist's ever-present, hovering fears of failing, and also the fears of succeeding, that kept him from fully using his talents at work. He was a procrastinator, putting off important decisions, doubting the ones he made. And he sometimes resented those who were more confident and decisive than he was. Though they were no longer so incapacitating, Michael also had specific fears, phobias—of planes, bridges, and of urinating in public bathrooms. Accompanying all these fears, weaving in and out of every challenge and decision, was the fear that his body, succumbing to some siren song of destruction, would betray him.

Sometimes, Michael woke at three or four in the morning, sure that something terrible had happened to, or was about to befall, his sons or wife. And always, at work or at home, when his back or neck or knees ached or his gut rumbled or it was hard to start his stream of urine, Michael quietly panicked. Pain in his chest, his neck, or his left arm was a sure sign of an impending heart attack. GI or urinary symptoms portended cancer.

On his first visit, Michael "assured" me that he really did have "prostate problems," swollen ankles, pain in his knees, and periodic infections.

He also had "digestive disturbances" that the specialists had called irritable bowel syndrome but that they were unable to treat. There were intermittent pains in his chest, neck, and head, and sometimes cramping, and even a "stabbing" sensation that defied diagnosis. He weighed too much and couldn't cope with his craving for sweets, and was worried about diabetes.

Psychiatrists had bestowed half a dozen different diagnoses on Michael: anxiety, phobic and panic disorders, and dysthymia among them. He had most recently been diagnosed, once again, with a "major depressive disorder" and also told he had a somatization disorder—he converted emotional conflict into physical (somatic) symptoms.

Over the years, cognitive behavioral therapy had helped Michael to identify his negative, self-destructive ways of thinking—"I'll always be sick," "I'll never be able to stand up on my own," "I can't possibly get on a plane"; offered him a view of himself that was both more realistic and optimistic—"I'm not feeling well now, but it will likely pass"; and helped him to begin to deal with some situations, such as flying, that had caused him great anxiety. And psychotherapy—exploring his emotional history and his family relationships—had explained the origins of some of the patterns of thought and action that burdened and limited him.

Still, in spite of his and his therapists' best efforts, Michael felt besieged by anxiety and hobbled by low energy, unhappy, and painfully stuck.

Meanwhile, after many years of thorough examinations, repeated lab tests, and reassuring words, Michael's internist was at his wit's end. He doubted the wisdom of more diagnostic workups and was no longer convinced that the small army of pills he'd been prescribing—drugs for possible prostate infections and drugs to slow the gut's activity, drugs to decrease muscle pain and lower elevated blood pressure, drugs to reduce anxiety and antidepressants to improve mood—were doing much good.

Though Michael liked and respected his internist, he'd begun to feel offended by the man's growing skepticism, and his impatience with Michael's persisting symptoms. Michael knew what he felt, even if it didn't fit any textbook picture. And it worried him that the psychotherapist on whom he had long depended, and his CBT therapist as well, now seemed as clueless as he did. Michael knew that something was still very wrong and that he needed help, but he didn't want to take any more pills—particularly antidepressants, which had previously aggravated his prostate, upset his gut, and diminished his sex drive. And so he had come to see me.

SEEING THROUGH TRADITIONAL CHINESE GLASSES

Michael's doctors and therapists had approached his physical and emotional symptoms as manifestations of several separate and distinct disease states that, for reasons they could not explain, continued to be resistant to treatment. As I asked him questions based on Chinese as well as Western medicine, I began to understand why.

Michael's physical and emotional symptoms were, in fact, all part of larger patterns that clinicians trained in Western medicine and psychology didn't, or simply couldn't, recognize. The analogy that comes to mind is to the three-dimensional comics of fifty years ago. When you looked at their pages without the appropriate pink-lensed glasses, they were just a bunch of blurry, fuzzy red and green lines. When you put on the glasses, a clear picture, one with color and depth, emerged. Chinese medicine provides glasses that enable us to see, amid an apparently chaotic welter of physical, emotional, and mental symptoms, clear, true pictures—and to treat them in a way that can successfully address all these issues and the imbalances they signify. What follows are a few frames of that Chinese medical worldview.

The Yin and Yang of Depression

According to Traditional Chinese Medicine, when we are healthy, we live in and according to the Tao, "the way." It is like a river of thought and feeling, physiology, attitude, and action that is flowing, ever changing, ever new. And it is, as Lao-tzu wrote, also impossible to define: "The way that can be described," as Milton learned, "is not the way." Definition, or even its attempt, removes us from the flow. Only direct experience opens us to it.

In ordinary life we perceive and experience the Tao according to its two primary qualities, which the Chinese call *yin* and *yang*. *Yin* means "the shady side of the hill." It is feminine, damp, dark, deep down, and slow. *Yang*, "the sunny side," is masculine, dry, bright, quick, superficial, and up. Everything on our planet, our entire universe, in fact—including the organs in our body, the illnesses and conditions that afflict us, our ways of looking at the world, and the moods we experience—may be described as either yin or yang. When yin and yang are in balance, we are healthy. When one or the other is in excess or deficient, we will probably experience disturbing physical and emotional symptoms.

Someone with a yang-excess depression is likely to be highly anxious, agitated and irritable, and to have trouble sitting still or concentrating—Milton, for example. This picture may be accompanied by excessive appetite, nightmares, phobias, and suicidal thoughts. Yang-deficiency depressions (which are usually related to conditions of yin excess), are characterized by fear, indecision, inactivity, and hopelessness. Theresa and April come to mind.

Yin-excess conditions are usually chronic and include such symptoms as sensitivity to cold, loose bowels, shallow breathing, and slow pulse. Yin-excess depressions are characterized by extreme fatigue, lethargy and weakness, markedly diminished interest in life and its pleasures, excessive sleeping, loss of appetite and interest in sex, and constant guilt and brooding. That's how Dorothy felt when she first came to see me. In yin-deficiency depressions, as in yang excess, there is nervousness and agitation.

The Three Treasures

There are, the Chinese tell us, "three treasures"—*shen* ("mind or spirit"), *qi* ("energy"), and *jing* ("essence"). Though these three are the fundamental substances of life, qi is regarded as the most basic. Qi is "the root of a human being." It is the refined energy that nourishes the body and mind, as well as the dynamic functioning of all the organs. It circulates constantly through the lines on the body that correspond to the internal organs, the meridians on which the acupuncture points lie. Qi is also the shield that protects us against adverse climates, microorganisms, and, most important when we consider depression, stress.

A person who has been under stress for a long time may, like Dorothy when she first came to see me, have deficient qi as well as yin excess. Symptoms of fatigue will likely be present, along with an incapacity to enjoy life. When the qi does not flow smoothly through the meridians, it is said to be "stagnant." This stagnation may occur when strong emotions—chronic anger, continual anxiety, unresolved grief—persist for a long time without release and relief. Qi stagnation often manifests as a depression characterized by frustration and angry outbursts, abdominal distention, migratory aches and pains, phobias, and preoccupation with one's physical condition.

In addition to *shen, qi,* and *jing,* the Chinese describe two other vital substances, blood and moisture (the bodily fluids). Blood stagnation often accompanies qi stagnation and may be associated with a variety of pains and dysfunctions, as well as such psychological symptoms as anxiety, agitation, and sudden irritability.

When *shen,* the spirit or mind, is disturbed, as it often is in depression, there may be a sense of disorganization and symptoms of lethargy, exhaustion, and worthlessness, as well as difficulty thinking, insomnia, and anxiety.

The Five Elements

The body's organs—the heart, lungs, liver, kidney, spleen, and so on—are regarded as the source of the vital substances and the sites of their transformation. These are the organs we see when we do an autopsy or open our anatomy books, but, according to Chinese medicine, they also partake of something larger, unrecognized in our Western understanding of anatomy and physiology. This larger quality is variously called a phase or element in which the organs, specific emotions, times of day, seasons, colors, tastes, sounds, and the like are all linked. There are five of these elements—wood, fire, earth, metal, and water—and each element has its own picture.

The traditional Chinese physician understands that the liver, which is linked to wood, is the primary agent of protection against stress and emotional trauma, and that, as such, it is often first affected in depression. The liver keeps the body, mind, and spirit in a state of working harmony by storing and releasing qi and blood; and it overcomes incipient stagnation by continually moving the qi.

When the forces of resistance become too great, when, for example, someone is unable to find relief or release from a persistent emotion, the liver's capacity to move energy becomes overwhelmed, and stagnation— emotional and physical stuckness—occurs. Then the liver's characteristic emotions of anger, frustration, and resentment, and the depression that may accompany them, may emerge.

Stagnation in the liver and of the qi affects the rest of the body as well. Some of this effect is direct. The stagnation in the liver meridian (which runs from between the first and second toe, up the inside of the leg, and through the front of the abdomen) compromises the functioning of organs through whose territory this line of energy passes. The accumulation of this stagnant energy in the pelvis, abdomen, chest, and throat may cause inflammatory problems in the genitals (and, in women, menstrual irregularities); flatulence, bloating, and other digestive symptoms; and pain in the chest and constriction in the throat. In addition, because anger causes the qi to rise, there may be pain in the head and neck.

In a way and to a degree that depends on each person's particular makeup and experience, the dysfunction in the liver will also affect the other organs and elements. For example, the spleen is the organ of transportation and transformation, of sugar metabolism (in Chinese medicine the spleen includes the pancreas), of some aspects of sexual functioning, and of the emotion of sympathy. If the spleen is vulnerable, because of heredity or loss or poor diet, the liver may suppress its function still further. The resulting condition, called "spleen dampness," is accompanied by such varied symptoms as fatigue, abdominal bloating and swelling in the lower leg, sugar cravings and weight gain, and excessive worrying.

PUTTING IT ALL TOGETHER: MICHAEL'S TCM DIAGNOSIS AND TREATMENT

This picture of liver qi stagnation and deficiency, and spleen deficiency and dampness, is, in fact, the one that I found in Michael. Virtually all of his physical and emotional symptoms seemed completely unrelated and untreatable to his psychologist and his internist, and, indeed, to Western medicine, but were a part of this picture: worry about his family; excessive preoccupation with physical symptoms; irritability; insecurity about his life's direction; chronic, low-grade depression; phobias; abdominal bloating and prostatitis; chest, head, and neck pain; and fatigue.

History-taking is important in Traditional Chinese Medicine. Physical diagnosis is central. TCM understands that every part of the body is a hologram, a microcosm of the whole person. By examining the microcosm—specific regions of the body—the TCM practitioner can diagnose the state of the whole. The function of our organs, the movement and strength of our qi, stagnation in blood, and disturbances in *shen*—the general and specific state of our physical, mental, emotional, and spiritual well-being—can all be read by a trained practitioner: in the color, contours, and coating of the tongue; in the pain and swellings of the abdomen; and, especially and most precisely, in the strength, size, and shape of the pulse of the radial arteries that come close to the surface of our wrists near our thumbs. This pulse, which Western medicine perceives as a single entity, the Chinese routinely divide into twelve: three superficial and three deep pulses on each radial artery.

I asked Michael to lie on my treatment table while I looked at his tongue, felt his belly, and took his pulse. Afterward, as he breathed slowly and deeply, I needled specific acupuncture points to build up his qi and stimulate its movement, and to break up the stagnation and resolve the dampness that his history suggested. Twenty minutes later, the uncomfortable feeling in his gut had diminished. He felt that his limbs, and his head and neck, were moving a little more easily. When he got off the table, he said he had "more energy," and that he felt "more relaxed," and "happier."

This is one of the beauties of acupuncture. The person receiving it not only can get results over time, he may well experience small but gratifying immediate changes. Greater calm, decreases in pain, easier breathing, better digestion, more energy, and improved mood may well follow a single treatment.

Although the most striking effects of a single acupuncture treatment may not last long—a few hours or a few days—there appears to be a cumulative process at work. Over a series of ten or twelve weekly treatments, for example, energy builds, tension in mind and body dissipates, mood improves, sleep becomes deeper, and physical symptoms abate. It is as if a new, more balanced being, less burdened and more sure-footed, a little more supple and alert, is growing within us.

MICHAEL MOVES AHEAD: HOPE, HERBS, AND HAPPINESS

Shortly after I began acupuncture with him, I asked Michael if he would be willing to take Chinese herbs. I explained that my choice of herbs, and my way of combining them, would be guided by the same history and physical findings, and based on the same perspective, as the acupuncture. Because he felt immediately different after each acupuncture treatment, and generally better over time, Michael was feeling more adventurous and hopeful, and eager to add another aspect of Chinese medicine to his healing program.

I prescribed several combinations of herbs—a total of forty individual ones—that have been traditionally used to treat the specific symptom pictures that Michael presented and the organs that were involved: herbs that dry out spleen dampness, move stagnant blood, mobilize qi, and quiet *shen*. Some of these herbs work synergistically, each enhancing the other's effect. Others balance out potential side effects: combining stimulating and relaxing herbs to produce a calm and yet energetic state rather than alternating agitation and lethargy. The herbs would, if properly chosen and balanced, work slowly and surely on most, or all, of Michael's symptoms.

Within a couple of weeks, Michael's bloating began to decrease, as did his difficulties with urination, the pain in his knees, and some of his anxiety. Now, his symptoms no longer seemed so threatening, so overwhelming. They had fit into a picture, and we were actually changing that picture. With his internist's blessing and supervision, Michael began to discontinue, one at a time, the drugs he'd been taking. Within two months, he'd stopped them all.

As the pain in Michael's chest eased, he became less irritable and fearful, less depressed, and more hopeful. He discovered, after five or six weeks, that he could move his head more freely. With enhanced motion, he discovered a new ability to "look around"—psychologically as well as physically—at the possibilities in his life. Before, significant changes had seemed impossible: Michael's gut had cramped and his urinary stream had faltered when he thought about taking on more responsibility at work, or being freer sexually or losing weight. Now, for the first time, he found himself wondering what challenge to tackle first: a better diet, his job, his marriage.

With my encouragement and supervision, Michael began a low-carbohydrate, high-protein diet that he'd tried before but that had never worked—perhaps because of the imbalances in his whole body. This time, he began to lose weight. He asked his wife to enter couples therapy. When, a few months later, a supervisory position was once again offered to him, Michael—anxious but determined—claimed it. Fear, the demon that had constrained his whole life, was yielding now to the courage that was growing in Michael, to his daimon.

Eight months after I began seeing him, Michael told me he'd not only lost weight and now felt physically well, but that a huge load of anxious preoccupation had lifted off him. The unpredictable storms of temper had dissipated, and he had far less foreboding about the future. Panic about his physical health—perhaps the most troubling of all his symptoms—came rarely and left quickly. Michael was traveling far more easily, handling challenges at work with some ease, and having "great sex" with his wife. To his enormous surprise and pleasure, he was, for the first time in his memory, neither anxious nor depressed—and happily moving ahead with his life.

LESSONS LEARNED

There are several points I want to make about this Chinese medical work with Michael, and about including Chinese medicine—and, potentially, other systems of traditional healing—as an integral and vital part of your journey through and beyond depression.

1 Traditional Chinese Medicine can make a major difference when you're depressed or in pain, or just feel "low energy" or out of sorts. I use it with just about all of my patients, and I could tell you many more stories other than Michael's—and so can my colleagues who practice TCM.

   In addition to our clinical observations, and those made over thousands of years by traditional practitioners, there is also a growing, if still limited, body of scientific research that supports the use of acupuncture in depression, as well as for pain and nausea and vomiting.

2 The results obtained in most research studies only hint at the power and utility of acupuncture. In them, points were chosen from a limited menu. There was no attempt to replicate the subtlety and complexity of the traditional Chinese approach: to design the kind of individualized treatment, based on history taking and examination of the tongue, belly, and pulse, that I did with

Michael. John Allen and his colleagues at the University of Arizona have recently completed an initial trial that uses a schema that approximates this approach and shows acupuncture to be as effective as a conventional antidepressant.

3 Acupuncture is only one part of the much more vast system of healing that is TCM. TCM includes herbs, the deep treatments of Chinese internal medicine that nourish, balance, and sustain the flow of qi and all of the body's substances and organs; the breathing exercises, movements, and visualizations of qigong and its sister art tai chi, which work directly on qi, decrease stress, enhance mobility, and improve our sense of balance and confidence; and the hands-on techniques of Chinese massage—tuina, acupressure, and hand and foot reflexology.

4 Finally, the Chinese worldview—with its abiding appreciation for working with, not against, nature's changes, for using all her bounty to help us regain harmony with our own nature—offers wisdom and guidance (remember Milton) as well as concrete tools for transformation.

The true test of what I believe to be Chinese medicine's great power to help us to transform our demons to our daimons, and move through depression, will come only when we use the entire integrated system to address the unique combinations of challenges and needs that characterize each of us.

And, I would add, the greatest benefits of TCM will be realized only when we make it a part of the integrative approach I'm describing here. What matters if you're depressed, anxious, out of sorts, or low in energy is, of course, what works. TCM can, as with Michael, be combined with a variety of kinds of psychotherapy and with all the techniques in this book. So far as I'm concerned, an approach in which this rich variety of therapeutic modalities complement and enhance one another's efficacy is ideal.

SUMMING UP

>> The demons that keep you confined in depression are your teachers. They conceal the daimon that can help free you from depression.

>> Meditation, quieting anxiety and binding you to the mast of awareness, helps you to observe, and eventually relax with your demons and uncover your daimons.

>> If you can't identify your demons, use the Inner Guide imagery to help you discover them.

>> Use the dialogue with the SPI to discover your own best ways of learning from and transforming your demon. Remember, the demon masks the daimon.

>> Music, books, and movies can hold up a mirror to your demon and allow you to more fully experience its impact on you.

>> Physical movement can energize you and help you move through the impasses and obstacles that your demons present.

>> You may need Saturnian times-out and -off from your customary activities—moratoria to provide time and space for your internal change.

>> Expressing the emotions you have suppressed, particularly your anger, can help free you from your demons and help you discover your daimons.

>> Don't be discouraged if your doctors and therapists cannot understand your physical and emotional symptoms or tell you they know of no treatment for the demons that trouble you. There are other ways to understand and deal successfully with what's happening to you.

>> Traditional Chinese Medicine (and other traditional healing systems) can give you this other perspective on your demons and give you a way to address the complex patterns of physical symptoms, thoughts, feelings, and behaviors that characterize your unique pattern of depression.

PRESCRIPTION FOR SELF-CARE:
Finding Practitioners of Chinese Medicine

Finding appropriate practitioners is an integral part of self-care. It requires a combination of persistence, knowledge, and discrimination. In chapter one, The Call, I discussed the variety of holistic or integrative physicians. In chapter two, I focused on how you can use your intelligence, research skills, and intuition to help you find the right Guide for your journey. Here I want to offer a schema for finding practitioners of Chinese medicine and using the Resources section in the back of the book to help you do it.

I'm going to focus on practitioners of acupuncture and Chinese herbal medicine in this prescription, but the same principles will help you to find other practitioners—a massage therapist, an Ayurvedic physician, or a Western herbalist.

Let's begin.

If you're looking for a practitioner of Traditional Chinese Medicine, start with the general category. In this case, it's best if you can find someone who works with both acupuncture and herbal medicine and is licensed (by his or her state) and/or certified by a respected accrediting organization. That means you want someone with an OMD (doctor of oriental medicine) degree from the United States or abroad, or someone licensed by a state where practitioners are required to pass exams in both acupuncture and herbalism; or someone licensed as an acupuncturist who has also studied herbalism.

Acupuncturists who do not work with herbs can also be extremely helpful (and some of them work quite skillfully with Western and other systems of herbal medicine). They are currently licensed in forty-one states. The crucial credential here for a non-physician acupuncturist—in addition to licensure—is certification by the National Certification Commission for Acupuncture and Oriental Medicine (NCCAOM). The NCCAOM exam guarantees extensive and intensive training in the principles and practice of Chinese medicine and a good grounding in Western medical science as well.

Physician acupuncturists obviously have extensive medical knowledge and experience. Their training in acupuncture may, however, vary significantly—from a minimum of 220 hours to many years of intensive education in acupuncture as well as herbalism and other aspects of TCM. You need to ask specifically about their training. Physicians who have taken only the minimal amount of training may still be helpful, but remember, they are at the very beginning of their learning curve.

In the Resources section you'll find contact information for the various national acupuncture organizations. Your state medical board (or one of the other specific licensing boards) can provide information about other practitioners (chiropractors, naturopathic physicians, and so forth) who may be licensed to practice acupuncture. These boards can also tell you whether or not licensure as an acupuncturist in your state requires herbal knowledge.

I recommend the following specific steps in finding qualified practitioners.

1 Ask your primary care physician or your therapist if she can refer you to a practitioner who is skilled in Chinese medicine and experienced in working with depression.
2 If you can't find this kind of trusted referral, get in touch with the appropriate national organization. These groups will help you to understand the education, qualifications, and scope of practice (for example, acupuncture or acupuncture and herbs) of each professional. They will also help you locate those in your area who are properly credentialed.
3 Ask if the practitioner you've located is covered by your insurance. In some states, MDs are more likely to be covered to do acupuncture than non-MDs.

4 If you're not covered by insurance, and finances are a significant issue, ask the practitioner, when you call, if she takes patients at reduced fees.

5 If you cannot find low-cost services from private practitioners, check accredited schools of Chinese medicine or acupuncture (or free clinics where acupuncturists work). Virtually every one of these institutions has low- or no-cost services available from practitioners in training.

6 If there is no private practitioner or school nearby, it may well be worth your while to make a trip to the nearest one. Though many acupuncturists like to see their patients on a weekly (or even more frequent) basis, less frequent treatments (with e-mail or phone consultations in between) can also be quite effective.

7 Keep in mind the following final words on herbalism and herbalists.

>> Chinese herbs (and other natural substances, including animal parts, minerals, and spices), like acupuncture points, must be selected by an expert according to the unique picture each depressed person presents.

>> Each of the herbs is generally used in combination with ten or a dozen or two dozen others that amplify their effects and prevent side effects, and these combinations are modified as the person being treated changes.

>> Herbalists trained in other systems of healing—Indian, Tibetan, African, American Indian, and traditional Western European—operate according to similar principles. For them, as well, the single word *depression* includes a multitude of complex symptom pictures.

>> One last, important consideration: The practitioner you consult should be using herbs that are free of impurities and dangerous adulterations. You should ask your herbalist where she gets her herbs and how she knows them to be pure.

The steps I've outlined here can be applied to finding other kinds of complementary and alternative practitioners: massage therapists and other body workers; Ayurvedic practitioners; yoga, tai chi, and qigong teachers; Western herbalists; chiropractors; and homeopathic physicians. In the Resources section are the national organizations that represent and/or credential these professions.

Though the level of scientific evidence for the effectiveness of these latter approaches to depression varies considerably—from significant to nonexistent (I've provided some brief notes on it in the Resources section)—all, like TCM, are aimed at helping to restore balance in our bodies, minds, and spirits, and to enhance our physical, mental, and emotional well-being.

CHAPTER 5

The Dark Night of the Soul

>>>>>> There may be a time at the beginning of, or later on in, our journey when any of us may feel overwhelmed, despondent, despairing. This chapter is about that time. It will help you see that the hopelessness you may feel can be a stage on your journey, not the permanent state you fear. Understand, too, that this hopelessness is actually a more urgent version of the Call, and that it can be a turning point in your life, rather than an end point.

I'll begin by discussing the importance of acknowledging to yourself the despair you feel and the suicidal thoughts that may come with it. I'll go on to encourage any of you who may be feeling this way to reach out to Guides who are capable of hearing what's happening to you and supporting you as you go through this difficult passage.

Then I want to focus on those times in our lives when the Dark Night of despair is most likely to loom; on how my patients have learned deeply from these times and moved through them with courage and grace; and, especially, on practical strategies we developed that will help and inspire you as well.

The suffering of the Dark Night may tempt even those of you who have doubted the wisdom of taking antidepressants to ask your physicians for the drugs. This is completely understandable. That's why I've chosen this part of the journey to give you guidelines for deciding whether, and when, you should turn to pharmacologic antidepressants, as well as information about the specific supplements that I prefer to use, whenever possible, in these situations.

I CAN'T GO ON

Sometimes the cause of our despair—our loss of hope—is unexpected and obviously devastating: the sudden death of someone we love or a diagnosis that predicts terrible suffering or imminent death. Sometimes it feels as if we've lost ground gained with great pain, slipped back downhill. We've failed at another attempt to break an old, persistent addiction or pattern, or lost a job that promised finally to end our poverty. The spouse or lover or friend or Guide we'd counted on has disappointed or disappeared.

"I can't go on" may be the first thought, or "I'd be better off dead." Often, it's just a flash, like a sign winking at the periphery of our vision. For most of us, these are shocking, truly terrifying, glimpses. We have responsibilities, people we care about, a life we've always assumed would offer us more, be better. These thoughts feel like the deepest betrayal of who we are, of those we care for, of our contract with life.

Then, even feeling as badly as we do, we blink or turn or shake our heads, and the sign fades. Over weeks or months, in moments of heightened disappointment, or extremes of loneliness, these thoughts may reoccur. The image may become clearer, more specific, active rather than passive: "I can end it all" or "I could use pills." The flash can become a strobe, insistent, hypnotic.

If depression is stigmatizing, suicidal thinking is a scandal. It is obviously dangerous to ourselves, but it also feels dangerous to talk about. In fact, it's more deadly when we keep it to ourselves. Many times, particularly among men and women who believe their profession should make them immune to, or masters of, such thoughts—soldiers, firefighters, police, and physicians—silence about suicidal thoughts feeds despair. But there is similar, silent, lonely suffering among people of all ages and occupations who feel ashamed of the "unacceptability," "weakness," or "immorality" of their suicidal thoughts. They clam up, grow more isolated, depressed, and, yes, more suicidal.

"The absolute worst thing," Alice, a seventy-year old retired nurse, a brilliant and humorous boot-tough woman with years of rarely remitting pain, told me, "is you can't talk about feeling this way without everyone freaking out or calling the police. So you shut up and you feel more depressed."

Unfortunately, many doctors and therapists really are—forgive the pun—deathly afraid of talking about suicide. We may ask about it, as we are taught to, in an initial interview, but many often give subtle (or not so subtle) signals that they would rather not hear about it too much or too often. Opening ourselves to our patients' suicidal thoughts and feelings invites more talk, more intimacy with a despairing person, and with the specter of the death they desire. Instead of listening carefully and asking questions, many physicians just reach for the prescription pad.

The prescription and the pills are, to be sure, aimed at stabilizing the patients, reducing the high anxiety that often fuels suicidal thoughts, and pushing these thoughts back, down, or out of their patients' minds. But the drugs also push these thoughts, and the disturbing challenges they raise to our purpose as healers, out the doctors' doors. I believe that this is one reason why so many primary care physicians dispense antidepressants so quickly—in one important study, three minutes was the average time it took—almost reflexively.

SPEAKING OF SUICIDAL FEELINGS

It's time for all of us—physicians, therapists, and patients—to bring these dark flashes of despair, these terrible preoccupations with death, out of the closet of fear and shame and into the open space of shared discussion.

We don't, as Alice wryly observed, "have to endorse suicide as a social policy." But we do have to honor it as a legitimate subject for discussion, and to understand and even respect it as an option, a decision, that humans have made and sometimes do make.

If we look clearly at our suicidal thoughts, urges, or imperatives, we will likely find that they are also another kind of Call—in fact, a demand—for change. It is when we feel we cannot stand the way things are now—the emptiness and pain of loss, the leaden weight of depression, the hopelessness about the future that burdens our days—that we are pulled toward suicide. "It has to stop," we say to ourselves. And, at least for this time, death seems the only change that's possible.

This desperate notion is often the product of our limited vision and our limited understanding, and of extreme narrowing in our conceptual and imaginative horizons. The task here is, as it so often is in the journey through depression, to quiet the agitation that may be propelling us toward self-destruction, to step back from the situation we're in and to take a fresh look at it.

If you can bring the meditative skills you've been learning to this formidable challenge of despair, you'll most likely see that even the most hopeless thoughts and crushed feelings really do—like all other thoughts and feelings—come and go. It is likely, too, that if you find someone with whom you can share your pain, he'll also help you to bear it—working with you to quiet the overwhelming sense of urgency and inevitability, offering you the safe place and the time and the perspective you need to find lifesaving alternatives.

A Turning Point, Not an End Point

The ancients knew that terrible despairing times could come as part of the natural evolutionary process that marks depression. Hippocratic physicians respected what they called "the healing crisis"—that point in a chronic illness or condition when a patient was poised between a descent toward debility and perhaps death, and a turn upward, toward health. Contemporary practitioners of traditional medicines—from American

Indian medicine men to Chinese herbalists—understand this as well. In Alcoholics Anonymous, it is a commonplace that we have to "hit bottom" before we can begin to rise up again. "It is darkest," the popular saying goes, "before dawn." The Chinese written characters tell us that crisis is a time of opportunity as well as danger.

In the sixteenth century, a Spanish monk who became known as John of the Cross first described this kind of crisis as the "Dark Night of the Soul." This fine, resonant phrase adds the gravity, dignity, and mystery of spiritual suffering and search to the personal, psychophysiological pain of the healing crisis.

As I've suggested, this stage on the journey, this Dark Night, shares some of the characteristics of the first one, the Call. There is, in both, confusion and recognition of distress and disturbance, a sense that prior efforts at understanding and problem solving have failed. And, indeed, this kind of Dark Night can signal the beginning of the journey. But it is, as its name suggests, different, too—deeper, darker, more laden with despair.

Still, there is also something deeply hopeful about the Dark Night of the Soul. Dark Nights by definition are limited. They are part of a natural process of change and progression, and they yield, inevitably, to brighter mornings.

Indeed, many aboriginal societies—from the Plains Indians to African forest dwellers—choose to make a Dark Night experience a part of the growth and healing of its members. Their young people experience rites of passage to adulthood in which they meet the community's greatest fears and terrors—at night, in a cave, in a tunnel, or in underground chambers. Sometimes, as in the healing temples of ancient Greece, this kind of immersion in darkness is a crucial element in the healing of serious illnesses, including depression. In many societies, future healers are marked out by their successful, early-life encounter with the unavoidable Dark Night of a life-threatening illness, a psychosis, or suicidal despair.

The Homeric hymn of Demeter and Persephone is, as psychologist Thomas Moore points out, particularly relevant to these Dark Nights. The Dark Night's ideal guide is Hekate, witch and healer and goddess of the moon. Hekate alone hears Persephone's cry. In the underworld, Hekate comes to her, as well as to her mother, Demeter, who is wandering distraught aboveground. Hekate brings news back and forth between despairing daughter and frantic mother, and wisdom, too: Separation and loneliness, darkness and despair, are inevitable; healing and wholeness come only when we accept them as part of—not apart from—our lives.

REACHING OUT TO GUIDES AND OTHERS

Very few of us can move through these Dark Nights alone and without guidance. Friends who are steadfast, unafraid, matter of fact, and loving can be of great help, but most of us also need a Hekate, a professional Guide who honors and is at ease in these darkest places. She comforts and reassures us by her presence and gives us pause and much-needed perspective. Our connection with her builds a bridge back to life, over which her words and gestures—sometimes warm, sometimes sharp, always understanding—help us walk.

Though the need may be more urgent, the ground rules for reaching out in the midst of despair are the same as the ones I described in the Guides chapter. So, too, are the means for deciding which friends and what professional Guide may be most helpful to you. If you are in despair and don't have a Guide, read over chapter two's Prescription for Self-Care, in which I describe in detail writing the lists of a prospective Guide's ideal and necessary characteristics. Use the Inner Guide imagery to help you make your choice. If you do have a Guide, now is the time to reach out to him.

There are also organizations that can provide significant help. They are not a substitute for a professional Guide—or for family and friends—but they are widely and easily available and free of charge. And the people who belong to them or staff them are ready to be there when you're in despair.

The 12-step groups—Alcoholics Anonymous (AA) is the prototype, but there are others that have been created for a variety of other issues and problems—can be lifesaving. They include Al-Anon for relatives and friends of alcoholics, Narcotics Anonymous, Overeaters Anonymous, and, particularly if you're depressed, Emotions Anonymous. Their names and contact information are in the Resources section. If these groups are relevant to your situation and you need a place to speak your pain, to feel accepted, to be with others, or just to be, get in touch.

If you feel suicidal, there are telephone hotlines that have been set up specifically for you. You can begin by contacting the U.S. National Suicide and Crisis Hotlines (see the Resources section). These organizations are staffed by people who are specifically trained to deal with despair, and with suicidal feelings, temptations, and acts. Many operate twenty-four hours a day, seven days a week. I certainly can't vouch for all of them, but the ones I've worked with over the years have committed, well-trained volunteers, people whose purpose is to be of service. They are supervised by a capable professional staff that is on call to the volunteers. Hotline volunteers are not a substitute for a professional Guide, but they can be enormously helpful during a crisis, and a source of ongoing support in times of need, as well as an emergency measure. Hotlines promise and preserve your anonymity.

There are Internet resources as well, which can be quite helpful, particularly for those for whom e-mail and instant messaging are as comfortable as the phone is for most older people. And they are even more anonymous than a hotline. Some of them are listed in the Resources section.

Finally, for desperate teenagers and their equally desperate parents, there are "runaway houses." These wonderful, kid-sensitive institutions, with which I worked for many years, not only welcome homeless and troubled teens, they specialize in helping parents and kids to sort out the ongoing despair-inducing quarrels that may push desperate teens into suicidal withdrawal or flight from their homes.

All these services and their contact information are listed in the Resources section. What follows here is an exercise to help you decide which of these resources might be of the most help to you.

First, take a look at the variety of resources listed. Then, if you feel like it, look at their Web sites (if you don't have a computer, the librarian at your local public library can help). Take notes if you want.

GETTING AN ASSIST FROM YOUR IMAGINATION

Get ready to ask your imagination and your intuition for guidance. Take some deep breaths first, allowing your belly to be soft, relaxing for a few moments in your chair. Now imagine yourself seeking out one or more kinds of help that seem most comfortable, most appropriate—going to a 12-step meeting, calling a hotline, sitting at the computer, or asking someone else for advice. Let each of the images unfold for a minute or two.

Write down in your journal what has come to you. What did you see yourself doing and how did each activity feel? If there was one that was satisfying and productive, even if it appeared only briefly, take the guidance you've been given, act on it, and get in touch. If you felt frustrated in finding an image of connection, try again later today, or tomorrow, or when you feel particularly in need and open to it.

And, of course, any time you feel the need for connection, with or without a guiding image, take the step toward help that feels right to you: There will likely be someone, or many someones, there for you.

DARK NIGHTS THROUGH THE LIFE CYCLE

Though Dark Nights may come at any time, I want to focus on three periods in our lives when they seem particularly prevalent and threatening, and on strategies and perspectives that you can use to live deeply in and to move more safely and wisely through them.

>> Adolescence, when hormonal surges overwhelm teenagers who are poised, uneasily and vulnerably, between parents' commands and peers' expectations, between the demanding aspirations and idealism of youth and the fearful uncertainties of adult reality.

>> Middle age, especially late middle age, when we may confront the limitations of careers and families that have defined and sustained us, and the loss of hope of becoming who or what we had once wanted to be.

>> Old age, when our physical and mental abilities wane, and we come ever closer to death, the time of our greatest loss, and of a night that many of us believe will never end.

ADOLESCENCE: SOPHIE'S CHOICE

Suicide is a specter that haunts modern American adolescents and the parents and professionals who care for them. In the last fifty years, the numbers of young people attempting and succeeding at suicide has increased alarmingly. One authoritative survey not long ago indicated that *one in five high school students has "seriously considered" suicide,* and that one in ten had attempted it. More and more of them are, by design or accident, eventually succeeding. Suicide is now the third leading cause of death for people between the ages of fifteen and forty-four and the second for college students.

It wasn't hard, then, to understand why Sophie's mother, Jane, called me in a panic. Sophie, who was sixteen, was just about to be released from the psychiatric ward of her local hospital after a second suicide gesture (or attempt—no one was quite sure which). Several months before, Sophie had cut her arm repeatedly. The razor slashes were not life-threatening. Still, they were bloody and serious. A few days before Jane called, Sophie had taken enough pills to threaten her life, but she'd done it in a house full of people. Sophie's efforts weren't determined enough to guarantee death, but she was certainly sending a powerful message of despair to all who cared to hear.

Sophie was a large, attractive young woman who wore an artfully decorated long dress on her first visit to me. She seemed at once impressive and agitated, an unwilling participant in our meeting, and also its chair. She began our talk by announcing, with a kind of defiant pride, that she'd been diagnosed as having both a "major depression" and "bipolar disorder." The antidepressants she'd been prescribed had variously made her feel "agitated," "unreal," and "doped up." She had briefly taken Lithium—a standard treatment for the alternating mania and depression that define bipolarity; this, she reported, "made me feel like liquid lead."

After offering her summary of her "misprescriptions," Sophie sat silently in my office. She had the air of contentious resolve that people who work with adolescents—and a number of parents—know all too well. Her upper body was immobile, but her knee bounced up and down, keeping time to some inner urgency. She answered my questions with few words, as if she'd been coached for the courtroom. "Yes" and "no" she said. "A few days ago" she felt she "wanted to die," but now she didn't.

Her mother, Jane, was thorough and thoughtful. She said Sophie had easily met all the normal benchmarks of early childhood physical and mental development. From her first two years on, it had been clear that Sophie was intellectually precocious—creative as well as brilliant—but also "obstinate." When her younger brothers arrived, she seemed to become combative and competitive. In recent years, she'd retreated from the family. She ate most meals by herself, and had traded her upstairs bedroom for a corner of the half-finished basement, where she barricaded her quarters with piles of unwashed clothes and books.

When Sophie spoke, she was animated but cryptic. She was firmly convinced that her mother had "contempt" for her and was a "total phony." Her father was "hopeless," and her brothers "annoying," but not of central importance. She couldn't, or wouldn't, explain much more, but assured me that it was all "quite obvious."

Sophie and Jane agreed that a recent attempt at family therapy had been "catastrophic." Sophie and her brothers had argued at full volume until the boys began to cry; Sophie's father was enraged at everyone; and Jane suffered silently.

Jane said Sophie occasionally excelled in school, but was most often an "underachiever." Sophie acknowledged that she skipped "boring" classes sometimes, drank beer and smoked pot and had a few friends whom her mother had accurately labeled as "dubious." Her present psychotherapist was "nice but not very helpful." She would "obviously" like to feel better.

When I asked if there was any way that I might be able to help—a question I've found that is crucial to finding the common ground necessary for a therapeutic connection, and for passage through the Dark Night—she was thoughtful. After a while, she said she might like to do something about her "health," particularly about her weight. I told her that I worked with diet and meditation and acupuncture and that I would teach her things she could do to help herself. She nodded. When I asked, she said she was "willing" to see me again.

A few days later, while her mother sat in the waiting room, I met with Sophie alone. She professed indifference to her family and her school and said she was "bored" with questions about "my adolescent emotional life." She brightened considerably, but briefly, only when we talked about politics or poetry, the small-mindedness of self-important teachers, or her weight.

Kids' Despair Is a Family Affair

It occurred to me several times, as I tried to mine information and feeling from her, that it might make far more sense to see Sophie and her mother together. There, it seemed, was a place of conflict and connection, and also of a mystery whose solution might be lifesaving: What made Sophie so sure that this apparently kind and concerned mother was a total phony? Why was she sick enough of her and of her own life to try twice to kill herself?

There is, in this era of energetic diagnosis and biological explanation, a pronounced tendency to see, and understand and treat, children largely in isolation from their families and their environment. The kid manifests the symptoms and therefore has the problem. Let's label it and prescribe for it. This recapitulates, in a narrow, medicalized way, the psychoanalytic bias toward individual treatment. It also ignores a wealth of information, derived from decades of therapy with whole families, and a much larger body of anthropological understanding that tells us that families and the culture that helps to form them shape their children, and that interventions with these groups can restore lost balance to both the child and her family.

Neither Sophie nor her mother was enthusiastic about our meeting together, but each had to admit it made some sense. Theirs was the closest—and now the most conflicted—relationship in the family. Jane was deeply concerned about Sophie's welfare and her survival. Sophie acknowledged that her mother could, if she had a mind to, be her best ally in bringing about any changes she might hope for. And what I was suggesting seemed "harmless," just speaking and listening, no analyzing or interpreting, no arguing even, just paying attention to, being present with each other. Perhaps, without Sophie's father and brothers, they could at least talk.

I asked Jane and Sophie what each wanted, and requested that each listen silently while the other spoke. They did, with some help—my hand held up like a traffic cop's now in Sophie's direction, now in Jane's—talk, and even listen, to each other.

Sophie was clear about a number of issues. She did not want to take medication; be diagnosed as, or told that she was, crazy or depressed; argue incessantly with her father; or continue at the school she was attending; and—and she was especially emphatic about this—she didn't want to live at home any longer. She felt trapped in a family that was "making me crazy." She'd become suicidal, it seemed, because she felt there was quite literally "nowhere else to go."

Jane said she wanted Sophie to feel better, to stop hurting herself, to stop yelling so much, and to live up to her potential in school. She wanted Sophie to know that, as a mother, she was desperate because nothing she did or said seemed to help.

By the end of the session, Sophie was speaking in full, animated sentences and her knee was at rest. When I asked about the change Sophie said, still grudging, that "if" she was feeling better, it was because her mother was, for once, actually seeing and listening to her.

The resilience of young people and their capacity, when met with honesty and love, to forgive and move on and ahead is remarkable, and remarkably hopeful. I used to see this kind of startling shift daily, years ago, when I worked with runaway kids and their families—the surprising reassurance and hope, the reversion to calm and a semblance of sanity, that even a very few minutes of respectful, parental attention could give despairing adolescents. Runaways—there were more than one million of them each year when I created and directed a national program for them in the mid-1970s—often left their homes because they felt there was no way to be themselves, to be at once separate and dependent while they stayed there. Sophie, unable to leave home or stay, and frantic because of it, had felt compelled to opt for a permanent way out. And now her mother's clear caring was offering other real, though still unclear, possibilities, and hope.

In the following weeks, after I met with Sophie and her mother, I also treated Sophie with acupuncture and engaged her in her own care. For skeptical Sophie, each acupuncture session was "rather interesting"—"It does relax me," she had to admit, and "while you had the needles in, I had such a bright memory of my sweet little dog." And each item on my prescription pad—cutting down on sugar, caffeine, and beer; adding supplements; writing in her journal; taking long walks—was a welcome challenge. The simple injunctions addressed her concerns—her excess weight and her anxiety; offered her the opportunity to express herself; and encouraged her to have healthy time out of the house. They didn't imply that she was ill or defective in any way, and allowed her to define herself apart from her conflict with her parents.

In our fourth joint meeting, Jane agreed, much to Sophie's astonishment, that her daughter needed to go to boarding school. It seemed, after years of fruitless quarrels, so obvious. Still, there were significant practical and financial issues: Sophie, whose school record was none too good, had to be accepted; there would not be much money for college if she went to private school now; and her father had to be persuaded. Still, it was possible.

On their sixth visit, Jane, who suddenly seemed as disturbed as when Sophie was suicidal, stunned Sophie, and me, with her "confession." "I never really thought you were crazy or even deeply disturbed," she said. "Nor did I believe you were most at fault in the conflict with your father." Jane told us she had made a "conscious choice" to keep the peace with her husband. And so, in spite of what she really thought and felt, she had sided with him against Sophie; agreed with his assessments of Sophie's flawed character and serious psychopathology; and enforced his dictates as if they were her own.

Sophie was livid. But she was also relieved. After a few minutes of loud and angry invective, her body relaxed and her face softened, as if the world had just warmed and brightened. She'd been right all along. Her mother really was, at least in this most important area, a liar and a hypocrite. It was no wonder she'd felt so crazy and desperate.

Over the next weeks, past grievances and mutual mistrust receded into the background as Sophie and her mother drew on a small, but deep, reservoir of mutual good feeling. Checking out schools together, puzzling over financial forms, talking with Sophie's father, they freshened and replenished it. There were still blowups about money—Sophie's father was reluctant to spend so much of her college fund on high school—but Jane, now championing her daughter's needs, and Sophie prevailed. Within weeks, they had found a school that promised to foster Sophie's creativity, challenge her mind, and channel her aggression and rebellion into intellectual combat. At her admissions interview, Sophie, who ordinarily put her worst foot forward, was fluent and charming.

There were certainly fights in the months prior to Sophie's going away, but they had a different, ordinary, nondesperate quality: low-stakes disputes about curfews and drinking, and which clothes to take and how many to bring, and the necessity, or not, for a dorm room refrigerator. Jane's honesty had created a bridge over which Sophie could approach her, a basis for a working partnership and a foundation for ongoing trust. There were no more threats of suicide, no need to consider medication.

Four months later, Sophie left for boarding school. Freed from fruitless combat with her parents, she began to use her fine mind well, to enjoy her school and the academic challenges it brought. She made some friends and felt a satisfying self-reliance rather than a disabling, angry self-assertion. There were, of course, challenges, as Sophie met her own very real demons—a perfectionism that made her approach papers and tests slowly and fearfully, as if they were wild beasts, and merciless doubts about her own integrity. Still, she was far more open and accessible, deeply engaged with her life and her work, and, if sometimes overwhelmed, definitely not depressed. On the phone and at home, Sophie began to confide in her mother. She was far less inclined to be disabled or even discombobulated by her interactions with her father and her brothers. She had moved through the Dark Night of her despair.

Sophie and Jane's story is not exactly Persephone and Demeter's. Still, Sophie had long lived in stubborn silence in a bare underworld of pain, razors, and pills that pulled her toward death. And Jane, undone by her own deception, as well as her daughter's distress, had been wandering in fruitless search. Sophie's strangled cries had to emerge, be heard, interpreted, and related by me, Hekate's stand-in here, to her mother. Jane had to face her fear of her husband and admit to, and stop, the compliant, cowardly behavior that had deformed her relationship with her daughter. And both women needed to move beyond their perceived powerlessness, through remembered loss and persistent pain, to truths that gave them new life and returned them more honest, more whole, more wise to each other.

So it is with so many of the young people who think about and attempt suicide. They and we need to understand that the darkness of their mood and the disturbance in their lives don't have to be permanent. They need to be invited to express the pain that propels them toward death. And we adults need to hear and respect that pain, perhaps confessing, as Jane did, the fear that has made us judge, distance ourselves from, and try to constrain them.

We need instead, drawing on all the reserves of our family and community and culture, to understand that it is change and growth these near-adults want—an end, not to life, but to excruciating, apparently irremediable stuckness. Our job is to give shape and structure to the painful passage of these young people through these times of darkness, confusion, and despair. Then they will very likely move on, as Sophie did, to the next steps of their journey, away from suicidal desperation, toward the light.

HOLDING THE LIGHT FOR OUR CHILDREN

I'm writing these notes for adults, who are more likely to be reading them, but it would be an excellent idea for you to share them (and perhaps this whole book) with the young people you're concerned about. In fact, it's far easier, far more respectful, to engage adolescents as full collaborators as they navigate the Dark Night of their despair. Let me spell this out.

1 Young people, whether or not they admit it, want to feel better. We need to ally ourselves to this hope and this possibility.

2 Adolescents like Sophie may believe, because of previous experience, that there is no way out. Still, they are almost always responsive to genuine efforts to take a fresh, broader look at their situation, to efforts that provide alternatives to past, failed perspectives or solutions.

3 It's enormously useful to seek compassionate, evenhanded, "outside" help, a Guide—someone who can aid both the young person and her family in taking this broader look and developing alternatives.

4   This effort must begin by clarifying why the young person feels so helpless and hopeless, by listening carefully and respectfully to her point of view. Simply rushing to prohibit behavior or prescribe medication can be both demeaning and anxiety provoking, and is, in any case, unlikely to be effective.

5   This work must be collaborative. Young people should be engaged in their own care. I often describe my work with them—as I did with troublemaking, sugar-craving Dominique and angry and bewildered Jenny, as well as with Sophie—as "an experiment," one in which they are the primary investigators. That makes it interesting, challenging. It shows respect for their ability to help themselves. It also gives them a sense of control in situations where they may have felt powerless or victimized. I do this not only with teenagers but with kids as young as four or five.

6   Children, in general, have an even greater capacity to use, enjoy, and profit from the techniques that I describe in this book than do adults. Their youthful brain's capacity for learning and change, and their less fettered imaginations, make it quite easy for most children to effectively use mind-body techniques such as Soft Belly and guided imagery, to learn and enjoy the dialogues and drawings (I'll talk about the latter a bit later), to express themselves freely, and to channel their agitated energy into exercise, movement, dance, and expressive meditations.

7   Parents—and those of us who work professionally with children—need to be willing, as Jane was, to look at how our own concepts and behaviors may be foreclosing options for the young people we care about. Once we see what's getting in *our* way, we can get out of *their* way, as Jane did, and help them find their path to healing.

8   We should not aim for some imagined perfection of our child's behavior but for a fruitful, productive way out of the closed trap of despair. Our children's goal should not be to fulfill

adult expectations, but to take the next steps in their own life journey.

9 This is a process that takes time and patience. But in my experience, it often takes far less time than we fear and, indeed, far less than the experts may have estimated.

LATE MIDDLE AGE: MADELEINE'S DARKEST MOMENT

If we are depressed in our middle years, once again or still, we may feel even more discouraged than in earlier times. This may be in part, as research has shown, because second and subsequent episodes of depression seem to come more rapidly, and with less provocation. It may also be because in this later stage of life we may feel a kind of cumulative vulnerability. Tactics that worked well before—talk therapy, self-care, medication, Chinese medicine, exercise, and so forth—may seem to have simply been temporary fixes. Despair may threaten us, and sometimes suicide begins to seem almost sensible.

Erik Erikson, the psychoanalyst who wrote so eloquently about all the stages of the life cycle, described the central task of middle and late middle age as maintaining generativity in the face of stagnation. Generativity includes ongoing creativity and sharing ourselves and what we have learned—in our profession or our craft, and in the span of our lives—with the wider world, and especially with those who are younger, our children and grandchildren and those of others. Stagnation, the antonym that Erikson also describes, is very much like stuck, but it's darker, more dense, and more tenacious.

In middle and, especially, late middle age we come up against, or at least glimpse, the limits of our lives. We may find ourselves losing physical force and sexual ardor as well as the hope and imagination of youth. Loneliness and loss—of parents and friends to death and disability, and of children to the wider world—can, when we focus on them, stretch like a desert in front of us. Fresh ideas may flow less faithfully. Names begin to trickle away.

. . .

Madeleine was facing the loss and challenges of this time in life with fewer resources and less hope than many. I'd been seeing her every month or two for most of the previous ten years. When she first came to me, she'd had lower back pain, irritable bowel syndrome, and anxiety as well as depression. Her husband had died years before, leaving her childless, and she hadn't found another fulfilling, long-term relationship. Though she was a fine writer and linguist, and had always loved to travel, the world had seemed barren to Madeleine, life an ordeal. She always seemed to have to try so hard to secure a small measure of family support, to make friends, to gain favor at her job.

Dissatisfaction and hurt, worry and bitterness, were written in the creases of her forehead and echoed by her belly's turmoil. Along with painkillers, anti-inflammatories, and antispasmodic drugs for her back and gut, she'd taken antidepressants for six months. The first had given her "a little lift" for some weeks, but had also upset her gut, made her more anxious, and deprived her of sleep. The second had damaged her liver.

With diet and exercise, acupuncture, herbs, and meditation, Madeleine's back got better and so did her gut. She stopped the SSRI she was then taking as well as the other medication. Meditating—learning to relax and watch rather than being entrenched in or overwhelmed by her relationships—helped her begin to disentangle herself from her family's insults and indignities. As Madeleine started to appreciate her role in conflicts with her bosses, as well as her skill in their service, she seemed more realistic and felt less resentful. Madeleine's successes at a new job gave her satisfaction, and her social life picked up. Living alone and often lonely, skillful but unfulfilled at work, she wasn't exactly happy or satisfied, but she was certainly, as she put it, "OK."

"I Can't Keep Feeling Like This"

And then, as her sixtieth birthday approached, she wasn't. The glass that might have been half full emptied out. "My parents," she began one day several years ago, "were depressed. My sisters and brothers are depressed and, no matter what I do, I am, too, much of the time. I'm lonely ninety-nine percent of the time. I know, things look better on the outside. And I'm definitely less dysfunctional, more aware. Still, I stumble and get in my own way. I feel I have to perform in order to get any response. Most of all, I feel so alone, so terribly lonely. There's no cushion of family or friends. I want drugs," she concluded, as sad and disappointed to ask as she was challenging. "No matter how bad they are. Or," she added reluctantly, "to hear some wisdom. I can't keep feeling like this day after day, year after year." Madeleine is slumped in her chair as she says these last words, her jaw set in pain and defiance, her demand and her desperation heavy in the room.

I have to agree that things look bleak. Though Madeleine is less dependent on her family's approval, their coldness still has the power to chill and disappoint her. She does need, for as long as she is able, to hold on to jobs with obvious limitations and disappointments. She is a woman without independent means, alone and sixty, whose family history shadows her future.

I sit with Madeleine. No wisdom certainly, not even any words, come to me as I feel the difficulty of her present situation, her loneliness, her lifelong pain, like a knife pulled slowly across skin. Something opens in me, empathy, kinship, respect.

I tell Madeleine—wondering if I am pushing too hard, but believing and feeling that it is right and necessary and respectful—that when nothing seems to bring our spirits up, it's actually a time to go deeper, to exhume the buried thoughts and feelings that chain our hearts and minds to the past, in order to free ourselves. I ask her to do the full hour of Dynamic Meditation that years before had been my daily practice: fifteen minutes of fast, deep breathing, followed by fifteen minutes of emotional catharsis (shouting out feelings, letting the body be moved by them, pounding pillows), ten of jumping up and down, ten of silent, still watchfulness, and, finally, ten of dance.

Waiting while Madeleine considers my prescription, I imagine her among the Plains Indians, who on wilderness vision quests come to know the wildness of their own minds and hearts.

"This will not be easy," Madeleine pauses, choosing her words carefully, "for a very depressed person."

"Yes," I say, agreeing. "Let's see what happens. If something more, some biological boost, is needed, we'll use that, too."

Two weeks later, Madeleine is back. "I'm doing Dynamic every day, and I'm sore as hell." Emotions that had simmered for years are coming together in a dense, odorous soup. "The words keep coming up during the catharsis, 'angry,' 'sad,' 'miserable,' 'lonely,' 'friendless,' 'scared,' 'tired.' I can't stand it! My pain is more acute than ever, and I stumble around all day like a bull in a china shop."

Madeleine did, however, feel more energized, loosed slightly from her customary posture of aggrieved victimization. "While I'm pounding and shouting, I see more clearly what those others—relatives, bosses, colleagues—are like. And I also see what I do to get myself in trouble, how my expecting to be hurt is a red flag to those who wind up hurting me." On the mornings after she did Dynamic Meditation, she felt "more likely to take a walk, more interested in other people, maybe even ready to call someone up." Still she "couldn't see how much longer I can take this." The pain of her losses and loneliness was so sharp. It was so hard to reach out, and it hurt so much when her tentative moves toward others were ignored or rejected.

"I Deserve Respect"

Madeleine returns a week later. Her words are now angrier. They have attitude as well as energy. She's hurting more acutely, but she's also taking far more responsibility for what happens to her. People are no longer "cruel"; they now "piss" her off. She tells me that a friend her age who was also alone felt "terrific." Surprisingly, to her as well as me, this gave Madeleine hope for herself. But it also made her feel worse about her own inability to deal with her loneliness, the lack of love in her life, and her future. "This woman feels like a whole person just as she is, no man, no kids, sixty years old, and not rich." Madeleine is realizing how her perspective has shaped her feelings and also how far she is from where she wants to be. She says she'll continue to do Dynamic Meditation, but she insists she needs "something else or something more, a physiological boost."

Madeleine's request seems reasonable. She's done so much on her own, is learning so much, and is planning to continue, to push on deeper. Why not see if supplements can give her the physiological boost she's asking for and help her move through this dark time more easily? I prescribe S-adenosylmethionine (SAMe) for her, a supplement that helps our bodies produce more of several neurotransmitters, including serotonin, dopamine, and norepinephrine (I'll talk in detail about SAMe a little later). I suggest 400 milligrams in the morning and 200 milligrams at lunch time, an amount that may soon boost her energy and is unlikely to produce unpleasant side effects.

A week later, the circumstances of Madeleine's life remain the same and the bouts of despair still come, but there is a shift in her attitude toward them. "I don't feel so reactive, so out of control. I feel physically less sad. What I mean is, my body has some bounce. I know that Dynamic has raised my energy and what we're talking about is giving me more perspective, more hope, but I think it's the SAMe, too, and there are none of the negative effects of the drugs. And even if it's some kind of placebo effect, I'm going to keep taking it. I'm beginning to get that meditative perspective you've talked about for so many years."

One morning, not long after, during the cathartic part of Dynamic Meditation, Madeleine found herself shouting phrases that surprised her—"I deserve respect," and then, "That means I should give myself respect." "That astonished me," Madeleine says. "It's the kind of thing all the self-help books tell you about, but it wasn't coming from someone's sermon. It was coming from inside me."

Madeleine began to feel significantly better about herself, more comfortable about reaching out to others. Before she felt there was "no one" in her life with whom she could be honest. Now, when she "goes into a dark hole," she is able to "raise my head a bit" and discover—on the phone, via e-mail, or at church—"four or five" other women who are willing to listen to her, to share their own experiences, their own disappointments and depression, as well as their humor and hope. Madeleine feels as if she's "rejoining the human race."

Madeleine speaks up more at work in the ensuing weeks: "When things get impossibly chaotic ... I refuse to shoulder the blame." She starts looking at ads for jobs where she might feel more welcome, make better use of her talents, and, especially, be helpful to troubled young people who need the skills she can share with them. A month later, in a booming real-estate market, she sells her apartment, then panics, "I may never be in one this good." She breathes fast and shouts and dances and calms down. Two weeks later she's bought another nicer, less expensive place.

"A predictably calamitous" family visit devastates Madeleine for a few days before she further loosens family ties, "so I can more easily start over." In previous years, she notes, this "might have undone me. I do," she observes, surprised but very pleased with herself, "handle things better."

"Yes!" I say, not pumping my fist, but feeling like it. Madeleine has moved willingly, determinedly, into and through the places of her deepest hurt and darkest fears, and she is emerging less burdened, more generous, more content, happier than I've ever known her. She is rising up from lifelong victimhood and resentment to claim the life of her later years, inspiring me with her tenacity and courage. And now she is taking, and very much reminding me and all of us to take, the later-life troubles that inevitably come—and what a fine phrase of forward movement this is— in stride.

OLD AGE: THE AMBASSADOR AND THE SCIENTIST

The despair of old age is a terrible thing. I think of Lear, betraying and betrayed, alone and howling; of old people wasting away, moaning for death to come.

There comes a time when we know that we will die and know, too, that we are actually headed in that direction. The prince Siddhartha Gautama met this reality as a young man and, in time, woke up, became enlightened, and was called the Buddha. The present Dalai Lama, one of the Buddha's great heirs, once told me that from the age of eight on, he has thought daily about death.

This doesn't mean we should resign ourselves to death or decay. This is a very bad idea and a major contributor to depression, as well as to earlier death. If anything, old age should signal a more pressing need to care more lovingly, and with far more consistency, for our bodies and minds, and to share ourselves more fully with others. In fact, the approaches that I present in this book are even more important and effective for the elderly. Exercise—fitness generally and flexibility in particular—seems to have an even more powerful positive effect on the health and mood of older people than on the young, as do good diets, mental activity, and active engagement with other people.

Still, the coming of old age is a time for us to accept what is inevitable as *gracefully* (what a nice word that is, implying the beneficence of a higher power, as well as physical fluidity and ease) as we can. It's an opportunity to address—even perhaps embrace, against all reason—the challenges and wonder and mystery of all that comes our later-life way. Old people have many reasons to despair, many losses, many pains, including, most particularly, the growing certainty of their decline and the realization that there is, as the saying goes, "no hope of getting out of here alive."

All of us need to acknowledge, before we can adequately deal with them, these simple facts of our lives. Resistance to them causes us pots full of misery that we don't need, compounding our pain with resentment, limiting the possibilities that *are* given to us, souring the sweetness of what is happening now.

I am, at sixty-six, a beginning student in this class, but I've had some remarkable teachers, including two older men, both diagnosed with depression, who came to be friends as well as patients. One succumbed to illness and old age with a quiet resentment that drained his days of joy, and went decorously to his death. His resignation made his family and friends almost as sad as did his passing, and is a warning to us against old age's temptations to despair. The other, no less angry and at times despairing at his "terminal diagnosis," embraced the intellectual and physical challenges of his illness, reached out with wonder to all who gathered around him, and left us with love.

The Ambassador

The ambassador, a handsome, courtly man, was one of our country's great men, a statesman. As he approached eighty, his days were filled with sadness for the loss of his dear and, to him, incomparable wife, and punctuated by evidence of his waning physical power and shrinking (though still considerable) mental range. He had dutifully taken, along with medications for his cardiac arrhythmia and joint pain, the variety of antidepressants his doctors had prescribed. They did no good for him; in truth, he had not expected that they would.

The ambassador came to see me in order to mute the pleadings of his friends and relatives, but with little hope. Several years had passed since his wife's death, but he couldn't, wouldn't, let himself move on. His mourning had clotted to melancholia. The beautiful and kind women who sought him out all paled in comparison to his late wife. He was inconsolable, and his misery weighed on those who cared about him. "I'd like"—and he smiled self-deprecatingly as he said it—"to please them."

The ambassador had recently refused government positions as a senior counselor and resigned his posts on the boards of Fortune 500 companies and of charities that worked to improve the environment and reduce global suffering. He still stoically attended A-list dinner parties—"more relic to be observed than participant to be engaged"—but he'd stopped playing poker and golf. His inability to count cards, his topped drives and shanked irons, mocked years of bold betting, smooth backswings, and near-par rounds.

The ambassador seemed to enjoy our meetings. He smiled with benign fascination at my efforts to argue, analyze, meditate, and tease him out of his funk, and he asked thoughtful questions about my family and my work overseas with people traumatized by war. Still, he seemed to endure, at best observe, rather than embrace the life that was left to him. It was as if he believed that each of us has a quota of energy and excellence and he had used his up. His interest in his children, and their children, waned, and he slowly, gently excused himself from their lives.

At the urging of his close friends and family, and with my encouragement, the ambassador did marry again—an intelligent, warm, beautiful woman who loved him. And he loved her, too, and enjoyed her tender companionship. But still he faded. It was as if living less passionately, gracefully, and elegantly than he had held little interest for him. The flesh disappeared from his fine bones. His heartbeat became less strong, more irregular. The ambassador gave up; eased slowly, resigned and graceful, into a final descent toward death.

The Scientist

Another older man, I'll call him the scientist, leapt into the life that was left him. He had phoned me after he'd done some research on alternative therapies for the recurrent cancer that his oncologist said would soon—in months, weeks perhaps—claim his life. He was a world-class scientist and had become an expert in the disease that threatened to claim him. He knew that the odds that the recommended conventional therapy would save, or even extend, his life slightly were pitifully long. And he thought it highly unlikely that any alternative would help. "I'm a conventional man and exceedingly skeptical," he told me on that first call. Still, he wanted, "if there's at least a plausible mechanism of action, to explore other possibilities. Another game," he added slyly, "in which I can play."

The scientist lived, against all odds and everyone's predictions, for another five years. I consulted with him about the various therapies—conventional, complementary, and alternative—that he was exploring and using, and walked with him through the despair that at times overcame him. He was at least as proud and competitive as the ambassador and, as some of the alternatives lost their power to slow his cancer, as despairing about his diminished mental and physical capacities and his dwindling reserves of energy. He mourned his inability to climb and bike, to surf and sail, or even, as time went on, to walk briskly. He hated the way his elegant clothes fell from his cancer-diminished body. But there was something wondrously different about the way the scientist dealt with disappointment, depression, and even despair, a difference that became a legacy for all who knew him.

The scientist never stopped experimenting and engaging those of us who cared for him—his colleagues, his students, his family—in his search for health. He wanted to explain what he was learning, what was happening to him, to his wife and daughters, his friends and doctors. His language became less academic, simpler, more enthusiastic. And always there was a sense of possibility and adventure, a hope—for he was a true physician—that his experience might also be useful to others with cancer.

"See what we've learned about the Chinese herbs, how they stop the growth of my cancer cells when they're combined with them in a petri dish," he announced with glee on one visit. And on the next, "Take a look at the latest research on this vaccine."

In his worst time, in the months before he died, when the alternatives appeared to be losing their power, when the experimental chemo was, it seemed to friends and family, doing more harm than good, and weakness was seeping all through him, dampening his enthusiasm and depressing his mind, he joined a mind-body skills group I was leading. He was tired and discouraged and even, as his pain worsened, despairing. And he was predictably skeptical—"I'm not much of a group person"—but still curious. "I've never done this," he said.

On the last day of the group, we did three drawings—a reprise of an exercise we'd done in the first session. "Imagine yourself as you are now," I instructed, and played some music to help us summon up the mental images we would translate into pictures. When I stopped the music, I asked our group to draw the mental images that had come to them. I put on the music again: "Imagine how you would like to be" was the instruction this time. I continued to play the music for a while and then turned it off so they could draw. Finally, I asked them first to imagine and then draw "How you'll get to where you want to be" (I'll do this exercise in detail with you in the Prescription for Self-Care at the end of this chapter).

After we'd completed all three images and done the three drawings, each of us, in turn, showed our drawings, putting them side by side in the center of the circle, comparing them with the ones we'd done on the first day of our group.

When the scientist's turn came, he leaned forward. He pointed to his first set of drawings, noting small dark figures. His hope for the future, his second drawing, focused on an intravenous drip of a new, more effective chemotherapy, a masked surgeon, and diagnostic tests. The people were grim, widely separated, looking past one another.

Then he showed us the first drawing in the set he'd just completed, "Myself as I am now." "Everything looks different. All these people"—his wife, daughters, colleagues, cancer therapists—"are closer to me. And you guys in the group are here, too," indicating, he "suspected," his growing appreciation of the powerful importance of emotional support. "I look more at home," he said, "even in this first picture."

In the second drawing of that same set, the one of "How you would like to be," he was bathed in light, his arms were extended, his hands open, and there was a sweet smile on his face. The colors were far lighter and brighter than those he'd used on the first day; the darkness was present but not dominant. We group members were in a circle around him, our hands clasped. "I look so open. I'm letting go," he said, surprised, pointing. "And all of you are there, around me, with me, ready to catch me and hold me."

He shook his head and grinned as he turned over the third drawing, the one that told him, and us, how he would get to such a peaceful place. He was a boy in this picture, a stick figure. His head was in the lap of another stick figure, "my long-ago-dead grandmother."

He went on: "My parents were great, but pretty straitlaced. But my grandmother just lavished love on me. As you gave us the image and the music played, I could see her and hear her, too. It was definitely," he said, with the wonder of the child he was a very long time ago, "her soft voice, with that little lilt of an Irish accent that we all teased her about. She appeared to me while we were letting the image come. I loved her so much as a boy, and I haven't thought of her in years. And she said to me, while I listened to that flute music, 'I am here. I love you. Everything will be all right.'" He was crying as I'd never seen him before.

"I've never believed in all this touchy-feely stuff, in spirits, or life after death. I'm a scientist," he explained, summoning a bit of self-importance that made him smile, "but I cannot deny how much better I feel, and how much more hopeful I feel, and how happy I am to tell all of you about it."

CONSIDERING MEDICATION AND ITS ALTERNATIVES

Dark Nights, and particularly those that go painfully on and on, are the time when even the most skeptical and parsimonious of prescribers, like me, considers recommending antidepressant drugs. The length and intensity of the suffering of the person in front of us, and the inadequacy of previous approaches, heightens the urgency.

In the following section, I'll begin by sharing with you some of my reasoning about when antidepressants should be considered. Then I'll discuss some of the substances—the amino acid precursors and the herb that I sometimes prescribe before referring my patients for antidepressants. They are substances that can produce potent biochemical and psychological changes that are very similar to those of the drugs without many of their harmful side effects. Finally, I'll discuss the situations in which I think it is reasonable to explore the use of antidepressant drugs.

I'll start with my thoughts about using drugs with depressed kids. First of all, I haven't needed or wanted to prescribe antidepressants for children or adolescents, who, I believe, are far too quickly and scandalously often medicated. Using the approach I describe here, I didn't need to use them with Dominique or Jenny or suicidal Sophie, or the many other young people I've worked with over the years.

I believe antidepressants suppress the emotions that adolescents need to experience and express. Their short-term effects may well include increased agitation and distress, the likely reasons why antidepressants have been shown to *increase* suicidal thinking in children, adolescents, and young adults, too. Their long-term negative effects on developing brains may be quite significant and are, in any case, still unknown. And last, but not least, they give kids the generally erroneous, and sometimes quite debilitating, message that they are sick and must depend on a pill for their well-being and sanity.

All this doesn't mean you can't use the *Unstuck* approach with kids on antidepressants—just that it's a very good idea to help them get off the drugs as quickly and safely as possible.

I personally don't use antidepressants with adults either, but on occasion I do refer them to physicians who are skilled in and conservative with their use—that is, likely to use them sparingly and for short periods of time. I make these referrals only after I've done my best with all the approaches and techniques I've described on these pages. Or, if someone doesn't want to use this approach and explicitly asks me to.

Before I make these occasional referrals, however, I'm likely to explore the use of three nonprescription remedies that work—as antidepressant drugs do—directly on neurotransmitters: the supplements S-adenosyl-methionine (SAMe) and tryptophan (and its derivative 5-hydroxytrypto-phan, or 5HTP) and the herb Saint-John's-wort (*Hypericum*). All three have been demonstrated in some studies to provide symptom relief that is, for most people, as effective as the antidepressants, and far less fraught with unpleasant or destructive side effects.

Though I have seen each of these remedies provide relief of specific symptoms, including insomnia, agitation, rumination, pessimism, procrastination, and exhaustion, I don't prescribe them lightly or routinely. They all may have some of the same limitations as chemical antidepressants: the tendency to flatten out the emotional highs and lows that may be necessary to calling for and catalyzing change; side effects that, if less severe and prevalent than those of drugs, can still be distressing; a feeling of dependency on the supplements and a subjective sense, in some of those who take them, that their condition is a disease that calls for medication; and, in the case of Saint-John's-wort, quite serious interactions with other medications.

I use these supplements only occasionally. So far, of the people I've discussed in this book, only Madeleine, and Maria and Darla, the two overwhelmed procrastinators, have taken them.

Here I want to present some of the evidence for each of the three non-prescription supplements and suggest some situations in which they might be helpful. Though they don't require a prescription, if you are considering these remedies, I strongly urge you to work with someone who is knowledgeable about them—a psychiatrist or holistic MD or DO, a naturopathic physician, a chiropractor who is an expert in nutrition, a qualified nutritionist or dietitian, or, in the case of Saint-John's-wort, an herbalist. You can use the Resources section to help find these professionals.

And *don't*—I repeat *don't*—use these remedies if you are still taking antidepressants. Remember, they work directly on the very same neurotransmitter pathways as the prescription drugs. You need to find a professional who can help you get off one and on the other, or to combine them in a way that works safely for you.

SAMe

The supplement that I'm most likely to use is S-adenosylmethionine (SAMe). SAMe is called a methyl donor because it releases a methyl molecule into the body, one composed of a carbon atom attached to three hydrogen atoms. This molecule is essential to the production of the neurotransmitters serotonin, norepinephrine, and dopamine, precisely the ones at which antidepressants, and stimulant drugs such as Ritalin and the amphetamines, are targeted. Instead of blocking reuptake of these transmitters, as many chemical antidepressants do, SAMe seems to encourage the body's production of all three of them.

Some of the studies on the efficacy of SAMe are of poor quality, and even the better ones have many of the same flaws as the studies on antidepressant drugs. Still, the overall data is somewhat encouraging. According to a review of some fifty studies by lead author Richard Brown, a Columbia Medical School psychiatrist who regularly uses SAMe clinically, the bottom line is that SAMe relieves symptoms of depression significantly better than placebo, and often as well as chemical antidepressants (it's been compared to both imipramine and SSRIs).

Brown's and other published articles show that SAMe has far fewer and less severe side effects than the SSRIs. The ones most often observed in studies, and those I've seen in my clinical experience, include agitation and GI hyperactivity, headaches, and emotional numbing. Withdrawal symptoms appear to be minimal. There have been no reports of suicide, though, to my knowledge, this has not been explicitly studied. One million Europeans have been reported to have taken SAMe (which also appears to give some relief from joint pain) regularly.

I'm most likely to use SAMe with people who have a chronic, recurrent depression and a persistent sense of being overwhelmed and unable to do more, coupled with a desperate need to find some temporary relief from the pain of their discouragement and struggle.

I sometimes use SAMe with those who have terrible trouble with procrastination and avoidance—for example, Darla, the graduate student who, in spite of using many of the approaches in this book as well as cognitive behavioral therapy, couldn't complete her research papers. Most often, they take SAMe, which begins to act more quickly than antidepressants, for a few weeks or months to help them through a crisis. Then, as they continue to use the *Unstuck* approach and feel better, they tend to "forget" to take SAMe. Finding they still feel well, they taper off and stop. On a few occasions, others I've worked with, such as Madeleine, have stayed on SAMe for a year or two while they've continued to use the approaches in this book.

I've also used SAMe, sometimes for long periods, with people with chronic pain, advanced cancer, chronic wasting neurological disorders, and severe lung disease. It seems, often without troubling side effects, to give them an energy boost, to improve their mood, and to enhance their capacity to deal with overwhelming and disabling illness.

Tryptophan and 5HTP

Over the years, I've occasionally used several neurotransmitter "precursors," particularly tyrosine and phenylalanine, which increase norepinephrine and dopamine production, and tryptophan and 5-hydroxytryptophan (5HTP), which enhance serotonin production. These amino acids are known as precursors because in the body they are converted to neurotransmitters.

Perhaps because they facilitate production rather than interfere with breakdown of neurotransmitters, precursors tend to have fewer side effects than drugs. At this time, however, I do not use either tyrosine or phenylalanine with my patients. I prefer SAMe, which seems more effective and has more recent research studies to back it up.

I still sometimes use tryptophan, or the more easily available 5HTP (into which tryptophan is converted), to help depressed people who, in spite of all the other approaches I've used, have not improved. I'm most likely to use it with depressed people who also have significant trouble sleeping and, rarely, with people who aren't depressed but can't sleep.

There are a few controlled trials and a number of less rigorous studies that show that 5HTP and tryptophan supplementation can improve mood and decrease emotional distress better than placebo. There are also studies that demonstrate the ability of tryptophan and 5HTP to promote sleep. Both tryptophan and 5HTP appear (though this has not been at all well studied) to have fewer and far less devastating side effects than SSRIs.

Because of the dangerous, and sometimes lethal, allergic reactions that were reported some years ago, tryptophan is still not widely available over the counter in the United States (though it is in Canada and Europe and can easily be prescribed in the United States). I want to emphasize that these reactions to tryptophan were *not* side effects. As far as investigators have been able to determine, they came from one contaminated batch. They were the result of a specific and, in a number of cases, deadly manufacturing defect that had nothing to do with the substance itself.

Saint-John's-wort (*Hypericum*)

For many centuries, Saint-John's-wort has been used by herbalists to treat neurological disorders and to enhance the body's resistance to infection, as well as to improve mood. In recent years, scientists have explored its mode of antidepressant action (it raises levels of serotonin, probably increases norepinephrine and dopamine, and possibly boosts other neurotransmitters as well) and have compared its efficacy to that of chemical antidepressants.

In dosages of 300 milligrams of extract (standardized to contain 0.3 percent of the compound hypericin, which is one, but by no means the only one, of the active ingredients in the herb) given three times a day for four weeks, Saint-John's-wort has proved significantly better than placebo. In some studies, it has been as effective as SSRIs in relieving the symptoms of mild to moderate depression—with far fewer side effects. In a recent large-scale multisite study, Saint-John's-wort was not more effective than placebo for people with more severe depression, but neither was the chemical antidepressant to which it was compared.

This data is both useful and misleading. It's useful because it documents the very real antidepressant effectiveness of Saint-John's-wort. The studies on Saint-John's-wort—and its widespread use in Europe and the United States—also help, more generally, to open our minds to the possibility that there are equally effective, less harmful, and less expensive natural alternatives to antidepressant drugs for depression.

The studies on Saint-John's-wort are also, in important ways, misleading. This is because they perpetuate two misguided notions: that there is, or could be, a single treatment for everyone's depression, and that herb and drug prescribing are basically the same. Some well-trained Western herbalists believe Saint-John's-wort is inappropriate and even contraindicated for certain kinds of depression. Even more important, Saint-John's-wort, even when appropriate, may be far more effective if it's used as one element in a complex, multipart herbal formula.

I rarely prescribe Saint-John's-wort, strongly preferring to work with combinations of Chinese herbs. Some of my patients have, however, taken it with some benefit, usually for brief periods, when they were just starting with me or during times of very significant stress. Some people I've worked with, particularly those with chronic physical illnesses, including neurological disorders and cancer, have found that it's been quite helpful to them over long periods of time.

An important cautionary note with Saint-John's-wort: It induces a liver enzyme system that accelerates the breakdown of a number of drugs, including the antiretroviral medications that are used to treat HIV/AIDS, thereby rendering them less effective, or even ineffective. As I've said before, a physician, a nutritionist, or an herbalist should be consulted if you are thinking of taking Saint-John's-wort. He or she should be informed of all the other medications that you're taking and should work closely with you if you decide to discontinue an antidepressant and start Saint-John's-wort.

Other "Natural" Antidepressants

There are a number of other substances that in the last ten years have been heavily promoted as antidepressants. These include, most prominently, the herb *Rhodiola rosea* (which has long been used in Asia) and L-theanine, which is present in green tea. Though the studies on their use in depression are not at this point impressive, both herbs seem to work to moderate the intensity of the stress response. You can check the references in the Notes section to find out more about them. I don't currently use them with my patients.

IF YOU FEEL YOU DO NEED ANTIDEPRESSANT DRUGS

In this book, I've been describing a comprehensive, integrative, and individualized approach in which even the deepening of depression and despair can signal progress in a journey toward healing. From this perspective, antidepressant drugs are, even for those who are despairing or suicidal, a last resort rather than a first choice. Still, there may come a time when the pain becomes too intense and intractable, when these drugs are a reasonable remedy: "In extreme situations," Hippocrates admonished, "extreme remedies."

If this time comes, if you are convinced, after working with a good Guide for several months and using the approach I'm sharing with you in *Unstuck* (including the precursors and Saint-John's-wort), that you need something else or something more, *or* if you are feeling consistently overwhelmed, desperate, and hopeless, then you may indeed want to ask for a referral to a psychiatrist or other physician who is an expert in prescribing antidepressant medication.

What follows are some guidelines to help you decide if you want and need to take medication, and some guidance in finding a professional who can skillfully and thoughtfully work with you.

FINDING A PHYSICIAN-PHARMACOLOGIST

It's vitally important that the physician who prescribes your medicine be a good one—for you. It is abundantly clear—and the power of the placebo effect on depression is well documented—that here, as in every other therapeutic relationship, the quality of the connection, and the faith and trust that the physician inspires in you, can make a significant difference in the treatment outcome.

Here is a checklist to review if you're thinking of going to a physician for antidepressant drugs. You may want to ask yourself these questions and take these steps before you decide to ask for, and use, antidepressants. Afterward I make some suggestions for finding an appropriate physician-pharmacologist.

>> Have you given your work with your Guide a fair trial?
>> Have you discussed with your Guide the possibility of taking medication? What are the results of that discussion?
>> Do you think you might do better with another Guide? If so, have you explored other possibilities?
>> Have you ruled out the potential physical causes and contributors to depression discussed in chapter one, "The Call"? Have you taken steps to find help for any imbalances that may have been discovered?
>> Have you been actively engaged in the *Unstuck* approach and the Prescriptions for Self-Care? In what ways are you satisfied with the results? What are its limitations for you?

>> Have you consulted a practitioner of Chinese medicine? Have these approaches helped?

>> Is there more you feel you should be doing? Are you willing to do it?

>> Have you consulted a qualified health professional about SAMe, tryptophan, 5HTP, and Saint-John's-wort? If you've used any of these for at least two weeks, have they been helpful?

>> What is still troubling you? Use the Inner Guide imagery or dialogue with an SPI to help you decide what to do about it.

>> Do you now feel you want to look into taking medication?

If, after this inquiry, you feel that you do want to take medication, ask your Guide or your primary care physician for a referral to an expert in pharmacological treatment—a psychopharmacologist who specializes in this treatment or another physician with long experience in using these drugs. That person should be humane, thoughtful, committed to psychological exploration and psychotherapeutic approaches as well as medication, and, ideally, encouraging about, or at least accepting of, the approach in *Unstuck*.

If you go for a consultation with this psychopharmacological expert, make sure you discuss with her everything else that you're doing—including, and especially, all the supplements you may be taking—and be sure that you feel comfortable sharing with this person what you're taking and who you are.

Remember that all decisions about your welfare, and what best serves you, are ultimately yours. And understand, even as you take the drugs, that they, too, can be an aid on your journey. They are not its end point.

SUMMING UP: MOVING THROUGH THE DARK NIGHT

›› At some point in our lives, any or all of us may lose hope. This time may be called the Dark Night of the Soul.

›› Remember, even Dark Nights are part of a natural process of change. Dark Nights do most often yield to brighter mornings.

›› The despair and even the suicidal feelings that accompany these Dark Nights are actually the Call to change.

›› Now is a time to open yourself to possibilities you've never dreamed of, and to call on a skilled, courageous Guide to help you discover and realize them.

›› Let the stories of Sophie, Madeleine, and the scientist inspire you. Read them over. Let them remind you that times of despair whenever they come can, with care and courage, become times of the most profound, life-affirming change.

›› Times of despair are times when many of you may want to use antidepressant drugs.

›› Before you do so, consult with your Guide and explore, with a skilled professional, the possibility of using natural, nonprescription, mild-side-effect precursors and supplements.

›› If you do decide to take antidepressant drugs, make sure you follow the steps I've suggested for finding a skilled and compassionate physician.

›› Regard drugs as an aid on your journey, not a cure-all or end point.

PRESCRIPTION FOR SELF-CARE:
Imagining an Alternative

Like my friend the scientist, most of us have the capacity, even when we are most despairing, to conceive of change and to imagine at least the first steps by which we can bring it about. I know this seems unlikely—the nature of despair is to feel bereft of possibility.

Still, I've seen it happen over and over—in my private practice, in our groups at The Center for Mind-Body Medicine, and even in the midst of population-destroying wars.

The exercise we use, the one with which the scientist and his fellow group members worked, is a simple sequence of drawings. It invites your imagination to roam, free of the constraints of conscious thought, of the dismal logic of depressive thinking. It may be profound and useful at any time on your journey. When you are in despair, it can be a life changer, even a lifesaver.

You'll need some crayons or, better yet, because they're brighter and bolder, some markers, and three sheets of blank paper (or three pages in your journal). You can use music, like a gentle meditative melody (see the Resources section), to help you on this journey of the imagination.

Here are the instructions:

Begin with Soft Belly, breathing deeply for several minutes, allowing your belly to be soft, as you've done before, relaxing with each exhalation. Then . . .

Imagine yourself as you are now.

Let the image unfold. You may find yourself in a real-life situation or one you've never experienced. Alone or with others. At work or home. Indoors or on a city street or in nature. Pay attention to the images that arise. Feel the feelings that come. Listen for words or sounds. Take a few minutes to do this.

Now, open your eyes and draw what you've experienced. Your drawing can be abstract or realistic. It can fill most of the page or only a part of it. Use words if you'd like, as well, to clarify or to describe more fully what you're representing.

You may be self-conscious. Most of us who as children endured the limitations of our own artistic productions, as well as the criticisms of adults, are self-conscious. But there are no grades on this exercise, no judgments. Take 5 minutes or so. Now put this paper away. Next . . .

Imagine how you would like to be.

Sit comfortably again, breathing deeply, doing Soft Belly. This time, imagine how you would like to be. For several minutes, let this scene unfold with all its visual images, sounds, and feelings.

Open your eyes and take 5 minutes to draw what you've experienced on the second sheet of paper. Now put this paper away as well. Finally . . .

Imagine how you'll get from "where you are now" to "how you want to be."

You're ready now for the third drawing. This time, as you sit comfortably for a few minutes, allow an image to come of how you will get from "how you are now" to "how you want to be," from drawing one to drawing two. Your mind may argue with your intention. "How can I do that?" "If I could do that, I wouldn't be so desperate to know what to do or how to do it." Let those thoughts come and go, and stay with whatever images arise. They may make no sense to you as they form. That's OK. Let them unfold.

Open your eyes and put what you've experienced on paper, again allowing the drawing to take form as it needs to, noticing but not dwelling on the disbelief that may accompany your efforts. Take 5 minutes or so for this third drawing.

Now look at your three pictures in turn, and write your responses to each of the following questions in your journal:

>> What do you see in each drawing?
>> What shapes and colors and words?
>> What does each drawing evoke in you as you look at it now?
>> Does it seem different from when you drew it?

Now, compare the first two drawings.

>> What changes are there between the first and second drawings? In form? Color? Subject matter? Theme?
>> What do these changes tell you about "who and how you are now" and "who and how you would like to be"?
>> What do you think and feel about your vision of who you'd like to be?
>> Is this vision of the future surprising or predictable?

Now, look at the third drawing again.

The first drawing is an assessment of your present status, a reflection of your state of mind. The second represents possibility and illustrates your capacity for, or the difficulty of, hope. The third is a function of your intuition as well as your imagination and may, like the scientist's, be both surprising and profoundly useful, as well as reassuring. You may find that you really are able to see and move beyond your constrained hope and present, limited, despairing vision.

What do you see in this third drawing? How does what you've drawn relate to your present situation and to its resolution in the second drawing? What are the steps—of thought, feeling and/or action—that it suggests to you? After he looked at this third drawing, the scientist knew he had to devote attention to the spiritual life he had long neglected. The closeness to his grandmother that he "saw" and the words of hers that he "heard" were, indeed, helping him do what his second drawing had shown: relax, open up, share who he was and everything that was happening, everything he was learning, with those who cared for him.

Are you willing to take these steps? If not, why not? What are you waiting for? What can you do, right now, or very soon, to make this vision of change and healing a reality?

Write down in your journal answers to these questions and anything else that comes to you.

These drawings may be for you, as they were for the scientist, a revelation. You can look at them when you are feeling despairing, put them on the wall to remind yourself of what is possible.

It can be quite helpful to repeat these drawings in a few days or a few weeks. Like the scientist's, yours may change significantly when you do them again. Comparing them allows you to recognize changes in your attitude and outlook, and in your capacity to open yourself to the power of your intuition. New images may well come, giving guidance for necessary change, allowing you to make closer connections with your own long-buried capacity for wonder and hope.

CHAPTER 6

Spirituality: The Blessing

>>>>>> Just about everyone who makes the journey out of depression feels, sooner or later, a connection to something larger than himself that touches and transforms his life. Both this connection and that larger "something" are what we often call "spiritual."

The idea of the spiritual may seem remote, otherworldly, and unattainable to some of you. Some of you may dismiss it as marginal or trendy, or, on the other hand, confuse it with religion. In fact, the spiritual dimension of our lives can be as real, immediate, and accessible as the physical and emotional dimensions. And, it does not require belief in order to experience it, or dogma to define it.

In many of the world's languages (for example, Hebrew, Greek, Sanskrit, and Chinese), words for "spirit" are identical or close to those for "breath." This etymological connection gives us a feeling for the naturalness of the spiritual and of its central importance. In the great cultures that used these languages, spirituality, like breath, was intimately associated with the beginning and end of life, and also with every moment of it. And like breath, spirituality was understood to connect us in every moment to the larger world beyond our bodies and minds.

Though the spiritual is quite real, this connection between ourselves and something greater than ourselves is not easy to put into words: "The way that can be described," Lao-tzu observed, "is not the way." Often when we try, we sound vague, improbable, or both.

In fact, we know the spiritual realm best when we experience it directly. Time-honored paths to this experience include exercises designed to move us beyond the physical and mental realms in which we ordinarily move (exercises like the ones I've already taught you that often make use of breath) and stories.

In this chapter, I'll begin by describing the spiritual as a stage in the journey through and beyond depression. I'll tell you some stories—true-life spiritual tales—of people you've already met who have actually transformed their depression to delight. And, as we approach the end of our journey together, I'll give you practical tools and techniques: new perspectives to help you change your attitudes and beliefs, new ways of approaching prayer and religion, and meditations that will invite forgiveness and love, the greatest spiritual blessings, into your life.

GLIMPSES OF LIGHT

Our experience of the spiritual often begins with a glimpse: Milton finding surprising ease in reading Lao-tzu; April transforming her hated yellow slicker into her beloved purple coat; Madeleine speaking her own self-affirming words; the scientist hearing his grandmother's voice and turning in wonder to the members of our group.

Many of us have been given these glimpses before, in childhood. They are a very important part of what makes us human. Perhaps you can remember them, or reexperience them now, as you watch a child absorbed in the play of light on a window or the progress of a bug across the grass. There's appreciation in these childhood moments; a joyful gratitude for what we see, hear, and feel; an unquestioned sense of peace and connection to our own nature and to nature—delight.

These glimpses may come and go, lost and recovered, over and over. In time, in many of us, this experience and this understanding may be overcast by the doubts, disappointments, and distrust that growing up brings us.

For some lucky souls, this experience—these early glimpses—becomes a guiding vision, a course from which inevitable deviations are continuously corrected. Sometimes, though, it's only after we've been through the worst, most painful, darkest times of depression, when all hope has been stripped away, that this vision emerges again with stability and clarity. Dante feels hope as he emerges from the Inferno's deepest frozen darkness into the morning of the Purgatorio. Dorothy, Sophie, Madeleine, and the scientist are finally able to move again, holding the light in their eyes, only after they've lived through the most intense stuckness, the darkest night. This evolutionary process is what places this stage, the Blessing, after the Dark Night of the Soul.

THERESA CALLS AGAIN

It had been more than two years since I'd last seen Theresa. She'd moved from Washington, D.C., to teach in the South, not far from where she grew up. I heard a summer smile in her greeting and imagined her standing among plants on her front porch. "My life," she said when I asked about it, "has been a series of divine interventions."

"Tell me," I said.

And she began, looking back on what had happened since the time we'd last met, looking inside at what had made it all possible.

Ten years before, we hadn't spoken explicitly of the spiritual dimension of Theresa's life, but our work, she assured me, had helped her to understand and claim it. Perhaps then she was too uncertain or shy to discuss it. Now, looking back, it was "crystal clear."

"My depression and the sad state of my spiritual life were two sides of the same coin," she told me now. "First, I needed to look at myself psychologically, to see that I was depressed; that mine were ordinary human problems; that I wasn't this bad, immoral woman, self-indulgently sleeping with guys who turned out not to love me; drinking too much. I needed to see how what I did, and the sad, confused way I felt, connected to my childhood—to that lonely little girl with her desperate desire to please. And I needed to get my life on a track that worked for me.

"But, then, in order to get over my depression, I needed to feel my spiritual side. And by my spiritual side, I don't mean hearing the commandments of an old man sitting up in the clouds. I'm talking about needing to find the heart, or the soul, or the divine in me.

"When I came to see you, I was confused and upset and lost. I had low self-esteem. I knew I didn't want to 'medicate.' I'd already been medicating with alcohol. I was looking for some kind of balance and harmony."

The way I'd approached her, and what I suggested, it turned out, had helped her to experience her "spiritual side" as well as her basic sanity. My hopefulness, my understanding that depression was a journey not a disease, was the crucial starting point for Theresa. My assurance that medication was a part of her problem, not its solution, was vitally important, as was my encouraging her to reach out to Barbara, to do yoga and practice Soft Belly, and to take the herbs I prescribed. Together, these told her she wasn't sick, that there was hope, and that she could do something—many things—to help herself.

But there was more, she wanted me to know, things it turned out I'd forgotten: "You told me to read *The Trial* by Kafka, and that was very good for a reader like me. I saw myself in that book, those never-ending accusations that I was making toward myself, and I had to see that truth and *understand*"—and here she is emphasizing, underlining—"*that I was doing it to myself.*

"And then, a little while later, you had me put on music and dance in front of a mirror, so I could let it all hang out and release the tension. It got me moving and also it got me bonded with me. I didn't have to look outside of me for approval or stimulation. It was *me* who was feeling and moving."

Theresa began, through her work with me and meditation, and in psychotherapy, to develop "some emotional radar . . . to sense what I was feeling—anxious, sad, angry—that something was off-kilter, or not enough. And I learned"—very like, I thought, Odysseus tied to that mast—"not to react against it. I realized it was okay to feel the pain. It was just my feeling.

"And everything I was learning with you seemed a spiritual teaching as well as a psychological one. It was just like what I was hearing at Sunday services at Unity" (a New Thought church, like Mary Baker Eddy's Christian Science, that emphasizes contact with the divine within us, and also the ways in which our beliefs create our reality). "So all of that was working on me, helping me to open up to my own healing power, letting me feel that I'm not just OK, that I'm basically good and a child of God." And all these experiences coming together, Theresa now supposed, led her to make a pilgrimage to the shrine of one of India's great modern saints, Ramana Maharshi.

In 1896, at the age of seventeen, Ramana left home and moved into a largely silent life of solitary meditation. He had, without the guidance of a teacher or guru, a fundamental spiritual insight—that he and the absolute (Brahman or God) were identical, that his body would die but his consciousness was immortal—"A living truth," he said, "that I experienced directly."

Ramana retired to the South Indian hill of Arunachala, asking himself one question over and over for decades, "Who am I?" The years passed, and without apparent effort, he drew to his hill seekers, sages, and students from around the world.

I'd been surprised several years before when Theresa, a civil rights activist, feminist, and Christian, told me she was going to Arunachala. When I'd asked her why, she wasn't sure—perhaps it was Ramana's question, perhaps the promise of community. Going was, she had suspected at the time, more a matter of trusting the intuition she'd been cultivating, being "guided by spirit," than of weighing pros and cons.

Almost fifty years after Ramana's death, Theresa found, among the caves in his South Indian hill, in the shrine Ramana had built for his mother, an altogether unexpected peace. "I spent time all over the community, and I worked with Ramana's question—'Who am I?'—and it was all good. But that shrine resonated with me, moved me especially. I could feel the love, the nurturing, mothering energy that I never felt from my own mother." It filled Theresa; and I feel, as she tells me about it, that it continues to fill her, flow from her.

"I know I can choose to be bent out of shape or take responsibility, to suffer or be happy. And I choose to take responsibility. I'm seeing that it's OK to feel the pain. It's there. It's just my feelings. They don't kill me. Sitting with the pain has actually made me not tougher"—I hear the smile in her voice—"but stronger.

"When, after the time with you, I left Washington, my therapist—you remember, he and my internist both wanted me to take antidepressants—told me I'd had one of the most serious depressions he'd ever seen. And he was pleased and amazed at how good I was, without ever taking the drugs. And I'm much better now. The work with you, going to Unity, my time in India: It's still a process. I wake up each day and do my meditation and start my day in that centered spot, and I'm really happy, happier than I've ever been in my life."

Theresa tells me a story then, about a nephew with a serious drug problem and how she has learned to help him—and others—without sacrificing or burdening herself, as she always used to do. "My goal is to help him, and help him help himself in a way that nurtures us both. I've learned over these years that the only person who can help me is me. People can guide and comfort and support me, but nobody else can take on my burdens. And the same is true for him.

"I love him and I can help him and still let him go and trust that the divine that works through me works through him also.

"I no longer have the feeling that I won't get what I want. I *have*"—she emphasizes that wonderful present-tense word, so different from all the terms of loss and longing that marked her depression—"what I want. I feel whole and happy as I am. If I find a 'significant other' . . . that would just add to it.

"I thought of you the other day," she says, as we're coming to the end of our phone talk. "Everyone needs to be inspired the way you inspired me. Those exercises you teach work. When you're depressed, you need to see you're not alone. And all of us also need to be open to connect to something greater than ourselves."

I thank Theresa on the phone, and silently, too, for sharing with me what is possible. Freud wrote about replacing neurotic with ordinary unhappiness. Psychopharmacologists praise the restoration of the "pre-morbid personality." Theresa is showing me, telling us, what it means to move from being terribly, chronically, depressed to feeling blessed every day.

RECONNECTING WITH SPIRIT

Sometimes we experience the spiritual outside the frame of formal reli-gion—Ramana on his hill, the poet Wordsworth seeing "clouds of glory," and Theresa in the shrine to Ramana's mother. More often, a particular religious tradition and its practices set the stage and give form to these experiences—feeling the mercy of Jesus's mother, Mary, while praying to her or looking at a sculpture or painting of her. Always, though, there is a trajectory in the experience that takes us, like Theresa, beyond the prac-tice, deeply into the tradition's mystery, to something or someone greater than ourselves—Brahman, God, the higher power, nature, the Tao with its ceaseless flow. And this experience of that which is beyond us also allows us to feel more fully ourselves.

This process of spiritual awakening enlarges and enriches every aspect of our lives. In beginning to realize the divine beyond us, we begin to see and feel it in ourselves. Experiencing it within, we see and feel it every-where, we appreciate it, even love it, in others. Depression, a dismal cycle of fear, lowered expectations, and gloom, is transformed into a bright, self-sustaining circle of joyful experience, hope, and fulfillment.

We can think of depression as a kind of disconnection from the spiri-tual and this circle of ease and light and love. Look back, for a moment, at those whose stories we've shared: Odysseus, longing for home and the journey toward it; Dante, alone, immobilized, and fearful in the dark wood; Persephone and Demeter, frantic, separated from their sense of purpose and place as well as from each other; Theresa and April, Dorothy, and Michael, unfulfilled by lives of apparent adequacy, out of touch with their own true nature, fearful.

And what are all our demons but different forms of separation? In loneliness, we feel incomplete, divided within, and yearn for who or what is lost outside us. But it's true as well of anger and resentment, like Milton's, which kept him from the love for his son that would heal them both. Perfectionism, pride, and procrastination all lock us from joy in our daily experience, wall us off from the interaction and flow of life, keep us stuck.

So, when Theresa tells me that spiritual experience has been central to her psychological healing, I can only agree. In fact, my approach to this journey through and out of depression is, whether I call it that or not, a spiritual one.

The techniques that I've shared with you are ways to manage stress and improve mood, ways of relaxing and becoming more self-aware. If you've been traveling with me on this journey, you've learned to make healing use of your intuition and imagination, your mind and body, and you've invited depression's demons to yield your daimon. What you've done has, I hope, made you aware of, and helped you establish, or reestablish, your connection to the basic rhythm of your life; undermined the fear and hurt that have kept you stuck and separate. I hope, too, that these experiences have given you the chance to fulfill the longing that you have to be at ease and connected, to move lovingly into life's flow.

What we've done together is practical, shaped in many cases by centuries or millennia of use, grounded in and supported by science. And what we've done, the journey we've been on, is also spiritual.

MEDITATION: FINGERS POINTING AT THE MOON

Meditation is the opening to the ordinary miracle of our every moment, our every day, which, I believe, is the place where we most regularly and reliably encounter the spiritual. The words of a Zen master convey it well: "Enlightenment is simply this: When I walk, I walk. When I eat, I eat. When I sleep, I sleep."

The techniques I used with Theresa—in fact, all the approaches in this book—can be viewed as meditative. From Soft Belly to the Inner Guide, from more mindful eating to shaking and dancing, they are all designed to make it possible for us to live in a relaxed, moment-to-moment awareness.

That's the goal. The techniques are the means. There is a piece of advice that another Zen master once gave a student: Don't pay attention to the finger that's pointing at the moon, but to the moon at which the finger is pointing. All the techniques are just fingers. The goal, the moon, is living moment to moment with relaxed awareness in a state of continuous discovery, of interest, wonder, and delight.

It's important for you to understand that any form of meditation can work. The *Vigyana Bhairava Tantra,* an Indian text that is more than a thousand years old, gives a hint of the possibilities. One hundred and twelve kinds of meditation are described—meditations on the in breath and out breath, and on the space between breaths; moving meditations as well as sedentary ones; and a variety of ways to use sex as a meditation. *Tantra,* which in the modern mind has come to be equated with esoteric sexual practices, is actually the Sanskrit word for "method." Tantra can be sexual, because sex can be used as one of many methods for entering a meditative state, not because tantra is limited to sexuality. Any aspect of our lives, the *Vigyana Bhairava* tells us, will do, will offer us an opportunity for meditation. One of my favorites: "While sitting and swaying in an oxcart, go within the swaying."

For many of us who are depressed, or who just feel stuck, active meditation techniques are often the easiest and most effective routes to spiritual experience as well as improved mood and decreased anxiety. "You cannot use the mind," Shyam, my teacher, long ago explained to me, as he recommended Dynamic Meditation, "to move beyond the mind." For Theresa, dancing was key. At least for a few moments each morning, she realized, "This is me, this is my body, it's alive. I am different from, greater than, my depression." Sometimes she felt an energy that kept her going long after she would have thought she'd be tired. Even if this energized, relaxed appreciation left after a time, Theresa knew it could be reawakened the next day and the next.

FORGIVENESS

Forgiveness is advised and honored by every religion, and in every spiritual tradition I know of. Forgiveness is the antidote to the guilt and self-blame that are such disabling and stubborn parts of depression and to the frowning, hypercritical outlook that darkens the depressed person's view of the world. In forgiving, we open ourselves to others whom we have rejected, and reclaim parts of ourselves that we have condemned. Forgiveness, recent research tells us, is good for our physical health (in particular, cardiovascular health), enhances mood, and promotes optimism. Forgiveness is crucial to recovering our wholeness and to experiencing the blessing of the spiritual.

Forgiveness is, however, practiced with some difficulty. Scriptures and sermons urge it, but shame and social constraints often prevent us from the first step: acknowledging and dealing with our decidedly "unspiritual" faults and feelings—the crippling demons, particularly resentment, that make forgiveness so necessary.

Meditation is an excellent tool for making forgiveness possible and even practical. Moment-to-moment awareness and acceptance allow us to acknowledge the demons that prevent forgiveness—pride, perfectionism, resentment—and relax with them until they gradually loosen their hold on us. Meditation makes it so much easier for us to walk the walk, as well as talk the talk of forgiveness. Meditating on Lao-tzu's words, Milton let go of his long-held hostility and resentment and forgave his ex-wife.

It can be just that simple, but, of course, it's often not. So many of us have come to define ourselves by what is wrong with us or who is against us or whom we're against, or even what we might do wrong or who *might* hurt or harm us. It usually takes time and dedicated intention, as well as meditation, to free ourselves from this constricting, destructive, unforgiving way of being.

Sometimes our fears, hurts, and negative judgments, and the resentment to which they give rise, are fairly specific. They are directed toward one aspect of ourselves or one person—that man did me wrong, what he did was unforgivable—or toward a particular group—blacks, whites, Palestinians, Israelis. When we find ourselves rising in wrath, we insist that there are ample, incontrovertible reasons for the way we feel. We don't, we insist, harbor hatred for everything about ourselves, or resentment against so many others. Indeed, we may argue, as some of the most unforgiving people I've met do, that we *usually* behave with kindness and even generosity.

Still, the place where we are stuck, like a tiny splinter in a large foot, is exercising a subtle influence on the rest of our lives. There is a self-protective rigidity to our bodies when we condemn ourselves or others, a judgmental quality that gradually creeps into all our assessments. We may also, as we mental health professionals say, "project," believe that those we are judging—whom we will not forgive—are also judging us and even wanting to hurt us. "Judge not," Jesus wisely admonished, "that you be not judged."

We shouldn't be surprised. A tiny splinter, unremoved, can create a very significant systemic infection, making us limp and lurch. If we become aware, we can sense the consequences, feel ourselves clinging to past hurts, pulling the cloak of prejudice around us, choking with rage and resentment. Relaxing, removing the splinter, we can breathe and walk easily, open up, begin to let go of our grievances. Unhappiness may drain away. Now we are able to look at others and experience ourselves with compassion and joy. Now we are getting ready to see that forgiveness is not just a one-time thing, but a way of life.

Jodie Lets Go

I'm thinking, as I write about forgiveness, of three women in their sixties whom I knew and liked well. All were depressed when they came to see me. All had widely disseminated, much treated metastatic cancer. And all were, I discovered over time, scarred by suppressed rage and resentment, unable to forgive those who had hurt them or to forgive themselves for allowing the hurt to happen.

All of these women lived well beyond their oncologists' expectations.

But two of them could never or would never forgive the people who they felt had betrayed them—one's habitually unfaithful and spineless husband, the other's demeaning sister.

The hurt these two women harbored turned aside the flow of their lives, tainted the sweet taste of their last years. "I've been wronged," they said to themselves and me. "No matter how strong or loving I seem, inside I'm still a pathetic victim. And, I will not," they maintained, in words and gesture and deed, "even in my last years or days, let that son of a bitch, or that bitch, off the hook." But as far as I could tell, the hook was biting them far more than their tormentors. I felt unfinished business sitting with us at their death beds.

The third woman, Jodie, an entrepreneur and social activist, a secular Jewish woman with strong opinions and even stronger convictions, was of the same age and had the same life-threatening disease, the same diagnosis of depression, and the same disposition to blame, resentment, and revenge as the other two. It was her sister whom she would not, could not, forgive: her sister, Elaine, who clamored for center stage as a child, stole Jodie's boyfriends during adolescence, and betrayed her during a joint business venture.

When I first met her, Jodie, who often spent time with Elaine's son, Joshua, hadn't spoken to his mother, her sister, in nine years. One day, after many months of growing awareness—and of hard work with me, in our mind-body skills group, and with a yoga teacher—after her cancer had returned for a second time, Jodie was furious. She railed against the disease that might soon take her from her husband, children, and grandchildren, and against all the other disappointments that had come to her, including, most particularly, her sister's betrayal. Suddenly, she stopped, as if hearing herself for the first time. "Do you think I should forgive her?"

I let the question hang in the air—it needed to—as we sat quietly. At length, she sighed elaborately. "I'm going to forgive her." And then a great rush of laughter came from this small, determined woman, as if a dam had broken inside her. When she could speak again, she looked at me with exaggerated innocence: "Do you think I have to tell her?" Now we both cracked up.

A few days later, Jodie called Elaine, saying simply, without self-congratulation, that she wanted to let go of the past. Elaine, perhaps predictably, acted "as if nothing much had happened," but it didn't matter to Jodie. She knew she'd done what she had to. She told me that after the call, she'd actually felt as if "I were a larger person, as if I could breathe more freely." She realized she was smiling more at others and laughing more easily at herself.

Several months later, at the end of yet another cycle of chemotherapy, Jodie went to Joshua's wedding.

In the days before the wedding, she recalls, "I had diarrhea which I thought came from the chemo, and I couldn't do anything but sip ginger ale and eat some crackers. My dear Joshua's bride comes from a religious family, so there was more food than any ordinary person could imagine. Everyone from my family was there, all the nieces and nephews, my brother with his wife, and, of course, my sister, Elaine, Joshua's mother, who, as oblivious as ever—pardon my sharp tongue—had seemed to think my forgiveness was only her due.

"Joshua had asked me to give a toast. I thought about it during the days when I couldn't eat or go far from the toilet. And I thought about an article I had read on the difference between the 'persona,' the mask we put on for others, and the 'self,' who we really are. Though I felt so weak, and fearful about my cancer, I also felt so changed since I'd let go of my resentment, so much less a 'persona,' so much more my 'self.' I realized I was just plain grateful for my own life and my wonderful husband and my children and how beautiful my nephew was.

"When I arrived at the wedding, I saw the future there, in those children and the children they would have, but most of all, I saw the glorious present, Joshua's joy and his bride's and even my poor, pinched sister's happiness. And I felt my heart open to everyone there.

"And when I heard my sister belittling some of the other people and proclaiming her own importance with that air of condescension and complaint she has, I just thought, 'How sad. But that's not me. I'm not a part of that any longer. It's not what I need to make me happy.'

"Do you suppose," she asked, "I had to call my sister all those months ago and forgive her, and then on top of that, throw up and have diarrhea and clear out whatever else was stuck inside me so this could happen?

"I don't have it figured out, and I really don't have to, but I do know that this is who I am, that my heart is so much more gracious and generous."

Bringing Forgiveness into Our Lives

When we are resentful or harbor hate, we inevitably judge ourselves as well as others and separate ourselves from them. In extending forgiveness to those we believe have hurt us, we, like Jodie, open ourselves to a new kind of connection with them and with others as well. When we forgive, we are also aligning ourselves with the deepest wisdom of the world's religions and spiritual traditions—the understanding that in forgiving others we are demonstrating and discovering in ourselves the compassion that the divine—God, nature, the higher power—shows to us. And as we forgive others, we also begin to feel compassion for ourselves. The harsh voices of self-condemnation that contribute so painfully to depression and isolation decrease in volume and lose their insistence.

Some years ago, I learned a practical method to help me forgive myself and others. My friend Joan Halifax, an anthropologist and American Zen abbot who leads meditation retreats and works with the dying and with prisoners on death row, taught it to me. I've used it often myself and with many people who, like Jodie, find it hard to forgive. In fact, I now use it all the time to help my patients, students, and colleagues—here in the United States and in war and postwar situations overseas—to recognize and begin to let go of their hurt and envy, blame and resentment toward others and themselves. I'm sharing it with you because it's such a simple, direct way to bring forgiveness—and with it a direct experience of the spiritual—into all parts of your life.

FORGIVENESS MEDITATION

There are four steps in this meditation, which is also a kind of guided imagery. You can do it in silence or listen to a gentle melody while you do it.

Sit comfortably. Close your eyes. Breathe in through your nose and out through your mouth, allowing your belly to be soft. Breathing slowly and deeply, feeling yourself present, here and now, relaxing into your chair with each breath. Breathing in and breathing out.

Allow an image to come of someone toward whom you have anger or resentment. Let yourself see that person now, as if she were sitting across from you in a chair. Choose whomever you like. It doesn't have to be the person who has hurt you the most, just someone toward whom you hold resentment.

Look at that person and say to her, "I forgive you. For whatever you may have done to harm me, intentional or unintentional, I forgive you." Soften toward that person. Imagine her coming into your heart just for now. Breathe in. Hold her there, in your heart, for a moment, breathing in and breathing out, staying present with her, relaxing, feeling forgiveness for her, breathing. Allow yourself to be there for a minute or two more. Now let her go, saying, "I forgive you."

Be aware of yourself again, breathing in through your nose and out through your mouth, allowing your belly to be soft, breathing slowly and deeply, feeling yourself present, here and now, relaxing into your chair with each breath, breathing in and out.

Now, imagine someone whom you have harmed in some way. Imagine him as if he were sitting in a chair across from you. Choose whomever you like. It doesn't have to be the person whom you have most harmed. Just someone whom you have hurt and whose name or image comes to you now. Look at that person and say to him, "Forgive me for whatever I may have done to harm you, intentionally or unintentionally, forgive me."

Open your heart to this person and imagine him opening his heart to you. Breathing in, and breathing out, imagining your hearts melting together. Hold him in your mind and your heart for a few moments, breathing in and breathing out, staying soft, relaxing, feeling forgiveness flowing from him toward you, feeling your hearts melting together. Breathe for a few minutes more. Now, let him go, thanking him for the forgiveness that he's offering you, allowing yourself to feel the forgiveness flowing from him to you, the connection between the two of you.

Breathing slowly and deeply, feeling yourself present here and now, relaxing into your chair with each breath, breathing in and out.

Now, allow the image of yourself to come to you. Imagine that you're sitting in a chair across from yourself. Look at yourself and say to yourself, "I forgive you for whatever you feel you've done to hurt yourself; for however you've let yourself down, I forgive you." Feel the sensation of opening your heart to yourself, feeling the connection between you and the image of yourself sitting in a chair across from you, the connection between your hearts. Allow the sensation of opening and softening to spread from you to your image, from your image back to you, uniting you. Breathe in and out, staying soft, relaxing, feeling forgiveness, for a few moments more.

Now, allow the feeling of forgiveness to spread from you, from your heart, to all those on the planet who are in need of forgiveness. Allow this feeling to grow and expand, breathing in, breathing out, relaxing. Saying to yourself and to everyone on the planet who needs forgiveness, "I forgive you." Breathing in, breathing out, relaxing for a few minutes. Now let that image fade.

Feel yourself now, sitting in your chair, your back against the back of the chair, your seat on the seat of the chair, your feet on the floor, breathing deeply, relaxing.

When you're ready, open your eyes and bring your attention back into the room.

Now, if you feel like it, write about your experience in your journal.

RELIGION AND SPIRITUALITY

There is an important difference between spirituality and religion. Spirituality, as its consistent association with "breath" reveals, is intimately connected with life itself and with moment-to-moment awareness. Its experience—in the visions, words, and deeds of Abraham, Jesus, Muhammad, and Buddha—is the life-giving beginning of religion.

So long as religion is alive and vital, it is spiritual. When it calcifies with custom and dogma, it becomes something else, a reassuring institution, perhaps a source of good respectful values, perhaps a force for conformity and control, a habit. And yet religions, even those that may seem lifeless to some of us, still have in them, waiting to be discovered, or rediscovered, that living, breathing, beating heart of spirit.

The scientific literature contains many studies that tell us that religious observance is good for our general health and for our mood. Those who regularly attend a church or synagogue or mosque are less likely to become chronically ill or to suffer from depression. If they do become ill or depressed, they appear to be more likely to recover sooner.

Some of this effect is undoubtedly due to the social support that these institutions provide, a sense of belonging and reassurance that we know is, even in secular circumstances, health promoting. Some is due to the better habits that regular congregants may have: moderate or no smoking and drinking, more regular hours, and the good behavior that religious doctrine urges.

But there appear to be other factors as well, ones that are integral to religion and can enhance our sense of well-being, decrease our anxiety, and lift our mood. In the New Testament, the Christian apostle Paul names two of them, faith and hope. Faith is a belief in what we cannot grasp through the senses, in the existence of the divine, and in the efficacy of prayer and other forms of religious practice. Hope includes an expectation of help that is beyond our own power to bring about, that can sustain us when we are vulnerable or hurting.

Faith, Hope, and Placebo

The medical literature addresses the virtues of faith and hope in the secular concept of the placebo (from the Latin, "I shall please") effect. Placebo is sometimes defined as "the sum of the nonspecific factors in healing." It includes the contribution that our faith in and hope for the benefits of any treatment can make to its efficacy.

For millennia, physicians have understood that inert substances believed to be active—placebos—could bring about therapeutic benefits. They put this knowledge to practical use, prescribing sugar pills to "please" the patient when no active substance was likely to help, relying on a patient's belief in their efficacy to mobilize the body's innate healing power.

When modern drugs began to be rigorously tested, they were compared in the most careful studies to a "placebo control," from which they were indistinguishable in appearance, taste, etc. The difference between the effect of the drug and the placebo represented the therapeutic activity of the drug.

On the battlefields of World War II, Henry Beecher, who later became professor of anesthesiology at Harvard, was deeply frustrated by shortages of appropriate pain medication, but also gratified and fascinated by the power of inert, injected salt solutions to relieve wound pain. During the 1950s, he began systematically to look not at the power of drugs but at the ability of placebos such as the saline injections to simulate their effects. He reviewed the available medical literature and discovered that placebos were, on average, 35 percent as powerful as drugs that were known to be effective, *regardless of the drug being tested or the condition being treated.*

As a medical student listening to Beecher, I was amazed by the fact that placebos were 30 to 40 percent as effective as morphine, our most powerful analgesic, even when they were being used to relieve the often excruciating pain of heart attacks and of the dissecting aneurysms that bulged and tore the wall of the aorta.

Subsequent studies have shown that placebos may be even more powerful. One review of several treatments that later proved to be *ineffective*—surgery for asthma, an invasive procedure for stomach ulcers, and three different treatments of herpes simplex virus—indicated that up to 70 percent of the initially treated patients had "excellent or good outcomes." More recent research has shown that the placebo effect of substances believed to be antidepressants has actually been increasing over the years.

Beyond the Powerful Placebo

Still, there is, I believe, something else, beyond placebo, that can be mobilized, that is being mobilized, when we have a spiritual experience. Though we can observe its effects, it is by its very nature subjective and not easy to describe or define. It depends on an absorption in, a communion with, practices and beliefs that we call spiritual, and with the sacred realm that gives these practices and beliefs power and meaning. The French anthropologist Claude Lévi-Strauss, writing of indigenous people and this connection, called it "participation mystique." Instead of simply improving our health, it may transform who we are.

I believe this is particularly true for those of us who are in danger of losing or taking our lives, and in those of us who have all but given up on hope or help for ourselves. In the medical literature, these occurrences are referred to as "anecdotes" about placebo response, or as examples of "spontaneous remission." In the Christian tradition, they may be cited as evidence of being "born again," marking people who in times of deepest and darkest despair have been, often against all reason, inspired by hope and have found faith. This response and rebirth represents not merely a change in the way we think, but in the nature of the mind that is thinking.

After Saul, the callous tax collector, was struck down and had this kind of experience, he became Paul, the Christian apostle. The New Testament calls this change of mind by its Greek name, *metanoia*.

Sometimes faith and hope make it possible for us to experience the spiritual in a new way, and we are in turn immeasurably enhanced by it. So it was for Theresa as she opened herself to the calm of meditative awareness, invited her body to move freely, studied the teachings of a new church, and allowed herself to experience the devotion of an Indian spiritual teacher and his mother.

Others may discover the spiritual, and the faith and hope it brings with it, through an experience of immediacy and fresh truth in a religion that had for them long ago grown stale. Here is the description of Bill W., the founder of Alcoholics Anonymous, who had for years despaired of ever finding relief from his suicidal depression and alcohol addiction, and then discovered what he, and the generations of alcoholics he has inspired, have come to call a higher power. Bill, brought up Christian, tells us that he had, for most of his life, "gagged badly" on the idea, and even the name, of God. Then, suddenly, at the very bottom of the pit of his despair, he looked up to discover "the room lit up with a great white light. I was caught up into an ecstasy which there are no words to describe. . . . A great peace stole over me."

And listen to how Madeleine experienced it, months after she began doing Dynamic Meditation and had started on SAMe: "I went on a retreat where we read parts of the New Testament. I felt the faith and sincerity of the leaders and their commitment to the truth that there is darkness as well as light, and that both are a part of all of us. I'd read the Bible regularly since childhood and had been what I guess you'd call an observant Christian, but now I saw its authenticity with new eyes.

"We read passages in the Bible and then drew and danced out their meaning and expressed the fear and anger, the loneliness and confusion, that came up as we read and drew and danced. And as I did these exercises, I realized how far short I was of Jesus's example. I felt ashamed as well as pained.

"A couple of days into the retreat, I read again those lines I know so well about judging others, about ignoring the beam in my own eye and focusing on the mote in the eye of my neighbor. But this time it was different for me. I cried and cried, not feeling sorry for myself as the victim, or unworthy now, but just feeling such relief. 'I'm a sinner,' I said to myself, and then for the first time, '*and* I'm OK.'"

To her surprise, self-conscious, undemonstrative Madeleine joined the other retreat goers in a joyous dawn dance and "felt the experience so deeply, the spirit of being new."

In the months after the retreat, Madeleine felt "a subtle but powerful shift." I could see it, too, on her face during her visits to me, in sweet smiles and a softening of the sharp lines of hurt and worry and disappointment. Now when struggles arose, she didn't see them just as signs of her inadequacy or reminders of childhood deprivation. They were also, she now felt, spiritual challenges to be met—tests of her faith and hope and of charity as well—"I try to start each day afresh now. I bring intention to my life. I enjoy the blocks I walk in the morning and the weather in every season. I let the job wait until I get to the office. And once I'm there, I thoroughly enjoy the help I can give to those sweet, struggling kids. I love myself enough now—it's not perfect—and I can be more gentle with myself and with others. Perhaps," she hazards, "I'm actually beginning to live like a Christian."

PRAYER

Prayer is the spiritual practice most of us in the West know best. The origin of the word in the old French—"asking humbly and earnestly"—prescribes the appropriate attitude. Earnestness dissipates the cynicism and defensiveness within which we may wall ourselves in depression. Humbleness—humility—further undermines our rigidity and our desperate self-importance. It melts the fear that marks us off from one another, allows a space to grow within us, in which we can receive from others and accept our own, unmined, inner gifts. Humility invites us to open ourselves to and welcome that which is beyond us.

During our journey through depression, faith and hope may prepare us to hear the call to action and change, steady us in times of surrender, affirm us amid despair, and give a larger context and more luminous cast to our struggles and our lives. Prayer further focuses faith and hope and, over time, may invite them to be our constant companions. I have seen the power of prayer in my office and our trainings and in work around the world with people of every age, religion, and political persuasion.

For some of you, prayer has been a welcome and reassuring part of life since childhood. You will, I hope, come to it for hope and help as you move through and beyond depression. For many others of us, however, prayer is problematic, connected with memories of rote or dogmatic religious observance, about which we may have very mixed feelings. It can also be particularly uncomfortable for those of us who pride (and I choose this word knowingly) ourselves on our self-reliance, rationality, and secularism.

Praying for My Life

I speak from experience. Though I, like Theresa and Madeleine, had thought of myself as a seeker, maybe even a spiritual person, for much of my life, I, like them, had had my problems with an Old Testament God who seemed to me remote, forbidding, and punitive and a New Testament Messiah who seemed to demand exclusive allegiance.

I enjoyed saying grace before meals, singing Sh'ma Yisrael in synagogue, reading the Bible, and reciting the Lord's Prayer in my high school chapel. But I knew that something was missing from the way that I'd participated in these familiar Christian and Jewish rituals, that I was reserving some depth of feeling, missing an actual felt connection to the God whom I read about or thanked or praised.

And then, many years ago, climbing on a California cliff near Big Sur, it changed. A friend and I had walked down the trail to the beach to sit on the rocks that the waves crashed against, to swim a little and hunt for jade. Afterward, I decided to climb up the face of the cliff, perhaps eighty feet high and quite sheer. I was more than a bit afraid of heights, and almost completely devoid of experience or skill as a climber, but it felt like something I had to do—a challenge, a test of some sort.

My friend walked up the path we had come down, and I began to climb. The cliff felt almost perpendicular, but I persevered, tips of toes balancing on tiny ledges, fingers clinging to rocks that crumbled, scraping palms, arms, knees.

I kept going . . . and then I couldn't. I couldn't find a rock to cling to, and the dry earth drifted between my fingers and fled from my feet. There was no way up.

I called to my friend, at the top by now, but she had no rope, couldn't help. I turned around, my back to the cliff, and looked down, dizzy, as I imagined falling sixty feet onto the boulders below, knowing I couldn't survive. My frantic eyes couldn't find another way down. I panicked. I couldn't do this. I needed help.

I saw a man on the beach with a young child. I called—screamed, really; I couldn't be cool—to him. He looked up, moved toward me. I felt such gratitude for his effort. And I knew, even as I did, that there was nothing, no matter how kind and brave and skillful he was, that he could do to help.

And then, for the first time in my life, I really, sincerely, prayed. "God," I said, astonished to hear myself say it. "Please, I have so much more to do in this life. Please help me." I was surrendered in that moment, when my own resources were wholly inadequate, and the goodwill of others could only comfort, not correct, the situation. And, I suppose, I was in despair as well. Against what my mind believed, I was reaching out to the only power—nonhuman, nonrational—that in this impossible situation might possibly help.

There was a pause then, as I started to sway out from the cliff, a kind of stillness in the air. The sun glinted off the points of the rocks below me. I couldn't see or hear my friend above. The man on the beach and his son, holding hands, were looking up.

And then, without knowing how or where it had come from—for I definitely had not felt or seen it before—my right foot found a firm place, and then my left. And then I was sliding and scraping and clinging my way to the bottom of the cliff, knowing that I had asked, begged, and that I had somehow been given my life.

Prayer still doesn't come easily to me. But I have prayed again, with almost equal fervor, on two occasions: for the life of a girl who by all medical accounts "should have" been dead in a car crash for which my godson was responsible, and for Alice, my friend, when she lay for weeks in a coma during a terrible illness. And both times my prayers were answered. The girl survived and so did Alice.

I can't prove that prayer had anything to do with these enormous, highly improbable changes, these miracles. There are, to be sure, studies that show that prayer, or "healing intention" generally, can make a difference for those who do not know they are being prayed for—reducing the incidence of complications in people in coronary care units, altering heart rates in people who are carefully isolated from the prayerful healers, diminishing pain, and improving immune functioning in AIDS patients. And there are almost as many equally good studies that refute this "distant healing" effect. Both the hopeful and the disconfirming studies are important to me. *And* I have my own undeniable experience that exists alongside them.

So, even though my mind may still doubt, I know in my bones and being that prayer, with its admission of powerlessness and its surrender to some other power, can make, however it does, a difference.

Everyday Blessings

There is an energy in prayer for ourselves and others, a surrender, a connection to whatever or whomever we pray to, that I believe transcends religious categories and energizes us, and who or what we pray for, like some amplified current.

Over the years, I've also come to appreciate another, less urgent, kind of prayer. William Alfred, one of my college professors, suggested it to me. Bill was Irish Catholic, Brooklyn working class, a playwright, and an Anglo-Saxon scholar. He had a long, kind, and rather goofy face and was already oldish and baldish when, as a Harvard undergraduate fifty years ago, I first met him. In later life, leaning, stooped against Massachusetts winters in his old overcoat and smashed-in fedora, he was what the Greeks might have called the "genius"—the kindly spirit—of Harvard Square.

Bill worked all day writing and teaching, and then sat up half the night with friends and strangers who looked to him for solace and guidance, with students who were, like me, as thirsty for his kindness as for the books he opened to us. Then he went to early-morning Mass.

One day not so many years ago, near the end of Bill's life, he looked up from the lamb chops he was cooking for us, raised his eyebrows, and gave a small smile. "Don't you think it would be a good idea," he asked, "if sometimes instead of praying or asking for something for ourselves, or even someone else, we just said to God, 'Thank you for a very nice day'?"

These words return to me often. Sometimes I do exactly what Bill suggested—thank God for the trees outside my window or the sunlight coming through it, or moments with a friend or a patient, or a phone call from someone I love, feeling gratitude for what I've been given. When I'm feeling "blue," as Bill would say, or frustrated, I remember his words and see his smile and feel my own smile, blessing, even in the middle of distress, each moment, each day.

I've begun, still tentatively (I'm very wary of urging faith on anyone) to suggest Bill's prayer to others—those who are committed to some form of religious observance and those resistant to all forms. It's the kind of simple, unpretentious prayer that any of us can do every day, a ratification, a blessing really, on all our opportunities—for quietly meditating, or sharing food or feelings, or walking down the street, or taking a deep breath. I suggest you do it, too, whenever you'd like: "Thank you, God, for a very nice day."

We may come to prayer as a light in the darkest of nights, but it can become a ladder on which we climb out of desperation and a perch from which we can delight in all we see.

LOVE

Love can break the spell that depression casts on us. Many, many of us, when we are depressed, believe that the approving glance of the longed-for prince or princess will thaw the ice around our heart, that his or her lips or hands will kiss or caress us back into life. And, indeed, when we are feeling so discouraged about ourselves, the love of another is literally wonderful, full of wonder. It is as if the sun had suddenly risen in the middle of the Dark Night. We see more clearly, feel warmed, and move about more freely. It does sometimes work for us, as it did for Sleeping Beauty or the poisoned Snow White. But the happiness, the fulfillment, rarely lasts "ever after."

Others' love cannot ultimately sustain us. If we haven't changed what made us depressed—the imbalances and distortions that our demons cause, the unmet needs and unfulfilled potential—we will eventually drain the other's love of its healing force and warp it to fit our still-crippled form. We will, in short, repeat more or less the same patterns, with more or less the same depressing consequences. There will be new episodes of dissatisfaction, more loss and discouragement, our loneliness magnified now by repeated disappointment. Barstools and therapists' consulting rooms are littered with the bodies of those who have felt revived by love and then let down again.

The love that heals us, that allows us to let ourselves be loved, and to love ourselves, is of a different kind.

This love is at once lyrical and intimate, spiritual, demanding, and practical. It requires demonstration on a daily—actually, minute-by-minute—basis. The paintings of the cowgirls dancing around the beautiful blue boy, the great Hindu god Krishna, are emblems of the soul's continual longing for and connection to the divine, of the utterly surrendered devotional quality—*bhakti* is the Sanskrit word—of this love. We hear it, too, in Solomon's Song of Songs, feel it in Saint Francis's prayer, in the Sufi poetry of Rumi, and in the stories of Jesus's and Buddha's compassion.

I hear intimations of this love as Theresa tells me how she works and cares for her home, and her troubled nephew, and herself, as she graciously shares with me what she has learned and is learning. Theresa's no longer "resigned" to being without a man. She accepts the fact that there is no man in her life and she enjoys, actually loves, the life she is living without a man. There's nothing showy about her love, but it shows up everywhere in her life. For me, this love—the Christian apostle Paul called it "charity"—is the most visible, palpable, mark of the blessing that comes from spiritual experience. It is also the surest sign that we are moving not only through but beyond depression.

Meditation, which quiets our nervous systems and allows us to more calmly confront our demons, may open the door to love. Relaxing, becoming aware of and accepting of whatever we experience—interesting thoughts and "foolish" ones, good feelings and bad, fears and insecurities, and arrogance as well as kindness—is a kind of love for us as we are, with all our imperfections.

Active meditation helps to clear away the demons that have plagued us, gives us some space to begin to transform them, some energy to do it.

All these meditative practices help us to become aware that we have a choice—to open up to and embrace our experience rather than protect ourselves against it. So many of depression's demons are forms of self-protection. Perfectionism keeps us from being wrong and procrastination from failing or being hurt or moving on and ahead. Envy and resentment separate us from the one against whom we've developed a grudge, and feeling lonely certifies our isolation. When we eventually allow ourselves to appreciate what we've protected ourselves against, we are moving into the current of life, experiencing an expansiveness that is very much like love.

Love, in fact, is the primal force of connection. All our research, as well as our experience, tells us that this love makes it possible for children to thrive. It is the crucial healing element in our work with good Guides—*compassion,* after all, literally means "feeling with." Love is the force that unites our families and tribes and nations, and love is the experience that may invite us to extend ourselves beyond those families, tribes, and nations. Love is the solution that can dissolve the chains that link enemies in endless cycles of revenge.

Love also comes as a grace, and sometimes when we least expect it— through a romantic relationship when we are ready for it, or friendship, or, and perhaps most often for adults, through children. The connection to a child can open our hearts more widely than we had ever imagined; sustain us like life's blood through the darkest of nights; transform us in ways that we may find astonishing.

I have seen this again and again—in Theresa opening to her nephew, in Madeleine with her troubled teens; in my other patients and friends and in the people I teach here in the United States; in those I work with overseas, who have despaired after the wartime deaths of family members; and in myself as well. Love can color the gray of our days gold as we move, sometimes by improbable paths, through depression toward delight.

Love Comes to Dorothy

This is how it was for Dorothy, first accepting the painful loss of love and then finding it again, repeatedly, unexpectedly, gloriously, sadly, and, finally, with a joy she had never known.

Dorothy left Todd, separating but not divorcing, not exactly under but barely noticeable on the gossipy screen of Washington's political radar. Todd, professing some surprise, confided to his colleagues that "Dorothy needed her space." As she had feared, her sons did far more than acknowledge her departure. Arthur, her older boy, and very much his father's son, took a large step back in chilly disapproval. The younger son, tender-hearted Jake, was desperate and angry on his dad's behalf: "He needs you. He'll be lost without you. How could you be so selfish?"

For months after she left Todd, Dorothy nourished herself with calls to Aunt Grace and visits to Arthur's twins, hoped for Jake to forgive her, and pulled her work tight around her. She knew, she told me, that it was "absolutely right" to leave and she was content, and at peace, with her decision, but still, she sometimes felt "horribly sad and desperately lonely."

"I look at this little apartment of mine and I take a few of those deep breaths I've learned to do, and it seems to suit me so well, the way I've arranged the living room and the colors in the bedroom and the freedom to put my arms out and dance around anytime I want. But sometimes I feel like a fish out of water, and I gasp for air, and I hardly know who I am."

Then one evening, at one of the few dinner parties to which she, suddenly single at sixty, was still invited, she met a man or, rather, ran into someone she had known long ago and had never quite forgotten. He was, like Todd, a public person, but thoughtful—not just smart—about life, and genuinely kind where Todd was merely courteous. He admired Dorothy's work and loved her stories and looked directly into her eyes. And he was married.

For many months, it didn't matter. Or at least it didn't keep them apart. Decorous lunches in elegant restaurants were followed by steamy afternoons in Dorothy's apartment. There were weekends in out-of-the-way, unfashionable addresses on the shore and in the country, and walks and long talks and passion. "I have to say it, Jim, I'm in love. And I know he's married and that no matter how crazy his wife is—and, of course, *because* she's so crazy—he'd never leave her. And it causes me terrible pain to know that sometime soon I'll be alone again. But there is such joy. He asks me about the speeches he gives, we read poetry to each other, and the sex is so good. We're like schoolkids. And the man is seventy years old." She's blushing now. "I have to pinch myself to believe that it's not some romance novel fantasy."

After a year, Dorothy's lover did indeed leave, excusing himself, proffering gifts as he backed out of her life.

Dorothy was "devastated, utterly devastated, but not at all regretful. I'm desperately sorry we couldn't go on, but I'm really more sorry for him than hurt or angry. And, Jim Gordon, I cry myself to sleep sometimes. But then I think about him, about us and what I would have missed if we hadn't been together, and my heart just smiles."

For a while, Dorothy endured her sons' distance and displeasure, and then she began to speak more directly to them—"Honest speech without being so worried about hurting their feelings or shattering the image of the perfect, loving mother"—about her hurt and anger at the way they were treating her, her need to live a life that sustained her, and not just for Todd and the family. These talks with her sons scared her even more than leaving Todd: "They are my own flesh. But speaking to them, honestly now, strengthens me, is changing me in such good ways, and actually letting me love them more."

Her cancer returned and with it the need for chemotherapy. But as sick as she felt, and as angry as she sometimes was at the cancer and the side effects of her treatment, she seemed somehow settled, even calm, as if her life had made a circle that now contained and supported her.

And then, "something truly amazing happened." Jake's wife, Joan, asked Dorothy to accompany her when she went to a remote tropical country to adopt a child: "It took ten weeks and, of course, Jake, who works just like his father, couldn't be there for more than two. But I could, and I was so grateful that Joan asked me—even though it was one hundred and ten degrees, and the so-called five-star hotel had power only four hours a day, and the food was inedible. But it was so good to give that gift to Jake and to Joan and, as I soon realized, to myself.

"That little baby girl," whom they had to find and secure through a wilderness of bureaucracy that not even Senator Todd could tame, "has made all the difference. There are still days when I feel so alone and miss my lover. I also think, sometimes, and I'm embarrassed to admit it, about the parties at the Kennedy Center and the dinners at the White House I'd be going to if I were still with Todd. And the memory loss and the nerve pain from the chemo gets me down. But I have to tell you, Jim, I wake every morning and feel I have so much to be thankful for. And I feel the bond with Joan and remember the look in Jake's eyes when we came back with that little baby, and I glory in my time with that child." She pauses. "I feel this is what I've lived to do."

THE PROMISE OF RENEWAL

The journeys of the epic and mythic heroes—Odysseus, Dante, and Demeter—close with a communion that seals the death of the old and announces the birth in these heroes of a capacity for living and an understanding, a depth of connection and love, that illuminates their lives. Odysseus, returning after long and painful delay, becomes a true father and example to his son, clears his palace of his wife, Penelope's, freeloading suitors, and meets her as his own and his equal. After his descent into the inferno, and his ascent of purgatory, Dante travels through paradise with his beloved Beatrice, toward the Virgin Mary and a vision of "the love that moves the sun and the other stars." Having lost Persephone—and herself—to darkness, Demeter embraces her returned daughter with hard-earned, luminous, and enduring warmth and wisdom.

All these journeys are inspiring, but as I write about and am taught by Theresa and Dorothy, it's Demeter whose journey seems to me most relevant and most deeply courageous. Demeter and Dorothy, forced by the necessity of their life's journey to give up what had been most dear to them—their ideas about themselves; the lovely, ordered world over which they presided; their children—must find their way through the darkest despairing depression before they return, renewed and changed, to those they love, before, in fact, they are able to feel the fullness of love. Before their painful, courageous journey, their affection was certified by custom and duty. After, it is wholehearted, without fear or expectation.

Demeter's immersion in and movement through the darkness that precedes healing and rebirth is also being replayed now, in Theresa's and Dorothy's lives, and with perhaps surprising frequency in the journey of so many of us who've been depressed and despairing: In April's dark, constricted passage through self-destructiveness to self-realization; in Milton's movement through resentment to compassionate fatherhood; in Michael's full-bodied meeting with his wife and his life; in Madeleine's celebration of what once burdened her; and in the scientist's embrace of the spirit of his grandmother; and, perhaps, also in your life.

I feel it now, too, almost every day in my own life and I see it more and more in all the people with whom I work. I offer it to you: the continuing, humbling realization that there is so much we cannot control; a growing trust in the necessity and power of surrender; knowing not to hope for love, and that love is our only hope.

Different traditions call this experience by many names: God's grace, or realization, enlightenment, healing, cure, or the blessing of the journey. But I keep coming back to *spiritual,* a word that is linked in so many languages to breath. It is for me a dynamic day-to-day word that reminds us that our lives, however troubled by depression, can ultimately be as easy, as natural as our inhaling and exhaling, as taking in and letting go, as we connect with what once seemed beyond us, with what is within us, with each breath we breathe.

SUMMING UP: SOME NOTES ON SPIRITUALITY

>> The spiritual dimension of our lives is both beyond and within us.
>> The spiritual is as real and relevant to the healing of depression as all the mental, physical, and emotional techniques we have been learning and using.
>> Spirituality is accessible to all of us whether or not we belong to any religious group.
>> *Breath* and *spirit* are intimately connected in many traditions and languages.
>> Meditative breathing techniques bring us into the present moment and are time-honored ways of disrupting depression and giving us direct access to spiritual experience.
>> Active expressive meditations use our body to raise our energy and can dispel the mental chatter that distracts us from spiritual experience.
>> Spiritual experience requires ongoing attention and nourishment and often deepens immeasurably over time.
>> Belief and faith in something or someone beyond us can open the door to the spiritual. Hope holds that door open.

>> Spiritual belief and practice are powerful forces for transforming Dark Nights into mornings of joy and brightness.

>> A prayerful, earnest, and humble attitude undermines pride and resentment and focuses our belief.

>> Forgiveness—of ourselves and others—can be a crucial step toward the openness, acceptance, and delight of the spiritual realm.

>> Love is the most fundamental spiritual experience and the most powerful of spiritual forces.

>> Love may begin with the smallest kind of appreciation of what is. Love can, if we devote ourselves to it, eventually color and transform everything we feel and do.

PRESCRIPTION FOR SELF-CARE:
Experiencing the Spiritual for Yourself

I'm going to offer you a prescription here—a meditative experiment that I hope will help you to experience the spiritual. It's a Tibetan Buddhist practice called *tonglen,* and doesn't require a "belief" in God. It may seem a bit improbable, even against the grain of your logical mind, but increasingly it is being embraced by people of many religious backgrounds.

Tonglen may give you, as it has given me and countless people I've worked with, a direct experience of spirituality and love. And it may transform the way you deal with the challenges that life brings to you.

Tonglen
This Tibetan Buddhist meditation practice, which literally means "taking and sending," invites us to accept, to take in and heal, the pain (physical, psychological, and spiritual) of another, and to use this experience to accept and heal our own pain, and the pain of the world, as well.

Though there seems to be a variety of ways to practice *tonglen*, all have the common denominators I've just described, and all may seem, at least at first, counterintuitive, if not threatening. "I'm already in pain," you may think, "still sometimes depressed, confused, anxious. What business do I have taking on someone else's pain?" You may wonder if it's dangerous.

I had these concerns when I first read about and began to practice *tonglen* many years ago. So did Thomas, a fifty-year-old, divorced cancer surgeon who came to me "because I feel so sad and lonely, so incapable of really caring about anyone else or, for that matter, myself."

The first few times Thomas practiced *tonglen,* he was restless and resistant. His efforts, during a sad time alone in a beautiful place, were difficult, unremarkable at best. Still, Thomas persevered. He was a man who rarely turned from a challenge, and *tonglen* seemed a way, at least in theory, to imaginatively understand others who were difficult or distant or simply hard for him to figure out. Even if it didn't help them, he thought, maybe it would help him. He practiced from time to time at his sick mother's bedside and with the image of a colleague whose casual cruelty had baffled him. And he did it several times with patients who were suffering terribly from cancer and its treatment.

Five years ago, *tonglen,* which until then was still an occasional practice and an "interesting" experience for Thomas, became very important. His ex-wife was suddenly in the hospital, very close to death. There wasn't much he could do, except keep an anxious eye on the medical situation, question the doctors, and lobby for a little more attention and comfort for her. As she struggled through surgical and medical emergencies that many times could have claimed her life, Thomas found himself horribly worried, sometimes panicky and overwhelmed, and often frustrated. He wanted to do more.

He decided then that every day when he visited her, he would practice *tonglen,* that he would sit in her room in the intensive care unit and breathe with her, bringing her pain into his body and allowing it to work on him, and, he hoped, to help him to heal her.

For the first week or so, he focused on present, life-threatening, physical issues—her compromised circulation and blood clots, the surgical infections, the congestion in her lungs. He soon began to visualize the years of physical pain she'd been through, the frustration and sadness and the deep emotional hurt he'd given her. As he sat with her during weeks of coma, and for four months after she awoke, he felt himself relaxing, coming close to her, helping, maybe even relieving her of some pain. Doing it, he felt he was somehow also clearing away some of his own hurt and shame, and bringing himself closer to his ex-wife than he'd ever been to anyone. *Tonglen* was allowing him to care, simply, sweetly, without fear, in a way he never had before.

Thomas didn't know—nor do I—if his *tonglen* practice had any effect on his ex's rather remarkable survival. What I do know is that it opened a path between her and Thomas, through all their mixed feelings and grievances, a path on which, five years later, they are still walking together.

I often use and recommend *tonglen,* which is now a regular part of our trainings in mind-body medicine. I recommend it to you as a practical tool for dealing with the pain and suffering of those you care about; as a practice for developing compassion and understanding for those who threaten and frustrate you; as a means to feel the commonalities between your own suffering and that of others everywhere on the planet; as a way of using your compassion for others to heal your own hurt; and as a way to directly experience that realm we call spiritual.

. . .

Here are the instructions for *tonglen*. You may want to record—and play—these so your own voice can guide you as you do this practice.

Begin by sitting comfortably. Allow your breathing to deepen. Let your belly be soft, breathe deeply in through your nose and out through your mouth, and relax into your chair, perhaps saying to yourself "soft" as you breathe in and "belly" as you breathe out. Breathe comfortably for several minutes, relaxing.

Now I'd like you to imagine, as Thomas did, someone you would like to help or heal. It can be someone very close to you, or someone you don't know so well. Imagine that person lying on a couch or a bed, and imagine yourself sitting with him or her, breathing deeply and relaxing.

Using your imagination, bring into the room with you deities, saints, or beings from your own religious tradition or others, or people you know or have heard or read about who represent or exemplify compassion. They are coming to add their compassion to yours, to help you give and receive. Let them find their places around you and the friend to whom you're bringing healing. Notice the light of love and healing that comes from them. See them, feel them, acknowledge them.

Now focus your attention back on your friend. Become aware of her suffering—physical, emotional, spiritual. Locate this pain and suffering in her body, perhaps in her chest, belly, fingers, hands, her head, perhaps even around her body. Visualize and feel it. It may appear as inky black smoke or tar, or some thick gooey gray or white stuff like sludge.

Take some time to appreciate all the physical hurt there may be in her organs and torso, limbs and head. Become aware of the emotional and spiritual hurt, the sense of loss and abandonment, fear, resentment, depression, and despair that may be there in your friend. Let your imagination also locate these other kinds of pain as smoke or sludge in the contours and organs of her physical body. Take some more time to do this.

Imagine now that you have, in your own chest, a crystal sphere of love and compassion. It has light within it and is covered with a crust of black tar, or a heavy sticky white paste that represents all your own physical, emotional, and spiritual pain, all your suffering.

As you breathe in, gradually, with each breath, inhale the physical, emotional, and spiritual pain of your friend, as if it were black or white or gray smoke. Understand that inhaling the hurt and suffering of another can help to heal you, as well as the other person. Take your time, locating the pain and hurt in all the places of her body, inhaling, breath by breath.

As you breathe in the smoke of your friend's pain, imagine that it's circulating around the crystal sphere in your chest, slowly wearing away the crusted covering of your own pain. Imagine your friend's dense darkness and clotted fear and pain, now converted to smoke, rubbing off, scouring the heavy covering of the crystal ball of light in your own chest.

Allow this process to take place. Breathe in, take in the darkness and opacity and the obstacles and stuckness, the hurt and suffering of your friend. Take it in as smoke, and allow it to rub away your own hurt and pain, hopelessness, despair, and suffering.

Perhaps as you do you'll become aware of the particular hurts and pains, prejudices and resentments, that are being rubbed away in yourself. Perhaps you'll realize some of the ways in which your suffering, your limitations, your blind spots, are like those of the person whom you're helping to heal.

And as the coating—the darkness and density in your own chest—begins to be rubbed away, become aware of the light of compassion and love within the crystal sphere, within your chest, the light in your heart.

As this light grows stronger and brighter, begin to send it back to your friend. Let it stream from your chest to her body. Let it fill all the places in your friend's body where before there was darkness or denseness, hurt and suffering and pain.

Let those beings, those spirits of compassion whom you brought into the room in the beginning of *tonglen,* help you, sending their light, along with yours, to your friend, filling her with light, surrounding her with light, surrounding you with light, filling the whole room with light. Enjoy this and enjoy the healing that has come, and will continue to come.

Now let that light expand from the room you're in, so it shines on everyone on the planet who is suffering—those you know and care about, and those you don't ordinarily care for, and all those you don't know at all. Let the light spread to everyone on our planet. Let this process continue for a few minutes.

After a few minutes more, become aware of yourself, breathing deeply, sitting in your chair, your back against the back of the chair, your seat on the seat of the chair, your feet on the floor. Breathe deeply, becoming aware of your soft belly. Breathe in, breathe out.

When you're ready, slowly open your eyes and bring your attention back into the room. After a few moments, you may want to write down in your journal what this experience was like. Here are some questions to help you organize your impressions of your experience.

>> Did compassionate beings take their place in the room with you? Who or what were they?

>> Did you see your friend? Who was it?

>> What did you learn about her, and her physical, emotional, and spiritual pain? What did it look like? Where was it in her body?

>> Could you imagine inhaling the smoke of her pain?

>> What was it like to take in her pain and suffering?

>> Did fear or disgust or added pain come up in you as you did?

>> Were you able to experience a bright crystal sphere covered with crust in your own chest?

>> Could you feel your own hurt as you inhaled the smoke into your chest?

>> Could you feel, as you continued to inhale, that the covering of that crystal sphere was being scoured or washed or rubbed away? What was that like?

>> Were there similarities between your suffering and that of your friend? Differences?

>> Did you send light to your friend? How did it look and what did it feel like?

>> Could you imagine sending light to all those on the planet who suffer? What was that like?

>> How do you feel now?

CHAPTER 7

The Return

The time after we've moved through depression, when its weight is lifting off and leaving us, is a time for celebration. We should savor the sights and sounds and movement of these days and weeks, as if we've just come out of a cave in which we've been trapped. Each glimpse of the bright world can awaken our eyes.

During this time, we also need to be relaxed and mindful, to hold our good feelings lightly, with gratitude and grace. Remember the cautionary tale of Dominique, who commemorated his ten days of sugar-free calm by consuming the Snickers bars that propelled him into a frenzy.

When I think of the return after the journey through and beyond depression, I remember stories from around the world in which the hero sets off to find the priceless jewel or the peerless bride. He travels long and far, overcoming countless obstacles, only to return home to discover that the jewel was sitting on his windowsill, that the ideal bride all along had lived next door. The scene of our lives may or may not be different, but, as we come to the close of this part of our journey, we have new eyes with which to see it.

TEN SUGGESTIONS

At the end of each of the previous chapters, I've shared with you a Prescription for Self-Care. This entire chapter is a prescription for thoughtfully, tenderly, caring for ourselves as we return from the journey through depression. It's also a recapitulation, a reminder of how you can use what you've learned—the perspectives and techniques and all the lessons that all our fellow travelers have taught us—to live fully and joyously, free of depression, as you take all the next steps of your life. I've grouped them into ten—not commandments—but lessons or suggestions.

1. Relax

Years ago, I had a tai chi teacher with the improbable, and entirely appropriate, name of Ben Lo. He was brilliant, graceful, tough. He could, with little effort, push around students like me who were half his age and twice his weight. Instead of just leading us through tai chi's wonderful, moving meditation, he would, on many occasions, have us hold positions that were quite difficult, particularly for Westerners unaccustomed to long squatting or, indeed, bending low.

One minute of holding a deep squat would find me breathing deeply, making sure my feet stayed rooted to the ground. At two minutes, I'd begin to tremble. At three or four, I'd be shaking hard enough—like a poorly planted tent pole in a storm—to throw me to the floor. At this point, Ben, bent far deeper in the same posture, breathing easily, smiling, would say, "Relax . . . relax . . . " I'd burst out laughing at the idea.

And yet, over the years, it's Ben, smiling, his movements as supple as a fish's, his breath as easy as a baby's, who comes to my mind. He reminds me that even in the most stressful situations—in fact, especially in the most emotionally as well as physically stressful situations—my job is simply to relax.

Relaxation is our birthright as humans. Whatever their material hardships, aboriginal and village people—hunter-gatherers, nomads, and preindustrial agriculturalists—live lives that are for the most part of far less stress than those of us who have material wealth and modern conveniences. The indigenous people I've visited spend far more time just sitting around, eating, sharing dreams and experiences, relaxing, than my friends in Washington or San Francisco, Tel Aviv, Beijing, or Johannesburg.

When the men in these societies work, they pause periodically to have a chat. And the work they do tends to be varied: hunting, fishing, chopping, carving, carrying, explaining, instructing—different activities at different seasons and times of day. No deadline-dominated eight hours in front of the computer.

Women in most of these societies, as in most societies around the world, work harder than men, but they, too, seem to have a far more relaxed life. They're almost always in groups: three generations—ten, fifteen, thirty women—caring for, teaching young children together. Lots of laughter, as well as cooking, cleaning, hoeing, harvesting. Very little rushing around. Definitely no carpools. This is the way our species has lived for most of its hundreds of thousands of years of history. This is our evolutionary heritage, a lifestyle for which our genetic programming has equipped us.

We cannot, of course, return to this condition, but we can learn from our ancestors and our aboriginal brothers and sisters and bring relaxation into our modern, or postmodern, lives. If we are to be depression-proof, healthy, and happy, we'd better.

Chronic stress, as we've discovered, predisposes us to later depression, and depression produces more stress. This stress is a hallmark of our most painful losses—of lovers, jobs, spouses, identities, and physical integrity. It is, in the stories I've shared with you, a major precipitating factor for episodes of depression throughout the cycle of our lives.

Relaxation allows us to roll with the punches that come with living. Relaxation is the foundation for psychological and physiological calm, the platform from which we can more serenely observe, experience, and deal with the demons that depression has revealed to us, that may appear again. Relaxation allows us to enjoy and employ our imagination; to make use of the verbal, written, and movement exercises we've shared; to find creative solutions to the ordinary dilemmas and the deepest challenges of our lives.

Set aside some time each day for relaxation. Soft Belly, which I shared with you and Theresa in the introduction, and which we've used in so many of our Prescriptions for Self-Care, is such a beautiful, simple way to do this—just about anywhere, anytime. If you have twenty minutes to do it, great. If you have five or three or even one, that's wonderful, too. Make, and take, the time.

Do Soft Belly whenever you feel yourself getting anxious, or ruminating about some real or imagined misfortune or fault, or reaching for food or drink you don't really need and may hardly even want, or obsessing about what you should or shouldn't do. Put signs up wherever you might need them—by the computer or on the refrigerator or in the car: BREATHE. SOFT BELLY. In time, even small amounts of stress or distress will become signals to stop and breathe deeply and slowly, to relax.

Ben Lo invited his students to relax in stressful postures, where activity or exertion was not only contraindicated but counterproductive and fruitless. But we can do this not only with tai chi, or yoga, as April learned to do, but in the midst of everyday challenges.

I have the opportunity to practice this several times a month when the planes in which I'm flying shimmy and shake, and the cup on my tray table slides and slops, and I bounce against my seat belt and my hands start sweating and I'm in total fight-or-flight mode. Since there's absolutely nothing I can do about the situation, I have to do something about my mind, my reaction to the situation. What I do is breathe slowly and deeply, allowing my body to relax into the jumping and bumping that a moment before was terrifying me; breathing through the fear and the illusion that I can control it; bringing my thoughts gently back from panic, relaxing into the jolts and dives; returning, paying attention to my breath, to Soft Belly; breathing, relaxing into the movement, breathing, relaxing, breathing, relaxing.

2. Move

Movement is a fundamental characteristic of human life. In depression it is disrupted. Sometimes, like Dominique, we're hopelessly and helplessly agitated. More often, like Theresa or Madeleine or Michael or myself, we alternate between bouts of self-flagellating agitation and defeatist exhaustion. Sometimes our body feels horribly burdened, unnaturally bound by gravity. Our face may look and feel frozen. Every action may be an ordeal.

As you emerge from depression and experience yourself more fully, you need to attend to signs and symptoms that announce anxiety and may signal discouraged withdrawal—the troubled pacing, the jittery knees, the creeping lethargy. You need to pay attention to your body, where your emotions are expressed, and to the messages it's conveying to you.

Begin by paying attention to your breath (and, yes, I know I'm repeating myself, but it bears repeating—we forget so fast and so often). Breathing is the most fundamental kind of movement, necessary for life and also capable of being altered to enhance every aspect of our living. Shallow breathing into a small portion of our chest—the kind that most people at most desks throughout the world seem to do—is both inefficient and anxiety producing. Remember, slow, deep, belly breathing brings you more life-giving oxygen, lowers your level of stress hormones and blood pressure, makes you feel calmer and happier.

To stay in physical and emotional balance, you also need to move the rest of your body and to do it every day.

Again, our hunter-gatherer forebears have much to teach. They moved throughout the day, easily, often, and in many ways—walking, lifting, pulling, carrying, and walking some more. When city people do this now, we call it cross-training. Aboriginal people and many rural people, even now, just call it "living."

I suggest that for the sake of simplicity, you make one physical activity your best friend and daily partner. It could be jogging, walking, swimming, yoga, tai chi. There is, as with a best friend, a security, a certain predictability, that is itself calming and encouraging. You may begin your activity in exhaustion or high anxiety, but you're likely to conclude by feeling both more energized and calmer. Fifteen or twenty minutes is fine, and more may feel better, particularly if you're highly agitated.

The more regularly you do your movement practice, the more likely you will appreciate it and its benefits: looser limbs, a clearer head, warmer hands, slower heart rate, sharper senses, and, yes, a better mood. The more likely, too, that you will bring the healing potential of hopeful anticipation to the activity—one of the characteristics of the therapeutically powerful placebo.

As one kind of movement becomes your best friend and partner, you will likely feel relaxed and comfortable enough to find other companions, other forms of movement, that are appropriate at particular times. If you're feeling cooped up in your house or in your mind, go for a walk. Or, if you're feeling at loose ends, do something useful, maybe even a household chore that someone else usually takes care of; or go food shopping, a nice activity if you don't regard it as demeaning or burdensome: walking the aisles of the supermarket, bending, reaching out, putting the food in the basket, taking it out, carrying the bags home, putting the food away.

If you're tired of standing or sitting and watching your child play soccer, walk along the sidelines as she runs, stretch while you do it. If you're feeling stuck mentally or physically in an emotion or with a demon, there's nothing like shaking to give you a few degrees of freedom.

If you work in an office or at a computer or, for that matter, in a consulting room, don't sit—earnest, hypnotized—for more than forty minutes at a time. That's a significant period even for an experienced meditator; much longer, the body grows stiff and attention tends to flag or become fixed. Get up. Put up another sign—or two—to remind you: One says BREATHE, the other, MOVE.

I suggest that whenever even the slightest urge appears, you dance, letting your arms and legs and body and head move as they will, as the body in its wisdom wants to move. Notice how you feel afterward. And no, you needn't wait for more scientific studies on the therapeutic value of dancing. Just do it and experience for yourself what happens.

As I suggested in chapter three, take some notes on your experiments with movement. The date and a few words will do: "Twenty minutes of walking in the morning. The air was crisp, and I felt it on my face and my arms, and felt my arms swinging when I walked. And I came back hungry and really tasted my cereal and fruit. Later on in the day, trying to write a report, I got all anxious and shook for two minutes and sat down again and was able to work."

Finally, I want to remind you that you can make beautiful and healing use of movement, even when you feel least able to. And any of us can do it.

Not long ago, I was supervising a group in Israel, a country long troubled by war and terrorism. Two men, trained by The Center for Mind-Body Medicine, were leading the group. Samuel's face was disfigured by a terrorist bomb. The other leader, Avi, was so crippled he could hardly stand. Samuel, I knew, still had the anxious hypervigilance of post-traumatic stress disorder; not long before, Avi had had all the symptoms of clinical depression. They had chosen to teach about movement, to teach, as each told us, about what they most needed to learn.

Samuel began by describing to us the moments before the bomb tore his face apart, and the horror after he woke up, immobile, his chest and face covered in bandages and held together by stitches. He said he had hated the pain of physical therapy, and hated even more the body and the twisted face that registered the pain. Loud noises, harsh voices, even the unexpected appearance of friends, might precipitate a panic attack.

Samuel told us he had panicked during the shaking in our first training but, helped by a friend, he had come back and tried again. Shaking and dancing among a hundred others, he told us, he discovered a pleasure in his body that he had not known in all the years since the explosion. He wasn't telling us about himself to gain our sympathy, he said—he didn't need it. He wanted only to share what had happened, to share how this exercise might also help us. That was his teaching story.

Then it was Avi's turn. He was going to demonstrate the shaking. "You may wonder how I will do this when, as you see, I cannot stand for long. But I will do it with you for a few minutes because this is, I've discovered, my best form of movement. And you can stand and do it, too.

Afterward, I will tell you how I feel, and since I have done this for myself every day since I learned it six months ago, and have felt good and proud of myself after, I expect I will feel good. And afterward you, too, can tell us how you feel."

3. Be Aware

Every stage of our journey, every step, is graced by and depends on awareness. Without it, we cannot recognize the good Guide or know when or how to surrender. Without awareness, demons remain demons, Dark Nights are impenetrable, and the blessing of the spiritual is a gilded but empty idea. With awareness, we are far less likely to become lost, disheartened, and depressed again, and more able to realize when we are headed in that direction. Awareness tells us when we are tense and need to relax, and which part of our body is most constricted, most in need of the deep, soft breathing that will unknot it. Awareness tells us which movement is right for us and at what moment.

"Cultivating awareness" is a phrase some writers use, and it's a nice one. Awareness must be recognized first as a necessary practice, planted in our understanding and gently encouraged in its growth. After some weeks or months of practice, a few deep breaths will prepare you and a simple, gentle, probing question may suffice to direct your attention: "What's happening now in my body?"

Alcohol can dampen or drown awareness. In fact, I think that many people, such as Theresa long ago, use it to that end. We don't want to know what we are really thinking or feeling, don't want to feel the pain or hear the Call and make the necessary change. Men, it seems, may be less likely to be diagnosed with depression partly because they are more likely to use drink to force feelings down.

If you drink, drink with awareness. Ask yourself if you're tasting or enjoying that good wine, or beer or whiskey, or just pouring it down; ask yourself if your mind is clear or careening toward oblivion. And if it's the latter, then know, like Theresa, that you need to attend to the feelings and hopes and possibilities that you are pushing down and aside.

Food, as I've said before, is a wonderful occasion for awareness.

Awareness tells us what we really want to buy and eat, or order in a restaurant, and how much. It reminds us of which foods are good for us and helps us to appreciate and maximize their benefits. If we stay aware as we chew and swallow and make decisions about another portion, we'll make wiser choices about the kind and quantity of our food, stay healthier, and enjoy our food far more. The habit of awareness about food, the enjoyment of food, can serve as a model for the rest of our lives.

I like to embrace awareness with my first waking moments—noticing, remembering my dreams as they recede, enjoying my eyes opening, registering the light in my room and my arms and legs stretching, the turning of my torso.

Write down your dreams when you first wake—otherwise you'll likely forget them—and the thoughts and feelings they evoke, perhaps to return to them later. They can be important teachers, reminding you of what or who you have been ignoring, sometimes answering questions and offering solutions to daytime problems.

Become aware, as you do your morning routine, of each action—washing, brushing your teeth, showering, and drying off. Appreciate the motions of dressing and the colors and contours, the textures and warmth of what you use to cover yourself.

And so it can go throughout the day. The walk to the bus, the usual commute, your colleagues at work, household chores, or getting the kids ready for school become, with your new eyes, interesting again.

When you bring awareness to it, just about every meeting or phone call loses its terror or tedium: It now seems an opportunity to connect with someone, or to meet a challenge, or just to feel some satisfaction in doing what needs to be done.

Awareness also enhances sleep. There is a large scientific literature on the contributions of the Mediterranean diet—high in olive oil and fish, vegetables and grains—to good health, but I suspect that the Mediterranean midday nap may also play a role. Disruptions of sleep are signs of stress and hallmarks of depression and can warn of its onset. Tending to your sleep, knowing when it is time for it, may help preserve you from depression.

At night, go to sleep when your body says you're tired, not when the

TV stops titillating. When you're fatigued during the day, don't take caffeine or other stimulants to stave off sleep, unless it's absolutely necessary. Take a nap instead. Fifteen minutes at the office, or in the (parked) car, as well as at home can be refreshing and refocusing.

4. Acceptance

Acceptance is the welcome we extend to awareness, the blessing we bestow on what is. It seems so obvious: Why shouldn't we accept what is? Yet it is very much at variance with the habits into which most of us have fallen—particularly those of us who are inclined to depression. We don't like or want to accept those parts of us that are or seem unworthy: our fears and hurts, our guilt and shame, our imperfections and resentment— all the demons that haunt and disturb us. We either deny that they exist until they overwhelm us or we damn ourselves repeatedly for them.

There's a paradox here: If we refuse to accept some part of ourselves, then we are, by definition, unworthy, and this feeling of unworthiness becomes the core of our depression. On the other hand, if we accept ourselves with our ignoble faults and perceived ugliness, with our self-deprecation and guilt, we have become, by this very act of acceptance, worthy—imperfect to be sure, but worthy—of acceptance.

In a way, *Unstuck* can be read as a manual of acceptance—of your bad moods and worst fears, of real or imagined shortcomings, of your disturbances and your depression, as well as of all that you regard as good and valuable. It is an invitation to acknowledge what you've been clinging to in order to let it go; to accept where you've been and where you are, so you can embrace what will be happening in the inevitable change of the next moment. There's a story about the playwright George Bernard Shaw. A friend told him that a famous intellectual had announced that she'd "accepted the universe." "Egad," Shaw is said to have remarked. "She'd better."

You have an ongoing opportunity to practice this lesson. Physical sensations are a great place to begin. They're easily accessible, and the rewards of acknowledging and accepting them are palpable. Instead of tensing your body against cramps, pain, or discomfort—and thereby aggravating it—or suppressing the pain with medication, you can breathe deeply into the pain and relax with it. Imagining the breath flowing into the part of your body that's troubling you, feeling it expand and soften, you may feel your pain diminish and quiet. Sometimes tears may come. Sometimes, with relaxation and acceptance, there will be laughter. You can breathe into your emotions as well—your inevitable feelings of anger, guilt, or loneliness—breathing, relaxing with the demons that may still trouble you from time to time, even when you're feeling good.

Other people will give you lots of opportunities to practice acceptance. You can begin by noticing negative judgments you make about their words or actions. When you observe yourself judging, breathe deeply a few times and ask yourself a couple of simple questions: "What am I judging?" "Is what I see in that other person something I find unacceptable in myself?" Often it is. In judging someone's defensiveness or obtuseness or anger, you may well be condemning attitudes or characteristics that you find unacceptable in yourself.

Take some more deep breaths, letting these judgments, like any thoughts that may arise when you're doing Soft Belly, come and go, bringing your mind back to the breath. Often, after only a few breaths, you may find yourself looking at the other person differently. His behavior or attitude is of significantly less emotional concern. After all, it's his. And, again, interestingly, accepting his limitations may make you less likely to judge the same or similar ones in yourself.

At The Center for Mind-Body Medicine, we see this process unfold in our trainings and groups around the world and here in the United States. Regular meditation at the beginning and end of the group, and our insistence on a meditative, relaxed, and aware mind throughout, remind all of us to be present, to watch and let go. The group is a safe, hospitable place for us to get to know ourselves, to be aware and relaxed with others.

Again and again, group members find that after days together, or months of weekly meetings, the man who at first seemed the most obnoxious or least sympathetic, has other sides, struggles, tender places.

Meanwhile, all of us in the group are becoming aware of the ways in which his behavior and attitudes may mirror our own. And we've been watching the changes in our attitude as his changes. In beginning to accept him, in understanding that there are many sides to him, that he is both similar to us and different, we find we begin to accept—and to extend compassion to—ourselves as well. As the group continues, all of us have the sense that we are in it together, learning about ourselves from one another, sharing difficulties and possibilities.

The classes and retreats, the meditation centers and monasteries that I list in the Resources section are also places where this kind of acceptance can unfold, schools for both awareness and acceptance. Set aside some time for them.

5. Have Patience

Some years ago, I commented to an old and close friend that it was hard for me to learn a new language—I'd taken a few Portuguese lessons—because it seemed to me the process should go so much faster. "I guess I'm a little impatient," I said, with a modest smile. "A little?" he responded, with amusement.

And, I assure you, I'm not the only one. Almost everybody who is depressed, or anxious, or in psychological pain of any kind, wants it over *now*. And impatience with our moods and pains makes them far less tolerable, makes it far more likely that we will compound our depression by condemning ourselves for staying depressed, for not moving through it faster.

Impatience is another form of nonacceptance. Your time of unhappiness and confusion or of depression has, I hope, helped you to practice patience, which does not come naturally or easily to most of us. Deciding not to take drugs, or drink too much, to relieve your discomfort and distress, you can set the stage for your lessons. Paying attention to what you do to help yourself—the decreased anxiety and enhanced sense of well-being that follows slow, deep breathing, the lightening of your mood after exercise or imagery, the satisfaction of doing tasks you've avoided—you've likely discovered both that change is possible and that it takes time and persistence. Observing that your mood may descend an hour or a day later, you come to know that this change is not necessarily permanent, that it is a process, not a product.

Some sense of urgency is, of course, necessary to move us onto the path of transformation. There's nothing virtuous or valuable about inefficiency or deliberate delay. And it's important to remember and heed this urgency when you feel yourself once again tormented by the demons that used to populate your depression. But the ongoing practice of patience is at least as important in preventing future episodes of depression.

If you don't react, or feel compelled to act, you may be less likely to say and do things and make choices for which you'll later condemn yourself, or to take actions you'll have to repair. If you become more patient, you will more easily accept what would before have frustrated and, indeed, depressed you—the time it may take to repair a troubled relationship or heal from a loss that has left you desolate, the measured courtship of a new lover, a boss's rebuke, even the slow pace of learning a new language.

You need to be patient with yourself as you continue to fill all the Prescriptions for Self-Care. Doing Soft Belly or mindfulness practice is a first step. Meditation slows you down and will help you to remember where you've been, and to appreciate where you are now, and what you're doing for yourself. It may help you remember that the habits of thought and feeling that got you stuck were years in the making, and to realize that time will be necessary, even after you're no longer depressed, to undo them. Meditation, and the patience it brings, will help you pay attention to, enjoy, and appreciate the small changes you continue to make and the benefits you feel.

Sometimes the exercises you do will reinforce your understanding that patience, not problem solving, is needed: Your Inner Guide or your drawings or dialogue may well let you know that it's not yet time to address a certain issue, or that you may need to relax more, or to try another approach. You need to listen.

It seems to me far better to learn the lessons our life has to teach, and to work with and even enjoy them, than it is to look for a quick fix—an infallible answer, a drug to work on us—to still our present pain.

6. Time Out

A friend and I were sitting with the enormously gifted and prolific painter Robert Rauschenberg. We were in his studio in Captiva, Florida, sipping Jack Daniel's with him in the early evening. He was describing his work habits, telling us that at around 10:00 p.m. or so, he would begin his customary nighttime painting. "Mr. Rauschenberg," my friend asked, "don't you ever want more time off?"

"Honey," Rauschenberg responded, without missing a beat, "I don't want time off. I want more time on."

I laughed, appreciating our host's energy, recognizing my own inclination in his. I want more time on, too—to love those who are close to me and to enjoy my life and do my work—but I have learned from my own experience and from the people whose stories I've told in this book that good time off is crucial to making my time on good for me.

I've learned to take this time off in the face of the world's apparent imperatives, as well as my own sense of responsibility and, yes, guilt. I've found that if I take this time to be with myself, I may discover new understandings and resources that will help me go where I need to, and to do it in the way it needs to be done. If I don't, I'm likely once again to become lost and stuck.

Meditation, those daily minutes of Soft Belly, or awareness, or shaking, is time off. So, too, is the time you take to consult your Inner Guide or write in your journal or take a long, pleasurable shower or a walk in nature.

Many of us resist, particularly those of us who are perfectionists and proud, who have the cruel conscience that characterizes depression: "It would be selfish," we say, "to take the time for ourselves." And yet we find that when we do take this time for ourselves, we have more to give, and we give it more freely.

I suggest that you give yourself these few moments every day, perhaps especially when you're most beleaguered. Everyone with whom I've worked who really wants and values it has found it possible—doctors and nurses running from one emergency to another, mothers with many children and little money, even people struggling to recover from, or live through, a war. All feel the benefit, and feel it even more when they're under the most pressure.

And there are longer times off, as well, that can give you new life. Remember Dorothy's retreat from responsibility, April's evenings of waitressing, Milton's long weekend with Lao-tzu, Theresa's weeks on Ramana Maharshi's peaceful hill.

These times out and off are nourishing, replenishing, and sacred, too. One of the first of the Old Testament commandments is to "remember the Sabbath day to keep it holy." Several thousand years later, the experience of modern Orthodox Jewish families confirms this wisdom. Every week, for twenty-four hours, usual activity stops. There are special blessings for each portion of time, extra attention paid to preparing and eating meals, honor for relationships with family and friends sometimes taken for granted, time to tell stories and walk and just be.

As we take this or similar time, all of us honor ourselves and our own creativity, as well as God, or nature, whose creation we are enjoying and celebrating. By stopping for a while, we are breaking up habitual behaviors and ways of thinking, giving ourselves each week, or each day, the opportunity for a new start.

7. Fear Not

Those who have been depressed often worry that this state will return to claim them. This is understandable. The experience is overwhelming, tenacious, and unhappy. Many of you have been discouraged because you've experienced it more than once.

Your fear is perhaps reinforced by a scientific and popular literature that is liberally veined with warnings. Depression, we are told, is not only an ominous disease, but one that is likely to become chronic and even more debilitating.

I don't dispute the data on the increasing likelihood of second and subsequent episodes of depression. I do think the interpretation is, at best, incomplete. People usually continue to have times of depression, I have observed, not because it's a chronic disease, but because they have not addressed the underlying reasons for it. I encourage you to see each subsequent episode of depression as another wake-up call, and the decreasing time between episodes as an intensification of your alarm system.

If we do not make the necessary changes in our work or our relationships or our attitude—the way we live and breathe and eat and exercise and deal with stress and other people and ourselves—we will, of course, continue to suffer the consequences. If we do address the causes, the results will likely be, as the stories I've shared with you indicate, quite different.

Your own worries and the warnings of medical experts may make you vigilant, if not anxious, looking over your shoulder for a pursuer who is likely to reclaim you, looking inward for telltale signs and symptoms, and anticipating stresses or strains that may distress or undermine you. Vigilance is entirely appropriate, but fear is likely to be debilitating.

Fear, which is the central element of prolonged stress, is, in one form or another, a major factor in depression—fear of the consequences of loss, abandonment, displacement, illness, death. Fear feeds depression, debilitating us further. And fearful belief in the inevitable chronicity of depression may well be self-fulfilling.

When I consider the possibility of depression reoccurring, the words *fear not* come to me. This reassuring phrase is an abiding part of our Judeo-Christian heritage and of the world's wisdom. In the Old Testament, in times of doubt and crisis, God says these words to Abraham and Jacob. In the New Testament, Jesus repeatedly uses the phrase to reassure his disciples and those who come for his help. After his enlightenment, Buddha is said to have spoken these words and made a gesture—right hand raised, palm out, fingers up, to signify to them: Fear not.

I hope you have discovered that depression is a sign of imbalance in your life and that it can be a starting point for a journey of self-discovery that can bring you wisdom and self-fulfillment. Now, when the troubles and temptations, or signs and symptoms, appear, you can look at them as signals that an ongoing attitude of awareness is necessary; you can see them as challenges rather than catastrophes. They can remind you to relax with, rather than react against, difficulty. They call you to accept rather than turn in fear from or deny some painful or unlovely part of yourself; to transform, not be trampled by, your demons; to trust in your capacity to heal yourself.

Theresa put it well: "Now when I'm feeling anxious, sad, or angry, I understand that these are *just* emotions, and I can allow them to be. And not react by panicking or medicating myself with alcohol or drugs. When something upsetting happens, I can be—and stay—bent out of shape, or I can choose to take responsibility: do my meditation, use all the tools I've learned, make sure I'm eating the right diet, and dancing; read the books that mean something to me; talk with my friends; find my balance again. It's OK to feel the pain. Pain comes to everyone. And I remind myself that accepting the pain before didn't kill me; sitting with the pain has actually made me not tougher, but stronger."

8. Ask for Help

It's humbling to deal with depression, to groan under its burden and confront demons whose deformities turn out to be our own. We learn, if we are on the path I've described, how much we can do to understand, help, and heal ourselves. We also begin to discover the vast, uncharted territories of thoughts and feelings that, if we are to stay on our path, we cannot control and have to accept, the unknown to which we must surrender. And we learn, too, in the face of our pride, the limits of our own unaided efforts, our need for Guides.

This well-earned humility is a good thing and a realistic response, especially in the darkest times of depression. It's also important to remember it when we're feeling better, more capable, stronger, less depressed, happy.

Humility will remind you of the binds and the blindness from which you've emerged, warn you against keeping satisfied company with the demons of pride, perfectionism, and resentment. Humility is the soil in which acceptance flourishes. Humility allows you to realize that you are not so different from those others who may seem better, or worse, richer, more self-reliant, or more beautiful, more or less troubled than you are. And humility will make it so much easier to admit you need help, to reach out to others when you need to, and to accept the help that they can offer.

Now might be a good time for each of you to acknowledge those who have helped you through hard times, to remind yourself of ongoing connections as well as old debt. These are the people who allowed you to be yourself, embraced and accepted you, and helped you to accept what sometimes felt unacceptable in yourself. Thinking of them now that you have moved ahead in your journey reminds you that it is possible to share what troubles you, to connect with others who care and for whom you care. Feeling affection for them is proof against whatever future loneliness you might face.

Not long ago, Madeleine gratefully made a list of these people for me, naming a few old friends she'd rediscovered, the leaders of her retreat, the formerly depressed women who were there when she needed them, some members of her church. She recalled the ways they had helped her, and expressed appreciation that they were still in her life and available to her. Then she invited all of them to dinner in her new apartment. Looking around her that evening, as they ate the food she'd prepared, she relaxed into the circle of friendship and healing.

9. Trust Your Inner Guide

Traveling with me on the journey through and out of depression, you've been learning to rely increasingly on your inner guidance, on the intuition and imagination you've mobilized through words and drawings, and in guided imagery, dialogue, and your journal. The people I've introduced you to have tested these techniques in times of great need—gaining confidence and direction in selecting a good Guide, discovering answers to previously insoluble dilemmas, and finding hope in the midst of despair. I hope you have, too.

As you emerge from the dark wood of depression, you can make regular, less pressured, more playful use of the approaches that I've taught you: to stay in touch with your unconscious wisdom; to deepen your experience of each day; to discover and enjoy the array of options and choices that are always available to you; to make decisions that are reliably in tune with who you are and what you really want.

Here are some suggestions for doing this on an ongoing basis.

Keep on writing in your journal—every day. It guarantees a time of reflection, expression, and release. It's an anchor, a safe home base. It will remind you of the range of your feelings, help guarantee that you become aware of old patterns—the seduction of demons—before they once again become habitual. Remember to record your dreams in your journal when you wake up and to write at other times that seem appropriate—at the end of the day, while eating lunch by yourself, or in spare minutes at the office or at home.

Use the Inner Guide imagery: The more you do this exercise, the easier it will be for you to use and benefit from it. Initially, feeling inexperienced, uncertain, and perhaps doubtful, the imagery may have required twenty difficult minutes. As time goes on, you'll often be able to do it more easily and quickly.

Ask your Inner Guide about the meaning of your dreams, or about decisions at work—how to deal with your boss and whom to hire and what project to do next. Ask about dilemmas at home—What am I doing to upset my wife or husband? And what does she or he really need to be happy? Or about issues at school—Should I write a paper on this or that subject? Ask X or Y out? And use your Inner Guide to help you when you want to create a new program of diet or exercise. The Inner Guide imagery is often powerfully informative and, as I've said, it becomes easier to use.

Consult your Inner Guide regularly, even several times a day if you feel like it. Our formal education has generally been heavy on facts, memorization, and analysis, but woefully light on developing intuition and creativity. Test scores and the bottom line rule. The Inner Guide offers you a practical way to address this imbalance, to bring your whole mind and being to daily decision making, problem solving, and living.

As you use this imagery, notice the difference between your preconceptions and fears about what the answers might be, and what they actually turn out to be. Keep track of how your guidance works out. Write all of this—preconceptions, questions, fears, answers, action steps, consequences, and next steps—in your journal.

We've discussed how to do written dialogues and drawings in chapters four and six. They tap into the same unconscious wisdom as the Inner Guide imagery, but the process and the parts of the brain mobilized are different. In your dialogue, you're doing something physical—writing—and dynamic, and producing a product. The activity, the dramatic interaction of the dialogue, its attention to a specific symptom, problem, or issue, can quickly promote focused understanding, and offer clear steps to resolution. Drawings are expansive, liberating, playful. The images you produce—of yourself and how you would like to be, and how you're going to get there—are true and hopeful mirrors and guides. If you look at them over time, they'll remind and inform you—in a way that is both concrete and symbolic—of what you're actually experiencing, and of what you want for yourself. They will also remind you, as you do them and gaze again at them, of the capacity that you have to imagine and navigate the ongoing journey from the present you know to the possible for which you hope.

10. Celebrate Everything

There's a world of difference between just existing and appreciating, enjoying, and celebrating existence. It's the difference between a dull dailiness that is hardly different from dysthymia and close enough to depression, and delight. To feel delight, to take pleasure in life, means opening yourself to fully experience whatever arises in the most intimate parts of your life, and in everyday, ordinary events.

Openness can't be selective. If you close yourself against pain, as many of us who've been depressed do, you're not likely to experience joy so fully. Sometimes, and especially in some children, this openness seems to be ongoing, almost constitutional. Sometimes it comes spontaneously, as a grace, after meditation, or dance, or intimate moments with a spouse, lover, friend, or child. Sometimes, particularly amid your daily responsibilities and habits, it's a choice, one you have to remind yourself to make. I need to remind myself daily, and so do the people I work with.

When I find myself uninterested in or bored by the people I'm with, or my surroundings, I close my eyes and take a few deep breaths, then open them to look with appreciation. For example, in the coffee shops where I often write, I'm now able to notice, appreciate, and enjoy what I previously ignored: the smile on the face of the one-year-old in her stroller; the swift motions of the barista preparing a latte; the impatient hands-on-hips stance of the man who is ninth or tenth in line for coffee, sweating in his overcoat. Meditation—quiet or expressive—is the ongoing means for creating this celebratory consciousness.

Love is the highest form of celebration. Of all the guides through depression and other difficult times, of all the guards against it, love seems to me the most sure-footed, the most reliably protective and sustaining. The unconditional love parents give their infants creates ease, balance, and assured self-love. This kind of care and affection, later in life, can repair damage that may have been done. Love to me is the essence of the "unconditional positive regard" (Carl Rogers's words again) that makes the good Guide—Athena, Virgil, Dante's Beatrice, Hekate, or Bob Coles, or any therapist or counselor—so good and good for us.

Love lost is more often than not a major cause of depression, and love recovered, in relationship with the same person, or another, is its most common remedy. But this kind of love, as psychologist Bruno Bettelheim famously said in another context, "is not enough." It is only when we feel love for ourselves that we are reliably able to feel we are loved; only when we are able to freely offer love to others that it carries us, like a boat on the sea, through the highs and lows of our daily lives.

Paul, in 1 Corinthians 13, is, I think, right about love. "Love suffers long and is kind. Love envies not. Love values not itself, is not puffed up, rejoices not in inequity, but rejoices in the truth." A tall order, or better said, a continuous challenge. The willingness to make love one's lodestar, often after many difficulties, is what I see when I look at the people whose stories I have shared with you in *Unstuck*. This acting out of love rather than fear or anger is the standard against which I measure myself and how I see myself behaving when all is well. It is one you can use as well.

There's a quote that I found not long ago in one of my bookstore browsings that sums up this ever-recurring starting place. It's attributed by the editor of the book, Daniel Landinsky, to Hafiz, a thirteenth-century Sufi whose poems Landinsky has collected and translated.

"What is the sign," a young woman asked Hafiz, "of someone knowing God?"

"Dear," he replied, "they have dropped the knife, the cruel knife most so often use upon their tender self and others. I have found the power to say no to any action that might harm myself or another."

This is such a good place to begin: vigilant for the harm you do to yourself, aware of, accepting, letting go of impulses and tendencies to martyrdom and guilt, your own inclination to pride or resentment, as well as your potential cruelty or indifference to others.

We all need to put away the knife when we're tempted to judge or gossip or criticize others, to tote up our own shortcomings, or blame and berate ourselves. Putting away the knife and knowing that we're doing it, every day, every minute, allows us to live without regrets or fears, with love, in that moment.

This may seem daunting, but it gets easier, becomes more interesting, even satisfying, as you relax, become more aware and accepting. It is, of course, harder when you're provoked, challenged, criticized; when you feel insecure, beset by your demons, inclined once again to react defensively, or be depressed.

There's another story that helps me when I'm feeling confounded or conflicted in these ways, when I feel the knots that once tied me in depression again tightening, a story I hope you, too, will remember and take to heart as we come to the end of this part of our journey together. Shyam, my Guide, teacher, and friend, told it to me long ago. It's about a famous samurai, a warrior who comes—after much suffering and with many doubts—to ask for help from a Zen master.

"What is the difference between heaven and hell?" the samurai asks with as much humility as he can muster.

"You muscle-bound moron," the master shouts at him. "That's the stupidest question. . . . "

The enraged samurai draws his sword.

"That is hell," says the master.

The samurai breathes deeply, slides the sword back into the sheath, and begins to smile.

"And that," concludes the Zen master, noting the easy motion, the relief, the relaxation, "is heaven."

ACKNOWLEDGMENTS

Many people have made the *Unstuck* journey with me. I have protected the identities of the ones whom I write about here, changing their names and important details about their lives, families, and work. My debt to all of them for what they have given to me and shared with you is enormous.

Dorothy is the only "composite" in the book. She is based on two patients who have been powerful teachers for me. Neither is a senator's wife, though both had husbands in public positions. I have, however, known a number of Senate wives and have used, with appreciation, details from their life experiences that they graciously shared with me.

Unstuck was conceived some years ago. I have, with occasionally frustrating but sometimes necessary interruptions and delays, written and rewritten it over time. I hope and believe this long gestation—and what I learned about myself and others during it—has made it more thoughtful, compassionate, and user friendly. During those years, my colleagues and board members at The Center for Mind-Body Medicine, our faculty, and all the men, women, and children I have worked with here in the United States and in war and postwar situations around the world have been my friends, teachers, and inspiration. They have helped me to understand the devastating impact of loss and given me a continuing education in human resiliency and the healing possibilities of self-awareness, self-care, and mutual support. Most of all, they have taught me about the power of hope and honesty, forgiveness and love. I particularly want to thank Dr. Susan Lord, who began our international work with me, always urged and helped me to look at what I wasn't seeing, and commented on earlier drafts of *Unstuck*.

I've had many Guides in my life. They've been there when I needed them and have inspired me with their wisdom, kindness, generosity, and humor. They include, in addition to Drs. Robert Coles and Shyam Singha and William Alfred, about whom I write, Drs. Edward Burchard, David Cheek, and Rudy Bauer, and Gregory Bateson, Rhonda Shomper, and Richard Polonchak. I'm grateful to my brothers, Andy and Jeff, my former wife and present dear friend Sharon Curtin, and my friends and fellow travelers on the healing journey Alan Cheuse, Kristin O'Shee, George Blecher, Howard Josepher, Lynne and Bill Twist, Allison Berardi, Joel Evans, Max Heirich, Isabel Letelier, Dave Levy, Penny George, Tina Linden, Gary Kaplan, Steve Blood, Dan Sterenchuk, and Lily Mondonedo, and my godchildren Matt, George, and Rosemary Lombard, for their unconditional love and support, and to Alan and George Blecher for reading drafts of *Unstuck* and helping me to head where I needed to go.

Many years ago, Peter Carlin, interviewing me for a magazine article on depression, first turned my attention to the possibilities of this book. Not long after, Dr. David Antonnuccio encouraged me to critically examine the research literature on antidepressants and their limitations. Much more recently, Dr. Robert Hedaya gave me expert commentary and advice on the almost finished *Unstuck*. Drs. Irving Kirsch, Ronald Kessler, Arif Khan, and Cynthia Murlow all helped me to appreciate the details and significance of their research.

Chris Tomasino, my literary agent, supported and encouraged me all the way with humor, insight, and energy, and helped me to bring out what was inside me. Jane Fleming, my editor at The Penguin Press, focused my efforts and made the book ever more accessible and practical. Ann Godoff, my publisher, got what I was doing from the get-go.

I've had wonderful help with research and the Resources section from talented, committed students—medical and otherwise—including Nina Wexell, Jake Hyman, Marika Alois, Jessica Ess, and, in the crucial last months of fact-checking, the painstaking, indefatigable Jason Wong. Chanelle Redman, my former assistant, lavished her love on transcribing and typing early drafts. Christine Fisher, who currently assists me, has been wonderfully competent and devoted as she helped me bring the manuscript to completion.

Several times, while I was writing *Unstuck,* Susan Lord's daughter, Jamie, now age six, asked if this book was "for me." It was and it is for Jamie, and for my son Gabriel, who is five. And it is also written in the hope that all of us will cherish the blessings that come from getting and being unstuck—the forgiveness and freedom, the love and joy—and share these blessings with all of our children everywhere.

RESOURCES

JAMES S. GORDON AND THE CENTER FOR MIND-BODY MEDICINE

www.jamesgordonmd.com. This is my Web site. It features additional Prescriptions for Self-Care, updates on the *Unstuck* approach, and up-to-date information on new ways to move through and beyond depression and distress. Please send me stories of your experience with *Unstuck* and your questions. I'll share some of the most inspiring stories and will answer some of your questions on the Web site.

The Center for Mind-Body Medicine (CMBM). This is the 501(c)(3) nonprofit educational organization that I founded in 1991 and continue to direct. Its goal is to make self-awareness, self-care, and mutual help—the approach I describe in *Unstuck*—central to medical and mental health practice, the training of health and mental health professionals, and the education of our children. Information about all CMBM programs is available on the Web site **www.cmbm.org.**

CMBM is a healing community and a community of healers. Our training programs in mind-body medicine and nutrition and our CancerGuides® training are open to all health, mental health, and education professionals as well as to those nonprofessionals who are committed to using our approach with others as well as with themselves. Our Web site has detailed information about all aspects of these trainings, including their content, dates, and locations. CMBM's model of mind-body skills groups is being used in the education of students in more than a dozen U.S. medical schools as well as in hundreds of hospitals and clinics and clinical practices in every part of North America.

CMBM's Global Outreach Program is currently working with populations traumatized by war and disaster in the Balkans, the Middle East (Israelis and Palestinians), and post-Katrina New Orleans as well as with U.S. soldiers returning from Iraq and Afghanistan. The method we use to heal post-traumatic stress disorder, depression, and anxiety in these populations is essentially the same as the one that I'm describing in *Unstuck*. In these programs, we first help health, mental health, and education leaders, as well as other community leaders, to deal with their own trauma and ongoing stress and then teach, supervise, and support them as they work with entire populations.

CMBM's program is currently central to Kosovo's community mental health centers, where it is available to two million people. It is being used by three hundred Israeli and ninety Palestinian leaders in mental health who are making it available to every sector of the population in Israel and Gaza, and by teams of Israelis and Palestinians working together. The CMBM model is also being widely used in public agencies, universities, and nonprofit and private settings throughout southern Louisiana and is beginning to be implemented by a core group of CMBM-trained military health and mental health professionals who are working with veterans returning from Iraq and Afghanistan.

CMBM and its faculty (there are currently twenty-five in the United States and forty-five more around the world) provide an initial training, an advanced training and practicum, ongoing supervision, and certification in mind-body medicine. Our faculty and others who are certified have received extensive training and supervision, are extremely knowledgeable about the CMBM approach, and are excellent resources for all readers of *Unstuck*. More than seventy CMBM-certified mind-body skills group leaders are available in the United States and Canada, and there are as many overseas. Many of them offer the mind-body skills groups that I discuss in chapter two and are qualified to be your Guides or to offer you informed referrals to Guides. The names, backgrounds, and contact information of faculty and those we've certified in the United States and Canada are available on our Web site.

Approximately six hundred North American clinicians have completed the advanced training and practicum and have therefore had some supervised experience using significant portions of the *Unstuck* approach. The remaining nine hundred have completed the initial phase of the training and have experienced the CMBM large- and small-group model and learned the science upon which it is based but have not completed the advanced training and practicum. All fifteen hundred may be appropriate as Guides or referral sources and may also offer mind-body skills groups. However, they vary significantly in their depth of understanding of the model and their experience in using it with individuals and groups. We cannot vouch for their expertise and experience. The names of those who have completed the advanced training are available by location on the CMBM Web site.

Although all fifteen hundred of these program participants have experienced the CMBM model, as with any health professional, make your own judgments about their appropriateness as Guides and referral sources.

The CMBM is a membership organization. Information about joining and about the benefits of public and professional membership may be found on the Web site. Donations to CMBM, which are fully tax deductible, are received with deep gratitude. Contributions may be made online or mailed to The Center for Mind-Body Medicine. They will go to CMBM programs that provide the *Unstuck* approach to populations traumatized by war and natural disasters and to disadvantaged U.S. communities where depression and post-traumatic stress disorder are widespread. Information about the work you support will be regularly posted on the Web site.

Address:	5225 Connecticut Avenue NW, Suite 414
	Washington, DC 20015
Phone:	202-966-7338
Fax:	202-966-2589
E-mail:	center@cmbm.org
Web site:	www.cmbm.org

Additional CMBM Resources

The Best of Stress Management (BSM). This multimedia kit offers you the experience of being guided in the mind-body skills that are central to the *Unstuck* journey in your own home. It is the closest approximation to actually being in a mind-body skills group and is proving enormously helpful to people who want to decrease stress, improve their mood, and take charge of their lives. In the BSM DVD, I provide an overview of mind-body medicine. The ten CDs, eight of which I recorded, take you through explanations and practice of many of the exercises that we use in *Unstuck,* including the Soft Belly, mindfulness, and *tonglen* meditations; the Lemon, Safe Place, and Inner Guide imagery; the dialogue with an SPI; and shaking and dancing. They also provide detailed, step-by-step guidance in other techniques that I've mentioned but that are not fully described here: mindful eating, biofeedback, and genograms. There's a digital biofeedback thermistor to measure hand temperature (which generally goes up as you become more relaxed) and a clear, user-friendly workbook to guide you in using these techniques. The kit includes appearances by my CMBM colleague Susan Lord, MD; and CMBM friends and advisors Herbert Benson, MD; Joan Borysenko, PhD; and Belleruth Naparstek, LCSW. Depressed and stressed-out people have described the kit as "comprehensive," "fun to use," "enormously supportive," and "the best self-care tool I've ever found."

BOOKS

Manifesto for a New Medicine: Your Guide to Healing Partnerships and the Wise Use of Alternative Therapies. James S. Gordon. Boston : Da Capo Press, 1996. *Manifesto* provides an overview of the New Medicine. It emphasizes the importance of self-care as the "true primary care," and also explores in considerably greater depth than in *Unstuck* many of the other approaches that I've integrated into my clinical practice: nutrition, acupuncture and herbalism, musculoskeletal manipulation, massage, homeopathy, and spiritual healing among them. There's a balance in the book between case histories that illustrate how an integrative medical practice can help you, and scientific references that support—and critique—the use of these complementary and alternative therapies.

Comprehensive Cancer Care: Integrating Complementary, Alternative and Conventional Therapies. James S. Gordon and Sharon Curtin. Boston: Da Capo Press, 2000. This book presents the best available information about complementary and alternative approaches that can be integrated into cancer care as well as practical ways to make this happen. It's based on CMBM's groundbreaking Comprehensive Cancer Care conferences and is widely regarded as *the* book to consult after you've received the diagnosis of cancer, the source of the best information on what you can do in addition to, or aside from, what your oncologist has recommended.

    The Best of Stress Management, Manifesto for a New Medicine, and *Comprehensive Cancer Care* can all be ordered through our Web site, www.cmbm.org.

Unstuck Resources

The resources listed below are keyed to the introduction and seven chapters of *Unstuck,* and the topics discussed in them.

INTRODUCTION: IS THERE SOME OTHER WAY?
MEDITATION

Independent Meditation Center Guide. Web site that allows users to search for meditation centers by type of meditation, geographic location, or name. Results include contact information, a link to each center's Web site, a brief description, and attendee comments, if available.

Web site: www.gosit.org

Vipassana Meditation. International home page of the organizations that offer courses in vipassana (awareness or mindfulness) meditation as taught by S. N. Goenka and his assistant teachers. Offers ten-day residential courses in vipassana meditation, for which there is no charge (all expenses are met by donations from people who have completed a course and wish to give others the opportunity to do so as well). Courses are offered at various locations worldwide.

Web site: www.dhamma.org

Shambhala. Global community of more than 170 centers and groups, all rooted in the contemplative teachings of Buddhism but available to practitioners of any tradition. Shambhala meditation centers offer instruction in mindfulness meditation free of charge. For those with little meditation experience, Shambhala offers introductory programs, which include open talks, meditation practice, group discussions, and personal interviews.

Web site: www.shambhala.org

The Transcendental Meditation Program. Official Web site for transcendental meditation. This concentrative meditation technique uses certain mantras, or sounds, to achieve a state of restful alertness. Provides referrals to certified instructors who have completed a six-month teacher training course.

Phone: 888-532-7686
E-mail: tminfo@tm.org
Web site: www.tm.org

CHAPTER ONE: THE CALL: FINDING THE RIGHT WAY
Western Medicine
PHYSICIANS

In the United States, the term *physician* is commonly used to describe a medical doctor holding a doctor of medicine (MD) or doctor of osteopathy (DO) degree. Although doctors of chiropractic medicine (DCs) and doctors of naturopathic medicine (NDs) are also physicians, only MDs and DOs are licensed to practice the full scope of medicine, including surgery. Those who hold an MD are sometimes referred to as allopathic physicians, while DOs are known as osteopathic physicians.

Training for MDs and DOs is virtually the same except that DOs also learn musculoskeletal manipulation. Students must complete four years of postgraduate medical education, pass standardized examinations, and complete at least one internship year to practice in the United States. To achieve board-certification status and specialization, graduates will undergo closely supervised, intensive residency and fellowship training for an additional three to eight years, depending upon the chosen field. Psychiatric residency training is four years long.

American Medical Association (AMA). The nation's largest medical association. Offers lists of more than 690,000 doctors, and includes their educational background, office hours, accepted insurance providers, and other helpful information for patients. All members must adhere to the AMA's Principles of Medical Ethics.

Address: 515 North State Street
             Chicago, IL 60610
Phone: 800-621-8335
Web site: www.ama-assn.org

American Osteopathic Association (AOA). The nation's primary association for certifying DOs and accrediting all osteopathic medical colleges and health care facilities. It represents more than sixty-one thousand osteopathic physicians.

Address: 142 East Ontario Street
             Chicago, IL 60611
Phone: 800-621-1773
Fax: 312-202-8200
E-mail: info@osteotech.org
Web site: www.osteopathic.org

NURSE PRACTITIONERS

Nurse practitioners (NPs) provide much of the same care as physicians, with duties including diagnosing and treating illnesses and disease, prescribing medications, as well as performing minor surgeries. Because the profession is state regulated, the educational requirements and methods of practice may vary. Most states require a master's degree and state licensure by the state board of nursing. National certification is provided by one of several professional nursing organizations such as the American Academy of Nurse Practitioners (AANP). A number of nurse practitioners are highly trained in the area of mental health.

American Academy of Nurse Practitioners (AANP). With more than 22,500 members and representing the interests of more than 120,000 NPs of all specialties, the AANP is the nation's largest professional membership organization. Its Web site provides an option to search for NPs in your local area. This is not a referral service, and members provide their own information.

Address: P.O. Box 12846
             Austin, TX 78711
Phone: 512-442-4262
Fax: 512-442-6469
E-mail: admin@aanp.org
Web site: www.aanp.org
Find an NP: www.npfinder.com

Integrative and Holistic Practitioners and Practices

American Holistic Medical Association (AHMA). Organization for physicians, medical students, and other health care practitioners who care for or are interested in caring for the whole person—body, mind, and spirit. Their integrative approach and their interest in nutrition make them appropriate for investigating the possible imbalances as well as the diseases and drugs that may contribute to depression. The AHMA provides board certification—which among other areas tests mind-body medicine and nutrition—in holistic medicine. The AHMA has a directory of more than seven hundred member MDs, DOs, and other health care providers with current unrestricted licenses. Membership is self-selecting for those who deliver care with a holistic philosophy, but this is not an enforced requirement.

> Address: P.O. Box 2016
>   Edmonds, WA 98020
> Phone: 425-967-0737
> Fax: 425-771-9588
> E-mail: ahma@holisticmedicine.org
> Web site: www.holisticmedicine.org

American Holistic Nurses' Association (AHNA). The AHNA is a membership organization open to nurses and other individuals interested in holistically oriented health care practices. Its philosophy and values, which include an emphasis on self-care and the idea that our physical and emotional problems "should be viewed as an opportunity for increased awareness of the interconnectedness of body, mind, and spirit," align closely with the approach offered in *Unstuck.* It offers a practitioner directory of holistic nurses by state, complete with full contact information.

> Address: 323 North San Francisco Street, Suite 201
>   Flagstaff, AZ 86001
> Phone: 800-278-2462
> Fax: 928-526-2752
> E-mail: info@ahna.org
> Web site: www.ahna.org

American College for Advancement in Medicine. A not-for-profit medical society committed to educating physicians and other health care professionals on the newest findings and procedures in preventive and nutritional medicine. Offers online and phone referrals to more than one thousand MDs, DOs, and other licensed health care professionals who practice alternative, integrative, and preventive medicine. Many use nutrition and chelation therapies.

> Address: 24411 Ridge Route Drive, Suite 115
>   Laguna Hills, CA 92653
> Phone: 949-309-3520
> Fax: 949-309-3538
> E-mail: info@acam.org
> Web site: www.acam.org

Institute for Functional Medicine (IFM). The Institute for Functional Medicine provides comprehensive, scientifically grounded training in using nutrition and supplements to treat and prevent chronic physical and emotional problems, including depression. IFM does not yet certify graduates of its program, but it provides a link to practitioners (mostly physicians, nurse practitioners, and dietitians) who have taken its training and are using nutrition as a significant part of their practice. An excellent resource for professionals who can help you optimize your health, though you will have to inquire about each individual's level of training and the degree to which they integrate nutrition into their work.

Address: 4411 Point Fosdick Drive NW, Suite 305
            P.O. Box 1697
            Gig Harbor, WA 98335
Phone: 800-228-0622
Fax: 253-853-6766
E-mail: client_services@fxmed.com
Web site: www.functionalmedicine.org

ORTHOMOLECULAR MEDICINE

Orthomolecular medicine is a medical approach that aims to correct individual biochemical imbalances and deficiencies in order to reestablish an optimum environment in the body. Orthomolecular practitioners use naturally occurring substances such as vitamins, minerals, essential fatty acids, amino acids, and trace elements. There is no single type of orthomolecular practitioner or physician, and licensure and certification do not exist in the United States. Orthomolecular physicians often specialize in treating diagnosed psychiatric conditions, including depression.

International Society for Orthomolecular Medicine. Society dedicated to advancing and increasing awareness of the field of orthomolecular medicine. Offers referrals to practitioners.

Address: 16 Florence Avenue
            Toronto, Ontario, Canada M2N 1E9
Phone: 416-733-2117
Fax: 416-733-2352
E-mail: centre@orthomed.org
Web site: www.orthomed.org

Orthomolecular.org. Web site offering an alphabetical list of practitioners who subscribe to an orthomolecular ideology.

Address: 3100 North Hillside
            Wichita, KS 67219
Phone: 316-682-3100
Fax: 316-682-5054
E-mail: support@orthomolecular.org
Web site: www.orthomolecular.org

NATUROPATHIC MEDICINE

A licensed naturopathic physician (ND) attends a four-year graduate-level naturopathic medical school. While NDs are educated in all of the same basic sciences as MDs, they are not required to complete a residency at the end of their medical training. Naturopathic physicians study holistic approaches to therapy with an emphasis on disease prevention and wellness. They complete training in clinical nutrition, acupuncture, homeopathic medicine, botanical medicine, psychology, and counseling. Naturopathic physicians must take professional board exams in order to be licensed by a state or jurisdiction as a primary care general practice physician. Currently, fourteen states, the District of Columbia, and two U.S. territories have licensing laws for naturopathic doctors. The scope of practice for NDs varies by state regarding such practices as performing minor surgeries and prescribing medications.

American Association of Naturopathic Physicians. National professional society representing licensed or licensable naturopathic physicians. Has a directory with referrals to more than seven hundred members who have completed postgraduate naturopathic medical education.

Address:	4435 Wisconsin Avenue NW, #403
	Washington, DC 20016
Phone:	866-538-2267
Fax:	202-237-8152
E-mail:	member.services@naturopathic.org
Web site:	www.naturopathic.org

CHIROPRACTIC

Doctors of chiropractic (DCs) are licensed to practice in all fifty states and the District of Columbia. In addition to passing a licensing exam, DCs must have completed a curriculum that includes a minimum of 4,200 hours, approximately four to five years of classroom, laboratory, and clinical experience. Basic science educational requirements for DCs are similar in length, intensity, and content to those of MDs. A major focus of the DCs' training is the manipulation of the spine. They cannot prescribe drugs or do surgery, and they usually don't have hospital or postgraduate residency training. Chiropractors can choose to specialize in a number of different areas. Requirements for certification in a specialty area vary by specialty. To become certified in nutrition (Diplomate American Chiropractic Board of Nutrition), chiropractors must complete 300 hours of course work and pass written and practical examinations.

American Chiropractic Association. Largest professional association representing doctors of chiropractic. Offers referrals to 21,500 member chiropractors. Provides the option of searching for chiropractors certified in different specialties, for example, those certified in nutrition.

Address:	1701 Clarendon Boulevard
	Arlington, VA 22209
Phone:	703-276-8800
Fax:	703-243-2593
E-mail:	memberinfo@acatoday.org
Web site:	www.acatoday.com

National Directory of Chiropractic. Comprehensive online resource with a database that represents the largest compilation of chiropractors in the United States. Offers referrals to more than sixty-five thousand chiropractors of all types and techniques of chiropractic care. Gives contact information, education, and techniques employed. Any chiropractor may list his/her practice in this directory.

Address:	7404 Union Park Avenue
	Midvale, VT 84047
Phone:	877-533-4199
Fax:	877-568-4694
E-mail:	support@chirodirectory.com
Web site:	www.chirodirectory.com

NUTRITION

Since the term *nutritionist* is not legally protected, nutritionists have highly varying levels of education. Some have PhDs or master's degrees; others do not. Dietitians, however, must have a bachelor's degree from an American Dietetic Association–accredited program. To become a registered dietitian (RD), dietitians must undergo national certification and testing. Licensed dietitians (LDs) hold a state license. Certified nutritional consultants (CNCs) are accredited by the American Association of Nutritional Consultants after passing eleven exams covering subject matter in basic sciences and nutrition.

American Dietetic Association (ADA). Nation's largest organization of food and nutrition professionals. Nearly half of all ADA members have advanced academic degrees and about 75 percent of members are registered dietitians. The remaining members are food service managers, consultants, researchers, dietetic technicians, students, etc. Offers referrals to member dietetics professionals. A subset of dietitians is particularly interested in complementary and alternative approaches (herbal therapies, elimination diets, etc.).

Address:	120 South Riverside Plaza, Suite 2000
	Chicago, IL 60606
Phone:	800-877-1600
Web site:	www.eatright.org

The Nutrition in Complementary Care Web site, which includes members' contact information, is www.complementarynutrition.org.

American Association of Nutritional Consultants. Professional association for nutritional and dietary consultants. Offers referrals to more than 2,500 members.

Address:	401 Kings Highway
	Winona Lake, IN 46590
Phone:	888-828-2262
Fax:	574-268-2120
E-mail:	registrar@aanc.net
Web site:	www.aanc.net

National Association of Nutrition Professionals. Nonprofit organization that represents holistically trained nutrition professionals. All professional members have graduated from approved institutions offering a curriculum that includes courses on such topics as nutritional herbology, environmental and cultural influences on health, nutritional supplementation, counseling, etc.

Offers referrals to more than 450 nutrition educators, consultants, and therapists who hold certification or degrees from approved schools.

Address:	P.O. Box 1172
	Danville, CA 94526
Phone:	800-342-8037
Fax:	510-580-9429
E-mail:	info@nanp.org
Web site:	www.nanp.org

HERBALISM

American Herbalists Guild. Nonprofit educational organization that offers referrals to two hundred professional member herbalists who have completed at least four years of education and clinical experience, have been approved by their peer review board, and have agreed to adhere to a professional code of ethics.

Address:	141 Nob Hill Road
	Cheshire, CT 06410
Phone:	203-272-6731
Fax:	203-272-8550
E-mail:	ahgoffice@earthlink.net
Web site:	www.americanherbalistsguild.com

HEAVY METAL TOXICITY

American Board of Clinical Metal Toxicology. Organization that certifies MDs and DOs in clinical metal toxicology. Offers referrals to doctors certified for proficiency in the extraction of toxins by chelation and other methods.

Address:	4889 Smith Road
	West Chester, OH 45069
Phone:	800-356-2228
Fax:	513-942-3934
E-mail:	treasurer@abcmt.org
Web site:	www.abcmt.org

LIGHT BOXES

Light boxes are for sale online and range in price from $189 to $479. The following companies make products that meet the requirements detailed in *Unstuck*. Look for products that offer a full spectrum of light that is 10,000 lux strong (10,000 lux is equal to 10,000 lumens per square meter).

Apollo Health
  Web site: www.apollolight.com

The SunBox Company
  Web site: www.sunbox.com

Full Spectrum Solutions
  Web site: www.fullspectrumsolutions.com

CANDIDIASIS

The Yeast Connection Handbook. William G. Crook, MD. Jackson, TN: Professional Books, 1997. An extended discussion of how yeast overgrowth may contribute to depression and other conditions and how dietary modification and medical treatment can reverse this process. The science is still uncertain, but there are hopeful case histories, interesting references, and much practical advice on diet.

ELIMINATION DIET BOOKS

Allergy Exclusion Diet. Carlsbad, CA: Hay House, 2002. Jill Carter and Allison Edwards's book provides a twenty-eight-day program designed to identify food allergies and sensitivities. It also offers a four-day rotation diet useful for dealing with these conditions.

Dealing with Food Allergies: A Practical Guide to Detecting Culprit Foods and Eating a Healthy, Enjoyable Diet. Janice Vickerstaff Joneja. Boulder, CO: Bull Publishing, 2003. This book describes a practical method of detecting food allergies and sensitivities and offers step-by-step instructions for preventing adverse food reactions. The book also includes food shopping tips, practical recipes, and information on reading ingredient labels.

CHAPTER TWO: GUIDES ON THE JOURNEY
The Professions
PSYCHIATRISTS

> Psychiatrists are MDs or DOs who have completed a four-year psychiatric residency that provides extensive supervised clinical experience and formal teaching in psychiatry. Psychiatrists understand the biological, psychological, social, and cultural aspects of mental and emotional problems and issues, and are qualified to order laboratory tests, prescribe medications, and offer psychotherapy. Psychiatrists can become board certified by the American Board of Psychiatry and Neurology, indicating that they have completed an approved training program and undergone an evaluation process assessing their ability to provide quality patient care in psychiatry.

American Psychiatric Association. Medical specialty society with more than thirty-five thousand member physicians. Has the APA Answer Center, which helps the public locate area psychiatrists.

Address: 1000 Wilson Boulevard, Suite 1825
           Arlington, VA 22209
Phone: 703-907-7300
E-mail: apa@psych.org
Web site: www.psych.org

PSYCHIATRIC NURSES

There are three levels of psychiatric nursing: licensed practical nurses (LPN), registered nurses (RN), and advanced practice psychiatric registered nurses (APRN). LPNs usually have one to two years of training and must operate under an RN or physician. RNs have a wider scope of practice than LPNs, and have completed either a bachelor of science degree in nursing (BSN), an associate degree in nursing (ADN), or a hospital-based diploma program. APRNs are educated at the master's or doctoral degree level, are qualified to practice independently, can prescribe medications in most states, and usually offer psychotherapy. The scope of practice and third-party reimbursement varies by state.

American Psychiatric Nurses Association. Professional membership organization with almost five thousand members who practice mental health nursing and can offer psychotherapy.

Address: 1555 Wilson Boulevard, Suite 602
           Arlington, VA 22209
Phone: 866-243-2443
Fax: 703-243-3390
E-mail: inform@apna.org
Web site: www.apna.org

PSYCHOLOGISTS

Psychologists have a doctoral or master's degree in psychology. A doctoral degree usually requires five to seven years of graduate study, including significant supervised experience doing a variety of kinds of psychotherapy. Common doctoral degrees held by psychologists are doctor of philosophy (PhD), doctor of psychology (PsyD), doctor of science (ScD), and doctor of education (EdD). While the PhD degree includes a dissertation based on original research, the PsyD degree is more focused on practical, clinical work and examinations. The ScD degree is equivalent to and is being replaced by the PhD degree. The EdD degree is similar to the PhD degree, but while a PhD is oriented toward research, an EdD may be more focused on testing and psychotherapy. A master's degree in psychology requires at least two years of graduate study, a period of supervised practical experience, and completion of a master's thesis. Psychologists must meet state licensing criteria, which generally include a period of supervised clinical practice, a licensing exam, and continuing education requirements.

There are many different schools of psychological thought. Cognitive behavioral therapy, which focuses on negative patterns of thinking and which has a strong scientific evidence base, can be extremely helpful to depressed people, especially in "dealing with demons." Its therapists seek to teach their clients not *what* to do, but *how* to do, using highly structured, instructive, goal-specific therapy sessions that usually incorporate daily homework and reading assignments and exercises to encourage clients to practice in their home environment the techniques they've learned.

Two other schools of psychology—humanistic psychology and transpersonal psychology—may be of particular relevance to the approach to depression detailed in *Unstuck*. While humanistic psychology acknowledges that the mind may be influenced by negative forces in childhood and society, it emphasizes the independent worth of human beings and their capacity for self-determination, personal competence, and self-respect. Transpersonal psychology focuses on spiritual development.

American Psychological Association (APA). Professional organization that represents psychology in the United States. APA is the largest association of psychologists worldwide. Offers a psychologist locator service.

Address: 750 First Street NE
　　　　　Washington, DC 20002
Phone: 800-374-2721
Web site: www.apa.org

Find-a-Psychologist.com. Web site that offers a directory of psychologists, including contact information, credentials, services offered, and a description of their practices. The site also has an option to search for licensed psychologists, psychiatrists, social workers, therapists, and counselors who offer therapy for depression.

Phone: 866-450-3463
Fax: 480-807-7962
E-mail: info@find-a-therapist.com
Web site: www.find-a-psychologist.com

National Directory of Psychologists. Online directory that provides contact information for psychologists in all fifty states as well as the District of Columbia. While only licensed psychologists are listed, degrees and credentials vary. When available, the directory also provides links to the psychologist's Web site and descriptive information about his or her practice.

E-mail: info@psychologyinfo.com
Web site: www.psychologyinfo.com

National Association of Cognitive-Behavioral Therapists (NACBT). Association dedicated to the practice and teaching of cognitive behavioral psychotherapy. Offers membership and certification of certified cognitive behavioral therapist (CCBT). CCBTs must hold either a master's or doctoral degree in psychology, sociology, psychiatry, or related field from an accredited university, have at least six years of postgraduate experience providing cognitive behavioral therapy, and complete certification programs recognized by NACBT.

Address: P.O. Box 2195
　　　　　Weirton, WV 26062
Phone: 800-853-1135
Fax: 304-723-3982
E-mail: nacbt@nacbt.org
Web site: www.nacbt.org

Association for Humanistic Psychology (AHP). Association of individuals who share a humanistic approach to healing. Offers referrals to AHP members, many of whom, but not all, are psychologists and psychotherapists. Other humanistic professionals include educators, consultants, social workers, nurses, etc.

Address: 1516 Oak Street, #320A
　　　　　Alameda, CA 94501

Phone: 510-769-6495
Fax: 510-769-6433
E-mail: ahpoffice@aol.com
Web site: www.ahpweb.org

Association for Transpersonal Psychology. Member association for individuals interested in transpersonal psychology. Membership is not exclusively for psychologists. Offers a directory of professional members, who include psychologists, medical doctors, nurses, etc.

Address: P.O. Box 50187
            Palo Alto, CA 94303
Phone: 650-424-8764
Fax: 650-618-1851
E-mail: info@atpweb.org
Web site: www.atpweb.org

SOCIAL WORKERS

Social workers usually have a master's degree (MSW) or bachelor's degree (BSW) in social work, but majors in fields such as psychology and sociology may qualify for entry-level jobs. BSW programs require at least four hundred hours of supervised field experience, while MSW programs require two years of education beyond the undergraduate level and nine hundred hours of supervised field instruction, much of which is likely to be in psychotherapy. The National Association of Social Workers offers voluntary credentialing to individuals holding a BSW or MSW who meet specific additional requirements for experience, supervision, education, knowledge, and skills as psychotherapists. Such credentials include the Academy of Certified Social Workers credential (ACSW), the qualified clinical social worker credential (QCSW), and the diplomate in clinical social work credential (DCSW). Standards for licensing vary by state.

National Association of Social Workers (NASW). Largest member organization of social workers. Provides a directory of licensed social workers who have met national standards established by the NASW Competence Certification Commission.

Address: 750 First Street NE, Suite 700
            Washington, DC 20002
Phone: 202-408-8600
E-mail: credentialing@naswdc.org
Web site: www.socialworkers.org

COUNSELORS

Forty-eight states and the District of Columbia have counselor licensure laws and programs. Usually, counselors need to have a master's degree in counseling, complete two years or three thousand hours of supervised clinical experience, and pass a state exam. Some states also have continuing education requirements. The National Board for Certified Counselors is the primary certifying organization for the profession, offering the designation "national certified counselor (NCC)" to individuals with a master's degree who can pass the board's National Counselor Examination for Licensure and Certification. In addition, two years of supervised counseling experience and other prerequisites are needed. While the NCC credential is not required for independent practice and cannot substitute for legislated state credentials, the credential does indicate that practitioners have met specific national standards. Pastoral counselors are unique in that they must be ordained priests, ministers, or rabbis in order to practice. The American Association of Pastoral Counselors certifies these professionals. There are different levels of certification, all of which require, as a minimum, a master's or doctoral level degree in divinity, theological/spiritual studies, biblical studies, or pastoral counseling; religious body endorsement to ministry; active participation in a local religious community; completion of a supervised self-reflective pastoral experience; three years in ministry; and 375 hours of pastoral counseling with 125 hours under supervision. Only Arkansas, Kentucky, Maine, New Hampshire, North Carolina, and Tennessee actually license the title pastoral counselor, but many other states license pastoral counselors as marriage and family therapists or professional counselors.

National Board for Certified Counselors. Professional certification board for counselors. Has a directory of counselors, all of whom hold the national certified counselor (NCC) credential.

Address:	3 Terrace Way
	Greensboro, NC 27403
Phone:	336-547-0607
Fax:	336-547-0017
E-mail:	nbcc@nbcc.org
Web site:	www.nbcc.org

American Mental Health Counselors Association. Professional membership organization that represents the mental health counseling profession. Offers referrals to more than 750 therapists with a variety of specialties, including depression.

Address:	801 North Fairfax Street, Suite 304
	Alexandria, VA 22314
Phone:	800-326-2642
Fax:	703-548-4775
Web site:	www.amhca.org

International Association for Counselors and Therapists. Multidisciplinary association that specializes in holistic techniques. Offers referrals to professional members who are licensed or certified counselors or mental health therapists with a strong interest in complementary therapies and approaches, including those discussed and taught in *Unstuck*.

Address:	RR 2, Box 2468
	Laceyville, PA 18623
Phone:	800-553-6886
Fax:	570-869-1249
E-mail:	info@iact.org
Web site:	www.iact.org

American Association of Pastoral Counselors. Nonsectarian organization that certifies pastoral counselors and accredits pastoral counseling centers. Has a referral directory that lists certified members.

Address: 9504A Lee Highway
           Fairfax, VA 22031
Phone: 703-385-6967
Fax: 703-352-7725
E-mail: info@aapc.org
Web site: www.aapc.org

The Safe Harbor Project. Has a directory of more than three hundred health professionals in a variety of fields (medical doctors, naturopathic doctors, acupuncturists, biofeedback practitioners, social workers, etc.) who offer alternative treatment of mental and emotional conditions. Each practitioner listed has responded to a questionnaire about practices and views and has stated that he or she meets certain criteria, including no psychosurgery, no shock treatments, and minimal or no psychiatric drugs.

Address: 787 West Woodbury Road, #2
           Altadena, CA 91001
Phone: 626-791-7868
Fax: 626-791-7869
E-mail: mail@alternativementalhealth.com
Web site: www.alternativementalhealth.com

Other Specific Therapeutic Approaches

PSYCHODYNAMIC PSYCHOTHERAPY

Psychodynamic psychotherapy is a form of verbal therapy derived from psychoanalysis and aimed at revealing maladaptive motives and conflicts of the clients' unconscious that may be contributing to their emotional problems. It is often the basis for training psychiatrists, psychologists, social workers, and counselors and is used in individual, family, group, and couples therapy to treat people experiencing sadness, confusion, anxiety, and depression. Therapists help clients to acknowledge the existence of their maladaptation and to develop a range of new options for problem solving. Psychodynamic psychotherapy demands a client's deep introspection and the ability to manage the strong emotions therapy may provoke. Great importance is also placed on the relationship between the therapist and client.

Many therapists practice psychodynamic therapy or use its principles in their practice. You will need to ask them about it. The standard listings of licensed professionals I've provided will often indicate whether or not the particular individual practices psychodynamic psychotherapy.

MARRIAGE AND FAMILY THERAPY

Marriage and family therapy is a form of psychotherapy that focuses on the systems of interaction among family members. This type of therapy emphasizes what goes on between the individuals rather than on the individuals themselves, and on how the interactions may be sustaining problems. Marriage and family therapists (MFTs) try to point out the patterns of interaction that the family may not have noticed, with the goal of altering these interactions by suggesting different ways of responding. Licensing and education requirements vary based on jurisdiction, but most states require MFTs to hold at least a master's degree and about three thousand hours of supervised work before sitting for a licensing exam conducted by the American Association of Marriage and Family Therapists.

American Association for Marriage and Family Therapy (AAMFT). Professional association representing more than twenty-four thousand marriage and family therapists, almost all of whom offer individual counseling as well. All members hold at least a master's degree, while one-fourth of members are MDs or have completed a doctoral degree. Offers a database that can be used to locate marriage and family therapists who are members of AAMFT.

Address: 112 South Alfred Street
           Alexandria, VA 22314
Phone: 703-838-9808
Fax: 703-838-9805
Web site: www.aamft.org

American Group Psychotherapy Association (AGPA). An interdisciplinary community that has been "enhancing practice, theory and research of group therapy" since its founding in 1942. It provides resources for the mental health professional who wants to become a certified group therapist (CGP), as well as the ordinary person who may seek to be a member of a group. It includes a tool to search for a CGP near you. Its three thousand plus members come from more than twelve different disciplines, including psychology, creative arts therapy, psychiatry, nursing, social work, alcoholism counseling, and marriage and family therapy.

Address: 25 East 21st Street, 6th Floor
           New York, NY 10010
Phone: 212-979-6627
           877-668-AGPA (2472) (toll-free)
Fax: 212-979-6627
E-mail: info@agpa.org
Web site: www.agpa.org

ART THERAPY

Art therapy is a mental health profession that uses the creative art process to improve the emotional, physical, and mental well-being of individuals. Through artistic self-expression, art therapists help clients to reduce stress, manage behavior, and increase self-awareness. Art therapists use the visual arts (drawing, sculpting, painting, etc.) and the creative process, as well as counseling and psychotherapy, to treat anxiety, depression, trauma and loss, addiction, and many other social and emotional difficulties. Professional art therapists hold a master's degree in art therapy or a related field and after graduation complete a minimum of a thousand hours of direct client contact. Completion qualifies an individual as a registered art therapist (ATR), or an

ATR-BC, upon achieving board certification as conferred by the Art Therapy Credentials Board (ATCB).

American Art Therapy Association. National nonprofit association dedicated to promoting the therapeutic use of art. Through journals and newsletters, offers directory of therapists and publications.

Address: 5999 Stevenson Avenue
            Alexandria, VA 22304
Phone: 888-290-0878
E-mail: info@arttherapy.org
Web site: www.arttherapy.org

Arts in Therapy Network. A 501(c)(3) not-for-profit organization providing an online community for creative art therapists (CATs) in the areas of music therapy, art therapy, and dance therapy. Offers referrals, ongoing events, and links to creative arts therapy organizations.

Web site: www.artsintherapy.com

DANCE THERAPY

Dance therapy is the psychotherapeutic use of movement as a process to improve cognitive, social, behavioral, physical, and emotional conditions. It is an expressive therapy based on the realization of the mind-body continuum, in which the body's movement may have a positive effect on mental well-being. Registered dance therapists (DTRs) hold a master's degree that includes 700 hours of clinical internship. Academy of dance therapists (ADTRs) must complete 3,640 hours of clinical work.

American Dance Therapy Association (ADTA). Establishes standards for professional practice, education, and training, and maintains a registry of dance/movement therapists.

Address: 10632 Little Patuxent Parkway, Suite 108
            Columbia, MD 21044
Phone: 410-997-4040
Fax: 410-997-4048
E-mail: info@adta.org
Web site: www.adta.org

MUSIC THERAPY

Music therapy is an established clinical and evidence-based health care profession that utilizes singing, creating, moving to and/or listening to music as forms of communication, self-expression, and self-discovery. Professional music therapists must hold a bachelor's degree or higher in music therapy from a program approved by the American Music Therapy Association, as well as complete 1,200 clinical training hours and a supervised internship. Board certification by examination is required for professional practice and the credential music therapist–board certified (MT-BC).

Professional music therapists are listed on the National Music Therapy Registry (NMTR) at 301-562-9330.

American Music Therapy Association (AMTA). Provides a current list of qualified music therapists nationwide and is free of charge.

Address: 8455 Colesville Road, Suite 1000
                Silver Spring, MD 20910
Phone: 301-589-3300
Fax: 301-589-5175
E-mail: findMT@musictherapy.org
Web site: www.musictherapy.org

BODY PSYCHOTHERAPY

Body psychotherapy is a branch of psychotherapy that emphasizes reciprocal relationships and interactions between the body and mind. Body psychotherapists combine "talk" therapy with bodywork, such as touch, exercise, and postural alignment, to increase awareness of bodily sensations, emotions, and behaviors. Ideally, a body psychotherapist should have a college degree, a graduate degree, and certification in body psychotherapy or body psychotherapy training from an advanced-degree academic program.

United States Association for Body Psychotherapy. The only national organization for body psychotherapy in the United States. Offers a locator service for member body psychotherapists who have given permission to list their names and contact information.

Address: 7831 Woodmont Avenue
                Bethesda, MD 20814
E-mail: usabp@usabp.org
Web site: www.usabp.org

GESTALT THERAPY

Gestalt therapy is an experiential form of therapy that was influenced by psychoanalysis but differs in that the emphasis is on discovery rather than interpretation. Therapists devise experiments that allow clients to become aware of their present perceptions, feelings, and actions. This awareness of present behavior helps clients to overcome their symptoms through self-acceptance and the ability to experience life in the present without the guilt of unfinished issues. The ultimate goal is full acceptance of what is, rather than focusing on trying to change. Although the process for becoming a certified Gestalt therapist varies slightly, most therapists are required to be licensed psychotherapists, complete two hundred hours of training, and pass a written examination.

The Gestalt Directory: Resource for those seeking a Gestalt therapist. Be aware that listings are self-administered and operate on the honor system. If you find a therapist who seems appropriate, you'll want to interview him or her about his or her experience.

E-mail: compass@gestalttherapy.net.

Web site: www.gestalttherapy.net

INTERPERSONAL THERAPY

> Interpersonal therapy (IPT) is a form of short-term psychotherapy that focuses on an individual's relationships with others and the concurrent progression of that individual's psychiatric symptoms. IPT, the use of which with depression has been studied scientifically, is often used to treat couples whose marital disputes may be contributing to their depression, as well as for individuals who are depressed. Although the focus with IPT is on resolving personality problems stemming from the unconscious and childhood experiences, IPT also seeks to reveal how a person's current relationships and behaviors may be causing or maintaining symptoms.

A number of therapists of all kinds have been trained in IPT. Check for training in it in their contact information or ask about it in person.

JUNGIAN PSYCHOLOGY (ANALYTICAL PSYCHOLOGY)

> Jungian psychology is based on the ideas of the Swiss psychiatrist Carl Jung, who sought to uncover and integrate the motivations that underlie human behavior through exploration of the unconscious mind. Jungian therapists seek to reestablish healthy communication between the conscious and unconscious by exploring the significance to clients of dreams, religion, spirituality, and mythology.

International Association for Analytical Psychology (IAAP): An accrediting and regulatory organization for all analytical psychologists' groups. IAAP membership is by application only, and demands rigorous training and supervised experience. The IAAP includes a database of member analysts who choose to publicize their contact information.

Web site: http://www.iaap.org/

Find an analyst: www.iaap.org/database_directory/viewdatabase_simple.php?

POSITIVE PSYCHOLOGY

> Positive psychology is a new branch of psychology created by the pioneering University of Pennsylvania researcher Martin Seligman, PhD, and his colleagues. It studies the aspects of life that promote individual happiness and enable communities to thrive. Positive psychological therapy is said to alleviate symptoms of depression as well as prevent disease and combat illness. Therapists help clients to focus on what makes life worth living rather than on the problems that may be causing symptoms. The goal is

to help clients have higher hopes and feel more engaged in life, regardless of their circumstances. Variations of positive psychology are often utilized in schools, the workplace, and in communities to promote overall well-being. Although this is a relatively new field, some therapists may hold a master of applied positive psychology (MAPP).

The Positive Psychology Center (PPC): A center at the University of Pennsylvania that promotes research, training, and education in positive psychology. Also provides links to several other centers involved in the field.

Address: 3720 Walnut Street, Solomon Labs
            Philadelphia, PA 19104
Phone: 215-898-7173
E-mail: seligmaninfo@psych.upenn.edu
Web site: www.ppc.sas.upenn.edu

GUIDED IMAGERY

The Best of Stress Management Kit. For more information, please refer to the text entitled The Center for Mind-Body Medicine at the beginning of the Resources section.

Academy for Guided Imagery. Provides the nation's only comprehensive, integrated curriculum for teaching interactive guided imagery skills. Also produces books, CDs, and DVDs, and offers workshops and self-study courses for health professionals, organizations, and the general public. Offers referrals to more than 750 health professionals who have completed the Academy for Guided Imagery certification program of 150 hours of course work and have been certified as Interactive Imagery Guides. There is no state licensure for Interactive Imagery Guides, and the Academy for Guided Imagery is the only official certifying body.

Address: 30765 Pacific Coast Highway, #369
            Malibu, CA 90265
Phone: 800-726-2070
Fax: 800-727-2070
E-mail: train@academyforguidedimagery.com
Web site: www.academyforguidedimagery.com

Belleruth Naparstek's Guided Imagery Center. Offers depression-focused guided imagery CDs that range in price from $17.98 to $20.00, as well as less expensive audiocassette tapes and MP3 downloads.

Address: 891 Moe Drive, Suite C
            Akron, OH 44310
Phone: 800-800-8661
Fax: 330-633-3778
Web site: www.healthjourneys.com

IMAGERY AND MEDITATION CDs

The following are CDs that have soft music that can be used for imagery and meditation.

Angel Love. By Aeoliah. Mild, flowing synthesizer chords accompanied by light pianolike tones.

Music for Sound Healing. By Steven Halpern. Features a peaceful combination of electric and grand piano, flute, and harp. Recommended by a number of physicians for relaxation and well-being.

Ancient Runes. By Deborah Martin and Preston Scott. Soft music composed of silver flute, river cane flute, bamboo and agave didjeridoos, synthesizer, and the natural sounds of an Ozark mountain rainstorm.

Earth Spirit: Native American Flute Music. By Carlos Nakai. This music by one of the leading American Indian artists has tracks featuring either the eagle's bone whistle or solo American Indian flute, with no extras or accompaniments. Works well for Inner Guide imagery.

Oriental Sunrise: New Music for Zen Meditation. By Riley Lee. Simple shakuhachi flute music with soft background sounds of nature. Works well for Safe Place imagery.

Spirit Wind. By Richard Warner. Continuous, slowly unfolding movement of bamboo and alto flutes, tuned glass crystals, chimes, finger cymbals, and synthesizer.

Quiet Heart. By Richard Warner. Calm and restrained solo bamboo flute music.

CHAPTER THREE: SURRENDER TO CHANGE
MIND-BODY SKILLS GROUPS

The Center for Mind-Body Medicine. Please refer to the text entitled The Center for Mind-Body Medicine at the beginning of the Resources section (page 347).

Benson-Henry Institute for Mind Body Medicine. Institute for the study and practice of mind-body medicine founded by Herbert Benson, MD, the pioneering Harvard researcher who wrote *The Relaxation Response* and many other books. Offers various mind-body medicine programs targeted toward ameliorating a variety of medical conditions and other concerns, including anxiety and depression. Offers professional training in mind-body medicine, but does not provide referrals to individuals who have completed their training program.

    Address: 824 Boylston Street
                    Chestnut Hill, MA 02467
    Phone: 617-732-9130
    Fax: 617-732-9111
    E-mail: mindbody@partners.org
    Web site: www.mbmi.org

Center for Mindfulness in Medicine, Health Care, and Society. Multidimensional center in the division of preventive and behavioral medicine at the University of Massachusetts Medical School. Founded by mindfulness meditation teacher Jon Kabat-Zinn, PhD, it offers an eight-week mindfulness-based stress reduction program as well as professional training programs, workshops, and retreats. Provides referrals to practitioners who have completed at least one of the organization's professional training programs.

    Address: 55 Lake Avenue North
                    Worcester, MA 01655

Phone: 508-856-2656
Fax: 508-856-1977
E-mail: mindfulness@umassmed.edu
Web site: http://www.umassmed.edu/cfm/index.aspx

YOGA

International Association of Yoga Therapists (IAYT). Nonprofit membership organization for yoga practitioners, teachers, researchers, and therapists, as well as health professionals who utilize yoga in their practice. Offers an online member directory, with the option of limiting the search to find only certain members (only yoga therapists who work with individuals on their specific problems and issues, for example). Listings include contact information as well as degrees and credentials. Education and training of yoga teachers and therapists varies widely; IAYT membership is the only requirement for directory listing.

Address: 115 South McCormick Street, Suite 3
            Prescott, AZ 86303
Phone: 928-541-0004
Fax: 928-541-0182
E-mail: mail@iayt.org
Web site: www.iayt.org

Yogafinder.com. Largest online yoga directory. Has search functions for yoga classes, events, retreat centers, music, and products. Results for classes indicate contact information, style of practice (Integral, Kripalu, etc.), links to Web sites, and class details.

Phone: 858-213-7924
E-mail: webmaster@yogafinder.com
Web site: www.yogafinder.com

LifeForce Yoga. Style of yoga developed by Amy Weintraub that is specifically intended to improve mood. In addition to listing private sessions and yoga retreats, the Web site includes contact information for yoga practitioners who have attended a forty-hour LifeForce Yoga training program.

E-mail: info@amyweintraub.com
Web site: www.yogafordepression.com

TAI CHI

American Tai Chi Association. National nonprofit organization that has a search engine for instruction in tai chi, a Chinese moving meditation with many different styles. Can search for tai chi coaches by geographic location, style, and desired benefit (stress reduction, for example). Listing in the database is open to all tai chi instructors, thus levels of training may vary.

Address: 2465 J-17 Centreville Road, #150
            Herndon, VA 20171
Email: contact@americantaichi.net
Web site: www.americantaichi.net

QIGONG

National Qigong Association (NQA). Nonprofit organization whose members range from supporters and general members with an interest in qigong (Chinese meditations that combine movement and attention to breath with imagery) to practitioners and professional members who are qigong teachers or healers or have written books and articles on qigong. Offers search functions for qigong teachers who have received two hundred hours of training in qigong, as well as NQA members.

> Address: P.O. Box 270065
>   St. Paul, MN 55127
> Phone: 888-815-1893
> Web site: www.nqa.org

Qigong Institute. Nonprofit organization dedicated to the promotion and advancement of qigong. Offers a directory of more than two hundred qigong teachers and therapists. Directory listings, however, are not limited to those who have received a prescribed amount of training. Qualifications of the instructors, therefore, may vary.

> Address: 561 Berkeley Avenue
>   Menlo Park, CA 94025
> E-mail: qi@qigonginstitute.org
> Web site: www.qigonginstitute.org

EXPRESSIVE MEDITATION

Best of Stress Management Kit. Please refer to the text entitled The Center for Mind-Body Medicine at the beginning of the Resources section.

Osho International Foundation. Nonprofit foundation that makes the work of Osho, formerly known as Bhagwan Shree Rajneesh, available through the osho.com Web site. It has a directory of Osho meditation and information centers around the world. Two types of meditation used in the *Unstuck* approach and practiced at these meditation centers are the Kundalini (shaking and dancing) and Dynamic Meditations.

> Address: Bahnhofstrasse 52, 8001
>   Zurich, Switzerland
> Phone: +41 (1) 214-6242
> Fax: +41 (1) 214-6203
> E-mail: oshointernational@oshointernational.com
> Web site: www.osho.com

BIOFEEDBACK

Biofeedback is a treatment technique in which people are trained to use signals from their own bodies to reduce stress and improve their health. This practice is intended to increase an individual's awareness and conscious control of physiological processes. While it is an unregulated field, certification in biofeedback is available from the Biofeedback Certification Institute of America (BCIA). BCIA-certified practitioners must hold a degree in an approved clinical health care field, meet education and clinical training requirements, and pass a written certification exam. Educational and training requirements are different for the different types of biofeedback, but they range from 28 to 48 didactic hours, 20 to 36 mentored clinical training hours, and 30 to 100 patient sessions. Biofeedback is widely used to decrease stress and improve mood.

Best of Stress Management Kit. Please refer to the text entitled The Center for Mind-Body Medicine at the beginning of the Resources section.

Biofeedback Certification Institute of America (BCIA). Organization that offers certification in three different types of biofeedback—general, EEG, and pelvic muscle dysfunction. Offers referrals to sixteen hundred practitioners who are trained and certified in various modalities of biofeedback therapy.

Address: 10200 West 44th Avenue, Suite 310
            Wheat Ridge, CO 80033
Phone: 303-420-2902
Fax: 303-422-8894
E-mail: bcia@resourcenter.com
Web site: www.bcia.org

MUSIC FOR ACTIVE, EXPRESSIVE MEDITATION

Adia. By Oliver N'goma. Distributed by Noli Productions, Gabon. Phone: 241-73-63-80. Copyright © 1996. Available through www.amazon.com (or order through your local music seller).

"You Can Get It If You Really Want." By Jimmy Cliff. *Ultimate Collection.* Copyright © 1976 Warner Bros. Available through www.warnerbrosrecords.com or www.amazon.com (or order through your local music seller).

Legend: The Best of Bob Marley and the Wailers. Deluxe edition copyright © 2002. Available through www.amazon.com or www.bobmarley.com (or order through your local music seller).

Osho Kundalini Meditation and *Osho Dynamic Meditations.* Distributed by New Earth Records, Inc., 154 Betassa Road, Boulder, CO 80302. Phone: 800-570-4074. Available through www.newearthrecords.com or www.amazon.com (or order through your local music seller).

Youssou N'Dour and Le Super Etoile Special Fin d'Année (1999). Available through www.youssou.com (or order through your local music seller).

CHAPTER FOUR: DEALING WITH DEMONS
Traditional Chinese Medicine
ACUPUNCTURE

Forty-one states as well as the District of Columbia require practicing acupuncturists to be licensed. Forty of these states require National Certification Commission for

Acupuncture and Oriental Medicine (NCCAOM) examinations, while California requires a state examination. Arkansas, California, New Mexico, and Texas also require licensed acupuncturists to have passed an examination in Chinese herbology. States without a practice-regulating licensure include North Dakota, South Dakota, Wyoming, Kansas, Oklahoma, Louisiana, Mississippi, Alabama, and Delaware. Education requirements vary by state, but they generally include completion of a three-year program. The title conferred also varies by state, most often being licensed acupuncturist (LAc), but may also be registered acupuncturist (RAc) or certified acupuncturist (CA).

National Certification Commission for Acupuncture and Oriental Medicine (*NCCAOM*). Nonprofit national certifying organization. Offers referrals to sixteen thousand acupuncturists, Chinese herbalists, Asian bodywork therapists, and Oriental medicine practitioners who have met certain education requirements and passed board examinations to become nationally certified. Education requirements for acupuncturists include graduation from a program accredited by the Accreditation Committee for Acupuncture and Oriental Medicine, completion of four thousand documented hours of training with an approved preceptor, or a combination of the two.

Address: 76 South Laura Street, Suite 1290
           Jacksonville, FL 32202
Phone: 904-598-1005
Fax: 904-598-5001
E-mail: info@nccaom.org
Web site: www.nccaom.org

American Academy of Medical Acupuncture (*AAMA*). A twenty-year-old organization that is specifically focused on training physicians in acupuncture. Offers referrals to nearly a thousand physicians (MDs and DOs) who have documented at least two hundred hours of education and training in medical acupuncture and have integrated acupuncture into their medical practice.

Address: 4929 Wilshire Boulevard, #428
           Los Angeles, CA 90010
Phone: 323-937-5514
Fax: 323-937-0959
E-mail: jdowden@prodigy.net
Web site: www.medicalacupuncture.org

Acufinder.com. Comprehensive online resource useful for searching for both national and international practitioners. Offers online referrals to twelve thousand acupuncturists who are state licensed or nationally certified.

Address: 825 College Boulevard, Suite 102–211
           Oceanside, CA 92057
Phone: 760-630-3600
Fax: 760-630-3676
Web site: www.acufinder.com

CHINESE HERBALISM

Many practitioners of Traditional Chinese Medicine (TCM) use herbs in treatment. Such practitioners may include licensed acupuncturists, doctors of Oriental medicine, and diplomates of Chinese herbology from the NCCAOM. Chinese medical doctors (CMDs) are also qualified in Chinese herbalism.

ORIENTAL MEDICINE

The NCCAOM offers certification in Oriental medicine, acupuncture, Chinese herbology, and Asian bodywork therapy. To become certified in Oriental medicine, individuals must complete a four-year formal education program and pass a national examination. There are only three schools in the United States that are accredited for a doctoral program. These programs award the title of doctor in Oriental medicine (OMD).

American Association of Oriental Medicine. National membership organization for providers of Oriental medicine. Offers referrals to ten thousand acupuncturist members who have completed training, passed a national certification exam, and are state licensed.

  Address: P.O. Box 162340
             Sacramento, CA 95816
  Phone: 866-455-7999
  Fax: 916-443-4766
  E-mail: info@aaom.org
  Web site: www.aaom.org

American Organization for Bodywork Therapies of Asia. Nonprofit professional membership organization representing practitioners, instructors, programs, and students of Asian bodywork therapies. Offers referrals to fifteen thousand shiatsu, acupressure, tuina, and other therapists who understand and make use of TCM principles and practices. Certified practitioners and instructors have a minimum of five hundred hours of training for a professional level of membership.

  Address: 1010 Haddonfield-Berlin Road, Suite 408
             Voorhees, NJ 08043
  Phone: 856-782-1616
  Fax: 856-782-1653
  E-mail: office@aobta.org
  Web site: www.aobta.org

AYURVEDIC MEDICINE

Ayurveda is a traditional holistic Indian medical system that seeks to balance and enhance the functioning of the body, mind, and spirit. Due to strict regulations, the most regularly practiced Ayurvedic treatments in the Western world are massage, dietary and herbal guidance, and yoga. In the United States there are a number of schools that teach Ayurvedic principles, but there is no consensus as to the graduation requirements. There is no formal certification or licensing in the United States other than that offered by the California College of Ayurveda, which offers certification as a clinical Ayurvedic specialist (CAS) after 1,732 hours of instruction and a six-month residency.

National Ayurvedic Medicine Association. National organization representing the Ayurvedic profession in the United States. Holds annual conferences at which participants can learn more about Ayurveda in practice.

Address:	620 Cabrillo Avenue
	Santa Cruz, CA 95065
Phone:	800-669-8914
Fax:	505-294-7572
E-mail:	info@ayurveda-nama.org
Web site:	www.ayurveda-nama.org

HOMEOPATHY

Homeopathy is an alternative medical system based on the principles that "like cures like," that a single remedy that particularly characterizes each person is effective for multiple symptoms, and that the remedy should be taken in an extremely small dose. Many practitioners around the world use homeopathic remedies to treat depression, and they offer case reports on their efficacy. There are, however, no good scientific studies on their use in depression. There are a variety of homeopathic board certifications recognized in the United States. Their credentials recognize individuals as proficient in classical homeopathy, but they do not constitute a license to practice. Statutes for practicing vary by jurisdiction.

North American Society of Homeopathy. National organization for homeopaths. Has a directory of registered homeopaths with a variety of certifications.

Address:	P.O. Box 450039
	Sunrise, FL 33345
Phone:	206-720-7000
Fax:	208-248-1942
E-mail:	nashinfo@homeopathy.org
Web site:	www.homeopathy.org

MASSAGE

Certification of massage therapists is available through the National Certification Board for Therapeutic Massage & Bodywork. To sit for one of the national certification examinations, candidates must have completed at least 125 hours of anatomy and physiology, 200 hours of massage and/or bodywork theory and application, 40 hours of pathology, 10 hours of business and ethics, and at least 125 hours of related course work. In some published scientific studies massage has been shown to decrease anxiety and improve mood.

National Certification Board for Therapeutic Massage & Bodywork. National certifying organization that offers referrals to certified practitioners.

Address:	1901 South Meyers Road, Suite 240
	Oakbrook Terrace, IL 60181
Phone:	800-296-0664
Fax:	866-402-1890
E-mail:	info@ncbtmb.com
Web site:	www.ncbtmb.com

American Massage Therapy Association. Organization that represents more than fifty-six thousand massage therapists in twenty-seven countries. Has a therapist locator service that offers contact information for more than fifteen thousand professional member practitioners. Professional members must have graduated from a 500-hour massage therapy training program, passed the national certification examination in therapeutic massage and bodywork, or possess a current license to practice.

Address:	500 Davis Street, Suite 900
	Evanston, IL 60201
Phone:	877-905-2700
Fax:	847-864-1178
E-mail:	info@amtamassage.org
Web site:	www.amtamassage.org

REFLEXOLOGY

Reflexology is a complementary therapy that is based on the same holographic understanding as TCM. It involves the stimulation of the hands, feet, and ears with the intention of affecting other, corresponding parts of the body and improving overall health. Since reflexology is not recognized by law, no formal training is required for practice. Some nurses and massage therapists, however, offer reflexology as part of their licensed practice. There are different certificate programs that reflexologists can complete, and the certifying organization will generally offer referrals to its associated practitioners. There are reports, but so far no clinical trials, on the positive effect of reflexology on depression.

American Reflexology Certification Board (ARCB). Independent testing agency for the field of reflexology. Offers referrals to a thousand reflexologists who have received national certification from the ARCB. This requires a minimum of 110 hours of training, 90 documented postgraduate sessions, and passing a national examination.

Address:	P.O. Box 5147
	Gulfport, FL 33737
Phone:	303-933-6921

Fax: 303-904-0460
E-mail: info@arcb.net
Web site: www.arcb.net

International Institute of Reflexology (IIR). Organization with more than twenty-five thousand members worldwide. Offers referrals to five thousand U.S. IIR graduates who have completed the 200-hour IIR Ingham Method of Reflexology certification program, passed a certification exam, and maintained continuing education in reflexology.

Address: 5650 First Avenue North
            P.O. Box 12642
            St. Petersburg, FL 33733
Phone: 727-343-4811
Fax: 727-381-2807
E-mail: iir@reflexology-usa.net
Web site: www.reflexology-usa.net

CHAPTER FIVE: THE DARK NIGHT OF THE SOUL
Support Groups
12-STEP PROGRAMS

This category includes a number of programs that follow a set of guiding principles for recovery from addictive or dysfunctional behaviors. Working through the 12 steps involves admitting a lack of control over one's addiction or compulsion, recognizing a higher power that can give strength, examining and making amends for past errors, learning to live a new life, and helping others who suffer from the same addictions or compulsions. Programs include Al-Anon, Alcoholics Anonymous, Emotions Anonymous, Narcotics Anonymous, Overeaters Anonymous, and many others. Each program's Web site contains a tool allowing users to locate meetings.

Alcoholics Anonymous. A 12-step program for alcoholics.
Address: P.O. Box 459
            New York, NY 10163
Phone: 212-870-3400
Web site: www.alcoholics-anonymous.org

Emotions Anonymous. A 12-step program for those working to improve their mental or emotional health, including those who are depressed.
Address: P.O. Box 4245
            St. Paul, MN 55104
Phone: 651-647-9712
Fax: 651-647-1593
E-mail: info@emotionsanonymous.org
Web site: www.emotionsanonymous.org

Al-Anon and Alateen. Twelve-step programs for family members and friends of alcoholics.

Address: 1600 Corporate Landing Parkway
            Virginia Beach, VA 23454
Phone: 757-563-1600
Fax: 757-563-1655
E-mail: wso@al-anon.org
Web site: www.al-anon.alateen.org

Narcotics Anonymous. A 12-step program for those working toward recovery from drug addiction.

Address: P.O. Box 9999
            Van Nuys, CA 91409
Phone: 818-773-9999
Fax: 818-700-0700
E-mail: fsmail@na.org
Web site: www.na.org

Overeaters Anonymous. A 12-step program for those working toward recovery from compulsive overeating.

Address: P.O. Box 44020
            Rio Rancho, NM 87174
Phone: 505-891-2664
Fax: 505-891-4320
E-mail: info@oa.org
Web site: www.oa.org

OTHER SUPPORT GROUPS

Depression and Bipolar Support Alliance. Patient-directed national organization focusing on depression and bipolar disorder. Offers up-to-date information on mood disorders that is reviewed by researchers and clinicians in the field to ensure medical and scientific accuracy. Provides a toll-free information and referral line, as well as a support group locator.

Address: 730 North Franklin Street, Suite 501
            Chicago, IL 60610
Phone: 800-826-3632
Fax: 312-642-7243
Web site: www.dbsalliance.org

Beating the Beast. Online support community for people with depression and related issues. This site strives to foster a "family" feel, and its information is centered around the personal experience of depression rather than the science behind it. Members can post and read entries on a variety of topics, such as medications, relationships, therapy, self-harm, suicidal thoughts, etc. Be advised, however, that there are no trained professionals on staff. The site also has a chat room.

E-mail: admin@beatingthebeast.com
Web site: www.beatingthebeast.com

SUICIDE AND CRISIS HOTLINES

National Suicide Prevention Lifeline. Network of crisis centers serving the entire United States. Calls from anywhere in the country will be routed, twenty-four hours a day, to the nearest available crisis center. Centers are staffed by employees and volunteers whose training varies by location. For instance, the crisis center located in Arlington, Virginia, requires its volunteers to complete a fifty-hour training program, while the center in Albuquerque, New Mexico, requires only forty hours of training. Supervision of volunteers also varies, but in most areas, volunteers and staff members work side by side.

Phone: 800-273-8255
Web site: www.suicidepreventionlifeline.org

RUNAWAY HOUSES

National Runaway Switchboard. Federally designated national communication system for runaway and homeless youth. Youth and family members can call 24 hours a day to speak with a staff member or volunteer who has completed a 36.5-hour training program and can help callers work through problems and find local help. While the call center is located in Chicago, the organization has a comprehensive national database and is able to provide local, community-based referrals. Assistance is provided in finding shelter, food, medical help, and counseling. The organization also provides crisis intervention, message relaying, and conference-calling services.

Address: 3080 North Lincoln Avenue
           Chicago, IL 60657
Phone: 800-786-2929
Fax: 773-929-5150
Web site: www.1800runaway.org

Herbs and Supplements

HERBS (SAINT-JOHN'S-WORT)

According to Mark Blumenthal, founder and executive director of the American Botanical Council, the most clinically studied and tested Saint-John's-wort products are the following.

Jarsin 300. Made by Lichtwer Pharma. In the United States, this product is imported and sold as Kira. Clinical research trials confirm optimal dosage of one 300-milligram tablet taken with water three times daily.

WS 5572. Made by Dr. Willmar Schwabe Group. This product is imported and sold in the United States by Nature's Way as Perika. Clinical research trials confirm optimal dosage of one 300-milligram tablet taken with water three times daily.

Saint-John's-wort extract. Made by Max Zeller Söhne AG. This product is not sold in the United States.

SUPPLEMENTS (SAMe AND 5HTP)

There is currently no external standard for evaluating supplement-producing companies. According to Dr. Joseph Pizzorno, one of the leading authorities on science-based natural medicine, Good Manufacturing Practices (GMP) and supplement evaluations by third parties are critical. Good Manufacturing Practices require that manufacturers, processors, and pack-agers take certain steps to ensure that their products are pure, safe, and effective. Organizations such as the Natural Products Association and United States Pharmacopeia are active in the realm of supplement quality control. Dr. Pizzorno recommends the following company, which makes both SAMe and 5HTP:

Natural Factors. Canadian-based company whose products undergo rigorous testing in accordance with United States Pharmacopeia guidelines. Meets GMP guidelines as well as all Health Canada and FDA regulations. Web site has a "where to buy" function, which lists natural foods stores in the United States and Canada that carry Natural Factors products.

CHAPTER SIX: SPIRITUALITY: THE BLESSING
Retreats

Retreat centers can be fine places to take steps on the *Unstuck* journey, to explore and experiment, recharge and renew. It is important to note, however, that these centers are not fully equipped to deal with serious psychological problems. While no one center focuses solely on depression, certain programs may offer, and many of the attend-ees may be looking for, emotional and physical healing as well.

RetreatFinder.com. Web site with a directory of more than fourteen hundred retreat centers. Can search for retreats by geographic location, environment, faith, and activity (yoga, art, spiritual studies, health and wellness, etc.). The teachings at many of these retreat centers are based on Christian and Jewish principles. Others are grounded in other religious and spiritual traditions.

Address: P.O. Box 1888
              Syracuse, NY 13201
Phone: 800-889-6906
E-mail: info@retreatfinder.com
Web site: www.retreatfinder.com

RESTORATIVE AND EDUCATIONAL RETREATS

Esalen Institute. Retreat center located on the beautiful Big Sur coastline of northern California. Provides a wide variety of educational and personal growth programs, with subjects such as meditation, yoga, spirituality, massage, transpersonal psychology, etc. Offers two- or five-day workshops and twenty-eight-day work-study programs on a variety of topics, as well as less structured personal retreats that include meditation, yoga, tai chi, and dance classes, and access to on-site hot springs.

Address: 55000 Highway 1
              Big Sur, CA 93920
Phone: 831-667-3005
Fax: 831-667-2724
E-mail: info@esalen.org
Web site: www.esalen.org

Feathered Pipe Foundation. Nonprofit organization that offers yoga and other retreats and workshops on various aspects of spirituality at several locations in Montana, Mexico, and India. Most retreats last one week.

Address: P.O. Box 1682
           Helena, MT 59624
Phone: 406-442-8196
Fax: 406-442-8110
E-mail: fpranch@mt.net
Web site: www.featheredpipe.com

Hollyhock. Educational and restorative retreat center located on Canada's Cortes Island. Offers workshops and retreats that are relevant to this center's five main themes, including well-being, wisdom practices, arts and culture, business and leadership, and world change and service. In addition to educational programs, Hollyhock offers a variety of activities, such as yoga, movement, meditation, hiking, sailing, and kayaking.

Address: P.O. Box 127, Manson's Landing
           Cortes Island, BC V0P 1K0 Canada
Phone: 800-933-6339
Fax: 250-935-6424
E-mail: registration@hollyhock.ca
Web site: www.hollyhock.ca

Kripalu Center for Yoga and Health. Retreat center located in the Berkshire Mountains in western Massachusetts that provides visitors with a vast array of yogic and spiritual options as well as integrative health care. Offers daylong intensive programs, weeklong retreats and workshops, and long-term residential opportunities.

Address: P.O. Box 309
           Stockbridge, MA 01262
Phone: 866-200-5203
E-mail: registration@kripalu.org
Web site: www.kripalu.org

Omega Institute. Center for wellness and personal growth with several sites in the United States, the Virgin Islands, and Costa Rica. Omega offers rest and rejuvenation retreats of varying lengths. Retreats include morning classes on a variety of topics, evening programs such as concerts, lectures, and dances, and optional yoga, meditation, tai chi, and movement classes. The institute also offers workshops on a wide range of topics, including empowerment, growth during difficult times, and yoga for sleep, as well as a range of spiritual practices. (I do five-day retreats based on *Unstuck* at the Rhinebeck, New York, location.)

Address (main campus):   150 Lake Drive
           Rhinebeck, NY 12572
Phone: 800-944-1001
Fax: 845-266-3769
E-mail: registration@eomega.org
Web site: www.eomega.org

MEDITATION RETREATS

Insight Meditation Society. Retreat center for the practice of vipassana ("insight") and metta ("loving kindness") meditations. The center is located in Barre, Massachusetts, and offers more than twenty-five meditation courses, ranging in duration from two days to three months. During most retreats, complete silence is maintained at all times, except during teacher interview periods.

    Address: 1230 Pleasant Street
                    Barre, MA 01005
    Phone: 978-355-4378
    E-mail: rc@dharma.org
    Web site: www.dharma.org/ims

Spirit Rock Meditation Center. Meditation center located in Woodacre, California. Focuses on vipassana ("insight") meditation and offers residential retreats as well as daylong programs and weekly classes. One of the founding teachers of this center is Jack Kornfield, who is one of the teachers who introduced Buddhist mindfulness practice to the West.

    Address: P.O. Box 169
                    Woodacre, CA 94973
    Phone: 415-488-0164
    Fax: 415-488-1025
    E-mail: srmc@spiritrock.org
    Web site: www.spiritrock.org

SPIRITUAL AND RELIGIOUS RETREATS

FindtheDivine.com. Web site that provides a state-by-state listing of spiritual retreats and programs. Results are primarily for Christian retreats, but some Jewish retreats are also included. Many of the centers listed at Find the Divine are for religious learning rather than spiritual exploration.

    E-mail: info@findthedivine.com
    Web site: www.findthedivine.com

The Abode of the Message. Sufi community and retreat center that is one of the nation's only Islamic-based retreat centers, though it welcomes people of all faiths. Offers a variety of individual retreats and other residence options.

    Address: 5 Abode Road
                    New Lebanon, NY 12125
    Phone: 518-794-8090
    Fax: 518-794-8060
    E-mail: programsoffice@theabode.net
    Web site: www.theabode.net

Dar al Islam. Religious retreat for Muslims and non-Muslims, with the stated purpose of bettering society through education, cooperation, and networking. Offers programs that are centered around bringing Muslims together, as well as programs that focus on reaching out to non-Muslims.

Address: P.O. Box 180
           Abiquiu, NM 87510
Phone: 505-685-4515
E-mail: rcoburn@igc.org
Web site: www.daralislam.org

Elat Chayyim Center for Jewish Spirituality at the Isabella Freedman Jewish Retreat Center. Center
for Jewish spirituality that offers retreats for people from all backgrounds. Focuses on developing and renewing Jewish spirituality, and on cultivating an awareness of the divine presence
in all aspects of life.
    Address: 116 Johnson Road
               Falls Village, CT 06031
    Phone: 800-398-2630
    Web site: www.elatchayyim.org

Gampo Abbey. Western Buddhist monastery that offers intense Shambhala Buddhist programs
and retreats. Many of the programs require at least a six-month time commitment and a disciplined lifestyle. Gampo Abbey is under the direction of Pema Chödrön, a leader in teaching
about meditation and how the Buddhist principles apply to everyday Western life.
    Address: Pleasant Bay, Cape Breton
               Nova Scotia, B0E 2P0, Canada
    Phone: 902-224-2752
    E-mail: office@gampoabbey.org
    Web site: www.gampoabbey.org

Upaya Institute and Zen Center. A Zen retreat in Santa Fe, New Mexico, with a variety of offerings that may combine experience of the nearby desert with topics such as mindfulness, gratitude, and death and dying. Led by Joan Halifax, PhD, who originally taught me the
Forgiveness meditation.
    Address: 1404 Cerro Gordo Road
               Santa Fe, NM 87501
    Phone: 505-986-8518
    Fax: 505-986-8528
    E-mail: upaya@upaya.org
    Web site: www.upaya.org

Zen Mountain Monastery. One of the West's most respected Zen Buddhist monastic training
centers. Focuses on teaching an accessible Western interpretation of the Buddha's original
lessons.
    Address: P.O. Box 197
               Mount Tremper, NY 12457
    Phone: 845-688-2228
    Fax: 845-688-2415
    E-mail: zmmtrain@mro.org
    Web site: www.mro.org/zmm/index.php

NOTES

Aust N Z J Psychiatry	*The Australian and New Zealand Journal of Psychiatry*
Australas Psychiatry	*Australasian Psychiatry*
Behav Med	*Behavioral Medicine*
Behav Neurosci	*Behavioral Neuroscience*
Behav Therapy	*Behavior Therapy*
Biofeedback Self Regul	*Biofeedback and Self-Regulation*
Biol Psychiatry	*Biological Psychiatry*
Bipolar Disord	*Bipolar Disorders*
BMC Complement Altern Med	*BMC (BioMed Central) Complementary and Alternative Medicine*
BMC Med	*BMC (BioMed Central) Medicine*
BMC Pediatr	*BMC (BioMed Central) Pediatrics*
BMC Psychiatry	*BMC (BioMed Central) Psychiatry*
BMJ	*BMJ (British Medical Journal, Clinical Research Edition)*
Br J Med Psychol	*The British Journal of Medical Psychology*
Br J Psychiatry	*The British Journal of Psychiatry*
Br J Sports Med	*British Journal of Sports Medicine*
Brain Behav Immun	*Brain, Behavior, and Immunity*
Brain Inj	*Brain Injury*
Braz J Med Biol Res	*Brazilian Journal of Medical and Biological Research*
Brief Treat Crisis Interv	*Brief Treatment and Crisis Intervention*
Cleve Clin J Med	*Cleveland Clinic Journal of Medicine*
Clin Chem	*Clinical Chemistry*
Clin Endocrinol (Oxf)	*Clinical Endocrinology (Oxford)*
Clin Investig	*The Clinical Investigator*
Clin Pharmacol Ther	*Clinical Pharmacology & Therapeutics*
Clin Psychol Rev	*Clinical Psychology Review*
Clin Rheumatol	*Clinical Rheumatology*
Clin Toxicol (Phila)	*Clinical Toxicology (Philadelphia)*
CNS Spectr	*CNS Spectrums*
Cochrane Database Syst Rev	*Cochrane Database of Systematic Reviews*
Cogn Behav Ther	*Cognitive Behaviour Therapy*
Complement Ther Clin Pract	*Complementary Therapies in Clinical Practice*
Complement Ther Med	*Complementary Therapies in Medicine*
Compr Psychiatry	*Comprehensive Psychiatry*
Curr Atheroscler Rep	*Current Atherosclerosis Reports*
Depress Anxiety	*Depression and Anxiety*
Drug Saf	*Drug Safety*
Electroencephalogr Clin Neurophysiol	*Electroencephalography and Clinical Neurophysiology*
Eur Arch Psychiatry Clin Neurosci	*European Archives of Psychiatry and Clinical Neuroscience*
Eur J Clin Nutr	*European Journal of Clinical Nutrition*
Eur J Neurol	*European Journal of Neurology*
Eur J Neurosci	*The European Journal of Neuroscience*
Eur J Nutr	*European Journal of Nutrition*
Eur J Pub Health	*European Journal of Public Health*
Eur J Pharmacol	*European Journal of Pharmacology*
Eur Neuropsychopharmacol	*European Neuropsychopharmacology*
Gen Hosp Psychiatry	*General Hospital Psychiatry*
Health Aff (Millwood)	*Health Affairs (Project Hope)*
Health Care Women Int	*Health Care for Women International*
Health Psychol	*Health Psychology*

Horm Res	*Hormone Research*
Hum Brain Mapp	*Human Brain Mapping*
Hum Exp Toxicol	*Human & Experimental Toxicology*
Humboldt J Soc Relat	*Humboldt Journal of Social Relations*
Indian J Clin Psychol	*Indian Journal of Clinical Psychology*
Indian J Med Res	*The Indian Journal of Medical Research*
Indian Pediatr	*Indian Pediatrics*
Infant Behav Dev	*Infant Behavior & Development*
Int Clin Psychopharmacol	*International Clinical Psychopharmacology*
Int J Behav Med	*International Journal of Behavioral Medicine*
Int J Cardiol	*International Journal of Cardiology*
Int J Neuropsycholopharmacol	*The International Journal of Neuropsychopharmacology*
Int J Neurosci	*The International Journal of Neuroscience*
Int J Psychiatry Med	*International Journal of Psychiatry in Medicine*
Int J Psychoanal	*The International Journal of Psycho-Analysis*
Int J Clin Experi Hypnosis	*International Journal of Clinical and Experimental Hypnosis*
J Abnorm Psychol	*Journal of Abnormal Psychology*
J Affect Disord	*Journal of Affective Disorders*
J Altern Complement Med	*Journal of Alternative and Complementary Medicine*
J Am Acad Child Adolesc Psychiatry	*Journal of the American Academy of Child and Adolescent Psychiatry*
J Am Coll Cardiol	*Journal of the American College of Cardiology*
J Am Coll Nutr	*Journal of The American College of Nutrition*
J Am Diet Assoc	*Journal of The American Dietetic Association*
J Behav Med	*Journal of Behavioral Medicine*
J Biol Chem	*The Journal of Biological Chemistry*
J Clin Endocrinol Metab	*Journal of Clinical Endocrinology & Metabolism*
J Clin Psychiatry	*The Journal of Clinical Psychiatry*
J Clin Psychol	*Journal of Clinical Psychology*
J Clin Psychopharmacol	*Journal of Clinical Psychopharmacology*
J Consult Clin Psychol	*Journal of Consulting and Clinical Psychology*
J Dev Behav Pediatr	*Journal of Developmental & Behavioral Pediatrics*
J Epidemiol Community Health	*Journal of Epidemiology and Community Health*
J Gerontol Nurs	*Journal of Gerontological Nursing*
J Health Soc Behav	*Journal of Health and Social Behavior*
J Holis Nurs	*Journal of Holistic Nursing*
J Music Ther	*Journal of Music Therapy*
J Nerv Ment Dis	*The Journal of Nervous and Mental Disease*
J Neural Transm	*Journal of Neural Transmission*
J Neuropsychiatry Clin Neurosci	*The Journal of Neuropsychiatry and Clinical Neurosciences*
J Neurosci	*The Journal of Neuroscience*
J Nutr Sci Vitaminol	*Journal of Nutritional Science and Vitaminology*
J Pers Soc Psychol	*Journal of Personality and Social Psychology*
J Psychiatry Neurosci	*Journal of Psychiatry & Neuroscience*
J Psychopharmacol	*Journal of Psychopharmacology*
J Psychosom Res	*Journal of Psychosomatic Research*
J Sex Marital Ther	*Journal of Sex & Marital Therapy*
J Tradit Chin Med	*Journal of Traditional Chinese Medicine*
J Urban Health	*Journal of Urban Health*
JAMA	*The Journal of the American Medical Association*
Life Sci	*Life Sciences*

Lipids Health Dis	Lipids in Health and Disease
Lung Cancer	Lung Cancer (Amsterdam)
Mayo Clin Proc	Mayo Clinic Proceedings
Med Hypotheses	Medical Hypotheses
Med Sci Monit	Medical Science Monitor
Med Sci Sports Exerc	Medicine and Science in Sports and Exercise
MedGenMed	Medgenmed: Medscape General Medicine
N Engl J Med	The New England Journal of Medicine
Nahrung	Die Nahrung
Nat Med	Nature Medicine
Nat Neurosci	Nature Neuroscience
Neuro Endocrinol Lett	Neuro Endocrinology Letters
Nutr Neurosci	Nutritional Neuroscience
Oral Surg Oral Med Oral Pathol Oral Radiol Endod	Oral Surgery, Oral Medicine, Oral Pathology, Oral Radiology, and Endodontics
Pain Manag Nurs	Pain Management Nursing
Pediatr Rev	Pediatrics in Review
Percept Mot Skills	Perceptual and Motor Skills
Pers Soc Psychol Bull	Personality and Social Psychology Bulletin
Pharmacol Biochem Behav	Pharmacology, Biochemistry, and Behavior
Philos Trans R Soc Lond B Biol Sci	Philosophical Transactions of the Royal Society of London. Series B, Biological Sciences
Physiol Behav	Physiology & Behavior
PLoS Med	PLoS (Public Library of Science) Medicine
PNAS	Proceedings of the National Academy of Sciences of the United States of America
Pol J Pharmacol	Polish Journal of Pharmacology
Prev Med	Preventive Medicine
Prog Neuropsychopharmacol Biol Psychiatry	Progress in Neuro-Psychopharmacology & Biological Psychiatry
Prostaglandins Leukot Med	Prostaglandins, Leukotrienes, and Medicine
Psychiatr Ann	Psychiatric Annals
Psychiatr Serv	Psychiatric Services (Washington, D.C.)
Psychiatry Res	Psychiatry Research
Psychol Bull	Psychological Bulletin
Psychol Med	Psychological Medicine
Psychol Psychother	Psychology and Psychotherapy
Psychopharmacol Bull	Psychopharmacology Bulletin
Psychosom Med	Psychosomatic Medicine
Psychother Psychosom	Psychotherapy and Psychosomatics
Qual Life Res	Quality of Life Research
Res Publ Assoc Res Nerv Ment Dis	Research Publications—Assocation for Research in Nervous and Mental Disease
Rev Gen Psychol	Review of General Psychology
S Afr Med J	South African Medical Journal
Seishin Shinkeigaku Zasshi	Psychiatria et Neurologia Japonica
Semin Fetal Neonatal Med	Seminars in Fetal & Neonatal Medicine
South Med J	Southern Medical Journal
Support Care Cancer	Supportive Care in Cancer
Trends Food Sci Tech	Trends in Food Science & Technology

INTRODUCTION: IS THERE SOME OTHER WAY?

1–2 **Joseph Campbell's groundbreaking studies** Campbell, J., 1949. *The hero with a thousand faces.* Bollingen Series 17. [New York]: Pantheon Books.

4–5 *Diagnostic and Statistical Manual of the American Psychiatric Association* (the DSM-IV) American Psychiatric Association. 2000. *Diagnostic and statistical manual of mental disorders:* DSM-IV-TR. 4th ed. Washington, D.C.: American Psychiatric Association.

5 **the most disabling of nonfatal conditions** Ustun, T. B., et al. 2004. Global burden of depressive disorders in the year 2000. *Br J Psychiatry* 184: 386–92.

5 **thirteen to fourteen million Americans** Kessler, R. C., et al. 2003. The epidemiology of major depressive disorder: Results from the National Comorbidity Survey Replication (NCS-R). *JAMA* 289 (23): 3095–3105.

6 **three million have a dysthymic disorder** http://www.hcp.med.harvard.edu/ncs/ftpdir/table_ncsr_12monthprevgenderxage.pdf.

6 **almost one-tenth of our adult population** http://www.hcp.med.harvard.edu/ncs/ftpdir/table_ncsr_12monthprevgenderxage.pdf.

6 **study estimated that one in five Americans** http://www.hcp.med.harvard.edu/ncs/ftpdir/table_ncsr_12monthprevgenderxage.pdf.

6 **another predicted** Lewinsohn, P. M., et al. 2003. Adolescent psychopathology: I. Prevalence and incidence of depression and other DSM-III-R disorders in high school students. *J Abnorm Psychol* 102 (1): 133–44.

6 **more than $50 billion** Greenberg, P. E., et al. 2003. The economic burden of depression in the United States: How did it change between 1990 and 2000? *J Clin Psychiatry* 64 (12): 1465–75.

6 **Depression … may predispose** Moussavi, S., S. Chatterji, E. Verdes, A. Tandon, V. Patel, and T. B. Ustun. 2007. Depression, chronic diseases, and decrements in health: Results from the World Health Surveys. *Lancet* 370 (9590): 851–58.

6 **depression is the leading cause of nonfatal disability** Ustun et al., Global burden of depressive disorders.

6 **the father of our Western medicine, Hippocrates** Hippocrates, 1950. Trans. J. Chadwick and W. N. Mann. *The medical works of Hippocrates.* Oxford: Blackwell Scientific Publications.

7 **For most of the last two thousand years** Horwitz, A., and J. Wakefield. 2007. *The loss of sadness: How psychiatry transformed normal sorrow into depressive disorder.* New York: Oxford University Press.

8 **a rough-and-ready division of depression** Mendels, J., and C. Cochrane. 1968. The nosology of depression: The endogenous-reactive concept. *Am J Psychiatry* 124 (11): S1–11.

8 *Diagnostic and Statistical Manual* (DSM-III) American Psychiatric Association. 1980. *Diagnostic and statistical manual of mental disorders.* 3rd ed. Washington, D.C.: American Psychiatric Association.

8 *only on the DSM symptoms* Horwitz and Wakefield, *The loss of sadness.*

8 **Some important studies** Elkin, I., M. T. Shea, J. T. Watkins, S. D. Imber, S. M. Sotsky, J. F. Collins et al. 1989. National Institute of Mental Health Treatment of Depression Collaborative Research Program. General effectiveness of treatments. *Arch Gen Psychiatry* 46 (11): 971–82, discussion 983; Shea, M. T., I. Elkin, S. D. Imber, S. M. Sotsky, J. T. Watkins, J. F. Collins et al. 1992. Course of depressive symptoms over follow-up. Findings from the National Institute of Mental Health Treatment of Depression Collaborative Research Program. *Arch Gen Psychiatry* 49 (10): 782–87.

9 **By the time the DSM-IV** American Psychiatric Association, DSM-IV-TR. 4th ed.

9 **Eager to save money** Cutler, D. M. 2004. *Your money or your life: Strong medicine for America's health care system.* New York: Oxford University Press; Olfson, M., S. C. Marcus, B. Druss, L. Elinson, T. Tanielian, and H. A. Pincus. 2002. National trends in the outpatient treatment of depression. *JAMA* 287 (2): 203–9; Zuvekas, S. H. 2005. Prescription drugs and the changing patterns of treatment for mental disorders, 1996–2001. *Health Aff (Millwood)* 24 (1): 195–205.

10 **189 million prescriptions for antidepressants** http://www.imshealth.com/ims/portal/front/articleC/0,2777,6599_18731_77056778,00.html.

10 **will pay about $12 billion for these drugs** http://www.imshealth.com/ims/portal/front/articleC/0,2777,6599_18731_77056778,00.html.

10 **"My belief is that today"** Alan Leshner, PhD, as quoted in Samuels, D. 1998. Saying yes to drugs. *New Yorker.* March 23, 48–49.

10 **no consistent pathological postmortem findings** Stockmeier, C. A., et al. 1997. Serotonin receptors in suicide victims with major

depression. *Neuropsychopharmacology,* 16 (2): 162–73; Lowther, S., et al. 1997. 5-HT1A receptor binding sites in post-mortem brain samples from depressed suicides and controls. *J Affect Disord* 42 (2–3): 199–207.

10 **The genetic association, though present** Sher, L. 2000. Psychiatric diagnoses and inconsistent results of association studies in behavioral genetics. *Med Hypotheses* 54 (2): 207–9.

10 **no consistent biochemical abnormalities** Valenstein, E. 1998. *Blaming the brain: The truth about drugs and mental health.* New York: Free Press; Sadock, B. J., V. A. Sadock, and H. I. Kaplan. 2005. *Kaplan & Sadock's comprehensive textbook of psychiatry.* 8th ed. Philadelphia: Lippincott Williams & Wilkins.

10 **Though some studies** Owens, M. J., and C. B. Nemeroff. 1994. Role of serotonin in the pathophysiology of depression: Focus on the serotonin transporter. *Clin Chem* 40 (2): 288–95.

10 **There is still no proof** Heninger, G. R., P. L. Delgado, and D. S. Charney. 1996. The revised monoamine theory of depression: A modulatory role for monoamines, based on new findings from monoamine depletion experiments in humans. *Pharmacopsychiatry* 29 (1): 2–11; Lacasse, J. R., and J. Leo. 2005. Serotonin and depression: A disconnect between the advertisements and the scientific literature. *PLoS Med* 2 (12): e392; Roggenbach, J., B. Muller-Oerlinghausen, and L. Franke, 2002. Suicidality, impulsivity, and aggression—is there a link to 5HIAA concentration in the cerebrospinal fluid? *Psychiatry Res* 113 (1–2): 193–206; Sadock et al., *Comprehensive textbook of psychiatry.*

11 **stress and the action of stress hormones are . . . causes** Lee, A. L., W. O. Ogle, and R. M. Sapolsky. 2002. Stress and depression: Possible links to neuron death in the hippocampus. *Bipolar Disord* 4 (2): 117–28; Sapolsky, R. M. 1996. Why stress is bad for your brain. *Science* 273 (5276): 749–50.

11 **antidepressants may be only marginally** Moncrieff, J., and I. Kirsch. 2005. Efficacy of antidepressants in adults. *BMJ* 331 (7509): 155–57; Kirsch, I, T. J. Moore, A. Scoboria, and S. S. Nicholls. 2002. The emperor's new drugs: An analysis of antidepressant medication data submitted to the U.S. Food and Drug Administration. *Prevention and Treatment* 5 (*Article 23*). http://www.journals.apa.org/prevention/volume5/pre0050023a.html.

11 **an increasing body of information** *Physicians' desk reference (PDR).* 2004. Montvale, NJ: Medical Economics Data Productions Company; Breggin, P. R., and G. R. Breggin. 1994. *Talking back to Prozac: What doctors won't tell you about today's most controversial drug.* New York: St. Martin's Press; Glenmullen, J. 2000. *Prozac backlash: Overcoming the dangers of Prozac, Zoloft, Paxil, and other antidepressants with safe, effective alternatives.* New York: Simon & Schuster; Black, K., et al. 2000. Selective serotonin reuptake inhibitor discontinuation syndrome: Proposed diagnostic criteria. *J Psychiatry Neurosci* 25 (3): 255–61; Coupland, N. J., C. J. Bell, and J. P. Potokar. 1996. Serotonin reuptake inhibitor withdrawal. *J Clin Psychopharmacol* 16 (5): 356–62; Lipinski, T. F., et al. Fluoxetine-induced akathisia: Clinical and theoretical implications. 1989. *J Clin Psychiatry* 50 (9): 339–42; Hansen, L. 2003. Fluoxetine dose-increment related akathisia in depression: Implications for clinical care, recognition, and management of selective serotonin reuptake inhibitor–induced akathisia. *J Psychopharmacol* 17 (4): 451–52; Montejo-Gonzalez, A. L., et al. 1997. SSRI-induced sexual dysfunction: Fluoxetine, paroxetine, sertraline, and fluvoxamine in a prospective, multicenter, and descriptive clinical study of 344 patients. *J Sex Marital Ther* 23 (3): 176–94; Modell, J. G., et al. 1997. Comparative sexual side effects of bupropion, fluoxetine, paroxetine, and sertraline. *Clin Pharmacol Ther* 61 (4): 476–87.

11 **the very real suicide risks . . . of SSRIs** Jick, H., J. A. Kaye, and S. S. Jick. 2004. Antidepressants and the risk of suicidal behaviors. *JAMA* 292 (3): 338–43; Gibbons, R. D., et al. 2007. Early evidence on the effects of regulators' suicidality warnings on SSRI prescriptions and suicide in children and adolescents. *Am J Psychiatry* 164 (9): 1356–63; Laje, G., et al. 2007. Genetic markers of suicidal ideation emerging during citalopram treatment of major depression. *Am J Psychiatry* 164 (10): 1530–38.

11 **well told in books that I list** Breggin and Breggin, *Talking back to Prozac;* Glenmullen, *Prozac backlash;* Horwitz and Wakefield, *The loss of sadness;* Healy, D. 1999. *The antidepressant era.* Cambridge, MA: Harvard University Press; Healy, D. 2006. *Let them eat Prozac: The unhealthy relationship between the pharmaceutical industry and depression.* New York: New York University Press; DeGrandpre, R. 2004. *The cult of pharmacology: How America became the world's*

most troubled drug culture. Durham, NC: Duke University Press; Leventhal, A., and C. Martell. 2005. *The myth of depression as disease: Limitations and alternatives to drug treatment.* New York: Praeger.

13 **approximately 30 to 35 percent versus 2 to 5 percent** Sadock et al., *Comprehensive textbook of psychiatry.*

13 **a real genetic contribution** Kendler, K. S., et al. 2006. A Swedish national twin study of lifetime major depression. *Am J Psychiatry* 163 (1): 109–14; Kramer, P. 2005. *Against depression.* New York: Viking.

13 **along with other critics** Joseph, J. 2001. Separated twins and the genetics of personality differences: A critique. *Am J Psychol* 114 (1): 1–30; Horwitz and Wakefield. *The loss of sadness;* Antonuccio, D. O., et al. 1999. Raising questions about antidepressants. *Psychother Psychosom* 68 (1): 3–14.

13 **a recent, landmark study** Caspi, A., et al. 2003. Influence of life stress on depression: Moderation by a polymorphism in the 5-HTT gene. *Science* 301: 386–89; Horwitz and Wakefield, *The loss of sadness.*

14 **the loss of cells in the hippocampus** Bremner, J. D., et al. 1997. Magnetic resonance imaging–based measurement of hippocampal volume in posttraumatic stress disorder related to childhood physical and sexual abuse—a preliminary report. *Biol Psychiatry* 41 (1): 23–32.

14 **these children appear to be more vulnerable** Levitan, R. D., et al. 1998. Major depression in individuals with a history of childhood physical or sexual abuse: Relationship to neurovegetative features, mania, and gender. *Am J Psychiatry* 155 (12): 1746–52.

14 **episodes of depression in adult life** Sheline, Y. I. 2003. Neuroimaging studies of mood disorder effects on the brain. *Biol Psychiatry* 54 (3): 338–52.

14 **changes in glucose metabolism** Drevets, W. C., et al. 2002. Glucose metabolism in the amygdala in depression: Relationship to diagnostic subtype and plasma cortisol levels. *Pharmacol Biochem Behav* 71 (3): 431–47; Kumar, A., et al. 1993. Regional cerebral glucose metabolism in late-life depression and Alzheimer disease: a preliminary positron emission tomography study. *PNAS* 90 (15): 7019–23; Liotti, M., H. S. Mayberg, S. McGinnis, S. L. Brannan, and P. Jerabek. 2002. Unmasking disease-specific cerebral blood flow abnormalities: Mood chal-

lenge in patients with remitted unipolar depression. *Am J Psychiatry* 159 (11): 1830–40; Goldapple, K., et al. 2004. Modulation of cortical-limbic pathways in major depression: Treatment-specific effects of cognitive behavior therapy. *Arch Gen Psychiatry* 61 (1): 34–41.

14 **similar changes can be provoked** Shamay-Tsoory, S. G., et al. 2005. The neural correlates of understanding the other's distress: a positron emission tomography investigation of accurate empathy. *Neuroimage* 27 (2): 468–72.

14 **decreases in hippocampal volume and in . . . brain cells** Rajkowska, G. 2000. Postmortem studies in mood disorders indicate altered numbers of neurons and glial cells. *Biol Psychiatry* 48 (8): 766–77.

14 **association between brain changes and depression** Rajkowska, G., et al. 1999. Morphometric evidence for neuronal and glial prefrontal cell pathology in major depression. *Biol Psychiatry* 45 (9): 1085–98; Sheline, Y. I. 2003. Neuroimaging studies of mood disorder effects on the brain. *Biol Psychiatry* 54 (3): 338–52; Macmaster, F. P., et al. 2008. Amygdala and hippocampal volumes in familial early onset major depressive disorder. *Biol Psychiatry* 63 (4): 385–90.

14 **One of the most striking and frequently cited studies** Rajkowska et al. Morphometric evidence.

15 *neuroplasticity* Eriksson, P. S., et al. 1998. Neurogenesis in the adult human hippocampus. *Nat Med* 4 (11): 1313–17; Kandel, E. R. 1998. A new intellectual framework for psychiatry. *Am J Psychiatry* 155 (4): 457–69; Pascual-Leone, A., et al. 2005. The plastic human brain cortex. *Annu Rev Neurosci* 28: 377–401.

15 **Psychotherapy . . . noted to change brain function** Goldapple et al. Modulation of cortical-limbic pathways; Martin, S. D., et al. 2001. Brain blood flow changes in depressed patients treated with interpersonal psychotherapy or venlafaxine hydrochloride: Preliminary findings. *Arch Gen Psychiatry* 58 (7): 641–48; Brody, A. L., et al. 2001. Regional brain metabolic changes in patients with major depression treated with either paroxetine or interpersonal therapy: Preliminary findings. *Arch Gen Psychiatry* 58 (7): 631–40.

15 **Exercise (at least in animals)** Trejo, J. L., E. Carro, and I. Torres-Aleman. 2001. Circulating insulin-like growth factor I mediates exercise-induced increases in the number of new neurons in the adult hippocampus. *J Neurosci* 21 (5):

1628–34; van Praag, H., G. Kempermann, and F. H. Gage. 1999. Running increases cell proliferation and neurogenesis in the adult mouse dentate gyrus. *Nat Neurosci* 2 (3): 266–70.

15 **meditation ... can change brain function** Lou, H. C., et al. 1999. A 15O-H$_2$O PET study of meditation and the resting state of normal consciousness. *Hum Brain Mapp* 7 (2): 98–105; Lazar, S. W., et al. 2000. Functional brain mapping of the relaxation response and meditation. *Neuroreport* 11 (7): 1581–85; Davidson, R. J., et al. 2003. Alterations in brain and immune function produced by mindfulness meditation. *Psychosom Med* 65 (4): 564–70; Davidson, R. J. 2004. Well-being and affective style: Neural substrates and biobehavioural correlates. *Philos Trans R Soc Lond B Biol Sci* 359 (1449): 1395–1411; Jevning, R., et al. 1996. Effects on regional cerebral blood flow of transcendental meditation. *Physiol Behav* 59 (3): 399–402.

15 **One recent remarkable study** Lazar, S. W., C.E. Kerr, R. H. Wasserman, J. R. Gray, D. N. Greve, M. T. Treadway, M. McGarvey, B. T. Quinn, J. A. Dusek, H. Benson, S. L. Rauch, C. I. Moore, and B. Fischl. 2005. Meditation experience is associated with increased cortical thickness. *Neuroreport* 16 (17): 1893–97.

15 **history of drug therapy for depression** Sadock et al., *Comprehensive textbook of psychiatry*.

15 **During the early 1950s, physicians noted that Iproniazid** Ban, T. A. 2001. Pharmacotherapy of depression: A historical analysis. *J Neural Transm* 108 (6): 707–16.

000 **monoamine oxidase inhibitor (MAOI) stopped the breakdown of neurotransmitters** Feighner, J. P. 1999. Mechanism of action of antidepressant medications. *J Clin Psychiatry* 60 suppl. 4: S4–11, discussion 12–13.

16 **"biogenic amine hypothesis"** Schildkraut, J. J., and S. S. Kety. 1967. Biogenic amines and emotion. *Science* 156 (771): 21–37.

16 **appeared to increase the amounts of the amines** Sadock et al., *Comprehensive textbook of psychiatry*.

16 **there were significant side effects** Sadock et al., *Comprehensive textbook of psychiatry; PDR;* Pies, R. W. 1998. *Handbook of essential psychopharmacology.* Washington, D.C.: American Psychiatric Association.

16 **found less than normal amounts** Sadock et al., *Comprehensive textbook of psychiatry.*

16 **people who had once been treated with antidepressants** Delgado, P. L., et al. 1999.

Tryptophan-depletion challenge in depressed patients treated with desipramine or fluoxetine: Implications for the role of serotonin in the mechanism of antidepressant action. *Biol Psychiatry* 46 (2): 212–20; Spillmann, M. K., A. J. Van der Does, M. A. Rankin, R. D. Vuolo, J. E. Alpert, A. A. Nierenberg et al. 2001. Tryptophan depletion in SSRI-recovered depressed outpatients. *Psychopharmacology (Berlin)* 155 (2): 123–127.

17 **with annual U.S. sales reaching $3 billion by 2000** http://www.imshealth.com/ims/portal/front/articleC/0,2777,6599_3665_1003704,00.html.

17 **made more serotonin available for intercellular transmission** Hyttel, J. 1994. Pharmacological characterization of selective serotonin reuptake inhibitors (SSRIs). *Int Clin Psychopharmacol* 9 suppl. 1: S19–26.

17 **no evidence that SSRIs ... are any more effective** Steffens, D. C., K. R. Krishnan, and M. J. Helms. 1997. Are SSRIs better than TCAs? Comparison of SSRIs and TCAs: A meta-analysis. *Depress Anxiety* 6 (1): 10–18; Anderson, I. M. 2000. Selective serotonin reuptake inhibitors versus tricyclic antidepressants: A meta-analysis of efficacy and tolerability. *J Affect Disord* 58 (1): 19–36.

17 **antidepressant drugs quickly increase brain neurotransmitter levels** Nutt, D. J. 2002. The neuropharmacology of serotonin and noradrenaline in depression. *Int Clin Psychopharmacol* 17 suppl. 1: S1–12.

17 **greater effect of the drugs is exerted on** Czeh, B., et al. 2001. Stress-induced changes in cerebral metabolites, hippocampal volume, and cell proliferation are prevented by antidepressant treatment with tianeptine. *PNAS* 98 (22): 12796–801; Sapolsky, R. M. 2001. Depression, antidepressants, and the shrinking hippocampus. *PNAS* 98 (22): 12320–22.

17 **Studies have shown** *PDR;* Breggin and Breggin. *Talking back to Prozac;* Glenmullen. *Prozac backlash.*

18 **large numbers have significant, unwanted weight gain** Sherman, C. 1998. Long-term side effects surface with SSRIs [prozac-type drugs]. *Clinical Psychiatry News* 26 (5): 1. Glenmullen. *Prozac backlash.*

18 **significant percentage . . . experience various kinds of sexual dysfunction** Montejo-Gonzalez et al. SSRI-induced sexual dysfunction; Modell, et al. Comparative sexual side effects.

18 **Almost 40 percent of all depressed patients** Kirsch et al., The emperor's new drugs.

18 **One well-documented study** Hoehn-Saric, R., J. R. Lipsey, and D. R. McLeod. 1990. Apathy and indifference in patients on fluvoxamine and fluoxetine. *J Clin Psychopharmacol* 10 (5): 343–45.

18 **SSRIs increase ... serotonin, at the expense of ... dopamine** Ichikawa, J., and H. Y. Meltzer. 1995. Effect of antidepressants on striatal and accumbens extracellular dopamine levels. *Eur J Pharmacol* 281 (3): 255–61; Glenmullen. *Prozac backlash.*

18 **disorders of movement that resemble ... Parkinson's disease** Di Rocco, A., et al. 1998. Sertraline-induced Parkinsonism. A case report and an in-vivo study of the effect of sertraline on dopamine metabolism. *J Neural Transm* 105 (2–3): 247–51; Lambert, M. T., C. Trutia, and F. Petty, 1998. Extrapyramidal adverse effects associated with sertraline. *Prog Neuropsychopharmacol Biol Psychiatry* 22 (5): 741–48; Leo, R. J. 1996. Movement disorders associated with the serotonin selective reuptake inhibitors. *J Clin Psychiatry* 57 (10): 449–54.

18 **potentially life-threatening damage to heart valves** Connolly, H. M., et al. 1997. Valvular heart disease associated with fenfluramine-phentermine. *N Engl J Med* 337 (9): 581–88.

18 *discontinuation syndrome* Black, K., et al. 2000. Selective serotonin reuptake inhibitor discontinuation syndrome: Proposed diagnostic criteria. *J Psychiatry Neurosci* 25 (3): 255–61; Coupland, N. J., C. J. Bell, and J. P. Potokar. 1996. Serotonin reuptake inhibitor withdrawal. *J Clin Psychopharmacol* 16 (5): 356–62.

18 **paroxetine (Paxil) is the most dramatic ... example** Belloeuf, L., C. Le Jeunne, and F. C. Hugues. 2000. [Paroxetine withdrawal syndrome.] *Ann Med Interne* (Paris) 151 suppl. A: A52–53.

19 **as much ... suicidal potential as the tricyclics** Fergusson, D., et al. 2005. Association between suicide attempts and selective serotonin reuptake inhibitors: Systematic review of randomised controlled trials. *BMJ* 330 (7488): 396.

19 **SSRI overdoses are less likely** Barbey, J. T., and S. P. Roose. 1998. SSRI safety in overdose. *J Clin Psychiatry* 59 suppl. 15: 542–48; Nelson, L. S., et al. 2007. Selective serotonin reuptake inhibitor poisoning: An evidence-based consensus guideline for out-of-hospital management. *Clin Toxicol* (Phila) 45 (4): 315–32.

19 **serotonin syndrome** Boyer, E. W., and M. Shannon. 2005. The serotonin syndrome. *NEJM* 352 (11): 1112–20; Brody, J. 2007. A mix of medicines that can be lethal. *New York Times,* February 27, 2007, http://www.nytimes.com/2007/02/27/health/27brody.htm.

19 **SSRIs may actually precipitate suicidal thoughts** Teicher, M. H., C. A. Glod, and J. O. Cole. Emergence of intense suicidal preoccupation during fluoxetine treatment. *Am J Psychiatry* 147 (2): 207–10; Teicher, M. H., C. A. Glod, and J. O. Cole. 1993. Antidepressant drugs and the emergence of suicidal tendencies. *Drug Saf* 8 (3): 186–212.

19 **effect is most apparent** Jick et al., Antidepressants and the risk of suicidal behaviors.

19 **epidemiological data from Great Britain** Healy, D. 2003. Lines of evidence on the risks of suicide with selective serotonin reuptake inhibitors. *Psychother Psychosom* 72 (2): 71–79.

19 **an *increase* in suicidal thoughts** Gibbons, R. D., et al. 2007. Early evidence on the effects of regulators' suicidality warnings on SSRI prescriptions and suicide in children and adolescents. *Am J Psychiatry* 164 (9): 1356–63; Mosholder, A. D., and M. Willy. 2006. Suicidal adverse events in pediatric randomized, controlled clinical trials of antidepressant drugs are associated with active drug treatment: A meta-analysis. *J Child Adolesc Psychopharmacol* 16 (1–2): 25–32; Leslie, L. K., et al. 2005. The Food and Drug Administration's deliberations on antidepressant use in pediatric patients. *Pediatrics* 116 (1): 195–204; Bridge, J. A., et al. 2005. The risks and benefits of antidepressant treatment for youth depression. *Ann Med* 37 (6): 404–12.

19 **with a strong "black box"warning** http://www.fda.gov/cder/drug/antidepressants/anti depressants_label_change_2007.pdf.

20 **only seventeen hundred were involved in placebo-controlled trials** Breggin and Breggin. *Talking back to Prozac.*

20 **file-drawer effect** Lieberman, J. A., J. Greenhouse, R. M. Hamer, K. R. Krishnan, C. B. Nemeroff, D. V. Sheehan et al. 2005. Comparing the effects of antidepressants: Consensus guidelines for evaluating quantitative reviews of antidepressant efficacy. *Neuropsychopharmacology* 30 (3): 445–60; Kirsch et al. The emperor's new drugs.

21 **many studies ... were flawed** Antonuccio, D. O., et al. 1999. Raising questions about antidepressants. *Psychother Psychosom* 68 (1): 3–14; Antonuccio, D. O., D. Burns, and W. Danton.

2002. Antidepressants: a triumph of marketing over science? *Prevention & Treatment* 5 (Article 25).

21 **few ... used "active" placebos** Moncrieff, J., S. Wessely, and R. Hardy. 2004. Active placebos versus antidepressants for depression. *Cochrane Database Syst Rev* no.1: CD003012.

21 **A recent study by the ... Cochrane Collaboration** Moncrieff et al. Active placebos.

22 **One "systematic review"** Williams, J. W., Jr, et al. 2000. A systematic review of newer pharmacotherapies for depression in adults: Evidence report summary. *Ann Intern Med* 132 (9): 743–56.

22 **another review** Khan, A., H. A. Warner, and W. A. Brown. 2000. Symptom reduction and suicide risk in patients treated with placebo in antidepressant clinical trials: An analysis of the Food and Drug Administration database. *Arch Gen Psychiatry* 57 (4): 311–17.

22 **Another review article** Storosum, J. G., et al. 2001. Short-term efficacy of tricyclic antidepressants revisited: A meta-analytic study. *Eur Neuropsychopharmacol* 11 (2): 173–80.

22 **a "Special Article"** Turner, E. H., et al. 2008. Selective publication of antidepressant trials and its influence on apparent efficacy. *N Engl J Med* 358 (3): 252–60.

22 **the improvement that was noted** Stahl, S. M. 1999. Why settle for silver, when you can go for gold? Response vs. recovery as the goal of antidepressant therapy. *J Clin Psychiatry* 60 (4): 213–14; Trivedi, M. H., A. J. Rush, S. R. Wisniewski, A. A. Nierenberg, D. Warden, and L. Ritz et al. 2006. Evaluation of outcomes with citalopram for depression using measurement-based care in STAR*D: Implications for clinical practice. *Am J Psychiatry* 163 (1): 28–40.

23 **does not appear that they are more effective** DeRubeis, R. J., et al. 1999. Medications versus cognitive behavior therapy for severely depressed outpatients: Meta-analysis of four randomized comparisons. *Am J Psychiatry* 156 (7): 1007–13; Elkin, I., et al. National Institute of Mental Health Treatment of Depression Collaborative Research Program. General effectiveness of treatments; Shea, M. T., et al., Course of depressive symptoms over follow-up.

23 **This multiyear, multicenter effort concluded** Elkin et al. *General effectiveness of treatments.*

23 **patients who received Imipramine** Shea et al., Course of depressive symptoms over follow-up.

23 **More recent research** Casacalenda, N., J. C. Perry, and K. Looper. 2002. Remission in major depressive disorder: A comparison of pharmacotherapy, psychotherapy, and control conditions. *Am J Psychiatry* 159 (8): 1354–60; Ekers, D., D. Richards, and S. Gilbody. In press. A meta-analysis of randomized trials of behavioural treatment of depression. *Psychol Med;* March, J., et al. 2004. Fluoxetine, cognitive-behavioral therapy, and their combination for adolescents with depression: Treatment for Adolescents with Depression Study (TADS) randomized controlled trial. *JAMA* 292 (7): 807–20; Schramm, E., et al. 2007. An intensive treatment program of interpersonal psychotherapy plus pharmacotherapy for depressed inpatients: Acute and long-term results. *Am J Psychiatry* 164 (5): 768–77; Thase, M. E., et al. 1997. Treatment of major depression with psychotherapy or psychotherapy-pharmacotherapy combinations. *Arch Gen Psychiatry* 54 (11): 1009–15; Keller, M. B., et al. 2000. A comparison of nefazodone, the cognitive behavioral–analysis system of psychotherapy, and their combination for the treatment of chronic depression. *N Engl J Med* 342 (20): 1462–70.

23 **one ... study noted a subgroup** Nemeroff, C. B., et al. 2003. Differential responses to psychotherapy versus pharmacotherapy in patients with chronic forms of major depression and childhood trauma. *PNAS* 100 (24): 14293–96.

23 **both antidepressant drugs and psychotherapy** Martin, S. D., et al. 2001. Brain blood flow changes in depressed patients treated with interpersonal psychotherapy or venlafaxine hydrochloride: Preliminary findings. *Arch Gen Psychiatry* 58 (7): 641–48; Roffman, J. L., et al. 2005. Neuroimaging and the functional neuroanatomy of psychotherapy. *Psychol Med* 35 (10): 1385–98; Goldapple, K., et al. 2004. Modulation of cortical-limbic pathways in major depression: Treatment-specific effects of cognitive behavior therapy. *Arch Gen Psychiatry* 61 (1): 34–41.

24 **Each of these techniques** References for the effectiveness of all of these techniques will be provided as each is discussed in the text of *Unstuck.*

28 **Every organ and every cell become more vulnerable** Lovallo, W. R. 2004. *Stress and health: Biological and psychological interactions.* Thousand Oaks: Sage Publications.

28 **those who do experience painful ... early-life losses** McLeod, J. D. 1981. Childhood parental

loss and adult depression. *J Health Soc Behav* 32 (3): 205–20; Meaney, M. J. 2001. Maternal care, gene expression, and the transmission of individual differences in stress reactivity across generations. *Annu Rev Neurosci* 24: 1161–92; Kaufman, J., P. M. Plotsky, C. B. Nemeroff, and D. S. Charney. 2000. Effects of early adverse experiences on brain structure and function: Clinical implications. *Biol Psychiatry* 48 (8): 778–90.

28 **people who are depressed or "stressed out"** Chrousos, G. P., and P. W. Gold. 1998. A healthy body in a healthy mind—and vice versa—the damaging power of "uncontrollable" stress. *J Clin Endocrinol Metab* 83 (6): 1842–45; Bremner, J. D. 2002. *Does stress damage the brain?: Understanding trauma-related disorders*. New York: W. W. Norton.

28 **Prolonged overactivity** Sulman, F. G., Y. Pfeifer, and E. Superstine. 1977. The adrenal exhaustion syndrome: An adrenal deficiency. *Ann N Y Acad Sci* 301:918–30.

28 **decreased metabolism in parts of the frontal lobe** Bench, C. J., et al. 1992. The anatomy of melancholia—focal abnormalities of cerebral blood flow in major depression. *Psychol Med* 22 (3): 607–15.

28 **Continuing high levels of stress hormones** Sapolsky, R. M., et al. 1990. Hippocampal damage associated with prolonged glucocorticoid exposure in primates. *J Neurosci* 10 (9): 2897–2902.

28 **abnormalities in the levels of the various neurotransmitters** Ressler, K. J., and C. B. Nemeroff. 2000. Role of serotonergic and noradrenergic systems in the pathophysiology of depression and anxiety disorders. *Depress Anxiety* 12 suppl. 1: S2–19.

28–29 **Low-income and unemployed people and those with fewer close connections** Kuruvilla, A., and K. S. Jacob. 2007. Poverty, social stress, and mental health. *Indian J Med Res* 126 (4): 273–78; Kessler, R. C., et al. 2003. The epidemiology of major depressive disorder: results from the National Comorbidity Survey Replication (NCS-R). *JAMA* 289 (23): 3095–3105; House, J. S., K. R. Landis, and D. Umberson. 1988. Social relationships and health. *Science* 241 (4865): 540–45; Berkman, L. F., and S. L. Syme. 1979. Social networks, host resistance, and mortality: A nine-year follow-up study of Alameda County residents. *Am J Epidemiol* 109 (2): 186–204; Hollingshead, A. B. and F. C. Redlich. Social

class and mental illness: A community study, 1958. *Am J Public Health* 97 (10): 1756–57.

29 **women are diagnosed** Kessler et al., The epidemiology of major depressive disorder; Nobel, R. E. 2005. Depression in women. *Metabolism* 54 (5): 49–52; Burt, V. K., and K. Stein. 2002. Epidemiology of depression throughout the female life cycle. *J Clin Psychiatry* 63 suppl. 7: S9–15.

29 **cognitive behavioral therapy** Hammerfald, K., et al. 2006. Persistent effects of cognitive-behavioral stress management on cortisol responses to acute stress in healthy subjects—a randomized controlled trial. *Psychoneuroendocrinology* 31 (3): 333–39.

29 **by writing in a journal** Pennebaker, J. W., J. K. Kiecolt-Glaser, and R. Glaser. 1988. Disclosure of traumas and immune function: Health implications for psychotherapy. *J Consult Clin Psychol* 56 (2): 239–45; Smyth, J. M., et al. 1999. Effects of writing about stressful experiences on symptom reduction in patients with asthma or rheumatoid arthritis: A randomized trial. *JAMA* 281 (14): 1304–9.

29 **Just by talking with another human being** Martin, S. D., et al. 2001. Brain blood flow changes in depressed patients treated with interpersonal psychotherapy or venlafaxine hydrochloride: Preliminary findings. *Arch Gen Psychiatry* 58 (7): 641–48; Goldapple, et al., Modulation of cortical-limbic pathways.

29 **easily learned mind-body approaches** Speca, M., et al. 2000. A randomized, wait-list controlled clinical trial: The effect of a mindfulness meditation–based stress reduction program on mood and symptoms of stress in cancer outpatients. *Psychosom Med* 62 (5): 613–22; Watanabe, E., S. Fukuda, and T. Shirakawa. 2005. Effects among healthy subjects of the duration of regularly practicing a guided imagery program. *BMC Complement Altern Med* 5:21; Rees, B. L. 1995. Effect of relaxation with guided imagery on anxiety, depression, and self-esteem in primiparas. *J Holist Nurs* 13 (3): 255–67; Lating, J., G. Everly, T. Peragine, M. Neel, N. Glick, and M. Sherman. Biofeedback-assisted relaxation as part of preincident stress-management training within a model of comprehensive crisis intervention: A pilot study. *Brief Treat Crisis Interv* 3: 437–443.

29 **shift brain functioning from areas of the cortex** Davidson, R. J., J. Kabat-Zinn, J. Schumacher, M. Rosenkranz, D. Muller,

S.F. Santorelli, F. Urbanowski, A. Harrington, K. Bonus, J. F. Sheridan. 2003. Alterations in brain and immune function produced by mindfulness meditation. *Psychosom Med* 65 (4): 564–70.

29 **regulate the level of our neurotransmitters** MacLean, C. R., et al. 1997. Effects of the transcendental meditation program on adaptive mechanisms: Changes in hormone levels and responses to stress after 4 months of practice. *Psychoneuroendocrinology* 22 (4): 277–95; Infante, J., et al. 2001. Catecholamine levels in practitioners of the transcendental meditation technique. *Physiol Behav* 72: 141–46; Infante, J., et al. 1998. ACTH and beta-endorphin in transcendental meditation. *Physiol Behav* 64 (3): 311–15.

30 **significant thickening** Lazar et al. Meditation experience.

30 **Physical exercise has similar direct effects** Soares, J., M. G. Naffah-Mazzacoratti, and E. A. Cavalheiro. 1994. Increased serotonin levels in physically trained men. *Braz J Med Biol Res* 27 (7): 1635–38; Carr, D. B., et al. 1981. Physical conditioning facilitates the exercise-induced secretion of beta-endorphin and beta-lipotropin in women. *N Engl J Med* 305 (10): 560–63; van Praag, H., et al. 2005. Exercise enhances learning and hippocampal neurogenesis in aged mice. *J Neurosci* 25 (38): 8680–85; Ransford, C. P. 1982. A role for amines in the antidepressant effect of exercise: A review. *Med Sci Sports Exerc* 14 (1): 1–10.

30 **exercise may *by itself* be as effective** Dimeo, F., et al. 2001. Benefits from aerobic exercise in patients with major depression: A pilot study. *Br J Sports Med* 35 (2): 114–17; Babyak, M., et al. 2000. Exercise treatment for major depression: Maintenance of therapeutic benefit at 10 months. *Psychosom Med* 62 (5): 633–38; Blumenthal, J. A., et al. 1999. Effects of exercise training on older patients with major depression. *Arch Intern Med* 159 (19): 2349–56.

30 **eliminating or cutting down significantly on certain foods** Christensen, L., and R. Burrows. 1990. Dietary treatment of depression. *Behav Therapy* 21: 183–93.

30 **Some depressed people seem to have sensitivities to foods** Parker, G., and T. Watkins. 2002. Treatment-resistant depression: When antidepressant drug intolerance may indicate food intolerance. *Aust N Z J Psychiatry* 36 (2): 263–65.

30 **Inadequate levels of some nutrients** Brozek, J. 1957. Psychological effects of thiamine restriction and deprivation in normal young men. *Am*

J Clin Nutr 5: 109–18; Gilbody, S., T. Lightfoot, and T. Sheldon. 2007. Is low folate a risk factor for depression? A meta-analysis and exploration of heterogeneity. *J Epidemiol Community Health* 61 (7): 631–37; Tiemeier, H., et al. 2002. Vitamin B_{12}, folate, and homocysteine in depression: The Rotterdam Study. *Am J Psychiatry* 159 (12): 2099–2101; Hvas, A. M., et al. 2004. Vitamin B_6 level is associated with symptoms of depression. *Psychother Psychosom* 73 (6): 340–43; Tiemeier et al. Vitamin B_{12}, folate, and homocysteine in depression; Penninx, B. W., J. M. Guralnik, L. Ferrucci, L. P. Fried, R. H. Allen, and S. P. Stabler. 2000. Vitamin B(12) deficiency and depression in physically disabled older women: Epidemiologic evidence from the Women's Health and Aging Study. *Am J Psychiatry* 157 (5): 715–21; Kinsman, R. A., and J. Hood. 1971. Some behavioral effects of ascorbic acid deficiency. *Am J Clin Nutr* 24 (4): 455–64; Rasmussen, H. H., P. B. Mortensen, and I. W. Jensen. Depression and magnesium deficiency. *Int J Psychiatry Med* 19 (1): 57–63; Eby, G. A., and K. L. Eby. 2006. Rapid recovery from major depression using magnesium treatment. *Med Hypotheses* 67 (2): 362–70; Maes, M., et al. 1999. Lower serum zinc in major depression in relation to changes in serum acute phase proteins. *J Affect Disord* 56 (2–3): 189–94; Maes, M., et al. 1994. Hypozincemia in depression. *J Affect Disord* 31 (2): 135–40; Benton, D. 2002. Selenium intake, mood and other aspects of psychological functioning. *Nutr Neurosci* 5 (6): 363–74; Benton, D., and R. Cook. 1991. The impact of selenium supplementation on mood. *Biol Psychiatry* 29 (11): 1092–98; McLeod, M. N. and R. N. Golden. 2000. Chromium treatment of depression. *Int J Neuropsychopharmacol* 3 (4): 311–14; Davidson, J. R., et al. 2003. Effectiveness of chromium in atypical depression: A placebo-controlled trial. *Biol Psychiatry* 53 (3): 261–64.

30 **Acupuncture can improve mood** Han, J. S. 1986. Electroacupuncture: An alternative to antidepressants for treating affective diseases? *Int J Neurosci* 29 (1–2): 79–92; Luo, H. C., Y. K. Jia, and Z. Li. 1985. Electro-acupuncture vs. amitriptyline in the treatment of depressive states. *J Tradit Chin Med* 5 (1): 3–8; Han, C., et al. 2004. Clinical study on electro-acupuncture treatment for 30 cases of mental depression. *J Tradit Chin Med* 24 (3): 172–76; Manber, R., et al. 2004. Acupuncture: A promising treatment for depression during pregnancy. *J Affect Disord* 83

(1): 89–95; Schnyer, R. N. and J. J. Allen. 2001. *Acupuncture in the treatment of depression: A manual for practice and research.* London: Churchill Livingston Press.

30 **Saint-John's-wort has demonstrated** Schrader, E. 2000. Equivalence of St. John's wort extract (Ze 117) and fluoxetine: A randomized, controlled study in mild-moderate depression. *Int Clin Psychopharmacol* 15 (2): 61–68; Szegedi, A., et al. 2005. Acute treatment of moderate to severe depression with hypericum extract WS 5570 (St. John's wort): Randomized controlled double-blind non-inferiority trial versus paroxetine. *BMJ* 330 (7490): 503; Kasper, S., et al. 2006. Superior efficacy of St. John's wort extract WS 5570 compared to placebo in patients with major depression: A randomized, double-blind, placebo-controlled, multi-center trial [ISRCTN77277298]. *BMC Med* 4:14; Kalb, R., R. D. Trautmann-Sponsel, and M. Kieser. 2001. Efficacy and tolerability of hypericum extract WS 5572 versus placebo in mildly to moderately depressed patients: A randomized double-blind multicenter clinical trial. *Pharmacopsychiatry* 34 (3): 96–103; Lecrubier, Y., et al. 2002. Efficacy of St. John's wort extract WS 5570 in major depression: A double-blind, placebo-controlled trial. *Am J Psychiatry* 159 (8): 1361–66.

32 **hope is the necessary medium of this work** Kobasa, S. C. 1979. Stressful life events, personality, and health: An inquiry into hardiness. *J Pers Soc Psychol* 37:1–11; Taylor, S. E., M. E. Kemeny, G. M. Reed, J. E. Bower, and T. L. Gruenewald. 2000. Psychological resources, positive illusions, and health. *Am Psychol* 55 (1): 99–109; Buccheri, G.F., D. Ferrigno, M. Tamburnini, and C. Brunelli. 1995. The patient's perception of his own quality of life might have an adjunctive prognostic significant in lung cancer. *Lung Cancer* 12 (1–2): 45–58.

33 **Connection . . . is critical for almost all of us** House, J. S., K. R. Landis, and D. Umberson. 1988. Social relationships and health. *Science* 241 (4865): 540–45; Kawachi, I., and L. F. Berkman. 2001. Social ties and mental health. *J Urban Health* 78 (3): 458–67; Fu, S. Y., et al. 2007. The relationship between culture, attitude, social networks and quality of life in midlife Australian and Taiwanese citizens. *Maturitas* 58 (3): 285–95.

34 **Both concentrative and awareness meditation** Davidson et al. Delmont, M. M. 1984. Electrocortical activity and related phenomena associated with meditation practice: A literature review. *Int J Neurosci* 24 (3–4); 217–31; Infante, et al. Catecholamine levels in practitioners; Infante, et al. ACTH and beta-endorphin in transcendental meditation; Jevning, et al. Effects on regional cerebral blood flow; Lazar et al. Meditation experience; Lehmann, D., et al. 2001. Brain sources of EEG gamma frequency during volitionally meditation-induced, altered states of consciousness, and experience of the self. *Psychiatry Res* 108 (2); 111–21; A. Lutz, L. L. Greischar, N. B. Rawlings, M. Ricard, and R. J. Davidson. 2004. Long-term meditators self-induce high-amplitude gamma synchrony during mental practice. *PNAS* 101 (46): 16369–73; MacLean et al., Effects of the transcendental meditation program; Newberg, A., and J. Iversen. 2003. The neural basis of the complex mental task of meditation: Neurotransmitter and neurochemical considerations. *Med Hypotheses* 61 (2): 282–91; Tooley, G., et al. 2000. Acute increases in night-time plasma melatonin levels following a period of meditation. *Biol Psychol* 53: 69–78; Barnes, V. A., F. A. Trieber, and H. Davis. 2001. Impact of transcendental meditation on cardiovascular function at rest and during acute stress in adolescents with high normal blood pressure. *J Psychosom Res* 51: 597–605; Benson, H., et al. 1990. Three case reports of the metabolic and electroencephalographic changes during advanced Buddhist meditation techniques. *Behav Med* 16 (2): 90–95; Curiati, J. A., E. Bocchi, J. O. Freire, A. C. Arantes, M. Braga, Y. Garcia, G. Guimaraes, and W. J. Fo. 2005. Meditation reduces sympathetic activation and improves the quality of life in elderly patients with optimally treated heart failure: A prospective randomized study. *J Altern Complement Med* 11 (3): 465–72; Dwyer, J. H., C. N. Merz, S. Nidich, M. Paul-Labrador, D. Polk, M. Rainforth, R. Schneider, and I. Velasquez. 2006. Effects of a randomized controlled trial of transcendental meditation on components of the metabolic syndrome in subjects with coronary heart disease. *Arch Intern Med* 166 (11): 1218–24. Wenneberg, S. R., et al. 1997. A controlled study of the effects of the transcendental meditation program on cardiovascular reactivity and ambulatory blood pressure. *Int J Neurosci* 89 (1–2): 15–28; Zamarra, J. W., et al. 1996. Usefulness of the transcendental meditation program in the treatment of patients with coronary artery disease. *Am J Cardiol* 77 (10): 867–70.

34 **their positive effects on mood and anxiety**

Williams, K. A. et al. 2001. Evaluation of a wellness-based mindfulness stress reduction intervention: A controlled trial. *Amer J Health Prom* 15 (6): 422–32; Speca, A randomized, wait-list controlled clinical trial; Miller, J. J., et al. 1995. Three-year follow-up and clinical implications of a mindfulness meditation–based stress reduction intervention in the treatment of anxiety disorders. *Gen Hosp Psychiatry* 17 (3): 192–200. Kutz, I., et al. 1985. Meditation as an adjunct to psychotherapy: An outcome study. *Psychother Psychosom* 43 (4): 209–18; Kabat-Zinn, J., et al. 1998. Influence of a mindfulness meditation–based stress reduction intervention on rates of skin clearing in patients with moderate to severe psoriases. *Psychosom Med* 60 (5): 625–32; Brown, K. W. and R. M. Ryan. 2003. The benefits of being present: Mindfulness and its role in psychological well-being. *J Pers Soc Psychol* 84 (4): 822–48; Carlson, L. E., and S. N. Garland. 2005. Impact of mindfulness-based stress reduction (MBSR) on sleep, mood, stress, and fatigue symptoms of cancer outpatients. *Int J Behav Med* 12 (4): 278–85; Carlson, L. E., M. Speca, K. D. Patel, and E. Goodey. 2004. Mindfulness-based stress reduction in relation to quality of life, mood, symptoms of stress, and levels of cortisol, dehydroepiandrosterone sulfate (DHEAS), and melatonin in breast and prostate cancer outpatients. *Psychoneuroendocrinology* 29: 448–74; Finucane, A., and S. W. Mercer. 2006. An exploratory mixed methods study of the acceptability and effectiveness of mindfulness-based cognitive therapy for patients with active depression and anxiety in primary care. *BMC Psychiatry* 6: 14; Galvin, J. A., H. Benson, G. R. Deckro, G. L. Fricchione, and J. A. Dusek. 2006. The relaxation response: Reducing stress and improving cognition in healthy aging adults. *Complement Ther Clin Pract* 12 (3): 186–91; Teasdale, J. D., et al. 2000. Prevention of relapse/recurrence in major depression by mindfulness-based cognitive therapy. *J Consult Clin Psychol* 68: 615–23.

35 **"the relaxation response"** Benson, H. 1975. *The relaxation response*. New York: William Morrow.

35 **Slow, deep breathing also decreases our blood pressure** Elliott, W.J., and J. L. Izzo Jr. 2006. Device-guided breathing to lower blood pressure: Case report and clinical overview. *MedGenMed* 8 (3): 23; Bernardi, L., et al. 2001. Effect of rosary prayer and yoga mantras on autonomic cardiovascular rhythms: Comparative study. *BMJ* 323 (7327): 1446–49.

35 **PET scans and MRIs** Lou et al. A 15O–H$_2$O PET study of meditation; Lazar et al., Functional brain mapping; Davidson et al., Alterations in brain and immune function; Davidson, R. J. 2004. Well-being and affective style: Neural substrates and biobehavioural correlates. *Philos Trans R Soc Lond B Biol Sci* 359 (1449): 1395–1411; Jevning et al., Effects on regional cerebral blood flow.

41 **"archetypal" journeys** Jung, C. *Psychology and Religion*. 1960. New Haven: Yale University Press.

CHAPTER ONE: THE CALL: FINDING THE RIGHT WAY

48 *The Odyssey* Homer. 1992. *The Odyssey*. Trans. R. Fitzgerald. New York: Knopf.

48 **Dante Alighieri** Alighieri, D. 1974. *The Divine Comedy of Dante Alighieri*. Trans. J. D. Sinclair. New York: Oxford Univeristy Press.

48 **Greek hymn of Demeter** Luke, H. M. 1981. *Woman: Earth and spirit, the feminine in symbol and myth*. New York: Crossroad.

54 **Beck Depression Inventory (BDI)** Beck, A. T., et al. 1961. An inventory for measuring depression. *Arch Gen Psychiatry* 4: 561–71.

60 **Center for Epidemiological Studies scale (CES-D)** Radloff, L. 1997. The CES-D scale: A self-report depression scale for research in the general population. *Appl Psych Meas* 1 (3): 385–401.

64 **James W. Pennebaker and his colleagues and students** Pennebaker, J. W., J. K. Kiecolt-Glaser, and R. Glaser. 1998. Disclosure of traumas and immune function: Health implications for psychotherapy. *J Consult Clin Psychol* 56 (2): 239–45; Hemenover, S.H. 2003. The good, the bad, and the healthy: Impacts of emotional disclosure of trauma on resilient self-concept and psychological distress. *Pers Soc Psychol Bull* 29 (10): 1236–44; Smyth, J. M., et al. 1999. Effects of writing about stressful experiences on symptom reduction in patients with asthma or rheumatoid arthritis: A randomized trial. *JAMA* 281 (14): 1304–9.

69 **Sometimes the very drugs** Glenmullen, J. 2000. *Prozac backlash: Overcoming the dangers of Prozac, Zoloft, Paxil, and other antidepressants with safe, effective alternatives*. New York: Simon & Schuster.

69 **SSRIs . . . may provoke an agitated**

Lipinski, J. F., Jr. et al. 1989. Fluoxetine-induced akathisia: Clinical and theoretical implications. *J Clin Psychiatry* 50 (9): 339–42; Hansen, L. 2003. Fluoxetine dose-increment-related akathisia in depression: Implications for clinical care, recognition, and management of selective serotonin reuptake inhibitor–induced akathisia. *J Psychopharmacol* 17 (4): 451–52.

69 **It's well known that** Markou, A., T. R. Kosten, and G. F. Koob. 1998. Neurobiological similarities in depression and drug dependence: A self-medication hypothesis. *Neuropsychopharmacology* 18 (3): 135–74. Also, for example, John, U., C. Meyer, H. J. Rumpf, and U. Hapke. 2004. Depressive disorders are related to nicotine dependence in the population but do not necessarily hamper smoking cessation. *J Clin Psychiatry* 65 (2): 169–76; Schuckit, M. A. 1994. Alcohol and depression: A clinical perspective. *Acta Psychiatr Scand Sup* 377: 28–32.

70 **people improved significantly when they stopped** Christensen, L., and R. Burrows. 1990. Dietary treatment of depression. *Behav Therapy* 21:183–93.

70 **Aspartame (NutraSweet)** Walton, R. G., R. Hudak, and R. J. Green-Waite. 1993. Adverse reactions to aspartame: Double-blind challenge in patients from a vulnerable population. *Biol Psychiatry* 34 (1–2): 13–17.

70 **Hypothyroidism** Cleare, A. J., A. McGregor, and V. O'Keane. 1995. Neuroendocrine evidence for an association between hypothyroidism, reduced central 5-HT activity, and depression. *Clin Endocrinol (Oxf)* 43 (6): 713–19.

70 **diabetes** Anderson, R. J., et al. 2001. The prevalence of comorbid depression in adults with diabetes: A meta-analysis. *Diabetes Care,* 24 (6): 1069–78.

70 **lupus erythematosus** Nery, F. G., et al. 2007. Major depressive disorder and disease activity in systemic lupus erythematosus. *Compr Psychiatry* 48 (1): 14–19.

70 **cancer** Carney, C. P. et al. 2003. Relationship between depression and pancreatic cancer in the general population. *Psychosom Med* 65 (5): 884–88.

70 **acquired immune deficiency syndrome (AIDS)** Penzak, S. R., Y. S. Reddy, and S. R. Grimsley. 2000. Depression in patients with HIV infection. *Am J Health Syst Pharm* 57 (4): 376–86, quiz 387–89; Perry, S. W., III. 1994. HIV-related depression. *Res Publ Assoc Res Nerv Ment Dis* 72:223–38.

70 **Cushing's disease** Sonino, N., and G. A. Fava. 2001. Psychiatric disorders associated with Cushing's syndrome. Epidemiology, pathophysiology, and treatment. *CNS Drugs* 15 (5): 361–73.

70 **Addison's disease** Iwata, M., et al. 2004. [A case of Addison's disease presented with depression as a first symptom.] *Seishin Shinkeigaku Zasshi* 106 (9): 1110–16.

70 **autoimmune illnesses** Nery et al, Major depressive disorder and disease activity; Palkonyai, E., et al. 2007. Depressive symptoms in early rheumatoid arthritis: A comparative longitudinal study. *Clin Rheumatol* 26 (5): 753–58.

71 **strokes** Barker-Collo, S. L. 2007. Depression and anxiety 3 months post stroke: Prevalence and correlates. *Arch Clin Neuropsychol* 22 (4): 519–31.

71 **chronic fatigue immune deficiency syndrome (CFIDS)** http://www.cdc.gov/cfs/cfssymptomsHCP.htm.

71 **chronic pain** Ohayon, M. M., and A. F. Schatzberg. 2003. Using chronic pain to predict depressive morbidity in the general population. *Arch Gen Psychiatry* 60 (1): 39–47.

71 **diabetes** Anderson et al., Depression in adults with diabetes.

71 **heart disease** Kemp, D. E., et al. 2003. Heart disease and depression: Don't ignore the relationship. *Cleve Clin J Med* 70 (9): 745–46, 749–50, 752–54.

71 **infections** Abe, K. 1988. Depression after each respiratory tract infection in an adolescent girl. *J Nerv Ment Dis* 176 (9): 573–74; Fallon, B. A., and Nields, J. A. 1994. Lyme disease: A neuropsychiatric illness. *Am J Psychiatry* 151 (11): 1571–83.

71 **chronic obstructive pulmonary disease** Light, R. W., et al. 1985. Prevalence of depression and anxiety in patients with COPD. Relationship to functional capacity. *Chest* 87 (1): 35–38.

71 **multiple sclerosis** Zorzon, M., et al. 2002. Depressive symptoms and MRI changes in multiple sclerosis. *Eur J Neurol* 9 (5): 491–96.

71 **Parkinson's disease** Koerts, J., et al. 2007. Striatal dopaminergic activity (FDOPA-PET) associated with cognitive items of a depression scale (MADRS) in Parkinson's disease. *Eur J Neurosci* 25 (10): 3132–36.

71 **thyroid disease** Lee, I. T., et al. 2003. Relationship of stressful life events, anxiety, and depression to hyperthyroidism in an Asian pop-

ulation. *Horm Res* 60 (5): 247–51; Cleare et al., *Neuroendocrine evidence.*

71 **trauma to the head** Holsinger, T., et al. 2002. Head injury in early adulthood and the lifetime risk of depression. *Arch Gen Psychiatry* 59 (1): 17–22.

71 **Wilson's disease** Krishnakumar, P., and A. Riyaz. 2005. Wilson's disease presenting as depressive disorder. *Indian Pediatr* 42 (11): 1172–73.

72 **elevated levels of corticosteroids** Dinan, T. G. 1994. Glucocorticoids and the genesis of depressive illness: A psychobiological model. *Br J Psychiatry* 164 (3): 365–71.

72 **Very low levels [of coritcosteroids]** Heim, C., U. Ehlert, and D. H. Hellhammer. 2000. The potential role of hypocortisolism in the pathophysiology of stress-related bodily disorders. *Psychoneuroendocrinology* 25 (1): 1–35.

72 **chronic yeast infections** Crook, W., and M. Jones. 1989. *The yeast connection handbook.* 1999. Jackson, TN: Professional Books/Future Health.

73 **do implicate heavy metals** Cordeiro, Q., Jr, M. de Araujo Medrado Faria, and R. Fraguas, Jr. 2003. Depression, insomnia, and memory loss in a patient with chronic intoxication by inorganic mercury. *J Neuropsychiatry Clin Neurosci* 15 (4): 457–58; Powell, T. J. 2000. Chronic neurobehavioural effects of mercury poisoning on a group of Zulu chemical workers. *Brain Inj* 14 (9): 797–814; Otto, D., Y. Xia, Y. Li, K. Wu, L. He, J. Telech et al. 2007. Neurosensory effects of chronic human exposure to arsenic associated with body burden and environmental measures. *Hum Exp Toxicol,* 26 (3): 169–77; Schlegel-Zawadzka, M., A. Zieba, D. Dudek, J. Zak-Knapik, and G. Nowak. 1999. Is serum copper a "trait marker of unipolar depression? A preliminary clinical study. *Pol J Pharmacol* 51 (6): 535–38.

74 **a fascinating connection between** Logan, A. C., and M. Katzman. 2005. Major depressive disorder: Probiotics may be an adjuvant therapy. *Med Hypotheses* 64 (3): 533–38.

74 **may be significantly decreased by stress** Holdeman, L. V., I. J. Good, and W. E. Moore. 1976. Human fecal flora: Variation in bacterial composition within individuals and a possible effect of emotional stress. *Appl Environ Microbiol* 31 (3): 359–75; Lizko, N. N. 1987. Stress and intestinal microflora. *Nahrung* 31 (5–6): 443–47; Moore, W. E., E. P. Cato, and L. V. Holdeman.

1978. Some current concepts in intestinal bacteriology. *Am J Clin Nutr* 31 suppl.: S33–42.

75 **seem to benefit from repopulating** Gruenwald, J., H. J. Graubaum, and A. Harde. 2002. Effect of a probiotic multivitamin compound on stress and exhaustion. *Adv Ther* 19 (3): 141–50; Pimentel, M., E. J. Chow, and H. C. Lin. 2000. Eradication of small intestinal bacterial overgrowth reduces symptoms of irritable bowel syndrome. *Am J Gastroenterol* 95 (12): 3503–506.

75 **increase these beneficial bacteria** Pimentel et al., Eradication of small intestinal bacterial overgrowth; Kuda, T., T. Enomoto, T. Yano, and T. Fujii. 2000. Cecal environment and TBARS level in mice fed corn oil, beef tallow, and menhaden fish oil. *J Nutr Sci Vitaminol* (Tokyo) 46 (2): 65–70.

75 **work in concert with them** Gruenwald et al., Effect of a probiotic multivitamin compound.

75 **psychiatrist Norman Rosenthal** Rosenthal, N. 2006. *Winter blues: Everything you need to know to beat seasonal affective disorder.* Rev. ed. New York: Guilford Press.

76 **A number of studies** Magnusson, A., and H. Kristbjarnarson. 1991. Treatment of seasonal affective disorder with high-intensity light: A phototherapy study with an Icelandic group of patients. *J Affect Disord,* 21 (2): 141–47; Terman, J. S., et al. 1990. Efficacy of brief, intense light exposure for treatment of winter depression. *Psychopharmacol Bull* 26 (1): 3–11; Terman, M., J. S. Terman, and D. C. Ross. 1998. A controlled trial of timed bright light and negative air ionization for treatment of winter depression. *Arch Gen Psychiatry* 55 (10): 875–82.

76 **Though side effects** Terman, M., and J. S. Terman. 1999. Bright light therapy: Side effects and benefits across the symptom spectrum. *J Clin Psychiatry* 60 (11): 799–808, quiz 809.

76 **full-spectrum light may be helpful** Prasko, J., et al. 2002. Bright light therapy and/or imipramine for inpatients with recurrent non-seasonal depression. *Neuro Endocrinol Lett* 23 (2): 109–13; Martiny, K., et al. 2005. Adjunctive bright light in non-seasonal major depression: results from patient-reported symptom and well-being scales. *Acta Psychiatr Scand* 111 (6): 453–59; Yamada, N., et al. 1995. Clinical and chronobiological effects of light therapy on nonseasonal affective disorders. *Biol Psychiatry* 37 (12): 866–73.

76 **Subclinical hypothyroidism** Cooper, D. S. 2001. Clinical practice. Subclinical hypothyroid-

ism. *N Engl J Med* 345 (4): 260–65; Haggerty, J. J., Jr, R. A. Stern, G. A. Mason, J. Beckwith, C. E. Morey, and A. J. Prange, Jr. 1993. Subclinical hypothyroidism: A modifiable risk factor for depression? *Am J Psychiatry* 150 (3): 508–10; Monzani, F., P. Del Guerra, N. Caraccio, C. A. Pruneti, E. Pucci, M. Luisi et al. 1993. Subclinical hypothyroidism: Neurobehavioral features and beneficial effect of L-thyroxine treatment. *Clin Investig* 71 (5): 367–71.

80 **biochemical individuality** Williams, R. J. 1956. *Biochemical individuality: The basis for the genetotrophic concept.* New York: Wiley.

82 **Studies in the late 1970s** U.S. Senate Select Committee on Nutrition and Human Needs. 1977. *Dietary goals for the United States.* 2nd ed. Washington, D.C.: U.S. Government Printing Office, http://whqlibdoc.who.int/trs/WHO_TRS_916.pdf.

82 **Processed foods, it turned out** Senate Committee on Nutrition. *Dietary goals for the United States.*

83 **this modern, "civilized" diet** Burkitt, D. P. 1982. Western diseases and their emergence related to diet. *S Afr Med J* 61(26): 1013–15.

85 **a high glycemic (sugar) index** Jenkins, D. J., et al. 1981. Glycemic index of foods: A physiological basis for carbohydrate exchange. *Am J Clin Nutr* 34 (3): 362–66.

86 **by no means definitive** Westover, A. N., and L. B. Marangell. 2002. A cross-national relationship between sugar consumption and major depression? *Depress Anxiety* 16 (3): 118–20; Lien, L., et al. 2006. Consumption of soft drinks and hyperactivity, mental distress, and conduct problems among adolescents in Oslo, Norway. *Am J Public Health* 96 (10): 1815–20.

87 **carbohydrates are the engine that drives tryptophan** Madras, B. K., et al. 1973. Letter: Dietary carbohydrate increases brain tryptophan and decreases free plasma tryptophan. *Nature* 244 (5410): 34–35.

87 **sugars may also cause a release of beta-endorphins** Yamamoto, T., N. Sako, and S. Maeda. 2000. Effects of taste stimulation on beta-endorphin levels in rat cerebrospinal fluid and plasma. *Physiol Behav* 69 (3): 345–50.

87 **research . . . by Kathleen DesMaisons** DesMaisons, K. 1999. *Potatoes not Prozac: A natural seven-step dietary plan to control your cravings and lose weight; recognize how foods affect the way you feel; stabilize the level of sugar in your blood.* New York: Simon & Schuster.

89 **Robert Atkins** Atkins, R. 1984. *Dr. Atkins' nutrition breakthrough: How to treat your medical condition without drugs.* New York: William Morrow.

89 **Barry Sears** Sears, B. *Enter the Zone.* 1995. New York: HarperCollins.

89 **Vegetarians . . . must combine different foods** Messina, V., V. Melina, and A. R. Mangels. 2003. A new food guide for North American vegetarians. *J Am Diet Assoc* 103 (6): 771–75.

89 **Paleolithic ancestors** Eaton, S. B., and M. Konner. 1985. Paleolithic nutrition: A consideration of its nature and current implications. *N Engl J Med* 312 (5): 283–89.

90 **diet contains about 30 percent protein** http://www.mayoclinic.com/health/healthy-diet/NU00200.

90 **increase the [tryptophan] that flows into your brain** Moller, S. E. 1989. Neutral amino acid plasma levels in healthy subjects: Effect of complex carbohydrate consumed along with protein. *J Neural Transm* 76 (1): 55–63.

91 **our consumption of dietary fat** http://www.cdc.gov/od/oc/media/mmwrnews/n040206.htm#mmwr2.

91 **this saturated fat may be associated** http://whqlibdoc.who.int/trs/WHO_TRS_916.pdf; Ascherio, A., E. B. Rimm, E. L. Giovannucci, D. Spiegelman, M. Stampfer, and W. C. Willett. 1996. Dietary fat and risk of coronary heart disease in men: Cohort follow-up study in the United States. *BMJ* 313 (7049): 84–90.

91 **decreases . . . essential fatty acids** Simopoulos, A. P. 1999. Essential fatty acids in health and chronic disease. *Am J Clin Nutr* 70 suppl. 3: S560-69.

91 **prostaglandins** Norden, M. 1995. *Beyond Prozac: Brain-toxic lifestyles, natural antidotes & new generation antidepressants.* New York: HarperCollins; Lieb, J., R. Karmali, and D. Horrobin. 1983. Elevated levels of prostaglandin E$_2$ and thromboxane B$_2$ in depression. *Prostaglandins Leukot Med* 10 (4): 361–67; Nishino, S., R. Ueno, K. Ohishi, T. Sakai, and O. Hayaishi. 1989. Salivary prostaglandin concentrations: Possible state indicators for major depression. *Am J Psychiatry* 146 (3): 365–68; Ohishi, K., R. Ueno, S. Nishino, T. Sakai, and Hayaishi, O. 1988. Increased level of salivary prostaglandins in patients with major depression. *Biol Psychiatry* 23 (4): 326–34.

92 **fish high in omega-3 and decreased incidence of depression** Sanchez-Villegas, A., et al. 2007.

Long chain omega-3 fatty acids intake, fish consumption, and mental disorders in the SUN cohort study. *Eur J Nutr* 46 (6): 337–46; Tanskanen, A., J. R. Hibbeln, J. Tuomilehto, A. Uutela, A. Haukkala, H. Viinamaki et al. 2001. Fish consumption and depressive symptoms in the general population in Finland. *Psychiatr Serv* 52 (4): 529–31.

92 **people with bipolar disorder** Stoll, A. L., et al. 1999. Omega-3 fatty acids in bipolar disorder: A preliminary double-blind, placebo-controlled trial. *Arch Gen Psychiatry* 56(5): 407–12.

92 **point to the usefulness . . . in treating depression** Lin, P. Y., and K. P. Su. 2007. A meta-analytic review of double-blind, placebo-controlled trials of antidepressant efficacy of omega-3 fatty acids. *J Clin Psychiatry* 68 (7): 1056–61; Logan, A. C. 2004. Omega-3 fatty acids and major depression: a primer for the mental health professional. *Lipids Health Dis* 3: 25; Su, K. P., et al. 2003. Omega-3 fatty acids in major depressive disorder: A preliminary double-blind, placebo-controlled trial. *Eur Neuropsychopharmacol* 13 (4): 267–71; Sontrop, J., and M. K. Campbell. 2006. Omega-3 polyunsaturated fatty acids and depression: A review of the evidence and a methodological critique. *Prev Med* 42 (1): 4–13; Edwards, R., M. Peet, J. Shay, and D. Horrobin. 1998. Omega-3 polyunsaturated fatty acid levels in the diet and in red blood cell membranes of depressed patients. *J Affect Disord* 48(2–3): 149–55; Edwards et al., Omega-3 polyunsaturated fatty acid levels.

92 **OmegaBrite** http://www.omegabrite.com/.

93 **Significant intake of dietary fiber** Anderson, J. W., K. M. Randles, C. W. Kendall, and Jenkins, D. J. 2004. Carbohydrate and fiber recommendations for individuals with diabetes: A quantitative assessment and meta-analysis of the evidence. *J Am Coll Nutr* 23 (1): 5–17; Lupton, J. R., and N. D. Turner. 2003. Dietary fiber and coronary disease: Does the evidence support an association? *Curr Atheroscler Rep* 5 (6): 500–5.

94 **average American's intake is . . . 12 to 15 grams a day** Alaimo, K., et al. 1994. Dietary intake of vitamins, minerals, and fiber of persons ages 2 months and over in the United States: Third National Health and Nutrition Examination Survey, Phase 1, 1988–91. *Adv Data* 258: 1–28.

94 **more than 100 grams that our ancestors were** Leach, J. D. 2007. Evolutionary perspective on

dietary intake of fiber and colorectal cancer. *Eur J Clin Nutr* 61 (1): 140–42.

94 **Institute of Medicine (IOM)** http://www.iom.edu/CMS/3788/3969/18495.aspx.

95 **thiamine (B$_1$)** Brozek, J. 1957. Psychological effects of thiamine restriction and deprivation in normal young men. *Am J Clin Nutr* 5: 109–18.

95 **folic acid** Gilbody, S., T. Lightfoot, and T. Sheldon. 2007. Is low folate a risk factor for depression?: A meta-analysis and exploration of heterogeneity. *J Epidemiol Community Health* 61 (7): 631–37; Tiemeier, H., et al. 2002. Vitamin B$_{12}$, folate, and homocysteine in depression: The Rotterdam Study. *Am J Psychiatry* 159 (12): 2099–2101.

95 **pyridoxine (B$_6$)** Hvas, A.M., et al. 2004. Vitamin B$_6$ level is associated with symptoms of depression. *Psychother Psychosom* 73 (6): 340–43.

95 **B$_{12}$** Tiemeier et al., Vitamin B$_{12}$, folate, and homocysteine in depression; Penninx, B. W., J. M. Guralnik, L. Ferrucci, L. P. Fried, R. H. Allen, and S. P. Stabler. 2000. Vitamin B(12) deficiency and depression in physically disabled older women: Epidemiologic evidence from the Women's Health and Aging Study. *Am J Psychiatry* 157 (5): 715–21.

95 **vitamin C** Kinsman, R. A., and J. Hood. 1974. Some behavioral effects of ascorbic acid deficiency. *Am J Clin Nutr* 24 (4): 455–64.

95 **magnesium** Rasmussen, H. H., P. B. Mortensen, and I. W. Jensen. 1989. Depression and magnesium deficiency. *Int J Psychiatry Med* 19 (1): 57–63; Eby, G. A., and K. L. Eby. 2006. Rapid recovery from major depression using magnesium treatment. *Med Hypotheses* 67 (2): 362–70.

95 **zinc** Maes, M., et al. 1999. Lower serum zinc in major depression in relation to changes in serum acute phase proteins. *J Affect Disord* 56 (2–3): 189–94; Maes, M., et al. 1994. Hypozincemia in depression. *J Affect Disord* 31 (2): 135–40.

95 **selenium** Benton, D. 2002. Selenium intake, mood and other aspects of psychological functioning. *Nutr Neurosci* 5 (6): 363–74; Benton, D., and R. Cook. 1991. The impact of selenium supplementation on mood. *Biol Psychiatry* 29 (11): 1092–98.

95 **chromium** McLeod, M. N., and R. N. Golden. 2000. Chromium treatment of depression. *Int J Neuropsychopharmacol* 3 (4): 311–14; Davidson,

J. R., et al. 2003. Effectiveness of chromium in atypical depression: A placebo-controlled trial. *Biol Psychiatry* 53 (3): 261–64.

95 **are deficient in one or more of the essential micronutrients** http://www.health.gov/dietaryguidelines/dga2005/report/; http://www.who.int/nutrition/databases/micronutrients/en/index.html.

95 **study showed that dietary levels of selenium** Benton and Cook. The impact of selenium.

99 **mediated by other immune globulins, perhaps IgG** Isolauri, E., S. Rautava, and M. Kalliomaki. 2004. Food allergy in irritable bowel syndrome: New facts and old fallacies. *Gut* 53 (10): 1391–93; Sampson, H. A. 2003. Food allergy. *J Allergy Clin Immunol* 111 (2): 540–47; Atkinson, W., T. A. Sheldon, N. Shaath, and P. J. Whorwell. 2004. Food elimination based on IgG antibodies in irritable bowel syndrome: A randomised controlled trial. *Gut* 53 (10): 1459–64.

103 **elimination diet** Carter, J., and A. Edwards. 2003. *Allergy exclusion diet.* Carlsbad, CA: Hay House; Joneja, J. V. 2003. *Dealing with food allergies: A practical guide to detecting culprit foods and eating a healthy, enjoyable diet.* Boulder, CO: Bull Publishing.

CHAPTER TWO: GUIDES ON THE JOURNEY

110 **synchronicity** Jung, C.G. 1985. *Synchronicity.* New York: Routledge.

111 ***Manifesto for a New Medicine*** Gordon, J. S. 1996. *Manifesto for a new medicine: Your guide to healing partnerships and the wise use of alternative therapies.* Reading, MA.: Addison-Wesley.

111 ***Health* magazine** Carlin, P. 1997. Treat the body, heal the mind. *Health* Jan-Feb: 73–78.

120 ***Anatomy of Melancholy*** Burton, R. 1632. *The anatomy of melancholy: What it is, with all the kinds, causes, symptomes, prognostickes & seuerall cures of it: In three partitions, with their severall sections, members & subsections, philosophically, medicinally, historically, opened & cut up.* Corrected and augmented by the author. 4th ed. Oxford: Printed for Henry Cripps.

120 **Monkeys who lose their status** Raleigh, M. J., M. T. McGuire, G. L. Brammer, and A. Yuwiler. 1984. Social and environmental influences on blood serotonin concentrations in monkeys. *Arch Gen Psychiatry* 41 (4): 405–10;

McGuire, M. T., et al. Social dominance in adult male vervet monkeys: Behavior-biochemical relationships. *Social Science Information* 22 (2): 311–28; Sapolsky, R. 2004. Social status and health in humans and other animals. *Ann Rev Anthro* 33: 393–418.

120 **"self psychology"** Kohut, H., and C. B. Strozier. 1985. *Self psychology and the humanities: Reflections on a new psychoanalytic approach.* New York: W. W. Norton.

120 **"Mourning and Melancholia"** Freud, S. 1917. Mourning and Melancholia. *International Review of Psycho-Analysis* 4: 277–87.

120 **"hospitalism"** Spitz, R. A. 1945. Hospitalism. In *The psychoanalytic study of the child,* vol. 1, ed. R. S. Eissler. New York: International Universities Press.

120 **observations on monkeys by primatologist Harry Harlow** Harlow, H. F. 1962. Development of affection in primates. In *Roots of behavior,* ed. E. L. Bliss. New York: Harper; Harlow, H. F. 1964. Early social deprivation and later behavior in the monkey. In *Unfinished tasks in the behavioral sciences,* eds. A. Abrams, H. H. Gurner, and J. E. P. Tomal. Baltimore: Williams & Wilkins.

121 **on humans by psychiatrist John Bowlby** Bowlby J. 1980. *Loss: Sadness and depression.* Attachment and Loss, vol. 3. International Psycho-Analytical Library no. 109. New York: Basic Books.

121 **children who later received the comfort** Ainsworth, M., et al. 1956. The effects of mother-child separation: A follow-up study. *Br J Med Psychol* 29 (3–4): 211–47.

121 **fundamental importance . . . of a "basic trust"** Erikson, E. H. 1980. *Identity and the life cycle.* New York: W. W. Norton.

121 **"good enough mother"** Winnicott, D. W., Transitional objects and transitional phenomena: A study of the first not-me possession. *Int J Psychoanal* 34 (2): 89–97.

121 **importance of "maternal mirroring"** Kohut, M. 1971. *Analysis of the self: Systematic approach to the treatment of narcissistic personality disorders.* New York: International Universities Press.

121 **Loss and other traumatic early-life events** Bremner, J. D., et al. 1997. Magnetic resonance imaging–based measurement of hippocampal volume in posttraumatic stress disorder related to childhood physical and sexual abuse—a pre-

liminary report. *Biol Psychiatry* 41 (1): 23–32; Levitan, R. D., et al. 1998. Major depression in individuals with a history of childhood physical or sexual abuse: Relationship to neurovegetative features, mania, and gender. *Am J Psychiatry* 155 (12): 1746–52.

123 **unconditional positive regard** Rogers, C. R. 1951. *Client-centered therapy.* Boston: Houghton Mifflin; Rogers, C. R. 1961. *On becoming a person: A therapist's view of psychotherapy.* Boston: Houghton Mifflin.

124 **studies that use physiological measures** Martin, S. D., et al. 2001. Brain blood flow changes in depressed patients treated with interpersonal psychotherapy or venlafaxine hydrochloride: Preliminary findings. *Arch Gen Psychiatry* 58 (7): 641–48; Goldapple, K., et al. 2004. Modulation of cortical-limbic pathways in major depression: Treatment-specific effects of cognitive behavior therapy. *Arch Gen Psychiatry* 61(1): 34–41.

124 **Recent research on neuroplasticity** Eriksson, P. S., et al. 1998. Neurogenesis in the adult human hippocampus. *Nat Med* 4 (11): 1313–17; Goldapple et al., *Modulation of cortical-limbic pathways in major depression;* Kandel, E. 1998. A new intellectual framework for psychiatry. *Am J Psychiatry* 155: 457–69.

131 *Memories, Dreams, Reflections* Jung, C. G. 1963. *Memories, dreams, reflections.* Ed. A. Jaffe. Trans. R. Winston and C. Winston. New York: Pantheon Books.

133 **cognitive behavioral therapy** Beck, A. T. 1979. *Cognitive therapy of depression.* Guilford Clinical Psychology and Psychotherapy Series. New York: Guilford Press.

135 **"the language of the unconsicous"** Achterberg, J. 1985. *Imagery in healing: Shamanism and modern medicine.* Boston/New York: New Science Library.

135 **When you create mental images** Yoo, S. S., et al. 2003. Neural substrates of tactile imagery: A functional MRI study. *Neuroreport* 14 (4): 581–85; Bensafi, M., et al. 2003. Olfactomotor activity during imagery mimics that during perception. *Nat Neurosci* 6 (11): 1142–44; Kosslyn, S. M., and W. L. Thompson. 2003. When is early visual cortex activated during visual mental imagery? *Psychol Bull* 129 (5): 723–46; Laeng, B., and D. Teodorescu. 2001. Eye scanpaths during visual imagery reenact those of perception of the same visual scene. *Cognitive Science* 26 (2): 207–31.

135 **Mental images that make use of** Dossey, B. M., et al. 2000. *Holistic nursing: A handbook for practice.* 3rd ed. Gaithersburg, MD: Aspen Publishers.

135 **mental images may be able to decrease . . . anxiety** Krakow, B., et al. Nightmares in sexual assault survivors with posttraumatic stress disorder: A randomized controlled trial. *JAMA* 286 (5): 537–45; Montgomery, G.H., et al. 2002. Brief presurgery hypnosis reduces distress and pain in excisional breast biopsy patients. *Int J Clin Exper Hypnosis* 50 (1): 17–32; Urns, D. S. 2001. The effect of the Bonny method of guided imagery and music on the mood and life quality of cancer patients. *J Music Ther* 38 (1): 51–65; Rees, B. L. 1995. Effect of relaxation with guided imagery on anxiety, depression, and self-esteem in primiparas. *J Holist Nurs* 13 (3): 255–67; Stetter, F., and S. Kupper. 2002. Autogenic training: a meta-analysis of clinical outcome studies. *Appl Psychophysiol Biofeedback* 27 (1): 45–98.

137 **research . . . showing the usefulness of imagery** Weydert, J. A., et al. 2006 Evaluation of guided imagery as treatment for recurrent abdominal pain in children: A randomized controlled trial. *BMC Pediatr* 6: 29; Watanabe, E., et al. 2006. Differences in relaxation by means of guided imagery in a healthy community sample. *Altern Ther Health Med* 12 (2): 60–66; Roffe, L., K. Schmidt, and E. Ernst. 2005. A systematic review of guided imagery as an adjuvant cancer therapy. *Psychooncology* 14 (8): 607–17; Yoo, H. J., et al. 2005. Efficacy of progressive muscle relaxation training and guided imagery in reducing chemotherapy side effects in patients with breast cancer and in improving their quality of life. *Support Care Cancer* 13 (10): 826–33; Lewandowski, W., M. Good, and C. B. Draucker, Changes in the meaning of pain with the use of guided imagery. *Pain Manag Nurs* 6 (2): 58–67; Weydert, J. A., D. E. Shapiro, S. A. Acra, C. J. Monheim, A. S. Chambers, and T. M. Ball. 2006. Evaluation of guided imagery as treatment for recurrent abdominal pain in children: A randomized controlled trial. *BMC Pediatr* 6: 29; Crowther, J. H. 1983. Stress management training and relaxation imagery in the treatment of essential hypertension. *J Behav Med* 6 (2): 169–87.

137 **Imagery can also affect the immune system** Collins, M. P., and L. F. Dunn. 2005. The effects of meditation and visual imagery on an immune system disorder: dermatomyositis. *J Altern*

Complement Med 11 (2): 275–84; Gruzelier, J. H. 2002. A review of the impact of hypnosis, relaxation, guided imagery and individual difference on aspects of immunity and health. *Stress* 5 (2): 147–63; Achterberg, J., and M. S. Rider. 1989. Effects of music-assisted imagery on neutrophils and lymphocytes. *Biofeedback Self Regul* 14 (3): 247–57.

137 **imagery has been shown to improve** Bakke, A. C., M. Z. Purtzer, and P. Newton. 2002. The effect of hypnotic-guided imagery on psychological well-being and immune function in patients with prior breast cancer. *J Psychosom Res* 53 (6): 1131–37.

CHAPTER THREE: SURRENDER TO CHANGE

152 *Tao Te Ching* Lao-tzu and S. Mitchell. 1988. *Tao te ching: A new English version.* New York: Harper & Row.

158 **beginning to publish research** Gordon, J. S., et al. 2004. Treatment of posttraumatic stress disorder in postwar Kosovo high school students using mind-body skills groups: A pilot study. *J Trauma Stress* 17 (2): 143–47; Staples, J. K. and J. S. Gordon. 2005. Effectiveness of a mind-body skills training program for healthcare professionals. *Altern Ther Health Med* 11 (4): 36–41; Saunders, P. A., et al. 2007. Promoting self-awareness and reflection through an experiential mind-body skills course for first year medical students. *Med Teach* 1–7; Finkelstein, C., et al. 2007. Anxiety and stress reduction in medical education: An intervention. *Med Educ* 41 (3): 258–64.

160 **the grinding suppressed fury of hostility** Brummett, B. H., et al. 2005. Ratings of positive and depressive emotion as predictors of mortality in coronary patients. *Int J Cardiol* 100 (2): 213–16; Boyle, S. H., et al. 2005. Hostility, age, and mortality in a sample of cardiac patients. *Am J Cardiol* 96 (1): 64–66; Williams, R. B. 2001. Hostility and heart disease: Williams et al. (1980). *Adv Mind Body Med* 17 (1): 52–55.

160 **Fear, stress, and anxiety lower our immunity** Cohen, S., D. A. Tyrrell, and A. P. Smith. 1991. Psychological stress and susceptibility to the common cold. *N Engl J Med* 325 (9): 606–12; Koga, C., K. Itoh, M. Aoki, Y. Suefuji, M. Yoshida, S. Asosina, et al. 2001). Anxiety and pain suppress the natural killer cell activity in oral surgery outpatients. *Oral Surg Oral Med*

Oral Pathol Oral Radiol Endod 91 (6): 654–58; Segerstrom, S. C., D. A. Glover, M. G. Craske, and J. L. Fahey. 1999. Worry affects the immune response to phobic fear. *Brain Behav Immun* 13 (2): 80–92.

160 **Lack of close connections to others** House, J. S., K. R. Landis, and D. Umberson. 1988. Social relationships and health. *Science* 241 (4865): 540–45; Kawachi, I. and L. F. Berkman, Social ties and mental health. *J Urban Health* 78 (3): 458–67.

161 **Exercise—movement—alters brain chemistry** Soares, J., M. G. Naffah-Mazzacoratti, and E. A. Cavalheiro. 1994. Increased serotonin levels in physically trained men. *Braz J Med Biol Res* 27 (7): 1635–38; Carr, D. B., et al. 1981. Physical conditioning facilitates the exercise-induced secretion of beta-endorphin and beta-lipotropin in women. *N Engl J Med* 305 (10): 560–63; Ransford, C. P. 1982. A role for amines in the antidepressant effect of exercise: A review. *Med Sci Sports Exerc* 14 (1): 1–10.

161 **Exercise likely increases** Rhodes, J. S., et al. 2003. Exercise increases hippocampal neurogenesis to high levels but does not improve spatial learning in mice bred for increased voluntary wheel running. *Behav Neurosci* 117 (5): 1006–16; van Praag, H., G. Kempermann, and F. H. Gage. 2005. Running increases cell proliferation and neurogenesis in the adult mouse dentate gyrus. *Nat Neurosci* 2 (3): 266–70; van Praag, H., et al. 2005. Exercise enhances learning and hippocampal neurogenesis in aged mice. *J Neurosci* 25 (38): 8680–85.

161 **exercise . . . decreases people's depression scores** Nabkasorn, C., N. Miyai, A. Sootmongkol, S. Junprasert, H. Yamamoto, M. Arita, and K. Miyashita. 2006. Effects of physical exercise on depression, neuroendocrine stress hormones, and physiological fitness in adolescent females with depressive symptoms. *Euro J Pub Health* 16 (2): 179–84; Blumenthal, J. A., et al. 1999. Effects of exercise training on older patients with major depression. *Arch Intern Med* 159 (19): 2349–56; Babyak, M., et al. 2000. Exercise treatment for major depression: maintenance of therapeutic benefit at 10 months. *Psychosom Med* 62 (5): 633–38.

165 **There's evidence that yoga** Krishnamurthy, M. N. and S. Telles. 2007. Assessing depression following two ancient Indian interventions: Effects of yoga and Ayurveda on older adults in a residential home. *J Gerontol Nurs* 33 (2): 17–23;

Woolery, A., et al. 2004. A yoga intervention for young adults with elevated symptoms of depression. *Altern Ther Health Med* 10 (2): 60–63; Smith, C., et al. 2007. A randomised comparative trial of yoga and relaxation to reduce stress and anxiety. *Complement Ther Med* 15 (2): 77–83; Granath, J., et al. 2006. Stress management: a randomized study of cognitive behavioural therapy and yoga. *Cogn Behav Ther* 35 (1): 3–10; Brown, R. P. and P. L. Gerbarg. 2005. Sudarshan Kriya Yogic breathing in the treatment of stress, anxiety, and depression. Part II—clinical applications and guidelines. *J Altern Complement Med* 11 (4): 711–17; Michalsen, A., et al. 2005. Rapid stress reduction and anxiolysis among distressed women as a consequence of a three-month intensive yoga program. *Med Sci Monit* 11 (12): CR555–61; Khumar, S. S., P. Kaur, and S. Kaur. 1993. Effectiveness of shavasana on depression among university students. *Indian J Clin Psychol* 20: 82–87; Devi, S. K., J. P. N. Chansauria, and K. N. Udupa. 1986. Mental depression and Kundalini yoga. *Ancient Science of Life* 6 (2): 112–18.

171 **dancing, which has repeatedly been shown to improve mood** West, J., et al. 2004. Effects of Hatha yoga and African dance on perceived stress, affect, and salivary cortisol. *Ann Behav Med* 28 (2): 114–18; Kim, S., and J. Kim. 2007. Mood after various brief exercise and sport modes: Aerobics, hip-hop dancing, ice skating, and body conditioning. *Percept Mot Skills* 104 (3 Pt 2): 1265–70; Choi, P. Y., et al. 1993. Mood changes in women after an aerobics class: A preliminary study. *Health Care Women Int* 14 (2): 167–77; Goodill, S. W. 2005. Dance/movement therapy for adults with cystic fibrosis: Pilot data on mood and adherence. *Altern Ther Health Med* 11 (1): 76–77; Jeong, Y. J., S. C. Hong, M. S. Lee, M. C. Park, Y. K. Kim, and C. M. Suh. 2005. Dance movement therapy improves emotional responses and modulates neurohormones in adolescents with mild depression. *Int J Neurosci* 115 (12): 1711–20; Sandel, S. K., J. O. Judge, N. Landry, L. Faria, R. Ouellette, and M. Majczak. 2005. Dance and movement program improves quality-of-life measures in breast cancer survivors. *Cancer Nursing*. 28 (4): 301–9; Ritter, M. and K. L. Low. Effects of dance/movement therapy: A meta-analysis. *Arts in Psychotherapy* 23 (3): 249–60.

178 **dissipative systems** Prigogine, I., and I. Stengers. 1984. *Order out of chaos: Man's new dialogue with nature.* New York: Bantam Books.

179 **Archaic techniques of ecstasy** Eliade, M. 2004. *Shamanism: Archaic techniques of ecstasy.* 2nd pbk. ed. Bollingen Series 76. Princeton, NJ: Princeton University Press.

CHAPTER FOUR: DEALING WITH DEMONS

186 *The Republic* Plato. 2006. *The republic.* Trans. R. E. Allen. New Haven: Yale University Press.

188 **being combined with . . . psychotherapeutic approaches** Hoppes, K. 2006. The application of mindfulness-based cognitive interventions in the treatment of co-occurring addictive and mood disorders. *CNS Spectr* 11 (11), 829–51; Kingston, T., B. Dooley, A. Bates, E. Lawlor, and K. Malone. 2007. Mindfulness-based cognitive therapy for residual depressive symptoms. *Psychol Psychother* 80 (Pt 2): 193–203; S. H. Ma and J. D. Teasdale. 2004. Mindfulness-based cognitive therapy for depression: Replication and exploration of differential relapse prevention effects. *J Consult Clin Psychol*, 72 (1): 31–40; Teasdale, J. D., Z. V. Segal, J. M. Williams, V. A. Ridgeway, J. M. Soulsby, and M. A. Lau. 2000. Prevention of relapse/recurrence in major depression by mindfulness-based cognitive therapy. *J Consult Clin Psychol* 68 (4): 615–23.

188 *The Miracle of Mindfulness* Thich, N. H. 1976. *The miracle of mindfulness: A manual of meditation.* Boston: Beacon Press.

188 *Zen Mind, Beginner's Mind* Suzuki, S., and T. Dixon. 1970. *Zen mind, beginner's mind.* New York/Tokyo: Weatherhill.

213 *When Things Fall Apart* Chödrön, P. 1997. *When things fall apart: Heart advice for difficult times.* Boston: Shambhala.

215 **about lethargy in** *Care of the Soul* Moore, T. 1992. *Care of the soul: A guide for cultivating depth and sacredness in everyday life.* New York: HarperCollins.

216 **a moratorium** Erikson, E. H. 1964. *Childhood and society.* 2d ed. New York: W. W. Norton.

222 **the long-held anger of hostility** Brummett, B. H., et al. 2005. Ratings of positive and depressive emotion as predictors of mortality in coronary patients. *Int J Cardiol* 100 (2): 213–16; Boyle, S. H., et al. 2005. Hostility, age, and mortality in

a sample of cardiac patients. *Am J Cardiol* 96 (1): 64–66; Williams, R. B. 2001. Hostility and heart disease: Williams et al. (1980). *Adv Mind Body Med* 17 (1): 52–55.

222 **loneliness can diminish our immunity** Pressman, S. D., et al. 2005. Loneliness, social network size, and immune response to influenza vaccination in college freshmen. *Health Psychol* 24 (3): 297–306.

222 **Traditional Chinese Medicine (TCM)** Lake, J., and B. Flaws. 2001. *Chinese Medical Psychiatry.* Boulder, CO: Blue Poppy Press; Beinfield, H, and E. Korngold. 1991. *Between heaven and earth: A guide to Chinese medicine.* New York: Ballantine; Hammer, L. 1991. *Dragon rises, red bird flies: Psychology, energy and Chinese medicine.* Barrytown, NY: Station Hill Press.

233 **only hint at the power and utility of acupuncture** Han, J. S. 1986. Electroacupuncture: An alternative to antidepressants for treating affective diseases? *Int J Neurosci* 29 (1–2): 79–92; Luo, H. C., Y. K. Jia, and Z. Li. 1985. Electro-acupuncture vs. amitriptyline in the treatment of depressive states. *J Tradit Chin Med* 5 (1): 3–8; Han, C., et al. 2004. Clinical study on electroacupuncture treatment for 30 cases of mental depression. *J Tradit Chin Med* 24 (3): 172–76; Manber, R., et al. 2004. Acupuncture: A promising treatment for depression during pregnancy. *J Affect Disord* 83 (1): 89–95.

234 **John Allen and his colleagues** Schnyer, R. N., and J. J. Allen. 2001. *Acupuncture in the treatment of depression: A manual for practice and research.* London: Churchill Livingston Press.

CHAPTER FIVE: THE DARK NIGHT OF THE SOUL

242 **three minutes was the average time** Rand Corporation study (1993) as cited in Cowley, G. 1994. The culture of Prozac. *Newsweek* Feb. 7: 41–42.

243 **Hippocratic** Chadwick, J., and W. N. Mann. 1950. *The medical works of Hippocrates.* Oxford: Blackwell Scientific Publications.

244 **John of the Cross** John of the Cross. 1916. *The Dark Night of the soul.* Trans. B. Zimmerman. 4th ed. London: T. Baker.

244 **rites of passage to adulthood** Turner, V. W. 1969. *The ritual process: Structure and anti-structure.* Lewis Henry Morgan Lectures (1966). Chicago: Aldine.

245 **Thomas Moore** Moore, T. 2004. *Dark nights of the soul: A guide to finding your way through life's ordeals.* New York: Gotham Books.

248 **one in five ... students** Youth risk behavior surveillance: National College Health Risk Behavior Survey—United States, 1997. 1998. *Morbidity and Mortality Weekly Report* 47 (SS-3).

248 **Suicide is now the third leading cause** http://www.cdc.gov/ncipc/factsheets/children.htm.

252 **there were more than one million** http://www.clasp.org/CampaignForYouth/PolicyBrief/RunawayandHomelessYouthAct.

257 **Erik Erikson, the psychoanalyst** Erikson, E. H. 1959. *Identity and the life cycle: Selected papers.* New York: International Universities Press.

268 **why antidepressants have been shown to *increase* suicidal thinking** Jick, H., J. A. Kaye, and S. S. Jick. 2004. Antidepressants and the risk of suicidal behaviors. *JAMA* 292 (3): 338–43; Koizumi, H. 1991. Fluoxetine and suicidal ideation. *J Am Acad Child Adolesc Psychiatry* 30 (4): 695; King, R. A., et al. 1991. Emergence of self-destructive phenomena in children and adolescents during fluoxetine treatment. *J Am Acad Child Adolesc Psychiatry* 30 (2): 179–86.

270 **SAMe is called a methyl donor** Giulidori, P., et al. 1984. Transmethylation, transsulfuration, and aminopropylation reactions of S-adenosyl-L-methionine in vivo. *J Biol Chem* 259 (7): 4205–11.

270 **SAMe seems to encourage** Mischoulon, D., and M. Fava. 2002. Role of S-adenosyl-L-methionine in the treatment of depression: A review of the evidence. *Am J Clin Nutr* 76 (5): S1158–61.

270 **the overall data is somewhat encouraging** Mischoulon and Fava. Role of S-adenosyl-L-methionine; [Unidentified. n.d.] S-adenosyl-L-methionine for treatment of depression, osteoarthritis, and liver disease: http://www.ahrq.gov/clinic/epcsums/samesum.htm; Delle Chiaie, R., P. Pancheri, and P. Scapicchio. 2002. Efficacy and tolerability of oral and intramuscular S-adenosyl-L-methionine 1,4-butanedisulfonate (SAMe) in the treatment of major depression: Comparison with imipramine in 2 multicenter studies. *Am J Clin Nutr* 76 (5): S1172–76.

270 **Richard Brown** Brown, R. P., P. L. Gerbarg, and T. Bottigleri. 2002. S-adenosylmethionine for depression. *Psychiatr Ann* 32 (1): 29–44.

271 **SAMe has far fewer** Brown et al., S-adeno-sylmethionine for depression; Mischoulon and Fava, Role of S-adenosyl-L-methionine.

271 **One million Europeans** Brown et al., S-adenosylmethionine for depression.

271 **several neurotransmitter "precursors"** Growdon, J. H. 1979. Neurotransmitter precursors in the diet: Their use in the treatment of brain diseases. In Nutrition and the Brain Series, vol. 3., eds. R. J. Wurtman and J. J. Wurtman. Berkeley, CA: Raven Press; Meyers, S. 2000. Use of neurotransmitter precursors for treatment of depression. *Altern Med Rev* 5 (1): 64–71; Shaw, K., J. Turner, and C. Del Mar. 2001. Tryptophan and 5-hydroxytryptophan for depression. *Cochrane Database Syst Rev* (3): CD003198.

272 **There are a few controlled trials** Shaw, et al., Tryptophan and 5-hydroxytryptophan for depression.

272 **ability ... to promote sleep** Hartmann, E., and C. L. Spinweber. 1979. Sleep induced by L-tryptophan. Effect of dosages within the normal dietary intake. *J Nerv Ment Dis* 167 (8): 497–99; Nicholson, A. N., and B. M. Stone. 1979. L-tryptophan and sleep in healthy man. *Electro-encephalogr Clin Neurophysiol* 47 (5): 539–45; Hajak, G., et al. 1991. The influence of intravenous L-tryptophan on plasma melatonin and sleep in men. *Pharmacopsychiatry* 24 (1): 17–20.

272 **one contaminated batch** http://edition.cnn.com/HEALTH/9808/31/tryptophan/.

272 **For many centuries** Fetrow, C. W., and J. R. Avila. 1999. *Professional's handbook of complementary & alternative medicines.* Springhouse, PA: Springhouse Corp. Gupta, R. K., and H. J. Moller. 2003. St. John's Wort: An option for the primary care treatment of depressive patients? *Eur Arch Psychiatry Clin Neurosci* 253 (3): 140–48.

273 **compared its efficacy to that of chemical anti-depressants** Schrader, E. 2000. Equivalence of St. John's wort extract (Ze 117) and fluoxetine: A randomized, controlled study in mild-moderate depression. *Int Clin Psychopharmacol* 15 (2): 61–68; Szegedi, A., et al. 2005. Acute treatment of moderate to severe depression with hypericum extract WS 5570 (St. John's Wort): Randomised controlled double blind non-inferiority trial versus paroxetine. *BMJ* 330 (7490): 503.

273 **Saint John's wort has proved significantly better** Kasper, S., et al. 2006. Superior Efficacy of St. John's wort extract WS 5570 compared to placebo in patients with major depression: A randomized, double-blind, placebo-controlled,

multi-center trial *BMC Med* 4: 14; Kalb, R., R. D. Trautmann-Sponsel, and M. Kieser. 2001. Efficacy and tolerability of hypericum extract WS 5572 versus placebo in mildly to moderately depressed patients: A randomized double-blind multicenter clinical trial. *Pharmacopsychiatry* 34 (3): 96–103; Schrader. Equivalence of St. John's wort extract; Lecrubier, Y., et al. 2002. Efficacy of St. John's wort extract WS 5570 in major depression: A double-blind, placebo-controlled trial. *Am J Psychiatry* 159 (8): 1361–66.

273 **as effective as SSRIs** Schrader. Equivalence of St. John's Wort; Szegedi, et al. Acute treatment of moderate to severe depression.

273 **a recent large-scale multisite study** Hypericum Depression Trial Study Group. 2002. Effect of hypericum perforatum (St. John's wort) in major depressive disorder: A randomized controlled trial. *JAMA* 287 (14): 1807–14.

273 **An important cautionary note** Bilia, A. R., S. Gallori, and F. F. Vincieri. 2002. St. John's wort and depression: Efficacy, safety, and tolerability—an update. *Life Sci* 70 (26): 3077–96; Vorbach, E. U., K. H. Arnoldt, and W.D. Hubner. 1997. Efficacy and tolerability of St. John's wort extract LI 160 versus Imipramine in patients with severe depressive episodes according to ICD-10. *Pharmacopsychiatry* 30 Suppl. 2: S81–85.

274 **Rhodiola rosea** Kelly, G. S. 2001. Rhodiola rosea: A possible plant adaptogen. *Altern Med Rev* 6 (3): 293–302.

274 **L-theanine** Juneja, L. R., D. C. Chu, T. Okubo, et al. 1999. L-theanine—a unique amino acid of green tea and its relaxation effect in humans. *Trends Food Sci Tech* 10:199–204.

CHAPTER SIX: SPIRITUALITY: THE BLESSING

285 *The Trial* **by Kafka** Kafka, F. Trans. W. Muir. 1968. *The Trial.* New York: Knopf.

286 **Sunday services at Unity** http://www.unity.org.

286 **Ramana Maharshi** Maharshi, R. 1988. *The spiritual teachings of Ramana Maharshi.* Boston: Shambhala.

291 **Forgiveness is the antidote** Harris, A. H., et al. 2006. Effects of a group forgiveness intervention on forgiveness, perceived stress, and trait-anger. *J Clin Psychol.* 62 (6): 715–33; Brown, R. 2003. Measuring individual differences in the tendency to forgive: Construct validity and links

with depression. *Pers Soc Psychol Bull* 29 (6): 759–71; Luskin, F. M., K. Ginzburg, and C. E. Thoresen. 2005. The effect of forgiveness training on psychosocial factors in college-age adults. *Humboldt J Soc Relat* 29 (2): 163–84.

291 **recent research tells us** Worthington, E. L., Jr., et al. 2007. Forgiveness, health, and well-being: A review of evidence for emotional versus decisional forgiveness, dispositional forgivingness, and reduced unforgiveness. *J Behav Med* 30 (4): 291–302; Lawler, K. A., et al. 2003. A change of heart: Cardiovascular correlates of forgiveness in response to interpersonal conflict. *J Behav Med* 26 (5): 373–93; Lawler, K. A., et al. 2005. The unique effects of forgiveness on health: An exploration of pathways. *J Behav Med* 28 (2): 157–67.

295 **Joan Halifax, an anthropologist** Halifax, J. 1982. *Shaman, the wounded healer.* Illustrated Library of Sacred Imagination. 1982, New York: Crossroad.

298 **many studies that tell us that religious observance** Dwyer, J. W., L. L. Clarke, and M. K. Miller. 1990. The effect of religious concentration and affiliation on county cancer mortality rates. *J Health Soc Behav* 31 (2): 185–202; Gall, T. L. 2004. Relationship with God and the quality of life of prostate cancer survivors. *Qual Life Res* 13 (8): 1357–68; Harrison, M. O., et al. 2005. Religiosity/spirituality and pain in patients with sickle cell disease. *J Nerv Ment Dis* 193 (4): 250–57; Koenig, H. G., L. K. George, and B. L. Peterson. 1998. Religiosity and remission of depression in medically ill older patients. *Am J Psychiatry* 155 (4): 536–42; Oman, D., and D. Reed. 1998. Religion and mortality among the community-dwelling elderly. *Am J Public Health* 88 (10): 1469–75.

299 *regardless of the drug being tested* Beecher, H. K. 1955. The powerful placebo. *JAMA* 159 (17): 1602–6.

300 **One review of several treatments** Roberts, Alan, et al. 1993. The power of nonspecific effects in healing: Implications for psychosocial and biological treatments. *Clin Psychol Rev* 13: 375–91.

300 **More recent research** Walsh, B. T., et al. 2002. Placebo response in studies of major depression: Variable, substantial, and growing. *JAMA* 287 (14): 1840–47.

300 **"participation mystique"** Lévi-Strauss, C. 1962. *La Pensée sauvage.* Paris: Plon.

301 **the description of Bill W.** Zaleski, P., and C.

Zaleski. 2005. *Prayer: A history.* Boston: Houghton Mifflin.

305 **studies that show that prayer** Byrd, R. C. 1988. Positive therapeutic effects of intercessory prayer in a coronary care unit population. *South Med J* 81 (7): 826–29; Harris, W. S., et al. 1999. A randomized, controlled trial of the effects of remote, intercessory prayer on outcomes in patients admitted to the coronary care unit. *Arch Intern Med* 159 (19): 2273–78; Leibovici, L. 2001. Effects of remote, retroactive intercessory prayer on outcomes in patients with bloodstream infection: Randomised controlled trial. *BMJ* 323 (7327): 1450–1; Targ, E. 1997. Evaluating distant healing: A research review. *Altern Ther Health Med* 3 (6): 74–78; Astin, J. A., E. Harkness, and E. Ernst. 2000. The efficacy of "distant healing": A systematic review of randomized trials. *Ann Intern Med* 132 (11): 903–10.

305 **almost as many equally good studies** Aviles, J. M., et al. 2001. Intercessory prayer and cardiovascular disease progression in a coronary care unit population: A randomized controlled trial. *Mayo Clin Proc* 76 (12): 1192–98; Walker, S. R., et al. 1997. Intercessory prayer in the treatment of alcohol abuse and dependence: A pilot investigation. *Altern Ther Health Med* 3 (6): 79–86; Mathai, J., and A. Bourne. 2004. Pilot study investigating the effect of intercessory prayer in the treatment of child psychiatric disorders. *Australas Psychiatry* 12 (4): 386–89; Benson, H., et al. 2006. Study of the therapeutic effects of intercessory prayer (STEP) in cardiac bypass patients: A multicenter randomized trial of uncertainty and certainty of receiving intercessory prayer. *Am Heart J* 151 (4): 934–42.

308 **love makes it possible** Schore, A. N. 2005. Back to basics: Attachment, affect regulation, and the developing right brain: Linking developmental neuroscience to pediatrics. *Pediatr Rev* 26 (6): 204–17; Rohner, R.P., and R. A. Veneziano. 2001. The importance of father love: History and contemporary evidence. *Rev Gen Psychol* 5 (4): 382–405; Bowlby, J. 1990. *A secure base: Parent-child attachment and healthy human development.* New York: Basic Books.

CHAPTER SEVEN: THE RETURN

328 **Men . . . may be less likely** Angst, J., et al. 2002. Gender differences in depression Epidemiological findings from the European

DEPRES I and II studies. *Eur Arch Psychiatry Clin Neurosci* 252 (5): 201–9.

329 **Mediterranean diet** De Lorgeril, M., et al. 1998. Mediterranean dietary pattern in a randomized trial: Prolonged survival and possible reduced cancer rate. *Arch Intern Med* 158 (11): 1181–87; De Lorgeril, M., et al. 1996. Effect of a Mediterranean type of diet on the rate of cardiovascular complications in patients with coronary artery disease: Insights into the cardioprotective effect of certain nutriments. *J Am Coll Cardiol* 28 (5): 1103–8.

335 **I don't dispute the data** Post, R. M. 1992. Transduction of psychosocial stress into the neurobiology of recurrent affective disorder. *Am J Psychiatry* 149 (8): 999–1010; Kendler, K. S., L. M. Thornton, and C. O. Gardner. 2000. Stressful life events and previous episodes in the etiology of major depression in women: An evaluation of the "kindling" hypothesis. *Am J Psychiatry* 157 (8): 1243–51; Kendler, K. S., L. M. Thornton, and C. O. Gardner. 2001. Genetic risk, number of previous depressive episodes, and stressful life events in predicting onset of major depression. *Am J Psychiatry* 158 (4): 582–86.

BIBLIOGRAPHY

GENERAL TEXTS ON PSYCHIATRY

Sadock, Benjamin J., and Virginia A. Sadock, eds. *Kaplan and Sadock's Comprehensive Textbook of Psychiatry.* 8th ed. Baltimore, MD: Lippincott Williams & Wilkins, 2004.
This text is likely used by more mental health professionals than any other. It is certainly the best place to find comprehensive, densely referenced review articles that reflect the consensus of the psychiatric mainstream. There are long, useful entries on the history, epidemiology, genetics, and pharmacological treatment of depression. There are also good discussions of a number of psychotherapeutic approaches that may be applied to depression as well as other conditions.

Lake, James. *Textbook of Integrative Mental Health Care.* New York: Thieme Medical Publishers, 2006.
This is probably the most complete effort, to date, to present both an integrative perspective on psychiatry and reviews of the available research on particular alternative approaches and techniques. There's a useful chapter on depression that covers some of the same ground as *Unstuck* on the use of supplements.

OVERVIEWS OF DEPRESSION GROUNDED IN THE DISEASE THEORY

Kramer, Peter D. *Against Depression.* New York: Penguin Books, 2006.
This book, by the psychiatrist who wrote the 1993 best seller *Listening to Prozac,* is in part a critique of those, particularly literary and artistic types, who may have romanticized depression. Its most interesting chapters are on brain science and depression, where Kramer describes some of the most persuasive evidence for the biological basis of depression and recent efforts to develop more sophisticated pharmacological ways to address and prevent the damage that stress and depression does. Kramer is a passionate proponent of the disease theory of depression.

Solomon, Andrew. *The Noonday Demon: An Atlas of Depression.* New York: Scribner, 2001.
This literate, thoughtful book maps out much of the territory of anthropological and literary, as well as conventional scientific, thinking about depression. Antidepressant drugs are described at some length, but Solomon, who describes himself as chronically depressed and uses several medications himself, also points out their significant limitations.

Whybrow, Peter C. *A Mood Apart: Depression, Mania, and Other Afflictions.* New York: Basic Books, 1997. A well-written, scientifically grounded text by a distinguished psychiatrist who focuses on recent research on the psychobiology of depression, and its treatment with medication and cognitive behavioral therapy.

CRITIQUES OF THE DISEASE THEORY OF DEPRESSION AND OF ANTIDEPRESSANT DRUGS

Breggin, Peter R., and Ginger Ross Breggin. *Talking Back to Prozac: What Doctors Aren't Telling You About Today's Most Controversial Drug.* New York: St. Martin's Press, 1994.
An early, angry, and important response to the inflated claims surrounding the marketing and use of SSRIs by a psychiatrist and his collaborator wife who pored over FDA records. Dr. Breggin testified in numerous suits by patients and their families who claimed harm from the drugs. The title is a play on Peter Kramer's *Listening to Prozac.*

DeGrandpre, Richard. *The Cult of Pharmacology: How America Became the World's Most Troubled Drug Culture.* Durham, NC: Duke University Press, 2006.
A trenchant study—by a psychopharmacologist—of legal and illegal drugs and how their status and use has been shaped more by social, political, and economic forces than by scientific evidence. His chapter on SSRIs highlights some of their long-term side effects and their potential for producing suicidal and homicidal behavior.

Glenmullen, Joseph. *Prozac Backlash: Overcoming the Dangers of Prozac, Zoloft, Paxil, and Other Antidepressants with Safe, Effective Alternatives.* New York: Simon & Schuster, 2001.
Glenmullen, a Harvard psychiatrist, provides a detailed, extremely useful discussion of the scientific evidence on the limitations and hazards of antidepressants. He shows, with impressive documentation, that they are far less effective than advertised and have very dangerous short- and long-term side effects.

Healy, David. *The Antidepressant Era.* Cambridge, MA: Harvard University Press, 1997.
A fine, scholarly deconstruction of the development, use, and colossal overuse of antidepressants, written by a distinguished antidepressant researcher who has testified widely and effectively against the makers of these drugs.

Horwitz, Allan V., and Jerome C. Wakefield. *The Loss of Sadness: How Psychiatry Transformed Normal Sorrow into Depressive Disorder.* New York: Oxford University Press, 2007.
This is a careful, thoughtful, well-documented, critical study of how depression has been transformed into an ever-expanding disease category. The perspective and the references were particularly helpful to me. The book is remarkable for a self-critical introduction by Robert Spitzer, a psychiatrist who is one of the chief authors of the DSM description that Horvitz and Wakefield are critiquing.

Leventhal, Allan M. and Christopher R. Martell. *The Myth of Depression as a Disease: Limitations and Alternatives to Drug Treatment.* New York: Praeger, 2006.
This book, by two psychologists, presents some of the data (including unpublished data from FDA files) that shows the very limited advantages of SSRIs over placebo. They point out (though they don't analyze) what they call "woefully weak" evidence for the biological basis of depression, briefly critique the reductionist medical model, and focus on the advantages of considering depression as a learned experience and of using cognitive behavioral psychology to address it.

SELF-HELP BOOKS THAT FOCUS MOSTLY ON CONVENTIONAL CARE

Charney, Dennis S., and Charles B. Nemeroff. *The Peace of Mind Prescription: An Authoritative Guide to Finding the Most Effective Treatment for Anxiety and Depression.* Boston: Houghton Mifflin, 2004.

Two well-known psychiatrists who have done significant research on depression provide a popular overview of its pharmacological treatment, and of the use of cognitive behavioral and interpersonal therapies.

Copeland, Mary Ellen. *The Depression Workbook: A Guide for Living with Depression and Manic Depression.* 2nd ed. Oakland, CA: New Harbinger, 2002.
This book contains a series of chapters devoted to ways of thinking and feeling that are likely to lead to depression, and practical exercises designed to alter these patterns.

Hedaya, Robert J. *The Antidepressant Survival Program: The Clinically Proven Program to Enhance the Benefits and Beat the Side Effects of Your Medication.* New York: Three Rivers Press, 2000.
Clear, practical advice from a psychiatrist for enhancing well-being, decreasing stress, and dealing with drug side effects while you are on antidepressants. Hedaya integrates nutrition and mind-body approaches into his work and his guidance.

Norden, Michael J. *Beyond Prozac: Brain-Toxic Lifestyles, Natural Antidotes & New Generation Antidepressants.* New York: HarperCollins, 1995.
A useful introduction to the biology of depression and the use of both medication and supplements to address the physiological imbalances that have been described or hypothesized.

SELF-HELP BOOKS THAT EMPHASIZE NATURAL THERAPIES

Cousens, Gabriel. *Depression-Free for Life: A Physician's All-Natural, 5-Step Plan.* New York: William Morrow, 2000.
Cousens, a well-known integrative psychiatrist, focuses on the therapeutic use of vitamins, minerals, amino acids, and essential fatty acids.

DesMaisons, Kathleen. *Potatoes Not Prozac: A Natural Seven-Step Dietary Plan to Stabilize the Level of Sugar in Your Blood, Control Your Cravings and Lose Weight, and Recognize How Foods Affect the Way You Feel.* New York: Simon & Schuster, 1998.
This is a practical book for people whose depression may be related to sugar and carbohydrate sensitivity. It offers ways to become aware of and successfully respond to this biological vulnerability.

Emmons, Henry, with Rachel Kranz. *The Chemistry of Joy: A Three-Step Program for Overcoming Depression Through Western Science and Eastern Wisdom.* New York: Simon & Schuster, 2006.
This helpful book, by an integrative psychiatrist, combines some information about dietary supplements, medication, and meditation with a major emphasis on the psycho-typing system of traditional Indian Ayurveda and its use in depression.

Murray, Michael T. *Natural Alternatives to Prozac.* New York: William Morrow, 1996.
One of the earlier, simpler, and best of the books that discusses supplements, herbs, amino acids, etc. The author is a well-known naturopathic physician.

Ornish, Dean. *Dr. Dean Ornish's Program for Reversing Heart Disease Without Drugs or Surgery.* New York: Ballantine, 1992.
Ornish's program for reversing heart disease offers a good example of the effective use of a comprehensive approach, similar in some ways to the one I teach in *Unstuck*. Ornish includes nutrition and exercise, relaxation techniques, yoga, and group support. This is a wonderful example of the way clinical work with an integrative, nonpharmacological approach can provide significant benefits to people with life-threatening illness, and also yield persuasive research results.

Servan-Schreiber, David. *The Instinct to Heal: Curing Depression, Anxiety, and Stress Without Drugs and Without Talk Therapy.* New York: Rodale, 2004.
A good survey of some of the more important alternative therapies for depression, including acupuncture, eye movement desensitization and reprogramming (EMDR), omega-3 fatty acids, cognitive behavioral therapy, and a form of biofeedback that enhances "heart rate variability" and decreases stress.

Zuess, Jonathan G. *The Wisdom of Depression: A Guide to Understanding and Curing Depression Using Natural Medicine.* New York: Harmony Books, 1998.
This book, as its title suggests, shares with *Unstuck* a perspective that depression signals an imbalance in body, mind, and spirit. It is useful and hopeful.

GUIDES ON THE JOURNEY

Bolen, Jean Shinoda. *Goddesses in Everywoman: Powerful Archetypes in Women's Lives.* San Francisco: HarperCollins/Quill, 2004.
Bolen, a Jungian analyst, holds a bright psychological mirror up to the archetypes of the feminine. The book includes several chapters that explore the maturing of Demeter's earth wisdom; Persephone's emotional, psychological, and sexual awakening; and the relevance of both to modern women.

Campbell, Joseph. *The Hero with a Thousand Faces.* Bollingen Series. Princeton, NJ: Princeton University Press, 1949.
This book, rich with examples drawn from cultures around the world, presents the schema that I've drawn on (and modified) for *Unstuck.* Reading it may well deepen your understanding and enrich your experience of the stages on your own journey.

Chödrön, Pema. *When Things Fall Apart.* Boston: Shambhala, 1997.
One of the best books on dealing with the Dark Nights that may come to any of us, and one of the easiest to read and use. Chödrön is a Buddhist teacher who has been there. Her voice and her words, informed by decades of practice and counseling at the Abbey she leads, comfort, hold, and guide the reader.

Cutler, Howard C., and His Holiness, the Dalai Lama. *The Art of Happiness: A Handbook for Living.* New York: Riverhead Books, 1998.
The Dalai Lama, a wonderful example and guide, puts our day-to-day, moment-to-moment happiness front and center and encourages us and shows us how to achieve it by becoming more compassionate to ourselves and others. Howard Cutler, a psychiatrist who provides a psychological context for the Dalai Lama's comments, helps make the Dalai Lama's words and wisdom more accessible.

Dass, Ram. *Still Here: Embracing Aging, Changing, and Dying.* New York: Riverhead Books, 2001.
In this touching, humbling, inspiring, and useful book about aging, incapacity, the temptations of despair, and mortality, Ram Dass shares wisdom hard won from a debilitating stroke. Ram Dass is a courageous, playful seeker who inspired many with his earlier books *Be Here Now* and *The Only Dance There Is. Still Here* is, incidentally, a nice pun, signifying quiet mindfulness as well as persistence.

Dyer, Wayne W. *Inspiration: Your Ultimate Calling.* Carlsbad, CA: Hay House, 2006.
One of the more recent of Dyer's many best-selling books, this one, like several of his others, emphasizes the primacy of our connection to the spirit that is beyond and within us and the importance of tuning ourselves to its message. If, as he tells and shows us, we allow that connection to inform our thoughts and actions, life will flow naturally and harmoniously. He helps us understand that depression is a disconnection from, and an amnesia for, our connection to spirit.

Erikson, Erik H. *Childhood and Society.* New York: W. W. Norton, 1964.
A wonderful, illuminating book about how we grow up and how that growing up is shaped by, and in turn shapes, society. I have found Erikson, who is arguably the most important psychoanalytic and psychological thinker and writer of the last sixty years, to be a wise and encouraging guide on my own journey through the life cycle. Erikson's monograph *Identity and the Life Cycle* and his book on our later years, *Insight and Responsibility* (both of which I've also drawn on in *Unstuck*), are also enormously valuable.

Laing, R. D. *The Divided Self: An Existential Study in Sanity and Madness.* Baltimore, MD: Penguin Books, 1965.
An elegantly written description of the way people deny their "true selves" in favor of a false, socially accommodating self. A useful means of understanding many of the ways we deny our needs—and our demons—and deform our being.

Luke, Helen M. *Woman, Earth and Spirit: The Feminine in Symbol and Myth.* New York: Crossroad, 1984.
This book, written by a Jungian analyst, helped immeasurably to deepen my understanding of the myth of Demeter and Persephone. It illuminates the crucial importance of relationships and loss in depression and of the acceptance and love that help to bring healing.

Moore, Thomas. *Care of the Soul: A Guide for Cultivating Depth and Sacredness in Everyday Life.* New York: HarperCollins, 1992.
Moore draws deeply on the traditions of Renaissance humanism as well as modern psychology to enhance our appreciation of who, beyond roles or titles, we really are and can be. He has a wonderful discussion, which I've drawn on in *Unstuck,* of the need to honor and grow through the dark, depressed Saturnian times of frustration and inaction.

———. *Dark Nights of the Soul: A Guide to Finding Your Way Through Life's Ordeals.* New York: Gotham Books, 2004.
This valuable, learned book is a focused treatment of some of the issues Moore raised in *Care of the Soul.* It gives a fine perspective on a variety of soul-challenging experiences, including depression and despair.

PERSONAL NARRATIVES

Jung, Carl G. *Memories, Dreams, Reflections.* New York: Vintage, 1965.
This is the autobiographical account that I mention in the Guides chapter, chapter two. It is, I think, an extraordinary example of how one man, in his darkest times, found his deepest roots and discovered his life direction—through understanding his dreams and the creative use of solitude. I recommend this book to many people who are suffering a mid- or, indeed, late-life crisis.

Slater, Lauren. *Prozac Diary.* New York: Random House, 1998.
A personal narrative in which Slater gives readers a sense of the suffering that comes with depression, of the relief that antidepressants may bring, and of the very significant limitations of those drugs.

Styron, William. *Darkness Visible: A Memoir of Madness.* New York: Random House, 1990.
A beautifully written account of Styron's depression. It was on the *New York Times* best-seller list for some time, and continues to be widely read and cited. It's a curious book, though. The descriptions are elegant and easily recognizable to the depressed person, but Styron shows little understanding of what might have caused his condition or why his depression lifted.

PSYCHOTHERAPY

Rogers, Carl R. *On Becoming a Person: A Therapist's View of Psychotherapy.* Boston: Houghton Mifflin, 1970.
This is Rogers's classic book on personal growth and psychotherapy. It is thoughtful, gentle, and humane and will give you a good feeling for what unconditional positive regard can look and feel like.

Yalom, Irvin D. *Love's Executioner & Other Tales of Psychotherapy.* New York: Perennial, 2000.
In this collection of stories about his work with patients, Yalom, a professor of psychiatry at Stanford Medical School, gives a fine, nuanced sense of the process of psychotherapy from the clinician's as well as the patient's perspective.

MEDITATION

Begley, Sharon. *Train Your Mind, Change Your Brain: How a New Science Reveals Our Extraordinary Potential to Transform Ourselves.* New York: Ballantine Books, 2007.
This book, by the science columnist at the *Wall Street Journal,* summarizes some of the most interesting research from a recent conference organized for the Dalai Lama by the Mind and Life Institute. It presents, in clear, readable form, studies on neuroplasticity and the ways that each of us can use our mind, particularly through meditation, to improve our mood and alter the function and the structure of our brain.

Benson, Herbert, and Eileen M. Stuart. *The Wellness Book: The Comprehensive Guide to Maintaining Health and Treating Stress-Related Illness.* Secaucus, NJ: Carol Publishing, 1992.
An easy-to-read self-help guide. Each chapter focuses on a specific aspect of the mind-body approach, including meditation, exercise, nutrition, and stress management. It provides basic information and self-assessments and is full of illustrations and practical exercises.

Borysenko, Joan. *Minding the Body, Mending the Mind.* Reading, MA: Addison-Wesley, 1987.
A very good, readable, and practical introduction to the mind-body approach by a cell biologist and psychologist who's done laboratory research and clinical work at Harvard. Borysenko has a wonderful heart as well as an organized mind, and both are apparent here.

Brach, Tara. *Radical Acceptance: Embracing Your Life with the Heart of the Buddha.* New York: Bantam Books, 2003.
A clearly written, practical guide to bringing acceptance and compassion into every corner of our lives. Brach, who founded and directs the Insight Meditation Community in Washington, D.C., and is a psychologist, shows how Buddhist understanding and practice can help us find, amid the snares of desire and the faces of fear, our true longings and the courage to fulfill them.

Hanh, Thich Nhat. *The Miracle of Mindfulness: A Manual on Meditation.* Boston: Beacon Press, 1987; *Peace Is Every Step: The Path of Mindfulness in Everyday Life.* New York: Bantam Books, 1991.
These are wonderful and wonderfully practical books on mindfulness meditation by a Vietnamese Buddhist monk who was a heroic peace activist. They are ones I often recommend.

Kabat-Zinn, Jon. *Full Catastrophe Living: Using the Wisdom of Your Body and Mind to Face Stress, Pain, and Illness.* New York: Dell, 1990.
This book, by the founding director of a comprehensive program for the treatment of chronic illness at the University of Massachusetts Medical Center, gives a sense of the attitude that pervades that program—one of "mindfulness." It shows how yoga, meditation, and group support may be used in the treatment of chronic pain, anxiety disorders, depression, and other conditions.

Naranjo, Claudio. *How to Be.* Los Angeles: J. P. Tarcher, 1991.
A basic introduction to meditation that describes, and differentiates among, the three essential kinds—concentrative, awareness, and expressive. The book was written thirty years ago by a Chilean psychiatrist, and was updated in 1991.

Suzuki, Shunryu. *Zen Mind, Beginner's Mind,* ed. Trudy Dixon. New York: Weatherhill, 1970.
An elegant collection of talks by a great Zen teacher—very useful for those of us who spend too much time ruminating about the past or worrying about the future. I recommend it often.

YOGA

McCall, Timothy. *Yoga as Medicine: The Yogic Prescription for Health and Healing.* New York: Bantam Books, 2007.
This is an excellent compilation of the ways that yoga can be used to decrease stress, improve mood, and enhance physical and physiological functioning. There is a chapter on depression and one on anxiety and panic attacks as well as a number of others on common chronic illnesses.

Weintraub, Amy. *Yoga for Depression: A Compassionate Guide to Relieve Suffering Through Yoga.* New York: Broadway Books, 2004.
Weintraub combines clear step-by-step instruction in the appropriate yoga postures with a deep understanding of the psychological and spiritual aspects of depression. She is a fine teacher and a skillful guide on the journey.

TRADITIONAL CHINESE MEDICINE

Beinfeld, Harriet, and Efrem Korngold. *Between Heaven and Earth: A Guide to Chinese Medicine.* New York: Ballantine, 1992.
Probably the best and most complete introduction to the philosophy of Chinese medicine and acupuncture. It also gives a nice sense of those "Chinese glasses"—of how another culture views mind and body as inseparable and approaches all our conditions and illnesses in a more holistic way.

Flaws, Bob, and James Lake. *Chinese Medical Psychiatry: A Textbook and Clinical Manual.* Boulder, CO: Blue Poppy Press, 2001.
This is the most complete and thoughtful attempt to date to use the principles and practices of Chinese medicine to enrich psychiatric diagnosis and treatment. A rich but challenging reference volume.

Hammer, Leon. *Dragon Rises, Red Bird Flies: Psychology & Chinese Medicine.* Barrytown, NY: Station Hill Press, 1990.
A wise and comprehensive treatment of the five-element approach to Chinese medicine by an American psychiatrist. The emphasis is on psychological issues and conditions, including depression, and the utility of the five elements as a way of understanding, explaining, and addressing the imbalances that are present in them.

SPIRITUALITY

Rumi, Jelaluddin. *The Essential Rumi,* trans. Coleman Barks and John Mayne. Edison, NJ: Castle Books, 1997.
Rumi, the thirteenth-century Sufi (Islamic) poet celebrates the love of the soul for God in every encounter

and every moment. This book, which comes with a brief introduction to each of the sections, is a fine collection, but may be a little daunting. *Open Secret,* also translated by Moyne and Barks, is more accessible.

Buber, Martin. *Tales of the Hasidim.* New York: Schocken, 1991.
These stories of wise, wonder-working "zaddiks" give us a taste of the mystery, joy, and generosity experienced by the eighteenth-century Eastern European God-intoxicated Jews, the Hasidim. It has helped me to experience and reclaim the tradition into which I was born.

Dossey, Larry. *Healing Words: The Power of Prayer and the Practice of Medicine.* New York: HarperCollins, 1993.
A clear, well-written overview of the power of prayer to affect us physically, emotionally, and spiritually. The book, by an internist who has focused on the spiritual and energetic aspects of healing, is based on hundreds of published studies.

Gomes, Peter. *Strength for the Journey: Biblical Wisdom for Daily Living.* New York: HarperCollins, 2003.
This is one of several collections of the Reverend Gomes's sermons at Harvard's Memorial Church. In it, he enlarges our understanding of Biblical texts and illuminates events of the Christian calendar in ways that are immediately relevant and helpful. This book lives up to its title.

Isherwood, Christopher. *Ramakrishna and His Disciples.* Hollywood, CA: Vedanta Press, 1980.
The story of the Indian saint who gave himself, dancing and chanting in ecstasy, to a god equally female and male. This is a classic story of spiritual surrender.

Kornfield, Jack. *After the Ecstasy, the Laundry: How the Heart Grows Wise on the Spiritual Path.* New York: Bantam Books, 2000.
The title conveys Kornfield's understanding that those of us who enter the spiritual path must also deal with all the ordinary trials and troubles that beset any of us. Kornfield, a psychologist as well as a teacher of mindfulness meditation, helps readers to do this with grace and humor.

The Gift: Poems by Hafiz, the Great Sufi Master, trans. Daniel Ladinsky. New York: Compass, 1999.
A wonderful collection of poetry by the thirteenth-century Sufi poet who describes himself as a man "startled by God." Hafiz illuminates and celebrates the divine everywhere.

Lao-tzu. *The Tao Te Ching: A New English Version,* trans. Stephen Mitchell. New York: HarperCollins, 2006.
This is the intimate, very modern (alternating use of he and she) version that Milton first read. Each entry feels like an invitation to relax, let go, and unlearn those things that we thought we knew so well. Other translations that Milton—and I—have read and enjoyed include Gia-fu-Feng and Jane English's more austere version and Witter Bynner's mannered but elegant and revealing rendition.

Maharshi, Ramana. *The Spiritual Teaching of Ramana Maharshi.* Boston: Shambhala, 1998.
No book can convey Ramana's presence as the caves, trails, and gardens of Arunachula do. Still, this brief collection of his dialogues with seekers who visited him there invites us to drink from the cool, clear, and deep pool of his understanding. Carl Jung wrote the foreword.

Mitchell, Stephen, ed. *The Enlightened Heart: An Anthology of Sacred Poetry.* New York: HarperCollins, 1989.
A fine collection of religious and secular poetry that celebrates the individual human soul's quest to unite with the divine, and the reflection of that union that nature may give back to us. Selections range from the Psalms and the Upanishads to the Sufi poet Rumi and the less-known but remarkable fifteenth-century religious, Mechthild of Magdeburg, to Walt Whitman and Robinson Jeffers.

Neihardt, John G. *Black Elk Speaks*. Lincoln, NE: Bison Books, 2004.
An account of the way of life of an indigenous people, the Lakota Sioux, shortly before it was destroyed. *Black Elk Speaks* is a story of spiritual education and healing vision, and an inspiring example of hope emerging, even in the darkest of times.

Schachter-Shalomi, Zalman, with Joel Segel. *Jewish with Feeling: A Guide to Meaningful Jewish Practice*. New York: Riverhead Books, 2005.
This intimate, avuncular book by a modern Jewish mystic invites us to experience, here and now, the presence of the divine in our everyday life. Schachter-Shalomi is a wonderful storyteller with a knack for making ancient wisdom accessible, particularly to those who have been raised in, but who have become alienated from, Judaism. He is particularly good on honoring the Sabbath, prayer, and finding God's face in the natural world.

Shah, Idries. *The Sufis*. New York: Octagon Press, 1999.
I find this book, by one of the great modern Sufi teachers, to be the best general introduction to the Sufi way, its history, and its stories, as well as a fine complement to the poetry through which most modern Westerners encounter Sufism, an esoteric, mystical aspect of Islam. Shah suggests that Sufism may have influenced Western culture through Francis of Assisi, as well as the songs of the troubadors.

Warren, Rick. *The Purpose-Driven Life: What on Earth Am I Here For?* Philadelphia: Running Press, 2003.
This book, which has sold thirty million copies in hardcover, offers, within a Christian framework, step-by-step instruction for reconnecting to God and reaping the rewards—in peace of mind as well as purpose.

Yogananda, Paramahansa. *Autobiography of a Yogi*. Los Angeles: Self-Realization Fellowship, 1998.
This is one of the first spiritual books I read, a beautifully written and, to me and generations of seekers, utterly absorbing story of a man whose ordinary, troubled life becomes miraculous.

INDEX